The Anatomy of
Russian
Capitalism

The Anatomy of Russian Capitalism

Stanislav M. Menshikov

Translated from the Russian
by Rachel B. Douglas

EIR News Service
2007

Menshikov, Stanislav M. The Anatomy of Russian Capitalism.

Library of Congress Catalog Card Number: 2006937362

First English edition, 2007.
Translated from the first Russian edition:
    Stanislav Menshikov, Anatomiia rossiiskogo kapitalizma. Moscow: Mezhdunarodnye Otnosheniia, 2004.

Copyright © EIR News Service
All rights reserved.

ISBN 978-0-943235-22-6

Please direct all inquiries to the publisher:
Executive Intelligence Review
P.O. Box 17390
Washington, D.C. 20041-0390

On the cover: Proton booster rocket: NASA; LUKOIL filling station in Vails Gate, NY; shops on Tverskaya St., Moscow, 2001: EIRNS; Moscow street market, 1992: EIRNS; Red October candy factory, Moscow: EIRNS.

Printed in the United States of America

EIRBK-2006-1

Contents

Preface: Russia's Next Step   ix
          by *Lyndon H. LaRouche, Jr.*

Introduction to the English Edition   xiii

CHAPTER 1.   A General Description of Russian Capitalism   1

     1.1   Is this capitalism?
     1.2   Bolshevism in reverse
     1.3   The legacy of socialism
     1.4   Directors turned into capitalists
     1.5   Bankers as money-launderers
     1.6   Socialism: another source of capital
     1.7   Why not managerialism?
     1.8   A historical reminiscence
     1.9   Surplus value: a statistical study
     1.10 The distribution of profit by sector
     1.11 The nature of export superprofit

CHAPTER 2.   The Composition of Capital   39

     2.1   The accumulation of capital
     2.2   Consume, or resell?
     2.3   Where to hold capital: at home, or abroad?
     2.4   The relationship of industrial and banking capital
     2.5   The concentration of capital in the productive sector
     2.6   Where the oil giants came from
     2.7   The battle for metals
             Nickel: pre-existing concentration
             Aluminum: from disorder to monopolization
             The steel industry
     2.8   Sectors producing for the domestic market
             The automobile industry
             The food and allied industries
             Light industry

- 2.9 The defense industry
- 2.10 The oligarchy's industrial financial groups

CHAPTER 3.   State Capital, Millionaires and Managers, Small Business — 157

- 3.1 The state sector and the natural monopolies
  - The electric power industry
  - Natural gas
  - The railroads
- 3.2 The state and the defense industry
- 3.3 The state sector: the Kremlin oligarchical group, and some conclusions
- 3.4 Millionaires and managers
- 3.5 Small business and its prospects
- 3.6 The shadow economy, organized crime, and corruption

CHAPTER 4.   How Our Economy Works: Production and Income Distribution — 233

- 4.1 The composition of national income: the relationship of labor income to gross profit
- 4.2 Income distribution inequality, social stratification, and the middle class
  - The middle class
- 4.3 The composition of GDP: personal consumption, investment, and government consumption
- 4.4 GDP dynamics
  - The crisis and stagnation of 1992-1998
  - A period of growth (after 1999)

CHAPTER 5.   Economic Policy — 279

- 5.1 Structural reforms
- 5.2 Budget and tax policy
  - 1992-1997 budget policy
  - Budget policy in 1999-2005
- 5.3 Credit and monetary policy
- 5.4 Economic policy as a whole

CHAPTER 6. Russia, the World, and the Future   317
    6.1 Russia in the global capitalist system
           Raw materials dependence
           The problem of competitive power
           The problem of foreign investment
           Russian capital's transnational connections
    6.2 The inertial system of Russian capitalism
    6.3 Possible alternatives and policy solutions
           Policy recommendations

Glossary	377
Index	381
About the Author	396
Translator's Acknowledgments	398

Note on transliteration

Two systems for the transliteration of Russian into English are used in this book. Bibliographical references in the notes and under tables are given in the Library of Congress system. In the text, the transliteration is modified to better approximate Russian pronunciation.

PREFACE

Russia's Next Step
by Lyndon H. LaRouche, Jr.

In the aftermath of President Abraham Lincoln's defeat of the London-backed slave-holders' Confederate insurrection, the London-linked New York faction of U.S. finance unleashed a predatory looting of the physical assets of the territory formerly ruled by the defeated Confederacy. That operation, which was described then as "carpetbagging," is a term that pointed to the style of the personal baggage, in which the travelling, locust-like predators carried their personal effects.

When this English edition of Professor Stanislav Menshikov's book has been printed, Russia's President Vladimir Vladimirovich Putin will have delivered his landmark May 10, 2006 "state of the union" address. The President's address will have marked the probable close of what had been the demographically murderous, greatest carpetbagging swindle in history. The carpetbagging which Professor Menshikov's book describes, is the post-1989 looting of the territory of the former Soviet Union, a looting that, in fact, has also been the predatory ruin of most of the East European territory of the Comecon outside Russia then and now.

Ironically, it should be clear today, that no net gain was to be had over the long term, from that vast amount of looting done by the presumed victors over the Soviet system, such as President George H.W. Bush's USA and the relevant West European nations. Whatever the perceived benefits to anyone from the Soviet system's collapse, the current physical economic condition in Europe and the Americas today, is far worse than in 1989.

Since the earlier, Russian edition of this book appeared, relevant and crucially important additional elements in that story have been taken into account in the present English edition. With the book's completion, a chapter of world history is being closed.

It is now time to learn the lessons of Professor Menshikov's account, as they bear on the decisions which must be made now, as we enter what threatens to become the worst economic collapse the world will have experienced, since a period of horrifying religious warfare was ended by the crucial adoption of the 1648 Treaty of Westphalia. The methods and habits accumulated during looting of the former Soviet Union and associated Comecon nations, express the acquired habits that now threaten the ruin of the world as a whole, unless the adducible lesson of this experience of recent decades, described is this book, is learned and applied.

There was an earlier point in time, at which the worst of the effects of the post-1996 phase of the ruin of Russia might have been prevented. On April 24, 1996, I appeared as a featured guest at a Moscow seminar of a roster of distinguished leading figures of Russia. The hosts of the seminar represented as prestigious an assembly of responsible policy-shapers as one could have desired. The purpose of that meeting was to define a launching-point for a possible role of the USA, then under President William J. Clinton's leadership, in halting the carpetbagging process, and beginning new forms of collaboration between Russia and the USA, which might end the ongoing process of carpetbagging. Some in the USA strongly advised the Clinton Presidency against the course of action implied in that April 1996 Moscow seminar. On that account, the implied threat from President Clinton's political opposition, which included some of the most powerful predators of the Transatlantic financier community, was ominous.

This U.S. rejection of the course of action implied in that Moscow seminar, had serious consequences for not only Russia, but the world at large, including much of the worsening global economic nightmare which has been experienced to the present day.

It was soon apparent that U.S. failure to respond to the issues tabled at the Moscow seminar had been a grave mistake for the USA, too. The 1997-1998 world crisis of the financial-derivatives system, especially the GKO hedge-fund crisis and its aftermath of August-October 1998, was the consequence of the U.S. failure to seize that opportunity, which the Moscow seminar had signalled. To his credit, President Clinton proposed, in September 1998, to move toward a needed reform of the world monetary-financial order. The attempted impeachment of the U.S. President, organized by the very bitter, and very predatory opponents of his proposed reform, was the result. Now, ten years after that 1996 Moscow seminar, the U.S. failure to accept the implied cooperation from Moscow has come to menace not only the USA, but all of Western Europe, and much of other parts the world, as distant as Tokyo.

During the time the English edition of Professor Menshikov's book was being prepared for publication, there was the thought that the celebrated John Kenneth Galbraith, who had co-authored an earlier book with Professor Menshikov, would be a most appropriate contributor of an introduction to this edition. Concerns for Mr. Galbraith's health precluded his undertaking that chore. Since then, as we know, the venerable John Kenneth Galbraith has recently died. His association with the U.S. Franklin Delano Roosevelt administration, his association with President John F. Kennedy, and his role as a sometime senior advisor to President William J. Clinton, would have made him a most appropriate contributor.

The point to be stressed here and now, is that the presently on-rushing hyperinflationary spiral in world prices of primary materials of production, means that deep-going, and far-reaching reforms in the world economic order must be made, and that cooperation between the USA, among others, and Russia today, will be an essential part of any successful escape from the immediately threatened global catastrophe.

During 2006 to date, the rate of increase of the rate of inflation in primary commodities, is comparable to the pattern of increase of prices in Weimar Germany of the second half of 1923. In 1923, that inflationary crisis in Germany was the result of the predatory terms imposed by the financial interests represented by the Versailles Treaty organization. Today, the immediate cause of the world's present hyperinflationary crisis, is those same kinds of policies, recently operating world-wide, which were expressed by the carpetbagging operations against the territories of both the post-1989 Soviet Union and other territories of the former Comecon association.

In reflection on this experience from the period of world history since 1989, we should learn afresh, that looting one's neighbor, even a presumed adversary, is a bad policy, a policy which would probably cause ultimate suffering to the predator. We live on one planet, such that deductions from the physical and related well-being of any part of humanity, is a lowering of the conditions, under which the whole of the planet lives.

That is a well-known principle of natural law, called agapē in ancient Classical Greek, as in the Christian New Testament; it is also the principle set forth in the opening sentence of the great 1648 Treaty of Westphalia, on which the well-being of modern European civilization has always depended since. The rule of natural law, which is affirmed in the 1648 Treaty of Westphalia, is one that only fools violate. The rule is, that in all conflicts, the victor must benefit, not loot the vanquished—as President Franklin Roosevelt had intended to do as the close of World War II approached.

Therefore, I pray that you read this account by Professor Menshikov by that light. What happened to Russia, as he recounts that, not only could happen to us; it is, in effect, now happening to us in the USA, and to most of the world besides. The disease, which Professor Menshikov has described in these pages, is, in effect, now an economic global pandemic which we must all join to defeat.

May 14, 2006

Introduction to the English Edition

This book was first published in Russian in May 2004, two months after Vladimir Putin's reelection to a second term as President of the Russian Federation and six months after the arrest of Yukos Oil CEO Mikhail Khodorkovsky, who had been the wealthiest businessman in the country. At the time many people thought that the main motivation for the arrest was political, because Putin saw Khodorkovsky as a dangerous potential rival in the Russian power struggle. What this book shows, however, is that the conflict around Khodorkovsky reflects a deeper conflict within the Russian economy and the country's politics—between the state, and the industrial and financial oligarchy. In the years since publication of that first edition, that confrontation has become more acute.

After the collapse of Soviet power in 1991, there began a transition to a market economy and capitalism. Many people supposed that the Russian economy would proceed to develop in accordance with the neoclassical competition model, with private property distributed to a significant part of the population. The Russian Parliament adopted legislation in 1992 and 1993, designed to promote that model. Industrial enterprises that had previously been subordinate to ministries and other state agencies became independent and were converted to joint stock companies, with half their shares being designated for distribution to their employees, and the rest to the population at large through a voucher program.

In the event, things happened rather differently. By 1996-1997, ownership of facilities in key sectors of the economy had come into the hands of banking and financial oligarchs. Monopolies and oligopolies gained the upper hand over any sort of market competition. President Boris Yeltsin and his governments, with the exception of the short-lived Yevgeni Primakov cabinet in 1998-1999, promoted the creation of oligarchical capitalism and soon came under its control. The government turned into a management committee for the oligarchs' affairs. This book tells how that came to pass.

When Putin assumed power at the end of 1999, it was widely believed that he would be a puppet in the hands of the oligarchs. Grounds for this belief included the fact that the Yedinstvo (Unity) Party (later Yedinaya Rossiya, United Russia), to which Putin owed his first term as President, had been established with funds from Boris Berezovsky, one of the leading oligarchs at the time. But Putin's chief concern was to consolidate his own power as President, and he soon realized that being controlled by the oligarchs was a hindrance. He decided to free himself from that control. The first conflict between the President and the oligarchs developed over the broadcast media, which plays a major role in shaping public opinion. Berezovsky owned a controlling stake in ORT (Channel 1), Russia's most powerful TV company. The second most powerful television channel belonged to another oligarch, Vladimir Gusinsky. Putin managed first to force Berezovsky to surrender his control over ORT to the state, and then, acting through the state-owned company Gazprom, took control (of a "softer" kind) of Gusinsky's NTV. In both instances the President got the Prosecutor General's office to open criminal cases against these billionaires, forcing them to emigrate.

That was only the beginning of what Putin did to redistribute the oligarchs' property. The next step was to break Yukos Oil, transferring most of its oil extraction capacity (the Yuganskneftegaz company) to the state-owned oil company Rosneft. Then the state natural gas monopoly, Gazprom, took over Sibneft, an oil company that had belonged to billionaire Roman Abramovich. Thus Putin got rid of two more oligarchs—Khodorkovsky and Abramovich—and greatly enhanced the position of the state in the Russian oil industry.

Further on, the state-owned arms exporter, Rosoboronexport, took over the AvtoVAZ and KamAZ automobile producers. A state-owned aircraft production company has been established to unite all of the leading plants and design bureaus of this sector in a single holding company. In all, counting other companies and banks, at the beginning of 2006 the "Putin group" controlled assets with a market value of $245 billion, or 40 percent of the total market capitalization of companies listed on Russian stock exchanges. Before Gazprom relaxed restriction on trade in its shares, and the government returned to the oil industry in a big way, direct state participation in the economy was substantially less. This fundamental change in the structure of the Russian economy, which has occurred under Putin, is described in detail and analyzed in this new, English edition of *The Anatomy of Russian Capitalism*.

Two questions remain open, each of which directly affects Russia's future: 1) how far Putin will go in renationalizing the Russian economy, and 2) what role the state sector will play in the country's economic development.

In examining these questions from the standpoint of the struggle between Putin and the oligarchs for dominance in the political realm, as well as the economy, the first thing to look at is the dimensions of the capital controlled by each. Available data showed that the total personal wealth of Russia's fifty "dollar" billionaires was $192 billion at the beginning of 2006, an amount equivalent to 32 percent of the market capitalization of all Russian companies, both private and state-owned. These fifty people are the cream of the industrial-financial oligarchy, which Putin had grounds to consider a direct threat to his power as of 2004. But now things have changed. The total capital of the fifty oligarchs is now less than that of the "Kremlin" grouping, which controls 40 percent of the total market capitalization, a full eight percentage points more than the private oligarchs combined. Strictly on the basis of these quantitative measures, Putin could say, "Enough is enough. Let's stop. That's it." And the renationalization process would come to a halt.

But the President may have had other sources of inspiration. In the mid-1990s, when Putin was vice-mayor of St. Petersburg, he defended his dissertation for the *kandidat* degree in economics. In this paper he argued that the state ought to maintain ultimate control over all mineral resources. When he became President, he did not explicitly preach that principle, but we have often seen him apply it in practice. Lately he has extended it to some key manufacturing industries. He continues to take this line, running counter to the neo-liberal policy of minimizing the state's role in the economy, which the cabinet officials responsible for finance and economics espouse. These ministers, Alexei Kudrin and German Gref, even speak out from time to time against the expansion of the state sector, but they still enjoy the President's support in fiscal and monetary policy. The result is a contradictory situation, without clear indications for the future development of the state sector and its role in the economy.

One possible solution to the contradiction is the currently widespread hypothesis that what is occurring under Putin is not the partial renationalization of the economy, but rather what might be called "state privatization": transfer, to the "Kremlin" or "Putin" clan in the bureaucracy, of control over the financial assets and money flows of a large group of companies that are formally state-owned, but effectively are being transformed into a feeding trough for these new oligarchs. This school of thought holds that Putin and his close associates are becoming personally wealthy through the new redistribution of property. Putin has publicly denied that he would want to head Gazprom or any other business within the "Kremlin" group, when he leaves office in 2008. But those statements do not preclude his becoming the uncrowned monarch of this business empire. If that happens, the Kremlin industrial financial group will simply meld into the existing system of oligarchical capitalism, and will be one of its main branches, obeying its general laws and rules of conduct.

There is another scenario, which I personally prefer, but which is unlikely to come to pass without radical changes in economic policy. That would be the transformation of the state sector into the main engine of growth in the Russian economy, countering the stagnation brought on by the oligarchical form of organization. That is the main conclusion and policy recommendation to emerge from the present study.

The state ought to play a leading role in the Russian economy, if only because private capital refuses to invest in the science-intensive high-technology areas, where Russia potentially has major competitive advantages over other countries, including industrially developed ones. Only the state can break Russia's present tendency toward stagnation and open the doors to an across-the-board modernization of the economy, its production capacities, and forms of organization. Without leadership from the state, Russia will be unable to create modern economic infrastructure, revolutionize its transportation system, and cover the country with highway, communications and information networks. Without state leadership in the economy, Russia will continue chronically to lag behind the developed countries in labor productivity and standards of living, to depend on raw materials and fuels exports, and to suffer from an underdeveloped domestic market and unstable growth rates.

There would be no need for the state to take a leading role, of course, if the Russian economy were developing smoothly, and private capital were functioning as it should in a market economy. This is not the case. Private capital is invested primarily in export-oriented industries like oil and metals, which yield superprofit (rent), and in intermediary trade and finance operations, but not, as a rule, in manufacturing. There are two reasons for this pattern, the first being the consistently higher profit levels in the export sectors, and the second the small size of the domestic market, which renders most domestically oriented industries unprofitable. Those two reasons are subsumed by a single, primary cause: the excessive monopolization of the economy, resulting in too high a share of profit and too low a share of labor income in GDP. That is the diagnosis I give the ailing Russian economy in this book.

American readers may not immediately grasp the degree of monopolization in Russia, which justifies calling its economy "oligarchical." There is a fairly high concentration of capital in the United States; readers may think that Russian capitalism is merely following that model. A comparison of the two countries, however, reveals great dissimilarities and a deep abyss between them. The 25 biggest corporations in America, for example, account for 25 percent of the market value of all stock shares; the top 500 companies account for 63 percent. Those are high numbers, and they testify to the dominance of big business in the American economy. But in Russia, 50 companies account for over 90 percent of the total market value of shares listed on Russian stock exchanges. Obviously this bespeaks a far greater concentration of capital than there is in the USA.

The two countries also differ in the degree of concentration of personal wealth in the hands of the upper echelons of what may be called the financial oligarchy. The 50 richest people in Russia (each with a personal fortune of $1 billion or more) at the beginning of

2006 had $192 billion in total personal assets, an amount equal to 32 percent of the total market capitalization of companies listed on Russian stock exchanges. By comparison, the total personal assets of the top 50 billionaires in the United States in 2005 were 2.5 times greater in absolute terms than those of their Russian counterparts: $503 billion. But that figure equalled only 3.8 percent of total market capitalization, which is less by a factor of 8.4 than the relative size of the personal assets of Russia's wealthy. If we look at the 375 richest individuals in each of the countries (in the USA that means people with fortunes of $1 billion or more, while the level in Russia is $100 million or more), their total wealth equalled only 8 percent of overall market capitalization in the United States, but 43.8 percent, over five times more, in Russia. Taking note of the fact that another 48 percent is controlled by the Kremlin group, less than 10 percent remains for all other shareholders.

These figures reveal another contrast between Russia and the United States. In Russia, corporate stock shares are concentrated almost exclusively in the hands of either the state, or the top financial oligarchy, whereas in the USA millions of individual investors own shares, as do various financial and lending institutions. As of the beginning of 2005, almost 60 million American families, or 50.3 percent of the total, owned stock shares. In Russia, no more than 5 percent of all families are shareholders. In the United States in 2004, individual investors owned 38 percent of all shares, while banks, insurance companies, pension funds, and mutual funds held 48 percent. In Russia, where such financial institutions have not yet been developed, their share of ownership is negligibly small. Thus, not only is the domestic market for goods and services narrow, but the securities market is also extremely small, a factor that significantly retards capital investment and overall economic growth. It is apparent that in this area, too, it will be impossible to overcome stagnation and backwardness without the state taking the lead.

The contrasting composition of the American and Russian top layers of billionaires is also quite revealing. Thirty-two of the top 50 American billionaires, a strong majority, run companies in sectors such as finance, trade, and the mass media. None of this subgroup is directly involved with the physical economy, i.e., the production of material goods. The only group directly connected with the latest technological progress comprises businessmen involved in information technologies, represented by the owners of companies like Microsoft, Dell, Oracle and Google. The list of wealthiest American families includes no founders of auto, electrical engineering, aircraft, oil, aluminum, steel or other industrial companies—firms in what the noted American economist and politician Lyndon LaRouche classifies as the physical economy, comprising the backbone of America's industrial might. Those companies are headed not by billionaires, but by hired managers, as the result of a managerial revolution that took place over several decades in the 20th century. Personal wealth nowadays is acquired in different ways. But at least some of it is associated with major new companies that have succeeded in exploiting and promoting new technologies. Technological progress may have become limited to certain economic sectors, but it has not been totally suppressed by the drive to accumulate wealth; rather, the two impulses continue to interact.

Russian capitalism is young and has not experienced a managerial revolution. With the exception of the state sector, companies are still headed by the people who own the controlling stakes in them, and who generally acquired them at cut-rate prices when state-owned enterprises were privatized. The great majority of the 50 richest people in Russia own companies in the oil, non-ferrous metals, steel, coal, iron ore, copper, chemical feedstuffs, natural gas, and cement industries. There is only one high-tech billionaire among them, and he "inherited" his holdings from the state. Some of the billionaires, however, made their fortunes through financial operations, which they then used as a base from which to take over major banks.

While it might seem that the majority of Russia's oligarchs are directly involved in the physical economy, it must be borne in mind that they did not themselves establish the industrial enterprises they own, and that they have not yet set up any new ones, either in their own sectors or in others. Of special importance is the fact that not a single one of them has made his mark by turning out final products like machines, equipment, computers, transport and communications products, or consumer durables. They represent an amazingly unproductive generation of businessmen, who have managed to get rich by exploiting Russia's natural resources, but appear incapable of moving to the forefront of technological progress.

As a certain well-known economist once put it, "Monopoly breeds decay and technological stagnation."

An economy in such a condition is trapped. The only way out is to destroy its oligarchical structure, root and branch, with the state taking an active role.

That is the main subject and principal purpose of this book. It begins with a general characterization of Russian capitalism as a specific phenomenon that arose from the wreckage, and simultaneously on the basis, of state socialism. I say "wreckage," because the shock policy of the early 1990s—what I call "Bolshevism in reverse"—deliberately destroyed the previous economy's planning and distribution infrastructure, decreeing that private property be established in its place, without appropriate preparatory work being done to develop any market infrastructure. But the new system was heir to the surviving material base of the economy, in the form of tremendous production capacities, which were now placed at the service of their new owners and the new order of things. This material base, created for an entirely different purpose, became the foundation of the wealth of a new capitalist class.

That class actually began to take shape earlier, still under the planned economy, in the form of shadow economy operators and a certain degenerate layer of the economic elite in the socialist system. That background left an indelible mark on the new Russian capitalists, who were used to concealing their income, weaving webs of corruption, developing close relations with organized crime, and making money at state expense.

Currently some people maintain that the origin and history of the oligarchs' capital are of little importance, and that the only relevant question is for it to be utilized for the supposed good of the economy. In other words, the important process to focus on is the rapid and miraculous transformation of those former shadow economy operators and speculators, those capitalist pirates, into civilized businessmen who live by the customs and rules of the democratic West. There might be some logical basis for this argument, if the enrichment of that minority were occurring in a setting of overall improvement of life for the majority of the population (as happened in China, for example), or were based on technological innovation, rather than on speculation and natural rent from resources developed in the Soviet period. It might hold up, if the enrichment of that minority were due to overall economic growth and technological progress, rather than to robbery committed against the majority of the population. But that enrichment has ruined the economy and marked the new capitalist class as largely parasitical. Of necessity this book speaks loud and clear about the roots of these processes.

Unlike many other countries, Russia saw its capitalism spring up almost immediately in the form of major monopolistic concerns and banks. Though privatization was implemented, as a rule, on the basis of individual enterprises, within a few years they had merged and fused into large companies. In some sectors, such as oil and nickel, the state itself acted to create large concerns, which were then sold to private owners. Although private banks served as an initial venue for the accumulation of several multimillion-dollar fortunes, the banking sector developed at a significantly slower rate than did industry. Nonetheless, it was the banks that served as the focal points for the formation of the oligarchical financial groups, which seized control of all the most profitable sectors of industry.

With big business bloated out of all proportion, the role of medium-sized and small business in Russia is far less than it should be. This has various detrimental effects. The prevalence of monopolistic and oligopolistic organizations prevents the full-fledged development of competition, which, despite its limitations, can be a powerful factor in technological progress in a market economy. In addition, it blocks the development of a middle class, thereby stunting the development of the domestic market.

But if small business is underdeveloped in Russia, harmful phenomena such as the shadow economy, organized crime, and corruption at all levels of government are certainly overdeveloped.

This book demonstrates how the economic policy of neo-liberalism, pursued by several Russian governments since 1992, is often destructive and retards economic growth. It has put the emphasis on poorly prepared structural reforms, which only aggravated imbalances in the economy.

Chapter 6 shows the deterioration of Russia's place in the world economy: its extraordinary dependence on the raw materials sectors, the weak competitive power of its manufacturing industry, and the country's transformation into a peripheral zone of the industrial West. At the same time, Russia has failed to become a truly attractive market for the sale of Western industrial products or, unlike China, for foreign investment. Until very recently, the transnational ties of Russian capital have been underdeveloped and lopsided.

Only in 2006 did the transnational ties of Russian industrial companies begin to develop rapidly. In past years these ties had involved primarily foreign direct investment in Russian industry, and the purchase of Russian firms by foreign corporations. The biggest such deal was the sale of a 50 percent stake in the Tyumen Oil Company (TNK) to Britain's BP. Now, however, Russian companies are becoming active participants in the process, and have gone on the offensive.

Gazprom took the lead. The natural gas monopoly has moved to acquire gas distribution companies in several countries in the West. At the same time, Gazprom opened up trading in its shares to foreign portfolio investors, while a controlling stake remains state-owned. In addition, Gazprom has sent out new tentacles, building gas pipelines in northern and southern Europe, as well as the Far East. Another example is the IPO by the state-owned oil company Rosneft, which plans to place 49 percent of its shares in Russian and foreign financial markets. Several other Russian companies have also made their IPOs during 2006.

The new trend has a dual significance for the process of Russia's integration into the world economy. Russian companies are being transformed from simple sellers of their products on foreign markets, often through foreign middlemen, into active players in the capital markets, customers for the major western banks, and partners of elite financial and political groups on a world level. With expanded access to sources of foreign financing, they are in a position to break out of the narrow and limited Russian capital market. This is a good thing, though some dangers are entailed. As they become interwoven with the international financial system, our money markets grow more dependent on their fluctuations, and vulnerable to shocks from abroad. World money markets are a chaotic scene, where the speculative movements of portfolio and short-term capital are unpredictable. They experience periodic financial crises. Neither Russian capital, nor our government is ready for such turbulence.

Fluctuations on the Russian stock exchange are already quite significant. Minister of Economic Development and Trade German Gref has expressed some concern about these fluctuations, calling them a harbinger of a popping of the "stock market bubble." And a stock market crash could easily turn into a new edition of the 1998 crisis.

Russia's integration into the unstable financial markets of the West is encountering few obstacles, but the same cannot be said about its attempts to achieve integration in leading sectors of industry. The latest demonstration of the problem was centered on Arcelor, the Luxembourg-based steel company. A deal for the Russian steel company Severstal to acquire one-third of its shares occasioned a furious anti-Russian campaign in some quarters. The deal was cancelled, with Arcelor paying Severstal owner Alexei Mordashov a fine of 140 million euros, to be free of its entanglement with the Russian capitalist. Behind the scenes, it was Wall Street that orchestrated the parting of ways between Arcelor and Severstal. Goldman Sachs, known for its close ties with the Bush administration (its executive Henry Paulson had just been named U.S. Treasury Secretary), played a leading role. Their main motive is to block Russian access to advanced technologies in key sectors of industry, not to mention possible Russian control of major corporations in the West.

The last section of Chapter 6 summarizes what I call the inertial system of Russian capitalism. It is caught in a vicious circle of the economy's main biases: over-concentration on the fuel and raw materials industries and underdevelopment of the domestic market, due to poverty on a mass scale. Policy alternatives are offered as a way out of this macroeconomic trap: specifically, the state's taking a leading role, at least temporarily, as mentioned above.

Some readers may find my alternative program of reforms too radical. I would like to caution against jumping to such conclusions. Many of these recommendations echo recipes that have been used with success in developed industrial countries for many years. One proposal, for example, is to introduce a consistent policy of social partnership, based on an accord within the triangle of government, business, and trade unions, in order to rectify the macroeconomic imbalance between profit and labor income; to target capital investment, selectively, into priority sectors of the economy; and to bring about a more efficient and more just distribution of government social spending, as well as establish optimal levels of taxation.

I call for doing what was done in the USA after 1929: gradually to raise the share of labor income in GDP from its present level of 43-45 percent, up to 59-60 percent, and the share of personal consumption from 50 percent, up to the 67-70 percent range. This proposal obviously does not stem from radical leftist premises, but from the same plain common sense that prompted the American elite to accept the structural changes, needed in order to prevent a repetition of the Great Depression of the 1930s.

I present statistical evidence of the ability of American capitalism to thrive, on the whole, at average profit margins of just 6-7 percent in manufacturing, while our oligarchs, for some reason, complain that they can scarcely make ends meet at profit margins of 30, 50 or even 60 percent. Under those conditions it is, of course, impossible to have balanced growth of the economy as a whole, the free flow of resources from capital-surplus sectors into capital-deficit sectors, a normally functioning money market, or any properly functioning market whatsoever.

If Russia wants to develop as a normal, prosperous, civilized country with a decent standard of living for the majority of its population, it must make fundamental changes in Russian capitalism. Those changes cannot be merely cosmetic, daubing on some make-up to improve appearances, or creating the illusion of transparency. They must be thorough-going changes that make the market economy work in the national interest, move toward creation and modernization, achieve technological progress, and improve the people's welfare.

In conclusion, I would like to express special gratitude to my fine American colleague and friend Lyndon LaRouche, whose support has made it possible for this book to appear in the United States. It should be acknowledged that many of the concepts expressed by Lyndon, in his books and many public speeches, served as methodological points of departure for writing this book. More broadly, it may be said that Lyndon's inspiring ideas help thinking people in my country to better understand the processes taking place in the world. In that same spirit, I hope that my own book will promote a better understanding of Russia, in America.

Rachel Douglas has my thanks for undertaking the challenging work of translation, as well as for her many valuable observations, which helped me to update the English edition so that the factual material and analysis would include very recent events (through June 2006).

As always, Larissa Klimenko-Menshikova's help has been invaluable. The concept and execution of both the Russian and the English editions were discussed with her at every stage of the work.

Lastly, I am deeply grateful to all those who helped bring this book into being with their advice and critical remarks, especially to the authors of the numerous reviews that appeared in the Russian press and academic journals. Substantial improvements in the English edition were based on their suggestions.

Stanislav Menshikov
Moscow–Amsterdam, March 2006

1 A General Description of Russian Capitalism

A few years ago, when I initiated discussion of the first draft of this book with colleagues at Moscow State University, some of them questioned the propriety of even using the term "capitalism" with respect to Russia. They wanted to know why I supposed that the current Russian social order should be called capitalism. First of all, they argued, our society is a hybrid, which mixes various forms of economic organization, some of them non-capitalist. Secondly, what people in Russia call capitalism bears little resemblance to modern capitalism in the industrially developed West. Lastly, they thought it would be a bad idea to use the term "capitalism" because it was archaic and had a certain negative connotation.

For me, however, the term "capitalism" is neither obsolete, nor necessarily negative or derogatory. In many countries capitalism not only is nothing to be ashamed of, but it is held up as the highest achievement, the apotheosis of human civilization, or, in the words of the American sociologist Francis Fukuyama, a worthy "end of history."[1] In those countries wealthy people and capitalists are the pillars of society. They are the elite.

Admittedly the words "capitalist" and "capitalism" have been received with suspicion in Russia for a very long time. They bear the indelible stain of exploitation, of sweat wrung out of the workers, of dishonest profiteering, fraud, and usury. In the 19th century, Russian capitalists preferred to call themselves industrialists, entrepreneurs or merchants. Contemporary Russian capitalists likewise have formed "unions of industrialists and entrepreneurs," chambers of commerce and industry, industrial associations, and so forth. The President, members of the government, and many other politicians generally avoid the word "capitalism" when discussing the social system in Russia, preferring to say "market economy." It is worth noting, however, that in the Western literature these two terms are used interchangeably, and they are both applied to the situation in Russia today. Western authors are not plagued by doubts about defining capitalism as the predominance of private ownership of economic assets, in combination with market relations, as distinct from societies where there is no private ownership, or almost none, and no market serving as the main way to exchange products between economic agents. This understanding of capitalism is consistent with its scientific definition.

1.1 Is this capitalism?

In this book the concept of "capitalist" is used exclusively in its scientific sense, to denote an individual who privately owns means of production, whether solely, or jointly with others, and uses them to produce a saleable product by employing workers for monetary compensation. The types of capitalist activity are quite diverse. A capitalist may be an industrialist, meaning the proprietor of a manufacturing plant, factory, mine, quarry, farm, or any other production facility. He may be an entrepreneur in the broader sense, such as a merchant or the proprietor of a hotel, restaurant, or a transport or telecommunications company, who would not be called an industrialist. Lastly, a capitalist may be a banker or, broadly speaking, a financier: an entrepreneur who specializes in trading money-capital.

Accordingly, capitalism is defined scientifically as a society in which goods and services are produced primarily by privately owned businesses, which hire labor for monetary compensation and sell their output in the market. A society of this type has a legal basis for the private ownership of the means of production, the freedom to sell one's labor, and free competition in the market for goods and services. Politically, such societies have democratic institutions that guarantee basic rights for the individual, and the equal right of all citizens to take part in governing the state.

Of course, this broadest definition allows for some modifications and departures. Democracy in such societies may be incomplete, or even severely curtailed; historically capitalism in some countries was combined with overt despotism and de facto slavery. Capitalist forms may coexist with other forms of organization of production, but the former must be predominant, in order for the society properly to be called capitalist. Private property rights may be limited, but not to such an extent that the capitalist does not make decisions concerning what to do with his own property; he will not be compelled to subordinate his activity entirely to directives from the government, or stripped of the right to derive income from his businesses. Free competition may be limited, but total monopolies, as a rule, are excluded. Corrupt officials and criminals may play a role in the redistribution of income, but they are not the main players in the economy.

From these preliminary remarks, it is already apparent that Russian society diverges markedly from any pure model of capitalism. In fairness, it must be said that pure capitalism does not exist anywhere in the world, even in the most industrially developed countries. Since the peculiarities of our capitalism are the subject of this book, we shall analyze them in subsequent sections and chapters. For the moment, let us return to questions of terminology.

The Russian attitude toward capitalism is not limited to the traditional popular dislike of moneybags. The second half of the 19th century saw the emergence of theories that said capitalism could not develop on Russian soil, or could develop only in extremely abnormal forms. According to these conceptions, capitalist relations in agriculture (and Russia was primarily an agrarian country at the time) would be blocked by the traditional communal form of organization, which was incompatible with capitalism. As for urban areas, it was believed that capitalism would fail to develop in the cities because it was intrinsically incapable of creating a large enough domestic market for itself.

These views were opposed by other conceptions, which argued in favor of the viability of capitalism in Russia. One of these was the Leninist version of Marxism, which demonstrated convincingly that capitalism was developing quite well in Russia, although with certain peculiarities. V.I. Lenin believed that this was altogether a progressive tendency, since only the development of capitalism in the country could create a large and organized working class, which, according to Marxism, would be destined to replace capitalism with socialism. Lenin thought of capitalism as a short stage in Russia's development, and as a historical instrument for ripening its own contradictions and, ultimately, preparing the conditions under which it would be superseded.

Still another conception likewise viewed capitalism in Russia as viable, but held that capitalism itself would be the true pathway to Russia's "modernization" and transformation into an advanced industrial country. The high industrial growth rates experienced at the beginning of the 20th century would seem to have confirmed this theory, but World War I and the October Revolution of 1917 prevented it from being fully tested. Russian capitalism, being only in its early stages, was unable to withstand the social crisis, which was aggravated by the war; it fell victim to its own economic—and, even more to the point, political—backwardness.

In place of capitalism, the tasks of industrializing the country, and subsequently creating powerful, modern industrial, scientific, and technological capabilities, fell to the system variously known as socialism, state socialism, the command economy, or the centrally planned economy. We shall not analyze here in detail either how it functioned (that is described in our previous books, among other places), or the debate over its comparative shortcomings and advantages.[2]

Some works published in the late 1980s maintained that the economic development of Russia would have been faster, had Russia's old capitalism not been destroyed. Hypotheses of this type cannot be scientifically upheld or refuted, and must remain in the domain of speculation. Without question, however, the development of the economy would have been substantially different under the old capitalism; whether better or worse, is another question.

For example, Russia is a primarily northern country, whose enormous mineral resources are situated in areas that are accessible only with difficulty and have a climate inhospitable to human existence. It is doubtful that capitalist development would have been able to open up these resources for economic exploitation, without the intervention and assistance of a strong state. The planned economy was able to do this, albeit by sometimes less than humane methods. It is for this reason that by the late 20th century the Russian economy had acquired the peculiar composition that distinguishes it from most other countries: the predominance, on the one hand, of the fuel and raw materials sectors and, on the other, of an industrial, scientific and technological complex oriented toward military priorities. This unique composition, in turn, is what makes it so difficult for the Russian economy to adapt to a classical capitalist model and for the country to be transformed into an ordinary industrially developed market nation, oriented toward producing goods and services for personal consumption. An economy dominated by the extractive industries and heavy industry simply does not match the standard.

1.2 Bolshevism in reverse

Contemporary Russian reformers, and the Western scholars on whose advice they relied, proceeded from an extremely oversimplified notion of how such a transformation could occur. Their essential blueprint was almost a mirror image of the Leninist approach to building socialism. Lenin, following Marx, supposed that capitalism in its final stage would have created the complete material preconditions for socialism, and that it would suffice to change the prevailing mode of property ownership, replacing private ownership with state ownership, in order to obtain at least the bare bones of socialism. Then, by changing the system of distribution and putting it "at the service of the entire people," as he said, the economic framework created by capitalism would come to life as full-fledged socialism.

Things turned out to be rather more complex. Russian capitalism was underdeveloped from the standpoint of either the material base of production or the administrative infrastructure. Both of them had to be built up, which took many years, many lives, and many sacrifices by society.

The post-Soviet Russian reformers' blueprint followed Western neoclassical dogma, according to which, similarly, to restructure socialism into capitalism, it should suffice merely to replace state-owned property with private property, and the planned economy with the free play of market forces. In reality, this was "Lenin in reverse," since it was only formally that socialism had prepared the ground for capitalism, whereas in practice it had made this task extremely difficult, costing, once again, enormous social sacrifices in the form of an acute deterioration of living conditions for the majority of the population.

Nonetheless, both the Bolsheviks and the market reformers achieved their main goal: they truly did transform the formal basis of property ownership, and smash the old ways of running the economy. In that sense, we can talk about the emergence in today's Russia of a system with all the formal attributes of capitalism:

- As of 2003, 76.9 percent of the country's companies and other economic organizations were privately owned. Only 10.3 percent of them remained state property, whether at the federal or the municipal level, while 6.4 percent belonged to public associations, and the other 6.4 percent were held under mixed forms of ownership or belonged to foreign legal entities or individuals.[3]
- Out of 3 million private businesses, 2.1 million were large or medium-sized firms employing over 100 people. Forty percent of the country's working population was employed at such companies. If we exclude health care, education, and administrative agencies, where state ownership continues to predominate, over 50 percent of the remaining working population was employed in private business.

The revolution in ownership took place very rapidly. As recently as 1990, only 12.5 percent of all employed persons worked in the private sector, as against 82.6 percent in the state sector. Not even the Bolsheviks after their revolution moved as fast as the market reformers did, to destroy the old system of property ownership and the economic infrastructure. The Soviet leadership spent several years experimenting with a market economy under the New Economic Policy (NEP), after which it took almost ten years to develop a central planning and administrative apparatus. The market reformers abandoned central planning almost immediately, and yet a dozen years after the effective launch of their reforms, a modern market infrastructure had still not been fully created.

Macroeconomic data demonstrate the same contrast. Excluding the three years of the Civil War (1918-1921), it took nine years in the post-revolutionary period to restore Russia's pre-World War I level of gross domestic product (GDP). Fairly objective data from Western statisticians show that by 1929, GDP had attained 102.6 percent of its 1913 level.[4] The same set of data shows that average annual GDP growth was 6.1 percent during the subsequent decade (1929-1939). In 1939 the GDP of the USSR was 85 percent greater than the 1913 level.

In 2004, by contrast, thirteen years after the launch of market reforms, Russia's GDP had reached only 83 percent of its pre-reform peak (1990). If the Putin regime's growth program for the decade ending in 2010 is realized, the national product will reach only 110 percent of its pre-reform level by the end of that period. The contrast with reconstruction during the 1920s is significant.

Is it really more difficult to transform socialism into capitalism, than the reverse? If, as many people assert, the market economy is more natural than artificially imposed socialism, then it would seem that things ought to be otherwise. Or, is it rather the case that the legacy of socialism is much more difficult to overcome, because socialism is also natural for contemporary society? Let us try to sort this out.

1.3 The legacy of socialism

The socialism we inherited had several economic "layers," each of which met a different fate in the post-Soviet period and requires separate consideration:

- state enterprises in all sectors of the economy, under various systems of subordination to state administrative and planning agencies;
- collective farms, which were responsible for a substantial portion of agricultural production and were integrated into the overall state system of economic management in a special way;
- the state system of social distribution and provision of services, including public education, health care, pensions, and social protection, broadly construed.

All three of these layers comprised official socialism. But, in addition, deep within the official organizations, and sometimes alongside them, there were two other kinds of organizations, which are customarily called "shadow," underground, or illegal. They were:
- **the shadow economy, and**
- **organized crime.**

These additional sectors had found a home, to one degree or another, in the pores of official society. Their development was accentuated in the 1970s and 1980s. According to various estimates, the shadow economy accounted for as much as 15 percent of GDP by the latter half of the 1980s, which is only a little less than the State Statistics Committee (Goskomstat) estimate of the size of the shadow sector in Russia's market economy today. These figures do not, however, reveal the whole picture of the comprehensive interweaving and fusing of shadow businesses with legitimate ones. *In reality, by the 1980s this interweaving, rather than the formalities of planning or centralized management, had become the main feature of our economy.*

As shown in our earlier works,[5] practically every state enterprise had its shadow component. The state was only one of the actual owners, its role being evidenced in plan targets, personnel appointments, and the distribution of revenue, a significant portion of which went to the state budget. The other de facto owners were the people who managed the enterprise on a daily basis and had a real opportunity to make decisions concerning its material resources and financial flows, including in their own personal interest. The enterprise directors exercised these de facto, informal property rights jointly with a segment of the enterprise's labor force and with representatives of superior administrative and supervisory organizations, local authorities, law enforcement agencies, and so forth. Gradually organized crime took these informal property owners under its wing, though in some places organized crime became *their* tool.

The prevalence of this type of symbiosis varied among regions and republics. It most likely existed in the majority of enterprises and among a significant number of economic organizations. It was therefore quite natural that when, at the last national conference of the Communist Party of the Soviet Union (CPSU), enterprise directors put forward a slogan about eliminating the industrial-sector ministries, nobody seriously objected. The de facto owners felt encumbered by the formal fetters of state ownership and centralized administration, and were just waiting for the opportunity to get rid of them.

Thus, to use a well-known Marxist formulation coined in a somewhat different connection, capitalist relations had ripened in the interstices of state socialist society. But precisely for that reason, the initial privatization of Russian enterprises in 1992-1994 in significant measure represented the institutionalization of an already existing state of affairs. Property was transferred to the people who were in charge of it on a day-to-day basis. The former corps of directors, to a significant extent, turned into a class of private capitalists, or rather into the most numerous part of that class.

1.4 Directors turned into capitalists

Today many of the "red directors" still head their old enterprises, but now as the completely legal majority owners. Under the conditions established for privatization, half the shares of each enterprise were supposed to become the property of its work force as a whole, but in reality the directors and their associates usually succeeded in either buying up these shares, or obtaining a mandate to manage them.[6] Ownership of industry by workers' collectives quickly became a fiction. Reinstituting it is now highly unlikely, without a new social revolution. The transformation of the directors into capitalists is most likely irreversible.

Another segment of the new capitalist class was recruited from the ranks of former underground entrepreneurs, who had either been running the "red directors" from the sidelines, or made their personal fortunes by some other means, back in the pores of socialism. Such fortunes came into being, especially during the late Gorbachov period, primarily in wholesale trade, finance, and various types of intermediary business, as well as in organized crime. These fortunes then served as the source of outside investment to acquire controlling equity stakes in some major enterprises, at first by buying up vouchers and seizing control at voucher auctions,[7] then later using the "loans-for-shares" operation, through which several bankers came to head industrial empires.[8]

Thus one could say that the old shadow economy, having ripened in the interstices of state socialism and the planned economy, and having become an integral component of that system, smoothly developed into today's Russian capitalism. It is quite natural that in this process the new Russian capitalists, at least in the initial period, inherited the types of behavior and profiteering that had been typical of Soviet underground business and organized crime. This should come as no great surprise, insofar as these new capitalists had not "graduated from Harvard," as the saying goes. Indeed, a Harvard education was irrelevant in the Russian setting.[9] Those trained in America to bestow the benefits of free-market economics, in the manner of the gift-giving golden fish in the fairy tales of Pushkin and the Brothers Grimm, became easy prey for the local pikes and sharks, if they did not want to play by our rules. Those who did manage to adapt not only survived, but made a killing themselves.[10] On the whole, the Russian criminal milieu proved to be stronger than "proper" foreign business.

At the same time, the Russian shadow business world had to adapt to the new conditions of a relatively free market, liberated from the fetters of centralized planning and administration. Enterprises that no longer received orders regarding sales prices and volume of production (or turnover) of goods began to set their own, as they saw fit. The natural drive to maximize profit led them to raise prices arbitrarily, while minimizing output and sales in real terms. The result was an orgy of price hikes, during which the survival of any given company was, to no small extent, a matter of chance. Aggravating factors included the collapse of traditional ties between enterprises, regions, and republics, as well as a sharp contraction of aggregate demand on a national scale.

Under these conditions the top priority for the executives controlling a company, naturally, was to achieve a rapid increase in their personal fortunes, rather than to look after the firm's medium- or long-term interests. There were many techniques for doing this. The simplest and most accessible was to transfer state property (even before its formal privatization) to private control. This practice is known in the American literature as "asset stripping." This sort of "wild" privatization also continued after the state property had been formally transferred to private hands. Since only a relatively small portion of former state property had become the legal property of the executives who managed it, they had a direct interest in appropriating an additional margin for themselves.

All of these factors contributed to the disruption of economic life and the overall decline of the economy. It is surprising that only half of the GDP, and not more, was lost during those first years of the market reforms.

With a few exceptions, however, major personal fortunes did

not arise from the "wild" privatization phase. Far greater success in fortune-building was achieved by playing on the difference between domestic and world prices, and on the divergence between the exchange rate of the ruble and its real purchasing power. The price gaps were particularly large for fuel and other raw materials exports, and in office equipment and household appliance imports. Even without counting the direct appropriation of foreign-currency earnings from, say, the sale of oil under barter arrangements approved by the government,[11] extraordinarily high levels of super-profit could be had at the beginning of the 1990s from the resale of all kinds of raw materials in the West.

These were primarily accidental or "wild" operations, in that they were carried out by various middlemen, who did not necessarily have any direct involvement in oil or other raw materials extraction or processing. This market (as we shall see in Chapter 2) became relatively monopolized only in the mid-1990s, when a comparatively small number of major companies gained control of each of its segments. At that point, the "unorganized" private operators were driven out of the raw materials and fuel export markets, or taken over by the major firms.

Some traders who had made money on raw materials export operations did subsequently seek control of these companies.[12] The majority of such operations were only semi-legal. The special permissions required for export operations were issued in exchange for large cash bribes or agreement to provide some services in return.[13]

1.5 Bankers as money-launderers

Favorable conditions developed in the financial sector, as well, for the accumulation of capital on a large scale in semi-legal ways. The first private banks were created in this period, in order to consolidate money earned from operations in industry and trade, particularly the proceeds of "wild" privatization and speculative operations. Soon these banks found additional opportunities to build up their capital quickly, by exploiting the foreign exchange market and managing budget funds for various levels of government. Once again, legal and not entirely legal methods were combined. There were very few legislative or administrative restrictions, for instance, on the banks' foreign exchange operations. It was also quite legal for the banks to become officially authorized agents for handling federal and local budget funds, and those of certain government-financed organizations. In the absence of a state Treasury, and with the Central Bank unwilling to carry out such functions, the commercial banks were the only organizations physically able to service the government's money transfer needs. Taxes, duties, and other revenues were deposited in special government accounts at commercial banks, and then allocated according to payment orders issued by government agencies. Certain banks were assigned certain parts of the budgetary financial flows.

Some of the banks' revenue from this financial function came from entirely legal commissions, which could be 7 percent, 10 percent, or higher per annum. But most of their profit derived from the use of temporarily available government funds, which were on deposit but idle, for their own commercial gain. Since the spread between interest rates on loans and deposits was always at least three to one, that factor alone provided substantial, and still quite legal, income. The semi-legal side involved how, and for what price, the list of authorized banks was drawn up. In addition, the banks would deliberately delay action on payment orders, stretching out the time it took for budget monies to reach their designated destination.

Quite apart from these factors, the disorderly inflation of those days gave rise to schemes under which money assets could grow automatically, with no special effort by the financiers. One such scheme took advantage of the spread between the interest rate on bank credits and the rate of the ruble's devaluation against the dollar.

An example is what happened in 1995, when the average annual interest rate on ruble bank deposits was 320.3 percent. Despite the astronomical rate of inflation implied by that multiplier, the ruble fell by "only" 23.5 percent against the dollar during that year. A financier who had put, say, $10 million on deposit in a bank at the beginning of the year, in the form of 35.5 billion (pre-redenomination) rubles, saw it turn into 113.6 billion rubles, which by year's end he could convert back into $24.5 million. This meant a 250 percent increase of capital in dollar terms.

It is of particular importance that these gains happened automatically. The mechanism that produced them continued to function, as long as the spread between interest rates and the rate of devaluation of the ruble existed—until the 1998 crisis. Its profitability only diminished somewhat, as credit became cheaper. This source of enrichment played its part chiefly during the first years of reform, which was when the Russian banking empires came into existence.[14]

It was a priority for the financiers to establish control over large financial flows belonging to others, in this case to the government, and then put them to work as their own funds and get them to grow automatically. But the essential principle involved was the same as it had been in the old shadow economy: private capital took control over state property, treating it as its own, and appropriated the revenue it yielded. The only difference was the partial legalization of the process. Whereas under socialism it had been illegal from start to finish, in the new circumstances private income derived from state property could be legalized. Illegally obtained revenue was laundered.

Official agreements, under which a bank was temporarily allowed to use the property entrusted to it, with the obligation to pay a part of the associated earnings to the government, moved in the direction of legalizing these operations. But, insofar as these agreements covered only a small part of such revenue, while the banks had no legal right to appropriate the larger part, these operations as a whole teetered between legality and illegality.

1.6 Socialism: another source of capital

Another aspect of the socialist legacy also proved to be of some use in transiting to capitalism, namely, the main system for personal income distribution. Because it was useful, it lasted over a decade, despite the market reformers' attempts to dismantle it. Its staying power was not due to social unrest or popular resistance. The reformers carried out drastic experiments on the personal income of the majority of the population. By decontrolling prices and whipping up high rates of inflation, they managed to reduce incomes by one-half or two-thirds, without serious resistance. They slashed GDP and industrial output by one-half, reintroducing mass unemployment for the first time in decades. If they had really wanted to, they could also have liquidated the social support system. This did begin to happen to some extent, as we shall discuss below. At least temporarily, however, the main components were preserved:

- free basic health care;
- free secondary education;
- basically free higher education at state educational institutions;
- relatively low payments for housing and the most essential residential utilities.

For-fee services naturally appeared in all of these sectors as well, which sent the quality of the state services into a downslide. Nonetheless, the state services were preserved, despite strenuous efforts in the upper echelons of the government, and by the international financial institutions backing those upper echelons, to destroy them.

The reason would seem to be that this state of affairs was extraordinarily profitable for the new capitalist class. According both to Marx and to neoclassical theory, the required remuneration of labor (labor power) tends under equilibrium conditions to approximate the cost of reproducing that labor power, which includes not only what operatives spend on food, clothing and other immediate necessities, but also the costs of health care, education, housing, utilities, etc. If these social costs are subsidized by the state, businessmen are automatically relieved of carrying them. The main advantage of such a system for the capitalist class is that workers can be paid the lowest possible wage, with the capitalists bearing neither formal nor moral responsibility.

Of course, companies still have to pay the government their employees' social security deductions, as was the case under socialism, but those are much less than the amount the state continues to pay for social services. Thus it is obvious that the capitalist class directly gains from the preservation of the old system of social payments.[15]

Several indirect factors came into play, besides the direct benefits of the continuing existence of these social services. The delineation of for-fee and state-provided social services presumes the preservation of an extremely low wage level in the latter (for doctors, teachers, public utilities workers, etc.), which helps to legitimize an overall low wage level in the main sectors of the national economy, where the private sector now dominates. It was not until the middle of the current decade, that efforts to dismantle the Soviet social services and benefits system began in earnest. Yet the conditions for such a shift, namely an income revolution and the formation of a large middle class, still do not exist.

In the West, trade unions played a large role in making wages gradually approach the true value of labor. The trade unions also serve as a mass base for the social-democratic movements, whose successes within the capitalist system led to the creation of the general welfare state in Europe. Despite attempts to slash them in recent decades, state-funded social services have largely survived in the West, co-existing in various forms with free-market services. Difficult as it has proven to eliminate such state-funded services in the West, it is even more so in the former socialist countries, where they had become an organic part of the social system. Among other things, attempted changes in this area have provoked serious social protests.

1.7 Why not managerialism?

In the period when state socialism was just beginning to take shape, some theories predicted its inevitable degeneration. The founder of this tendency was Leon Trotsky, who saw Stalinism as a course toward a bureaucratic dictatorship that would inevitably be toppled by a genuine revolutionary workers' movement.[16] The Fourth International's ideologists kept their faith in such an outcome right up until the last days of the Gorbachov period, believing that the mass miners' strikes of that time, which were financed and, in part, organized from the USA, really reflected an imminent proletarian revolution against the Communist ruling clique.[17]

The first thorough attempt at a theoretical treatment of state socialism was James Burnham's 1940 book *The Managerial Revolution*, which approached the question from a standpoint fundamentally similar to that of Trotskyism, but reached very different conclusions.[18] Though the author subsequently became an extreme conservative, the analysis he published at that time proceeded according to the Marxist conception of the historical process as a succession of socio-economic formations. His view, however, was that capitalism would be succeeded not by socialism, but by a system he called "managerialism," after the name of its ruling class, the managers. The transition to this new system would take place everywhere, albeit in different forms. In the developed capitalist countries, the layer of hired managers was gradually pushing the capitalist property owners out of their ruling position, themselves becoming the dominant section of the ruling elite. In the USSR, the managers were the bureaucrats who had seized the commanding heights of the economy and the government.

Burnham saw managerialism as the latest system of exploitation, under which the ruling class, as usual, appropriates a significant portion, if not all, of society's surplus product. In the West, the managers shared this surplus value with other segments of the capitalist class. In the USSR, they were representatives of an exploiter state, which awarded them various sorts of privileges, placing them in a special position, relative to other layers of society. This idea was further developed in *The New Class*, by Milovan Djilas, the Yugoslav writer and former Communist Party leader.[19]

These critiques of state socialism contained a good deal of truth, but none of the authors from this school of thought captured the main historical direction of the socialist ruling elite: the transformation of a significant portion of that elite into a class of property owners, who built their fortunes through the direct expropriation of state property. This tendency is fundamentally different from what the Trotsky-Burnham-Djilas conception anticipated. They supposed that the "new class" would attempt to preserve its supremacy by means of unlimited state managerialism. Ultimately, however, the tendency that prevailed was toward the destruction, by the communist elite, of the very system that had made them the masters of society.

The forecast closest to reality, it should be acknowledged, was made not by any economist or political analyst, but by the satirist George Orwell. In *Animal Farm,* the ruling class of Pigs (i.e., the nomenklatura) achieves its ultimate goal of becoming equal to Man (i.e., private capitalists). There was a certain period of time when, among close friends, I used to like to call the late socialist regime "Piggism," and I thought of Boris Yeltsin as the classic example of a leader cast in the mold of Orwell's Comrade Napoleon.

Why did the "new class" ultimately prefer capitalism to managerialism? Chiefly, it was because the socialist ideology, associated with the state form of managerialism, sets strict limits on income, personal fortunes, the ability to bequeath fortunes, and power. Under state socialism the elite enjoyed certain privileges that put it a step, or even several steps, above the rest of the population, yet the difference between them was relatively small, and their income didn't even come close to the income and fortunes of managers in capitalist society, never mind major property owners. The main shortcoming of these privileges was their relative instability, insofar as they were associated with official posts. Losing the post or, in most cases, even just retiring, meant substantial material losses. Yet the habituation of the manager and his family to a certain standard of living generated a set of material requirements, which were extremely difficult to give up. Only a small minority of true believers in the ideals of equality could get used to the level of asceticism required. The majority of the elite viewed their privileges as their due for "service" to society—as having been acquired through particularly productive, skilled labor, and the devotion of their efforts and capabilities to the good of the nation. This self-conception as a kind of meritocracy gave rise to a sense of caste, of belonging to a special layer, the nomenklatura.

It was practically impossible under socialism, however, to preserve these privileges into old age or in the event of disability, or to bequeath them to heirs. Such limitations gave rise to a desire to break through them, a desire that pushed the nomenklatura toward crime. At times, the improper activities seemed to involve mere misdemeanors, such as the use of state-owned construction materials in building a dacha, trading favors in the arrangement of jobs or promotions for relatives, "help" to the right people in exchange for state funds and resources under their control, and so forth. The danger of being punished for such trifles served as an incentive to strike it rich, and provide for oneself and one's family for a long time to come. And if the trifles went unpunished, then they gradually grew into a mode of behavior, whereby the use of state property for one's personal benefit became the rule. In this situation, any notion of limits, beyond which such behavior would be intolerable, was gradually erased. Driving to eliminate all limits, and to make the system of personal enrichment entirely legal, became the natural thing to do. The best way to accomplish it was to reject managerialism in favor of capitalism.

It turned out, however, that socialist ideology was not the only obstacle to getting rich. Imagine a society in which property is substantially or even primarily state-owned, yet the prevailing ideology is non-socialist. Even in such a society, attempts by state officials to become rich at the state's expense would be considered illegal. In Western society, the reigning cynicism notwithstanding, state property is seen as public property, meaning that it belongs equally to all citizens. Government budget resources are the taxpayers' money. If an official steals from the state, he is stealing from everybody.

I have often discussed this with students and professors at universities in the West, where I taught for some period of time. As a rule, they thought that stealing from the state was a higher order of crime, than the mere embezzlement of private company funds. Stealing from the state is corruption; it is theft from all the citizens, whereas getting rich at the expense of other private individuals or companies is just a special kind of business. If a capitalist sells something to the state at an unfairly inflated price, he has committed a crime, whereas if consumers are willing to pay inflated prices in the market, that's their problem and their responsibility. Likewise, theft by managers, or other employees, from their own company is seen as a corporate problem, not a problem for society as a whole.

State ownership of property is seen in the West as something that impedes achievement of the highest possible levels of efficiency, because it limits or dilutes people's interest in making the highest possible profit. Neoclassical economic theory views state administration of the economy in this same light.

Managerialism, however, is quite compatible with capitalism. Though executives occupy a formally subordinate position in the Western elite, below the owners of large fortunes, the dividing line between them is not absolutely strict, insofar as upper management receives enormous salaries and other forms of compensation for refraining from robbery of the shareholders. Put another way, capitalist society has legalized the appropriation by executives of the significant portion of surplus value that is considered sufficient for integrating the executives into the capitalist class, with respect to their income and wealth.[20]

It follows that capitalist managerialism is a comparatively stable state of affairs, whereas state managerialism, especially socialist state managerialism, has within it the seeds of extreme instability, even decomposition. That does not mean, however, that a transition from state socialism to capitalist managerialism is inevitable by definition. To draw such a conclusion would be to absolutize material property relations as the decisive or sole factor in social development, ignoring or underestimating the role of ideology and religion in shaping and consolidating a social system. The political system is also important. The systems of state socialism that have existed to date were associated with totalitarian political regimes, which formally guarded the socialist order, while actually promoting the monopolization of political power by the elite and, consequently, the degeneration of the system. It is possible that in a rationally organized democratic socialist society, where the elite were effectively subordinated to society, rather than ruling over it, things might be different. That is, however, more a question of the hypothetical future, than of the real past.[21]

1.8 A historical reminiscence

As noted above, capitalism "came calling" on Russia three times during the past century and a half. The first time was in Tsarist Russia, starting in the second half of the 19th century. This was a spontaneous process, which developed quite slowly even after the elimination of serfdom. It came belatedly to Russia, by comparison with other European countries, never mind America. After the Revolution of 1905-1907, which shook the antiquated political superstructure to its foundations, a period of prolonged economic stagnation was superseded by rapid industrial growth, and capitalist reforms in agriculture, under the leadership of Prime Minister Pyotr Stolypin, who was murdered by a terrorist before he could accomplish most of his reforms. Despite the fact that the greater part of the economy remained underdeveloped, by world criteria of that time, major business concerns emerged in the country and began to lay the basis for a modern capitalist state.

The Bolshevik Revolution of 1917, with its program for the total nationalization of all sectors of the economy excepting agriculture, laid to rest whatever Russian capitalism had developed. At the end of the Civil War, however, in the early 1920s Lenin introduced limited capitalism, which he calculated would revitalize the destroyed economy and prepare it for socialism. This period went down in history as the NEP. It lasted for several years, ending in the late 1920s under Joseph Stalin. From that point until the end of the 1980s, over fifty years, there were practically no legal forms of private enterprise.

It would be a travesty of historical logic, therefore, to think that the new Russian capitalism of the 1990s had some deep roots, connecting it with the two earlier capitalist phases. Any representatives of the capitalist classes of those eras, who managed physically to survive the intervening periods of repression, had completely disappeared, of natural causes, by the end of the 20th century. And though their descendents survived, we have seen that the new capitalists did not emerge from their ranks. Thus the Russian capitalism of our time is based almost exclusively on the foundation built in socialist society's centrally planned economy.

Nonetheless, for primarily cultural historical reasons, several features are characteristic of all three phrases of Russian capitalism. The first is the tendency of the intermediary sectors of the economy to develop voraciously, at the expense of the productive sectors. This is not only because capital associated with trade and usury has historically taken precedence over industrial capital in every country. This rule may correctly explain 19th-century Russian capitalism, but the two later phases of capitalism did not develop in the traditional way. Both NEP capitalism and late 20th-century capitalism sprang up during profound economic crises involving severe inflation, when it was far more profitable to make money in trade and financial operations, than to produce goods. In both instances, there was no need to create new enterprises. The main thing was to take control of existing ones or expropriate them from the state. One of the most important requirements for accomplishing this was to have enough money, which could be earned only in the intermediary or speculative sectors.

The second feature that today's capitalism has in common with the past versions is its dependence and reliance on the state. From the 18th century on, the most successful entrepreneurs in Russia were those granted special rights by the state to develop mines and factories, exploiting the bonded labor force. Even after the abolition of serfdom, industrialists were able to count on substantial state support in the form of government orders and subsidies. This shaped the composition of the economy of that period, in that there were almost no successful Russian capitalists in the manufacturing sector (with the exception of the textile and defense industries), while the majority of large companies in the coal, steel, metals-processing, and machine-building industries belonged to foreign capital.

During the NEP, the new capitalists also avoided involvement in large-scale production. They concentrated on trade and profitable state concessions. This was understandable: the former industrialists had been expropriated, and most of them had emigrated, while the capitalism reborn with the initiation of the NEP was weak and depended on government purchases.

It is unclear whether this apparent tendency for Russian capitalism in every period to start developing primarily in capitalism's most primitive forms is "genetically" inherent to Russia, or if it was accidental. What is obvious, is that the parasitical quality was manifested even more starkly in the new Russian capitalism of the 1990s, than in the two earlier phases. Not a single new major plant was built during the first post-Soviet decade. The economy has survived exclusively by consuming the stock of productive capital, created under socialism. It is only natural to anticipate that such an economic system will be unviable, as its physical capital decreases.

In later chapters we shall examine whether this is a chronic feature of modern Russian capitalism, or a temporary condition that will be overcome in the years ahead.

1.9 Surplus value: a statistical study

Because of the peculiarities of Russian capitalism, some analysts have rejected the notion that the present-day Russian economic system is capitalist at all. The American Marxist economist David Kotz at one time was firmly of that opinion.[22] He reasoned that the greater part of profit in the Russian economy does not derive from surplus value created in industry, but constitutes rent from the exploitation of natural resources, which rent is converted into money not inside the country, but through export to international markets. Therefore the Russian economy is not a classical capitalist economy such as Marx analyzed. Later on, Kotz agreed that the Russian economy "was becoming" capitalist.

Kotz's conception is one of a number of hypotheses, based chiefly on the well-known distortion of the Russian economy in favor of the export sectors. We shall have occasion to return to this question in subsequent chapters. For the moment, let us begin by examining the essential content and provenance of surplus value in present-day Russia, and analyzing statistics that show its absolute and relative size.

We shall demonstrate below, that surplus value in Russia today plays a significant role both in the export sectors and in production for the domestic economy. Then we can estimate the gross super-profit of the export sectors, which derives from the spread between domestic and world prices; we can show that, although it is sometimes very large, the greater part of the surplus value nonetheless is of domestic origin. Russian capitalism makes a significant part of its money inside the country. Thus we shall be able to see that Kotz's hypothesis is not borne out by the statistics. Since working with statistics is always a painstaking endeavor, we should note that this section requires a certain level of concentration and patience on the reader's part.

Surplus value is defined as total gross profit and entrepreneurial income (before direct taxes) in an economy, i.e., the part of GDP remaining after compensation of employees has been subtracted. Whether or not net indirect taxes should be included in surplus value is a matter of debate. In this book they are not included. Relative expressions of surplus value may be obtained by comparing it with wages (this gives the "rate of surplus value," which characterizes the primary distribution of income in a society) or with the volume of output (to obtain one of the measures of profitability used in Russian statistics).[23]

Unfortunately, it is not easy to obtain reliable statistical values for these magnitudes. Official statistics use several concepts of profit: gross profit of the economy, net profit, and profit as shown in official financial statements. Gross profit of the economy (as calculated in the National Accounts System, or NAS) denotes profit, as such, plus consumption of fixed capital (roughly speaking, depreciation). Frequently, however, it is not broken out as a separate figure, but summed together with "mixed income," which is the income of small businesses, some of which do not employ paid labor. Consumption of fixed capital is likewise generally included in gross profit and does not appear as a separate category in current statistics.

These components were broken out, only in the Ministry of

Table 1.1 Various estimates of profit
(billions of redenominated rubles, 1995)

	IOT	NAS*	NAS**	IOT corr.***
GDP in market prices	1,659.0	1,630.1	1,585.0	1,659.0
Compensation of employees	498.9	707.9	696.8	668.9
Off the books	n.a.	170.0	160.0	170.0
On the books	498.9	537.9	536.8	498.9
Net indirect taxes	173.9	185.8	187.3	173.9
Gross profit of the economy + mixed income	986.2	736.4	701.9	816.2
Consumption of fixed capital	280.6	413.7	n.a.	280.6
Net profit and mixed income	705.6	322.7	n.a.	535.6
Net profit	392.0	(159.1)	n.a.	392.0
Net mixed income	313.6	(163.6)	n.a.	163.6
Gross profit of the economy (consumption of fixed capital + net profit)		(572.8)	n.a.	672.6
Gross investment in fixed capital	355.1	322.1	329.4	355.1
Taxes on profit	117.6	117.6	117.6	117.6
After-tax profit	n.a.	(133.1)	n.a.	199.9

Figures in parentheses are the author's estimates, based on comparisons with IOT data.
* RSY 1997 revisions of 1995 data.
** RSY 1998 revisions of 1995 data.
*** IOT data corrected after comparison with NAS.

Economics input-output tables (IOT) for 1995.[24] Subsequent official publications of the IOT, such as for 1998-1999 and 2000-2001, contained no data on consumption of fixed capital; it was merged into the broader category of gross profit. Since the 1995 data are the most detailed, we shall begin by comparing them with the NAS figures (Table 1.1).

The NAS calculates gross profit by subtracting from GDP all other components of income-formation: GDP in market prices, minus compensation of employees, minus net indirect taxes (not including subsidies) on production and imports. Net profit is calculated by subtracting, from gross profit, mixed income and consumption of fixed capital. Net profit as shown in the IOT, calculated by the same method, is significantly higher (by 56 percent in 1995) than net profit as calculated using the official financial reports filed by businesses. The IOT show 392 billion rubles net profit, whereas the financial accounts of businesses gave 250.6 billion rubles.

That discrepancy is due to the fact that the GDP estimates (whether in the IOT or the NAS) include an allowance for the shadow economy, whereas businesses' book profit includes accounting data from legal activities only. Indeed, if the two estimates are compared in a sector-by-sector breakdown, it is evident that they diverge only slightly in the main sectors of tangible goods production (industry, construction, transport and communications, agriculture), whereas 90 percent of the difference is attributable to trade and services, the areas in which the shadow economy's share is highest. It would be wrong to ignore this part of surplus value. Therefore gross profit will be one of the main points of departure for our analysis.

We should also note the very large discrepancy between the IOT and NAS estimates of total gross profit in the economy: the IOT estimate is 250 billion rubles higher, almost entirely because the NAS uses a higher estimate for compensation of employees than the IOT do (696.8 billion rubles in the NAS, as against 498.9 billion rubles in the IOT). By far the largest part of this 197.9 billion ruble discrepancy (160 billion rubles, or 80 percent) is accounted for by off-the-books wages—the shadow economy, once again. Restricting the comparison to reported wage payments, the difference is only 7 percent. When the IOT were drawn up, off-the-books wages were not taken into account in any direct form. But shadow sector income has been added to the NAS on the basis of highly provisional estimates, whose reliability cannot be taken for granted.

In recent years Goskomstat has estimated that the informal economy increases GDP by about 20 percent. In our base year, 1995, that amount was equal to 331.8 billion rubles. Thus off-the-books wages would comprise approximately half of all illegal operations, which is likely an overstatement of their weight.

Consumption of fixed capital presents additional difficulties. The methodology behind the calculation of this indicator is shrouded in secret. Yet the gap between consumption of fixed capital as reported in the IOT (280.6 billion rubles) and the NAS (413.7 billion rubles) is so huge—one estimate being 50 percent higher than the other—as to raise doubts about the calculations involved. The relatively higher estimate of fixed capital consumption in the NAS is also at odds with the indirect data obtained by looking at the reported share of depreciation within the composition of spending in major sectors of the economy. An artificially high estimate of fixed capital consumption, of course, reduces estimated net profit (by more than one-half).

In view of these considerations, we have provided corrected IOT data in the last column of Table 1.1. Since off-the-books wages were added to total labor income, the gross profit of the economy and mixed income have been reduced by a corresponding amount. The data on fixed capital consumption and net profit, however, were left unchanged. Summed together, they give gross profit, which was 672.6 billion rubles, or 40.5 percent of GDP. The corrected estimate of gross profit of the economy (column 2) is 572.8 billion rubles, or 35.1 percent of GDP. These figures are both high in comparison to the USA, where gross profit was only 21.8 percent of GDP in 1998.[25] In the chapters that follow, we shall return to the problems this gap creates for economic growth in Russia.

It goes without saying, that including fixed capital consumption in gross profit exaggerates the size of surplus value. But this is true only to the extent that depreciation allowances are really spent on replacement of worn-out physical capital. In the Russian economy, only a part of the depreciation allowance is actually used for that purpose. In 1995, for example, only 123.6 billion rubles of depreciation allowances, or 44.1 percent of the total, were spent on capital repairs and new investment. Roughly speaking, an estimated one-half of all depreciation represented an addition to surplus value. Thus overall surplus value in 1995 was 532 billion rubles, or 32 percent of GDP. The official book profit was less than half this amount.

Taxes on profit, which were relatively low that year at 117.6 billion rubles, amounted to only 30 percent of book profit and 22 percent of all surplus value. They did not substantially impede business, nor were they paid in full. The remainder of gross profit after taxes and investment in fixed capital was 199.9 billion rubles, or 12 percent of GDP. This is the profit available for personal use by the capitalist class. Thus the capitalist class spent for itself over one-third of gross after-tax profit. In the USA, corporate dividends are equal to less than 5 percent of GDP; and, since many people throughout society own shares, only a part of this income goes to the capitalist class.

We have made further calculations of surplus value in the Russian economy for 1995-2000, taking into account all of the consider-

Table 1.2 Surplus value in the Russian economy, 1995-2000

	1995	1996	1997	1999	2000
Surplus value (billions of rubles)	530.5	725.3	795.9	1,190.8	2,171.3
Surplus value, % of GDP	32.7%	33.0%	31.1%	26.2%	31.3%
Surplus value, % of wages	99.0%	92.3%	87.0%	81.2%	102.4%
Profitability of industrial production, %	20.1%	9.2%	9.0%	25.5%	24.7%

ations noted above (Table 1.2). Its relationship to wages was in the 81-102 percent range, which is typical of many capitalist countries with a medium level of development.

The profitability of production, or the share of book profit in sales, fell below 10 percent as an average for industry in the worst years, while reaching 25 percent during economic growth years.

Compare the results of these calculations with the new data, published by Goskomstat in its input-output tables for 1998 and 1999.[26] Unlike in the IOT for 1995, gross profit and fixed capital consumption are not broken out, and total compensation of employees does not include so-called off-the-books payments. Therefore the rates of surplus value, shown in Table 1.3, are somewhat overstated.

Although the data in Table 1.3 diverge somewhat from the preceding calculations, they confirm the general tendency: the rate of surplus value falls below 100 percent in crisis years, but may substantially surpass that level during years of economic growth. Overall profitability substantially surpasses crisis-year profitability, but practically

Table 1.3 Gross profit and compensation of employees in the IOT for 1998-1999
(billions of rubles)

	1998	1999
1. Gross profit	938.7	2,125.6
2. Compensation of employees	1,015.7	1,408.8
3. Rate of surplus value (%) (1:2)	92.4%	150.9%
4. Total value of goods and services produced	4,658.0	8,298.4
5. Overall profitability of production (%) (1:4)	20.2%	25.6%

Table 1.4 The distribution of profit in industry by sector, 1995-2000
(billions of rubles, unless % is indicated)

	1995	1997	1999	2000
Profit in industry, total	222.7	144.1	763.7	1,176.5
Profit by sector				
Fuel industries	33.6	31.7	201.5	426.7
Ferrous metallurgy	19.9	3.9	63.0	94.1
Non-ferrous metallurgy	20.9	8.7	154.7	214.6
Total for three export sectors shown	74.4	44.3	419.1	735.4
Total for three export sectors, as % of all industry	33.4%	30.7%	54.9%	62.5%
Total for sectors producing mainly for domestic consumption	148.3	99.8	344.6	441.1
Total for sectors producing mainly for domestic consumption, as % of all industry	66.6%	69.3%	45.1%	37.5%
Machine-building	37.1	20.7	89.3	110.0
Electric power	21.2	30.8	36.9	50.6
Total for machine-building and electric power, as % of all industry	26.2%	35.8%	16.5%	13.7%
Total for other sectors	90.0	48.3	218.4	280.5
Other sectors as % of all industry	40.4%	33.5%	28.6%	23.8%

Source: Calculated on the basis of RSY for 2000 and 2001. After 2000 the government statistics office ceased publication of gross reported profit of enterprises and replaced it with "net financial result" (equal to total profit minus total losses).

coincides with the profitability rate of growth years. Thus, the first stage of analysis shows that Russia's economy differs little from other capitalist countries in its overall parameters of the creation of surplus value. To the extent that there are discernable differences, they are chiefly found in a higher level of surplus value as a share of GDP.

1.10 The distribution of profit by sector

Now let us look at the distribution of profit and surplus value across the different sectors of the Russian economy. The available statistics on the reported book profits of enterprises provide a picture of the situation in industry (Table 1.4).

The table shows that the export sectors' share in aggregate

Table 1.5 Share of export industries in total gross profit of the economy
(billions of rubles and %)

	1998	1999	2001	2002
Gross profit of the economy	958.7	2,125.6	4,012.7	4,621.4
Oil and gas	65.2	195.5	383.8	486.4
Ferrous metals	15.4	57.2	53.6	78.3
Non-ferrous metals	35.5	124.2	141.2	136.8
Total, export-oriented industries	116.1	376.9	578.6	701.5
Export industries, share in the economy (%)	12.4%	17.7%	14.4%	15.2%
Share of oil and gas (%)	6.9%	9.2%	9.6%	10.5%

Source: IOT for Russia 1998-1999, pp. 52-53, 160-161; 2001, pp. 50-51; 2002, Table 4.1.

profit is subject to marked fluctuation, ranging from 30-33 percent in 1995-1997 to 63 percent in 2000. These changes, as we shall demonstrate below, are almost entirely a function of two factors: (1) the abrupt devaluation of the ruble after 1998, which caused a corresponding up-valuation of exported goods in ruble terms, and (2) the significant rise of world oil and natural gas prices. The second of these two factors comprises what is termed natural rent, which comes into being as a result of the large gap between domestic and foreign prices. We should note that this applies exclusively to the period of extraordinarily high world oil prices, but by no means to the entire period since Russian capitalism came into existence. During the years when it was just beginning to take shape (before the 1998 crisis), the export sectors played an important role, but they were far from dominating the economy. Two-thirds or more of the surplus value created in industry was associated with sectors producing mainly for the domestic market: machine-building and metal-working, electric power, the food-processing industry and light industry, the construction materials industry, etc.

As noted above, official data on gross profit by industry is not available for years after 2000. Instead, the government reports the "net financial result," which is the total gross profit minus total gross losses of enterprises. The share of the three major export-oriented industries (oil, natural gas, and metals) in the total for this indicator was 73 percent in 2000, 59.8 percent in 2001 and 59.5 percent

Table 1.6 Profitability of industrial production by sector, 1995-2001

(profit as % of gross value of output)

	1995	1997	1999	2000	2001
Industry as a whole	20.1	9.0	25.5	24.7	18.5
Fuel industries	20.8	13.1	44.5	51.1	35.9
Oil extraction	21.2	14.7	57.9	66.7	46.5
Oil refining	26.1	9.4	32.1	34.5	24.0
Natural gas	27.2	23.3	22.6	30.0	17.4
Ferrous metallurgy	22.1	3.6	28.2	25.6	12.5
Non-ferrous metallurgy	32.7	11.4	57.4	51.6	34.4
Electric power	17.5	14.1	13.7	13.5	15.7
Machine-building and metal-working	20.9	8.0	17.4	14.1	13.6
Chemicals and petrochemicals	20.0	4.3	22.3	17.0	11.5
Timber and paper	21.8	−5.5	23.9	16.5	11.5
Construction materials	17.9	5.6	8.6	9.0	9.8
Light industry	9.3	−1.5	9.5	7.2	5.4
Food-processing industry	16.3	8.4	13.0	10.1	11.5

Source: RSY 2000 and 2001.

in 2002. This is explained by record-high export prices for oil, gas, and metals, and would change drastically if world energy and raw materials prices were to fall.

Surplus value created or earned in industry, however, is only part of the total in the whole economy. According to the IOT for 1998, 1999, 2001, and 2002, the share of the three export-oriented sectors in total gross profit is much smaller than their share in total profit in industry (Table 1.5).

Thus the thesis that Russian capitalism is primarily of foreign origin, and that from the outset it thrived exclusively or primarily on export revenue, is incorrect.

Let us now examine the relative profitability of various sectors (Table 1.6).

Throughout the period, the oil industry was more profitable than the average level in industry as a whole, but until 1999 the difference was slight. Only in 1999-2000 did it become enormous: 58-67 percent, as against 25 percent for industry as a whole. Non-ferrous metallurgy became extraordinarily profitable during these years,

Table 1.7 Estimated superprofit from oil exports (before taxes and duties)

	1995	1996	1997	1998	1999	2000	2001	2003
Domestic price, $/metric ton	61.1	65.8	79.4	26.2	26.0	46.7	53.4	66.6
Export price, $/metric ton	101.0	127.6	116.9	74.9	105.2	174.8	151.8	182.0
Export price as % of domestic price	165.3%	193.8%	147.2%	285.5%	404.5%	374.5%	284.3%	273.3%
Price gap, $/metric ton	39.9	61.8	37.5	48.7	69.2	128.1	97.4	115.4
Oil exports, billions $	12.4	15.6	14.7	10.3	14.1	25.3	24.6	38.8
Oil exports, millions of metric tons	118.8	122.3	125.7	137.5	134.0	144.7	162.1	223.0
Profit from price gap, billions $	4.7	7.6	4.7	6.7	9.3	18.5	15.8	25.7
Cost of transport and related services	0.7	0.8	1.0	0.4	0.4	0.7	0.9	1.7
Profit from price gap, minus cost of transport and related services	4.0	6.8	3.7	6.3	8.9	17.8	14.9	24.0
Average exchange rate RUR/USD	4.554	5.126	5.785	9.695	24.623	28.135	29.172	30.145
Superprofit, billions of rubles	18.2	34.9	21.4	61.1	219.1	500.8	434.7	720.3
Book profit in the oil-extracting industry, billions of rubles	15.5	15.4	18.2	21.3	171.3	393.9	213.0	176.4

Sources: *Russian Economic Trends Monthly* (hereinafter RET), Oct. 2002; RSY 2004; author's calculations.

reaching a level of 52-57 percent. But the profitability of the steel industry was only middling during growth years, despite its export orientation. Machine-building (14-17 percent) and electric power (13-14 percent) lagged well behind the average level of profitability, while light industry and the food-processing industry were even lower, achieving profitability levels of no greater than 7-13 percent even in strong growth years. The data for 2001 are not strictly comparable with previous years, since "net financial result," rather than gross profit, was used for calculating profitability.

Profitability levels in the Russian economy are substantially higher than in U.S. industry. Average profitability (the ratio of pre-tax profit to sales) in American manufacturing industries, for example, was 8 percent, based on 1998 data, while the profitability of various sectors ranged from a high of 19.2 percent for the pharmaceuticals industry to 3.1 percent in the steel industry. Average profitability in the extractive industries ranged between 2.5 percent and 7.8 percent during 1990-1999 in the USA, while its range in the retail trade was from 1.3 percent to 3.4 percent.[27] American industry experienced strong growth, even with these relatively modest profitability levels. Russian businessmen, however, refuse to operate at such profitability rates, which they consider too low.

Let us attempt to estimate the size of the superprofit derived from the large difference between the prices of exported and domestically sold crude oil.

Table 1.7 shows clearly the comparatively small dimensions of oil superprofit before 1999, and its steep increase from that time on. Also visible are the factors in this growth: the sharp decrease of the domestic oil price expressed in dollars, by comparison with the period before the 1998 crisis, and the rise of prices on exported oil, which reached record highs in 2000-2001, before climbing even higher in 2002-2006. This is, of course, an approximation. But comparison of our results with reported oil industry profit shows that our estimate cannot be far off.

If we subtract export duties on oil (which averaged $23/metric ton in 2000) from the total shown in Table 1.7, the result is $14.5 billion, or 408 billion rubles, for crude oil alone, not counting refined petroleum products or natural gas. That is 14.7 percent of the total surplus value created in the economy. It is an enormous figure. But it fails to support the notion that the new class of owners of the means of production in Russia receives the greater part of its income in the world market, rather than inside the country.

1.11 The nature of export superprofit

The nature of export superprofit may be considered from the standpoint of theory, as well. According to neoclassical theory, any superprofit (called "economic rent") comes into being as an amount in excess of the customary rate of profit under conditions of market equilibrium and free competition. An excess amount of profit arises when the market price of a given commodity exceeds, for some reason, its average cost of production, including the normal cost of capital. This may happen either when monopolistic barriers hinder the market price from settling to a normal level, or when a producer has an opportunity to produce the commodity at costs below those incurred by his competitors.

Marxist political economy makes a distinction between rent, which arises as a result of barriers to the free flow of capital into agriculture or the extractive industries, and additional surplus value, which is the result of high productivity achieved by the introduction of new machinery or new technologies into the process of production. As a rule, such higher than usual margins of surplus value are temporary phenomena, lasting only until the new technology has come into widespread use. In neoclassical theory, the sectors in which temporary superprofit arises as a result of particularly favorable, transient conditions are called niches, and the entrepreneurs who shape their businesses to take advantage of such niches are named "rent-seekers."

Niches may occur not only for the pioneers of some new technology or the discoverers of new consumer products with unique features, but also as a result of unusual situations in the market. The superprofit received by exporters of Russian raw materials is of this latter type. The gap between world and domestic prices was the result of the Soviet market's prolonged isolation from any external environment, and of the peculiarities of price formation in a centrally planned economy.

There was a certain logic to those peculiarities. In the Soviet Union the government saw no need to impose high prices in order to appropriate the full amount of natural rent, when fuel or raw materials were sold inside the country. By refraining from such rent-collection, the government created an incentive for more rapid development of the manufacturing industries. Low prices on liquid fuels were also the prevailing practice in world markets from the 1920s until the early 1970s. During that period a few large, vertically integrated American, Anglo-Dutch, and French concerns were the main producers and suppliers of oil in the world. They saw no benefit in selling crude oil to their own refineries at high prices. World oil prices rose sharply beginning in 1973, after the majority of developing countries nationalized their oil industries, and the Organization of Petroleum Exporting Countries (OPEC) raised world prices several-fold, collecting the relevant natural rent for their own advantage.

Even after the events of the 1970s, the USSR was slow to raise its domestic oil prices, although it used the existing high world prices when selling oil outside the socialist countries. In 1991 the domestic price (producers' price) of crude oil in the USSR was only 70 rubles per metric ton, whereas the export price was $117. Depending on whether the official or the market exchange rate was used for a given year, the gap between these two prices could be either very small (differing by 20%) or very large (differing by a factor of 110). The true relationship lay somewhere in between those two extremes.

With the transition to a market economy, the gap between domestic and world prices might have been expected to shrink, since domestic prices ought to have been pulled toward world prices, as the domestic market became more open and less isolated from external markets. For export commodities, particularly oil, the changes that occurred were rather more complex (Table 1.8).[28]

Despite world oil price fluctuations, the domestic and export prices drew steadily closer for the six years ending with 1997. The gap would have closed even more quickly, had the ruble's exchange rate fallen in step with the decrease of its domestic purchasing power. Between 1992 and 1997, however, the domestic price of oil in rubles increased by a factor of 104, while the ruble's exchange rate declined only by a factor of 25. This discrepancy caused the domestic price in dollars to quadruple, reducing the export price to domestic price ratio from 7.4 to 1.9. The financial crisis of 1998 and the subsequent steep rise of export prices reversed this trend. It would take several years of significant do-

Table 1.8 Domestic and export oil prices, 1992-1999

1 Domestic prices, thousands of rubles/metric ton until 1998, rubles/ton after 1998
2 Domestic prices, $/metric ton
3 Export prices, $/metric ton
4 Factor by which export prices exceeded domestic prices

	1	2	3	4
1992	3.6	15.8	117	7.4
1993	31	17.1	105	6.1
1994	101	30.0	101	3.4
1995	282	61.8	108	1.7
1996	355	63.8	134	2.1
1997	376	63.1	119	1.9
1998	339	16.4	75	4.6
1999	1,000	37.0	107	2.9
2000	1,546	54.9	185	3.3
2001	1,504	49.9	156	3.1
2002	1,929	60.9	163	2.7
2003	2,065	68.8	182	2.6
2005 August	2,744	96.3	396	4.1

Sources: RSY 2000, RSY 2004, and *Ob ob"eme proizvodstva, oborote, zapasakh nefteproduktov i potrebitel'skikh tsenakh na nikh* (*Current Statistical Report on the Oil Market*), August 2005. This table, unlike Table 1.7, uses year-end prices, rather than average annual prices.

mestic price increases, in the setting of a stable ruble exchange rate and relatively stable world prices, for rapprochement of the domestic and world prices to resume. In 2000-2006, however, world oil prices exploded even more, inducing domestic prices to follow. In relative terms the gap remained approximately the same, oscillating around the factor of 3, while in absolute terms it increased to more than $100 per ton.

Thus far we have explored profit and surplus value only in the particular case of the oil industry, but it is clear that the relationship between domestic and world prices bears directly on the sources of surplus value and profit in the Russian economy as a whole.

The simplest version of this relationship occurs when domestically produced output is sold abroad at world prices. In that case the price gap allows the export sectors of the economy to realize an additional margin of surplus value (or, in neoclassical terms, rent). The source of this superprofit is that the greater part of the cost of production is paid at domestic prices, while a significant part of the output is sold at the higher external prices. But the products' being sold in foreign markets does not change the fact that the value was created by productive factors operating inside Russia. Newly created value in the export sectors is part of the gross domestic product of the Russian economy, not of any other economy.

If exported output is sold at below the world price, the price mechanism promotes the diversion of Russia's domestic product to the advantage of other countries. That is precisely the provenance of the fortunes of our early capitalists and their foreign partners, who bought Russian raw materials and fuels inside the country for essentially nothing, then sold them abroad at dumping prices, pocketing the difference, which was protected from Russian taxation. Though the undercharging currently occurs on a more modest scale in the case of export prices, some estimates place it at an average 20 percent off the declared price. Russian GDP and profit in our economy are correspondingly understated in value terms.

NOTES

1. Francis Fukuyama, *The End of History and The Last Man* (London: Penguin Books, 1992).

2. S. Menshikov, *Katastrofa ili katarsis? (Catastrophe or Catharsis?)* (1990; English edition: Interverso, 1991); *Ekonomika Rossii: prakticheskie i teoreticheskie aspekty perekhoda k rynku (The Russian Economy: Practical and Theoretical Aspects of the Transition to the Market)* (1996); *Novaia ekonomika: osnovy ekonomicheskoi teorii (The New Economy: Foundations of Economic Theory)* (2000); all from Mezhdunarodnye Otnosheniia publishing house in Moscow.

3. *Rossiiskii statisticheskii ezhegodnik (Russian Statistical Yearbook)*, hereinafter RSY, 2003, p. 315.

4. Angus Maddison, *Monitoring the World Economy 1820-1992* (Paris: OECD, 1995), p. 186.

5. S. Menshikov, especially *Katastrofa ili katarsis?*

6. Prominent examples of large- and mega-scale "red directors" would be Vagit Alekperov, the head of Lukoil, and former Gazprom head Rem Vyakhirev.

7. Kakha Bendukidze's control of Uralmash came about in this way, as did the Chernoy brothers' ownership of several aluminum combines. Boris Berezovsky's fortune emerged from speculation in trade and finance, thence to become the basis for his acquisition of several enterprises, not always by the traditional method of buying up shares. Vladimir Gusinsky's fortune originated with real estate operations, on the basis of which he created a media empire.

8. Vladimir Potanin gained control of Norisk Nickel and Mikhail Khodorkovsky took over Yukos Oil in this way.

9. A graduate of Harvard Business School did head the Vladimir Tractor Factory for a certain period of time, but he rather quickly realized the pointlessness of his attempts to introduce American practices in Russia and was forced to leave. The USA and Canada Institute of the Russian Academy of Sciences ran a joint program with a U.S. business school. The Russian managers who signed up for these courses learned to draw up business plans according to all the rules of American scientific practice. They graduated with high marks, but not a single one of these business plans was ever implemented.

10. It should be noted that American businessmen who mastered the ways of our shadow economy were quick to find a common language with the New Russian capitalists and politicians. Harvard Professor Andrei Shleifer and his colleague Jonathan Hay, who entered the country in the guise of consultants to our official agencies on privatization, did quite well in financial speculation in Russia. They were exposed by American (not Russian) law enforcement and left Russia in disgrace. An account of this and similar affairs appears in Janine Wedel, *Collision and Collusion* (New York: St. Martin's Press, 1998). James Giffen, who had gotten to know our commercial scene back in the Soviet period, became an adviser to the President of Kazakstan on oil and other matters. He also came under investigation by American prosecutors. Marc Rich, a fugitive from American justice living in exile in Switzerland since the 1980s, added quite a few millions to his wealth through his Russian operations in the early 1990s. Thanks to connections with Russian officials and shadow economy operatives, he was able to buy oil in Russia at a small fraction of the world market price (*International Herald Tribune*, Feb. 8, 2001). After its resale abroad, the profit was deposited in the foreign accounts of his counteragents inside Russia, among whom were officials and company directors. Aluminum and other raw materials were also resold in this fashion. After some time the Russian partners in these deals mastered the technique and squeezed Rich out of this type of business. Before leaving the U.S. Presidency, Bill Clinton pardoned him, along with some other swindlers, over the protests of U.S. prosecutors, who wanted to prosecute Rich not for fraud in Russia, but merely for tax evasion at home.

11. Several of our first multimillionaires (who soon fled abroad, it should be noted) had been granted permission to export consignments of oil belonging to the state, with a promise that the foreign-currency earnings would be spent on the acquisition of imported foodstuffs, equipment, etc. The exporter would pocket those earnings, to the tune of several tens of millions of dollars, while the relevant officials were bought off. Such cases of outright thievery are not considered here in detail.

12. It appears that this was the origin of, in particular, the fortune of Roman Abramovich, which appeared "out of nowhere" when he was engaged in the oil trade. He came to control one of Russia's seven largest oil companies, Sibneft, jointly with Boris Berezovsky for some time, before becoming its predominant owner. He sold it to Gazprom in 2005. Abramovich also shared control with Oleg Deripaska over Rusal, the major aluminum concern, before selling out to his partner in 2004.

13. Balkar Trading, for example, was originally founded as an automobile trading company, but the government granted it the right to export a large consignment of oil, in exchange for the promise to obtain a large foreign credit to finance the purchase of equipment for a Siberian machine-building plant. The credit never material-

ized, but the proprietors of the firm, including the Prosecutor General of the Russian Federation, were arrested and served time in prison. For a certain period there was also a category called "special exporters," a status determined by the Presidential Administration and upper echelons of the Government. Some public organizations were granted the right to import high-demand goods like alcoholic beverages duty-free and to trade them tax-free within the country.

14. The table below shows the relationship between the main parameters of this function for different years:

	Bank lending rate (%)	Devaluation of ruble against U.S. dollar (%)	Rate of increase of capital (multiple)
1993	356%	67%	2.1
1994	288%	65%	1.7
1995	320%	23.5%	2.5
1995	147%	16.7%	1.25
1996	47%	6.8%	1.38

Source: *Russian Economic Trends*, Oxford, U.K., Vol. 8, No. 4, 1999, pp. 119-120

15. In subsequent chapters we shall return to the question of income distribution in Russia today, and how it has changed. Without running too much ahead, it may be noted here that by 1995 wages as a percentage of GDP reached a low point of 21.6 percent, as against 47.5 percent in 1991. By comparison, employee wages in the USA were 39.2 percent of GDP in 1997. (Russian data: input-output tables for the years in question. U.S. data: *Economic Report of the President* for 1997. Other statistical tables.)

16. These ideas were fully developed in Leon Trotsky's book *The Revolution Betrayed*, which was published in the West (New York: 1937).

17. This author had several discussions on this topic, in Brussels, with the late Ernest Mandel, a prominent Fourth International theoretician, who could not accept the facts, but continued to issue one pamphlet after another about it.

18. James Burnham, *The Managerial Revolution* (New York: John Day Co., 1941).

19. Milovan Djilas, *The New Class. An Analysis of the Communist System* (New York: Praeger, 1957).

20. The position of capitalist managers in the USA is considered in S. Menshikov, *Millionery i menedzhery. Struktura finansovoi oligarkhii SSha* (*Millionaires and Managers. The Structure of the Financial Oligarchy in the USA*) (Moscow: Mysl Publishing House, 1966; English editions—Moscow: Progress Publishers, 1969, 1973). This was the first work to take up the concept of the integration of managers into the capitalist elite on the basis of income leveling between these two categories of the ruling class.

21. The theoretical question of overcoming the instability of state managerialism is considered in S. Menshikov, *Novaia ekonomika* (*The New Economy*).

22. David Kotz, "Is Russia Becoming Capitalist?"—paper presented at the American Economic Association Annual Convention in New York, January 1999.

23. Another expression of profitability used in our statistics is the profit-to-assets ratio, which is the ratio of profit to operating capital. We shall not use this measure in the current chapter, leaving it for later analysis.

24. Unpublished input-output tables for 1991-1995, compiled by the Institute for Macroeconomic Research (IMEI) of the former Russian Federation Ministry of Economics (later merged into the Ministry of Economic Development and Trade), are available to professional economic researchers. The tables contain data on the surplus product, wages, social services payments by businessmen, and pre-tax net profit for each sector of the economy, as well as the "mixed income" of small businesses, chiefly in agriculture, construction and retail trade.

25. *Economic Report of the President*, Washington, 2000, pp. 334-335.

26. *Sistema tablits 'rastraty-vypusk' Rossii za 1998-1999 gg. (Input-Output Tables for Russia, 1998-1999)* (Moscow: Goskomstat, 2002).

27. Calculated on the basis of *Statistical Abstract of the US*, 2000, p. 560.

28. The Goskomstat methodological guide defines the producer price, the base price and the consumer price as follows: "The base price is the price received by the producer per unit of goods or services, including any taxes that must be paid on products and any subsidies of products aside from import subsidies. The producer price is the price received by the producer per unit of goods or services, including any taxes that must be paid on products (exclusive of VAT, excise and import taxes) and excluding products and import subsidies due. In the oil and gas industry producer prices average 11.3 percent higher than the base prices. The consumer price is the price paid by the consumer when goods or services are provided. It includes intermediary trade costs or transport costs for delivery of goods, as well as taxes on products paid by the consumer." *Metodologicheskie polozheniia po statistike. Vypusk vtoroi. (Methodological Principles of Statistics. Second issue)* (Moscow: Goskomstat, 1998), pp. 133, 171.

2 The Composition of Capital

As outlined in Chapter 1, there were several sources of initial private capital formation in early-1990s Russia:
- money and other capital accumulated in the shadow economy during the Soviet period;
- fixed assets and working capital of state-owned enterprises that were privatized;
- speculative operations that took advantage of the gap between domestic and world prices, as well as between the domestic and external rates of devaluation of the ruble;
- state-issued credit, abatements and subsidies, management of government budget funds, underpayment of taxes, etc.

2.1 The accumulation of capital

The main problem in that initial period was not so much how to make use of money-capital, as how to accumulate it. Due to the general crisis in the economy, the ready sources of accumulation tended to be in the intermediary sectors of trade and finance, rather than in goods-producing industries. In the latter, the privatization process gave new private property owners control of a huge quantity of capital in the form of commodities and means of production, which, though they had been obtained at minimal cost, were difficult to convert into money. The normal way of effecting such conversion in a market economy, by selling the commodities produced, was only partly available, due to insufficient effective demand and the disruption of economic ties. Under these conditions, most enterprises cut production and raised prices, further aggravating the sales crisis. The steep decline of production continued without interruption for three years after President Boris Yeltsin's reforms were launched, until the early months of 1995.

Nonetheless, the statistics for this period show a fairly contradictory picture. Official reports indicate that profitability (gross profit as share of sales) was high in industry, reaching 38 percent in 1992, 32 percent in 1993, and 20 percent annually in 1994 and 1995. Those levels are much higher than profitability in industry in the late 1980s, when it averaged 12 percent. Only after 1995 did profitability fall to 9 percent and lower.[1] Thus, the years of high inflation were simultaneously high-profit years, despite the drastic slump in production. Statistics on barter also indicate a comparatively favorable situation for sales (albeit at a low level). The share of barter in industrial enterprise sales rose, but slowly. It was 6 percent in 1992, 9 percent in 1993, and 17 percent in 1994. Barter reached its peak level of 42-51 percent only much later, in 1997-1998.[2]

At the same time, only 36 percent of industrial enterprises were in good or satisfactory financial condition as of 1993; the following year, only 17 percent were. The ratio of companies' indebtedness to the value of their output rose. Most enterprises reported that their main problem was just to survive. Despite high rates of profit, companies had to share their earnings from inflation with the banks, even as interest rates on bank loans were 150-200 percent. Over 70 percent of all enterprises were forced to take out bank loans, most of them short-term loans to cover current expenses, necessitated by an acute shortage of working capital.[3]

One method of converting physical capital into money, used during this period, was to sell off fixed assets, chiefly equipment, or rent out industrial plant and facilities. Since the utilization of productive capacity fell to an average of 60 percent during these years, a significant portion of the equipment was idle, and not needed for the process of production. Some of it was mothballed and warehoused for better times, but another part was sold under the counter at cut-rate prices, often to dummy firms set up by managers at the privatized industrial enterprises.

Official statistics do not reflect this process very well, since they rely on company reports on the retirement of equipment. Some of the unused plant was rented to private firms, earning supplemental

Table 2.1 Assets of Russian enterprises and banks
(billions of rubles)

	1996	1997	1998	2000	2003
All fixed assets	13,072	13,286	14,126	16,605	25,764
Of which:					
State	5,752	5,979	6,357	7,140	10,821
Private	7,321	7,307	7,769	9,465	14,943
Enterprises' working capital	931	1,122	2,687	4,895	8,207
As % of all assets	11%	13%	26%	34%	55%
Total private business assets	8,252	8,429	10,456	14,360	23,150
Commercial bank assets	498	623	933	2,259	5,456.4
Total inside the country	8,750	9,052	11,389	15,334	28,606.4
Abroad	223	339	1,640	3,282	5,328.0
Grand Total	8,973	9,391	13,029	18,616	33,934.4
% of Grand Total:					
Inside the country	98%	96%	87%	82%	84%
Abroad	2%	4%	13%	18%	16%

Sources: RSY 1998, pps. 70-73, 691; RSY 2000, p. 269; RSY 2003, pp. 302-305; *Russian Economic Trends Monthly* (hereinafter RET2), #2, 2000, pp. 5-6, RET2 #5, 2001, Tables 7, 14.

income for the enterprises.

It is quite difficult to estimate the amount of private capital, accumulated during those first years and the following period. Official statistics report the value of fixed assets in the state sector and the private sector, as well as the value of physical working capital (without breaking it down by state and private sector). Some data are available on companies' financial investments. Since there had been no such investments in the Soviet period, we may provisionally presume that the rising amount of financial investments is approximately equal to the companies' financial assets. Beginning in 1998, there are data on companies' total current assets. Lastly, data on commercial bank assets are published regularly. All of these parameters, and their totals, are shown in Table 2.1.

Private capital's share of total state-owned and private assets sharply increased in the course of privatization, from 9 percent at the end of 1991 to 58 percent at the end of 1994, but it essentially stopped rising at that point. Most of what remained as state property was accounted for by buildings and facilities belonging to central and local government agencies, military facilities, assets of institutions in the healthcare, education, science, and culture sectors, part of the housing stock, transportation, and utilities.

At the end of 1997, privately owned fixed assets were worth an estimated 7.321 trillion rubles. Yet the state had received only 34.8 billion rubles from privatizing this property, or less than .05 percent of its value. Even after adjusting for the subsequent revaluation of assets due to inflation, the government's earnings equalled no more than 2 percent of the property's value. Thus, private capital acquired formerly state-owned assets as property, or obtained control over them,[4] virtually free of charge.

The new proprietors were stingy with new capital investment, which for several years failed to exceed depreciation. Growth of fixed assets in the private sector through investment commenced only with the post-1998 economic recovery, but it was still relatively small in real terms. Only in a few instances was there any commissioning of new capacities, not to speak of new plant construction.

During the eight years from 1992 to 1999, for example, only 7,400 MW of electric power generating capacity was brought on line, which was less than the *annual* new capacity added in the 1970s and 1980s. In the same period of time, steel-smelting capacity for 2.5 million tons was commissioned, about equal to the amount brought on line in 1990 alone. Two and a half thousand kilometers of new oil pipelines were laid, substantially less than what was built in 1985 alone. Commissioning of new machine-building capacity virtually came to a halt after 1994; up until that point, the only construction work done was to finish plants started in the Soviet era.[5] This depressing picture scarcely changed after the economy resumed growth in 2000-2005.

In 1997, new capacity accounted for only 2.7 percent of the value of total fixed assets in the economy. In 1999, that level was 3.4 percent. In the Soviet economy of the late 1980s, this figure had typically been higher than 11 percent. And only 18 percent of the new capacity was in the private sector.[6]

Even wealthy companies in the export sectors preferred to invest more in their own administrative buildings and other non-productive facilities, than in new plants. Taking into account the rising obsolescence of fixed assets (reaching an average of 60-70 percent for machines and equipment), it can be asserted that a significant part of privatized fixed capital was simply run into the ground. The annual replacement rate for fixed assets in the economy as a whole has been barely over 1 percent, as against 8-10 percent in the Soviet period.[7]

2.2 Consume, or resell?

Why did property owners develop such a peculiar attitude toward their capital? The general explanation is that assets obtained at such a low price are not adequately valued by their owners. For example, equipment with an original real value of 10 million rubles, physically depreciated by 45 percent at the date of its privatization, had a realizable value of 5.5 million rubles. But since the new owner had acquired it for a mere 1 million rubles, this equipment figured in his business plans in two different ways. One possibility was to continue using it for production for some period of time, yielding, say, 10 million rubles worth of output per year, while depreciating the equipment by 1 million rubles annually. If nothing was spent for maintenance or renovation, this depreciation represented a net, tax-free addition to profit. Sooner or later, over the course of five years or so, the equipment would wear out and be written off. The accumulated depreciation would be 5 million rubles. The net profit from this factor alone, minus the initial outlay of 1 million for privatization of the equipment, would be 4 million rubles.

The other approach was to sell the equipment immediately for 5.5 million rubles, netting 4.5 million after subtraction of the 1 million outlay for acquisition. The owner who did this would forego any profit he might have made from output, since such output would not be produced or sold.

If the new owner were to have paid the full book value (5.5 million rubles) for the privatized equipment, neither of these approaches would have brought him any profit. Instead of reaping a short-term superprofit by utilizing the equipment he had acquired almost for free, he would have had to spend his depreciation allowance to maintain the assets in working order and replace worn-out components. This would have cost him the depreciation allowance and part of his earnings. But privatization for next to nothing provided no incentive for normal capitalist economic behavior of that sort. Our example, of course, is an invented model that illustrates an extreme case, but this type of behavior on the part of the new Russian capitalists does go some way toward explaining the low level of capital investment in the economy and the increasing obsolescence of fixed assets on a national scale.

Another maneuver by new property owners who had invested money in a privatized company was to get it into shape for resale at a significantly higher price. Operations of this sort, of course, involved time and expense, but they had little chance of success in the overall economic crisis. Purely financial speculation and speculation on price spreads were much easier. Privatizing with intent to resell was therefore not very widespread, but it did occur.

An example of one such operation that failed was the purchase of the ZIL auto plant in Moscow, early on, by a trading company called Mikrodin. After several attempts to revitalize the production and sale of ZIL trucks, the new owners decided to declare bankruptcy. Ultimately, they were able to sell the factory, on less than favorable terms, to the Moscow city government, which wanted to preserve jobs at ZIL. An example of a successful operation of this type was the Chernoy brothers' acquisition of control over several aluminum plants in Siberia. Huge battles developed around these highly profitable factories. The Chernoys decided that the most advantageous course for them was to sell their controlling ownership stake to the even more freshly minted magnate Oleg Deripaska, evidently for much more than what they had paid during the initial privatization.

Kakha Bendukidze's purchase of the Uralmash heavy industrial machinery plant in Yekaterinburg is an example of an unconsummated operation of the same type. The new owner attempted to get profitable operations going at his newly acquired factory, but he found this difficult to do in the economic environment at the time. After several years of trying, Bendukidze began to sell off auxiliary components of the Uralmash complex (such as its steel-making capacities) in order to concentrate on developing its core business of heavy machine-building. Eventually, he sold out completely to the Vladimir Potanin group and moved to the Republic of Georgia, where he became the minister of economics of that Transcaucasus country.

Sectors producing for export, which guaranteed that superprofit could be made on the gap between domestic and world prices, offered ample opportunities for reselling privatized property to foreign investors. Here, however, the prevalent posture was to try to maintain control, and build up assets and market capitalization. The best the foreign oil companies could do was to acquire a certain portion of the stock in these Russian firms. Thus, eventually, BP bought half of Russia's TNK, and Conoco acquired a minority share in Lukoil. Foreign involvement in the Russian government-controlled natural gas industry is largely limited to portfolio investment and minority shareholding. The only major foreign shareholder in the natural gas sector is Germany's Ruhrgas, which eases Gazprom's access to the European market.

Early attempts by foreign capital to seize a strong position in the Russian steel industry were beaten back. In the non-ferrous metals sector, domestic companies reestablished their dominance after several years of foreign participation in control over the production and export of aluminum. Russian ownership of fixed assets in the country has noticeably increased in recent years, both in absolute terms and relative to the economy as a whole.

The new owners were more attentive to the circulating capital they acquired, than to the fixed assets. Physical working assets, meaning inventories of finished products and raw materials, could be sold under any circumstances (with varying degrees of liquidity) and thus converted into money. The working capital in money form, acquired through privatization, was scant and, as a rule, insufficient to sustain the process of production unless it was supplemented with expensive bank loans. But gradually, despite continuing complaints about the shortage of working capital, short- and long-term investment in financial assets began to increase the total of such funds in the economy. This is where a part of the profit, depreciation, and other disposable company funds would go. Working capital increased especially fast after 1999-2000, when the economy began to grow again. The share of working capital in total private assets increased from 11 percent in 1996, to 37 percent in 2000, and 55 percent in 2003. Thus, a qualitative shift occurred in the composition of assets: working capital, including financial resources, grew, as fixed capital stagnated.

Table 2.2   Russian capital abroad

(outflow shown as total for the year, assets shown for year-end, and assets in rubles calculated at year-end exchange rate)

Year	Capital outflow (billions of $)	Accumulated assets (billions of $)	Accumulated assets (billions of rubles)
1993	5.8	5.8	7.2
1994	3.4	9.2	32.7
1995	12.7	21.9	101.6
1996	18.6	40.5	225.6
1997	19.8	60.3	360.2
1998	17.3	77.6	1,640.5
1999	14.5	92.1	2,482.9
2000	25.0	117.1	3,297.9
2001	18.6	135.7	3,962.4
2002	19.9	155.6	4,823.6
2003	22.0	177.6	5,328.0

Sources: RET2, #2, 2000, pp. 3-4. RSY 2001, RSY 2002, RSY 2003, RSY 2004 Balance of Payments tables.

2.3   Where to hold capital: at home, or abroad?

The preference for financial assets over the physical assets involved in material production was also evidenced in the tendency to hold an increasing share of accumulated money-capital abroad. Our data (Table 2.1) show that by 2000, at least 18 percent of all private-sector assets were outside the country in one form or another. As of 2003 this level was 16 percent. The greatest increase in this category occurred in the period beginning in 1995.

In Table 2.2, assets abroad are estimated on the basis of data on capital outflow, published in *Russian Economic Trends* in February 2000 and the RSY for 2002, 2003, and 2004, using a method similar to the one employed by the Bank of Russia for such estimates. Capital outflow is calculated as the sum of three components:

- the portion of export earnings that is not repatriated;
- unreclaimed advance payments for imports that were not completed;
- the errors and omissions line of the official balance of payments report.

Table 2.3 "Errors and omissions" in total capital outflow from Russia
(billions of $)

Year	Errors and omissions	Total capital outflow	Errors and omissions as % of total outflow
1994	0.4	3.4	12%
1995	7.9	12.7	62%
1996	8.1	18.6	44%
1997	5.2	19.8	26%
1998	8.8	17.3	51%
1999	7.3	14.5	50%
2000	9.3	25.0	37%
2001	9.2	18.6	49%
2002	7.5	19.9	38%
2003	7.4	22.0	34%

Sources: Data on net capital outflows and "errors and omissions" from RSY 2002, p. 613; RSY 2003, p. 633; RET2, #6, 2001, Table 10; *Obzor ekonomicheskoi politiki v Rossii za 1998 god* (*Review of Economic Policy in Russia for 1998*), Bureau of Economic Analysis, 1999 (hereinafter BEA99), p. 625.

The first two components represent some of the most widely used ways of taking capital abroad, legally or illegally. Legal capital transfers occur when exporters leave abroad a portion of their foreign currency earnings, above the amount they are legally obliged to convert into rubles at the Bank of Russia. At various times, this portion has been 25 to 50 percent of officially reported export earnings. Illegal capital flight occurs when the exporter conceals part of his foreign currency earnings, for instance by understating the actual price of sale, and leaves these unreported funds abroad. Capital may also leave the country as payment for fictitious imports. For example, advance payment is made against an import contract, but the goods or services are not delivered, and the advanced monies are not reclaimed.

As for the third component, "net errors and omissions" in the balance of payments are calculated by subtracting all reported payments from all reported receipts. In international financial statistics, this line traditionally reflects the balance of unreported cross-border capital movements. In Russia's balance of payments, at times it accounted for a significant part of the total capital outflow.

The data in Table 2.3 show that from 1996 on, usually more than half of total capital outflow was associated with export-import opera-

Table 2.4 Capital flight as share of GDP

Year	Capital outflow (billions of $)	Capital outflow (billions of rubles)	GDP (billions of rubles)	Capital outflow as % of GDP	Gross domestic investment (billions of rubles)	Capital outflow as % of domestic investment
1994	3.4	7.5	610.7	1.2%	133.2	5.6%
1995	12.7	57.9	1,540.5	3.8%	327.9	17.7%
1996	18.6	95.3	2,145.7	4.4%	454.4	21.0%
1997	19.8	114.5	2,478.6	4.6%	482.5	23.7%
1998	17.3	172.4	2,741.1	6.3%	472.9	36.5%
1999	14.5	360.1	4,757.2	7.6%	741.1	48.6%
2000	25.0	703.6	7,063.4	10.0%	1,224.8	57.4%
2001	18.6	543.1	9,039.4	6.1%	1,685.8	32.2%
2002	19.9	618.9	10,853.4	5.7%	1,948.1	31.8%
2003	22.0	660.0	13,285.2	5.0%	2,417.7	27.3%

Sources: Data on GDP and gross domestic investment from RSY 2000, p. 265; RSY 2004, Tables 12.1, 12.9.

tions, that is, the activity of companies engaged in foreign trade. At the same time, firms that by no means specialized in foreign trade transferred tens of billions of dollars abroad through various other channels, primarily banking.

The estimates given here are lower than some of the ones found in the literature. Some published figures show Russian private assets abroad in the amount of $200 billion or even $300 billion. The latter estimate seems excessively high. First of all, the data shown here are very large in comparison with GDP and gross domestic investment (Table 2.4).

Even without taking into account the devaluation of the ruble in 1998-1999, capital flight rose to 6.3-7.6 percent of GDP and 36-48 percent of domestic investment (Table 2.4). In 2000, when each exported dollar began to be worth significantly more, the outflow of capital reached a record level of 10 percent of GDP, and stood at well over half the level of domestic capital investment. These data cannot be called understatements. And even 6 percent of GDP and 32 percent of domestic investment in 2001-2002 is abnormally high, considering how inadequate investment resources were in most industries.

The estimates in the range of $300 billion might be more plausible, if there were any reliable data to support the assertion that $100-200 billion left the country before 1993. But the so-called "Communist Party gold," allegedly spirited out of the country, has never been found, despite official and unofficial searches. Moreover, its putative value would not have been more than several billion dollars even by the most optimistic estimates. As for capital accumulated in the late Soviet-period shadow economy, we estimate it at 384 billion rubles.[8] If even 10 percent of this sum was taken out of the country, these shadow economy assets held abroad would equal something on the order of $3.8 billion, using the average market exchange rate of that period. Thus, these two components would raise the total of assets abroad by $8-10 billion at most. Even more important, they represent capital flight dating from the Soviet period, and are not typical of the processes that unfolded in the new capitalist economy of Russia.

Several reasons underlie Russian capital's preference for foreign investments over domestic. First of all, there is a certain level of mistrust in the Russian authorities. Although reform-era political regimes have been friendly to Russian capital, on the whole, apprehensions remain that the government authorities will move against it. Privatization would appear to be irreversible, and yet the numerous violations of law that occurred during that process tend to feed an atmosphere of uncertainty and instability. This mistrust was later aggravated by the Yukos Oil case, which showed that even the largest and presumably most influential company, and its billionaire owners, were not exempt from arrest, criminal prosecution, and lengthy imprisonment on charges of tax evasion and conspiracy to embezzle state-owned assets. The fact that some companies have been singled out for prosecution adds to the feelings of uncertainty.[9] The threat of more criminal prosecutions of companies and their owners amplifies the fears. It is therefore more comfortable to hold "extra" capital—monies that are temporarily idle and not invested in highly profitable operations—abroad.

Secondly, the criminogenic nature of the Russian business world prompts many capitalists to keep their personal funds abroad, as far away as possible from the turf of domestic criminal groups. This is not always an adequate defense against the long tentacles of the latter, which can reach across borders and around the world. As for organized crime's own capital, it gets laundered abroad on an appreciable scale. But law enforcement agencies view laundered

Table 2.5 Money-capital of businesses and organizations
(as % of working assets, except as noted)

	1993	1995	1997	1999	2001	2002
Money resources	8.6%	4.0%	2.9%	5.2%	6.0%	7.8%
Ruble accounts	2.5%	1.6%	1.3%	2.1%	3.0%	3.1%
Foreign currency accounts	4.3%	1.0%	0.8%	1.6%	1.1%	1.4%
Other money resources	1.8%	1.4%	0.8%	1.5%	1.9%	3.3%
Short-term financial investments	1.0%	1.8%	2.5%	7.0%	9.5%	8.5%
Total money resources and short-term investments	9.6%	5.8%	5.4%	12.2%	15.5%	16.3%
Bank accounts as % of total money resources and short-term investments	71%	45%	39%	30%	27%	28%
Short-term financial investments, billions of rubles	1.2	20.2	61.7	476.5	1,959.5	1,665.6
Total financial investments, billions of rubles	2.6	70.9	298.7	775.2	2,429.8	2,091.3
Short-term investments as % of all financial investments	46%	28%	21%	61%	81%	79.6%

Sources: RSY 2000, p. 526, 528, 545; RSY 2003, p. 576, 603.

criminal capital as a comparatively small portion of total capital flight from Russia.

Thirdly, investing idle money abroad is more reliable than making financial investments at home because the Russian banking system and capital markets are undeveloped and unstable. We shall return to the relationship between banking and industrial capital. At this point, it may be noted that Russian companies and entrepreneurs keep very little of their money in Russian banks.

Table 2.5 shows that money-capital, as such, comprised a comparatively small part of companies' total working assets. Money-capital, understood as the total of money in bank accounts and cash, plus fairly liquid financial investments, accounted for no more than 16 percent of working assets. Its fluctuations have depended on the financial condition of the country's enterprises. The share of money-capital fell as a function of the deterioration of the overall economic situation in

1993-1996, then increased quite sharply after the 1998 financial crisis. Typically, however, the share of funds on deposit in bank accounts, which had declined as the economic situation deteriorated, did not rebound to new highs after the financial crisis.

The combined share of on-demand deposit accounts and foreign currency accounts was only 3.7 percent in 1999, equal to its 1994 level, and much lower than in 1993. It is striking that the popularity of foreign currency accounts also gradually declined, despite the consistently high proportion of such accounts among all bank accounts (ranging from 38 to 65 percent in various years). The ratio of foreign currency account balances to annual new foreign currency deposits in corporate accounts fell from 24 percent in 1993 to 2-4 percent in 1998-1999. The financial crisis did long-term damage to corporate confidence in the banks as places to hold foreign currency, never mind ruble accounts, which were devalued by inflation.

At the same time, companies became more interested over the years in making financial investments. The level of short-term financial investments as a share of working assets increased from 1 percent in 1993 to 7 percent in 1999, while their share within money-capital rose from 29 percent in 1993 to 55 percent in 1999. Companies' financial investments include their investments in the securities and equities of other companies, monetary credits extended to other companies, and investment in interest-bearing government and municipal (or regional) bonds.

The rapid growth of short-term investments before 1998 was due to the boom in high-yield short-term government bonds, or GKOs, and a surge in the stock market. The crash of 1998 virtually wiped out GKO investments and significantly lowered share prices on the stock exchanges. The Russian Trading System (RTS) index had more than quadrupled from an average level of 80.9 in 1995, to 427.9 in 1997, but it fell to an average level of 106.9 for 1998. The stock market's subsequent recovery was gradual. By mid-September 2001, the RTS index was only slightly above 200.[10] In later years, however, there has been a new stock market boom. In late June 2005, despite the vicissitudes of Yukos Oil's affairs and their aftermath, the RTS index shot above the 700 mark. With the world commodity price inflation of 2005-2006, the RTS passed the 1,600 level in April 2006.

We do not have reliable data on the composition of Russian capi-

Table 2.6 Comparison of Russian commercial bank assets with Russian deposits in banks abroad

Year	Russian bank assets (billions of rubles)	Russian deposits in foreign banks (billions of rubles)	Deposits abroad as share of total bank assets (%)
1996	498	178	26%
1997	623	271	30%
1998	933	1312	58%
2000	2,259	2,626	54%
2003	5,456	4,262	44%

talists' assets held abroad. The data shown above indicate that less than one-tenth of their total is accounted for by direct investment. It is difficult to estimate the size of portfolio investments using official data alone. It is believed that the greater part (around 80 percent) of such assets consists of foreign bank deposits and, to a lesser extent, investment in real estate. If that estimate is correct, it means that Russian deposits in foreign banks are comparable to the total assets held by our commercial banks inside the country (Table 2.6).

To a certain extent, the sharp rise in the relative level of deposits in foreign banks, beginning in 1998, resulted from the devaluation of the ruble. Nonetheless, the fact remains that foreign, rather than Russian, banks have become Russian capital's main base of banking operations.

This development has colored Russian capitalism as a whole, accentuating its one-way relationship with the economy of its own country. Russia is its main source for the accumulation of capital, yet much of that capital is kept and used abroad. This tilt presents an obstacle to the economy's ability to grow.

Economists and government agencies, naturally, have repeatedly taken up the question of how Russian capital abroad might be repatriated. Various measures, from a possible amnesty for people who bring capital back home, to the complete deregulation of capital exports, have been proposed to attract those assets for purposes of investment in developing the Russian economy. Others have suggested the opposite: tighter currency controls in order to limit capital flight. None of these measures, however, is likely to yield any noticeable effect, without a fundamental change in the attitude of Russian capitalists toward investing in their own country. And that, in turn, would require some improvement of the investment environment:

- greater political stability;
- conditions for consistent growth of the domestic market, rather than orientation toward export;
- sweeping improvements in the banking system and stock market operations.

Equally necessary would be a radical shift in the criteria and guidelines by which Russian capital operates. What does this mean? Normally, capital will be readily invested if the anticipated return on investment exceeds some generally accepted minimum level. In Chapter 1 we showed that the level of return on investment in Russia today looks fairly high by international standards. It would seem to follow, that there should be great enthusiasm about investing in Russia. But the inordinately high level of surplus value in Russia's national product, by comparison with the advanced industrial countries, keeps the Russian domestic market relatively small, making it unattractive to invest on a large scale in industries that produce goods other than for export and/or consumption by the well-to-do minority of the population. This explains why there is an excess of money-capital, which readily leaves the country, though most domestic industries are starved for investment resources.

Those general observations do not, however, take into account the special psychology that Russian capitalists have developed, which gives them exorbitant profit expectations, even with the elevated risk levels taken into account. First of all, many of our firms are deterred from making new investments, by a fear that doing so could undermine their dominant market position, destroy the exclusive niche they have seized, and lower their profit. This behavior pattern may be called "the monopoly syndrome." It also includes the creation of numerous non-economic barriers to the emergence of competition, which is accomplished with help from the government apparatus and organized crime. Few people in Russia have adopted the customary attitude of Western entrepreneurs, who try to achieve a small per unit profit margin and high turnover, as opposed to a large per unit profit margin with small turnover. This still dominant Russian behavior pattern was inherited from the times of commodity shortages and a highly segmented elite market.

A second factor in the Russian capitalist's behavior is that he believes he can enjoy these unique business conditions only in Russia, whereas in the West he would have to submit to different rules of behavior. In other words, he views the investment of his capital abroad, where it earns comparatively low yields from short-term deposits in foreign banks, government bonds, and corporate securities, as a low-yield cash reserve, doubling as an insurance fund.

This bifurcation of capital into the part that is used inside Russia, with a high rate of return, and the part held abroad, which is a low-yield, but stable and fairly liquid reserve, makes some business sense, but only within limits. It is difficult to determine at what point it becomes unprofitable to hold such a reserve abroad. And even if that boundary is crossed, there is no guarantee that the extra capital will necessarily return to Russia, as opposed to being invested in other countries. If, for example, the rate of profit in Russia were to fall and approach the rate in the West, it is not out of the question that idle Russian money-capital would seek a haven there in the West, rather than at home.

There is another side to Russian capital's use of banks abroad. Major Western companies customarily keep a reserve fund on deposit in their banks, against which they receive various financial services and a line of credit that the company may use if needed. Russian companies that deposit their funds in banks abroad enjoy the same type of services, including ones Russian banks are unable to offer. The main type of activity involved here would be servicing of Russian companies' operations abroad, such as bank loans obtained to finance imports. This question should be considered as part of an analysis of the overall relationship between Russian industrial and banking capital.

2.4 The relationship of industrial and banking capital

Let us now compare the assets of enterprises with those of the commercial banks and with Russian deposits in banks abroad, using the data in Tables 2.1 and 2.6.

Table 2.7   Comparison of industrial and bank assets
(billions of rubles and %)

	1996	1997	1998	2000	2003
Assets of enterprises	8,252	8,429	10,456	14,360	23,150
Assets of commercial banks	498	623	933	2,259	5,456
Assets of commercial banks as % of assets of enterprises	6%	7%	9%	16%	24%
Deposits in banks abroad	178	271	1,312	2,626	4,262
Deposits in banks abroad as % of assets of enterprises	2%	3%	13%	18%	18%
Sum of commercial banks' assets and deposits in banks abroad	676	894	2,245	4,885	9,718
Sum of commercial banks' assets and deposits in banks abroad, as % of assets of enterprises	8%	11%	22%	34%	42%

The ratio of industrial to banking capital, shown in Table 2.7, is clearly not in the latter's favor. Until the 1998 crisis, bank assets equalled less than 10 percent of enterprises' assets. Only after the crisis did they break out of this range, reaching 16 percent in 2000 and 24 percent in 2003.

In the USA, by comparison, bank assets are equal to 47 percent of the assets of all corporations outside the financial sector. In combination with the assets of insurance companies, which also function as lending institutions, their total is equal to 65 percent of non-financial corporate assets, while the assets of all U.S. financial companies are equal to 97 percent of the assets of non-financial corporations. Thus the American banking and financial sector is approximately equal in size to the U.S. economy's non-financial sector, which includes all of industry, commerce, transport, construction, and non-financial services.

We may assume that the U.S. financial sector is overdeveloped, as a result of the speculative orientation of business. But even if we correct for this phenomenon, it is clear that fully developed interaction between the financial and non-financial sectors of the economy, which promotes normal economic growth, requires financial sector assets to be equal to at least two-thirds of the non-financial part of the economy. In Russia, however, even if the assets of non-banking financial and other lending organizations are included, the entire financial sector's level will not likely exceed 30 percent.[11] Even in simple quantitative terms, it is beyond any doubt that this sector is underdeveloped.

Russian capital's involvement with foreign banks has partially compensated for this shortcoming. If we include deposits in foreign banks, banking capital expressed as a share of non-financial sector assets rises to 34 percent in 2000 and 42 percent in 2003. It would be wrong, however, to view this as complete compensation, since banks abroad certainly cannot provide all the services the Russian economy needs. For them to do so would require, at bare minimum, the removal of any barriers whatsoever to the free movement of money from Russia to other countries and vice versa. Thus, currency deregulation would be in the interest of Russia's banking and industrial circles, a fact reflected in the programmatic declarations of their leaders. The extent to which such deregulation would really improve the availability of bank services to the Russian productive sector, however, remains unclear.

There is a qualitative social problem, namely, that relations between Russian banks and industry leave much to be desired. As we have noted, Russian companies are not eager to keep their idle money in banks inside Russia. At the end of 2000, only 1.1 trillion rubles out of 2.259 trillion rubles of bank liabilities, less than half, were in the form of ruble and foreign currency accounts combined, and 45 percent of those represented Russian citizens' personal savings. Thus, no more than 30 percent of total bank liabilities represented enterprises' deposits. And only 42 percent of total bank assets were in the form of loans to the private sector and non-financial government enterprises. Recent years have seen this share contract from 57 percent in 1995 and 47 percent in 1997, to 42 percent in 2000 and 45 percent in 2002.[12] If we subtract from this amount those loans that were made to private banks or individuals, the remaining total of loans to businesses as such accounted for only 30 percent of total bank assets, approximately the same share that enterprises' deposits represent within the banks' liabilities.[13]

Although many private banks were initially organized as adjuncts to large companies and were designed to service the latter, relations between the banks and businesses have not been stable.

Until the very recent past, over 90 percent of bank loans were short-term, for periods of less than one year.[14] Only a small portion of capital investment by companies is financed through bank loans. The main source of financing for capital investment is internal accumulation: companies' own profit, and depreciation allowances. So far, the issuance of securities like stocks and bonds is only ancillary. And when they are issued, Russian banks, unlike Western banks, play little role in underwriting and placing them.

Russian banks' lack of desire to extend credit to the productive sector was initially explained away by the superior profitability of other operations: speculating on exchange rates, investing in short-term government bonds, or unlawfully using the funds of state agencies for private money-making operations. As these sources of profit shrank and went into decline, it would seem that lending to businesses ought to have increased. But no such turnaround occurred. The explanation is to be found in the heightened risk associated with lending to anybody other than the most reliable borrowers, as well as in the lack of transparency in corporate financial accounting, which precludes any reliable assessment of companies' creditworthiness.

In the West, relations between banks and industrial companies are usually long-term and involve a high degree of trust. Bank employees are obliged to look after the interests of client companies' various subdivisions and facilities. At Chase Manhattan Bank in New York, for example, employees working in the industrial division used to be required to spend at least 40 percent of their work time on-site at the companies for which they were responsible.[15]

Russian banks do not advertise their policy in this regard, but available information indicates that they have only limited opportunities to devote that kind of attention to their corporate clients, let alone provide them adequate financial services. In fairness, it should be said that some of the larger private banks have begun to develop departments to service corporate clients. But their ability to satisfy companies' demand for long-term financing is limited, due to the predominantly short-term nature of their deposit base. This deficiency will not be corrected until insurance companies, private pension funds, and investment companies are more developed in Russia, and a specialized investment banking industry becomes an important factor in raising equity and bond capital for corporate clients. Russian capitalism has a long way to go before it reaches that point.

Alexander Mamut, a former head of MDM Bank, complains that not a single major Russian bank, with the exception of the state savings bank, Sberbank, can handle the financial needs of even a single major corporate client.[16] Yet these major enterprises and corporations are considered the most reliable borrowers. As head of the banking committee of the Russian Union of Industrialists and Entrepreneurs (RUIE) in 2000-2002, Mamut waged a persistent campaign for his proposal to cut the number of banks licensed for general operations, and enlarge them, in order to make the banking system "more reliable, more stable, more transparent and more attractive for investors." He proposed to reduce the number of banks licensed for general operations from the 255 in operation at the time, to several dozen. In addition, he wanted to liquidate all state-owned banks except for Sberbank, and limit Sberbank chiefly to lending to the population (mortgages and consumer credit), since its liabilities comprise chiefly individual deposits.

Mamut's proposal was criticized by small and medium-sized banks, which feared being edged out of the lending market. The major private banks that backed his project were criticized for trying to create a banking monopoly to serve major clients only.[17]

In this context we can look at the comparative size of banks and industrial companies, and the concentration of assets in banking and industry.

The number of lending organizations in Russia, most of which called themselves banks, initially grew very rapidly in the 1990s. By 1993, there were 1,700 such institutions, and 2,600 as of 1996. Only some of them had obtained the right to conduct banking operations such as soliciting deposits from the population and from organizations. There were 1,700 institutions that enjoyed this right as of 1998. Their number fell in the years that followed, but it was still significant: 1,311 at the end of 2000, and approximately the same number in 2003. The proliferation of lending organizations and banks may be attributed, first and foremost, to the fact that managing money, divorced from the production and sales cycles that characterize tangible goods production, was the simplest type of business someone could engage in. Under conditions of high inflation, it was very profitable. Moreover, many companies and organizations in various localities, not wishing to trust "outside" banks to handle their money, tried as much as possible to create their own banks, which they could control. The majority of such lending institutions, of course, were small, performed very limited functions, and were not commercial banks in the modern sense of the word.

In 2001, the 20 largest banks accounted for 45.7 percent of all commercial banking sector assets (Table 2.8). These assets were not evenly divided. Over half of the total belonged to two banks that are largely state-controlled, Sberbank and Vneshtorgbank (Foreign Trade Bank). Excluding these two, the 18 largest private commercial banks accounted for 27.7 percent of total private bank assets. By 2003, the picture had hardly changed. Thus, the extreme concentration of assets within the banking sector as a whole is chiefly due to the two state banks' huge share. The private banks are more fragmented, a certain degree of concentration notwithstanding. A leading bank such as Alfa Bank, for example, had only 2.6 percent of total banking sector assets in 2001. MDM Bank, whose top man was so actively promoting concentration within the sector, could boast of only 0.8 percent of the total assets. Obviously, the major commercial banks would like to expand their influence. It is also understandable that they aspire to eliminate the competition they face from Sberbank, whose assets are practically equal to the total assets of the 18 largest commercial banks. The very biggest of them is only one-eighth the size of the state-owned giant.

It is doubtful that Mamut's proposed reform, discussed above, could substantially improve the situation with bank lending to industry. If Sberbank's lending were redirected from industry into mortgage and consumer credit, the commercial banks would have to compensate for the enormous reduction in credit to industry, but it is unlikely that they would be capable of doing so. As of June 2001, Sberbank's commercial loans totaled 234 billion rubles, equal to the total lending of the 25 leading private banks.[18] The latter would have to double their lending, if they were to make up for what would be lost. It would be impossible to do this in any short period of time. The situation with credit availability to the non-financial sector of the economy would deteriorate.

We may also compare the dimensions of Russia's banks with those of its industrial corporations. Unfortunately, it is only rarely possible to make a direct comparison of their assets, since corporate reporting on assets is irregular. In most cases, therefore, it has been necessary to use sporadically published data on market capitaliza-

Table 2.8 Concentration of assets in the banking sector

	April 1, 2001		April 1, 2003	
	Assets, billions of rubles	Assets as % of all bank assets	Assets, billions of rubles	Assets as % of all bank assets
Total assets in the banking sector	3,155.0	100.0%	5,456.4	100.0%
1. Sberbank	620.8	19.7%		
2. Vneshtorgbank	164.9	5.2%		
Sberbank + Vneshtorgbank	785.7	24.9%	1,307.3	24.0%
3. Gazprombank	83.2	2.6%		
4. Alfa Bank	82.2	2.6%		
5. International Industrial Bank (Mezhprombank)	77.8	2.5%		
6. International Moscow Bank	70.1	2.2%		
7. Investment Bank and Trust (Doveritelny i investitsionny bank)	55.0	1.7%		
8. Rosbank	46.3	1.5%		
9. Bank of Moscow	46.0	1.5%		
10. Citibank	31.9	1.0%		
11. MDM Bank	25.0	0.8%		
12. Raiffeisenbank (Austria)	19.2	0.6%		
13. National Reserve Bank	18.7	0.6%		
14. Avtobank	16.3	0.5%		
15. Globex	16.1	0.5%		
16. Petrokommerts	15.8	0.5%		
17. Guta Bank	13.9	0.4%		
18. Yevrofinans	13.4	0.4%		
19. ABN AMRO Bank	12.9	0.4%		
20. Sobinbank	12.2	0.4%		
Total for 18 private banks (#3-#20)	656.0	20.8%	1,076.6	21.4%
Total for 20 banks	1,441.7	45.7%	2,383.9	47.4%
Total assets of all private banks	2,370.2	75.1%	4,149.1	76.0%
18 private banks, % of all assets of private banks		27.7%		25.9%

Table 2.9 Market capitalization of major industrial companies
(billions of rubles)

Oil and gas industry	
1. Gazprom	364.6
2. Surgutneftegaz	299.9
3. Lukoil	296.9
4. Yukos	255.8
5. Sibneft	62.3
Electric power industry	
1. Unified Energy Systems of Russia	141.1
2. Mosenergo	32.6
Metallurgy	
1. Norilsk Nickel	100.3
2. GMK* Norilsk Nickel	63.7
3. Cherepovets MK,** Severstal	25.9
Telecommunications	
1. Rostelecom	21.4
2. Moscow City Telephone Network	16.6
Civil aviation	
1. Aeroflot	9.3
Machine-building	
1. KamAZ	6.1
2. AvtoVAZ	5.9
3. OMZ (Uralmash-Izhora)	4.1

* GMK—mining and metallurgical works.   ** MK—integrated iron-and-steel works.

tion, obtained by multiplying the number of shares issued, by the current market price. Such data, of course, never coincide exactly with the volume of assets shown on the corporate books. Market capitalization fluctuates according to the situation in the stock market, sometimes exceeding the value of the assets, or lagging behind it during market downturns.[19] Nonetheless, data on capitalization approximates the relative size of the companies. Table 2.9 gives these data for several major sectors of the economy in 2001.

The companies shown in the table are among the 30 firms with the greatest market capitalization. They represent the backbone of

Russian industrial capital. It should be noted that food industry and light industry companies, as well as companies in the military-industrial complex (MIC), are practically absent from that top 30 list, which is dominated by companies from the fuel and energy sector, metallurgy, and, to some extent, telecommunications and civilian machine-building. The list thus reflects both the sectoral composition of the economy, and the nature of the concentration of capital within certain of the sectors, as will be discussed later in this chapter.

Let us now compare the banks and the major industrial corporations in size. Not counting Sberbank, whose 620 billion rubles in assets in 2001 made it 7.5 times larger than the biggest private commercial bank, the assets of the ten top private banks at that time ranged from 19.2 billion rubles to 83.2 billion. The capitalization of our selected ten major industrial companies ranged between 25.9 billion and 364.6 billion rubles. If we also take into consideration the scattered data available on industrial company assets, the top of the range will be 1.2 trillion rubles. No bank, not even Sberbank, comes anywhere close. And the major private commercial banks are dwarfed by the largest industrial corporations, which are concentrated in the fuel and energy sector and in the non-ferrous metals industry. The ratio of the five top industrial firms' capital valuation to the assets of the five top private commercial banks is 3.7 to 1. Looking at the companies' assets, rather than capitalization, the ratio will be 5 or 6 to 1.

The Russian banks' size is comparable with that of major firms in other sectors. The average capitalization of the six leading machine-building, telecommunications, and civil aviation companies, for example, was 10.6 billion rubles in 2001, while the top five commercial banks had average assets of 74 billion, and the top ten banks had average assets of 54 billion. It would appear that, though Russian banks do not have the resources to service the large corporations of the export-oriented sectors, they could very well handle the business of companies that produce primarily for the domestic market.

As of late 2004, the situation had not changed substantially. In September 2004 the capitalization of the ten largest industrial companies with their shares quoted on Russian stock exchanges ranged from 746 billion rubles (Lukoil) to 55 billion rubles (Megionneftegaz). The assets of the ten largest private commercial banks ranged from 175 billion rubles (Alfa Bank) to 39 billion rubles

Table 2.10 Size comparison of banks and industrial companies in the USA, Great Britain, Japan, and Germany as of 2001
(market capitalization, billions of $)

USA	Banks		
	1	Citigroup	250.1
	2	J.P. Morgan Chase	103.1
	3	Wells Fargo	89.3
	4	Bank of America	82.7
	Companies		
	1	General Electric	477.4
	2	Exxon Mobil	286.3
	3	Pfizer	263.9
	4	Microsoft	258.4
Great Britain	Banks		
	1	HSBC Holdings	140.6
	2	Royal Bank of Scotland	62.8
	3	Lloyds TSB	60.6
	4	Barclays	53.6
	Companies		
	1	Vodafone Group	227.2
	2	Royal Dutch-Shell	206.3
	3	BP (British Petroleum)	178.0
	4	GlaxoSmithKline	160.4
Japan	Banks		
	1	Mizuho Holdings	58.1
	2	Bank of Tokyo-Mitsubishi	46.9
	Companies		
	1	NTT DoCoMo	175.4
	2	Toyota Motor	123.8
	3	NTT	116.6
	4	Sony	67.1
Germany	Banks		
	1	Deutsche Bank	51.0
	2	Dresdner Bank	22.9
	3	Bayerische Vereinsbank / Bayerische Hypo Bank	22.2
	Companies		
	1	Deutsche Telecom	94.7
	2	Siemens	75.8
	3	Bayer	35.5
	4	BASF	27.8

(Promsvyazbank). The three major state-controlled banks—Sberbank (1.793 trillion rubles in assets), Vneshtorgbank (359 billion) and Gazprombank (287 billion)—still towered high above the largest private banks.

For the sake of comparison, Table 2.10 shows the relative sizes of major banks and industrial corporations in the four leading industrial countries.

The average ratio of the selected companies' capitalization to that of the selected banks is 2.5 in the USA, 2.4 in Great Britain, 2.6 in Japan and 1.8 in Germany.[20] Thus, in those countries the banks are approximately two to three times larger, relative to industrial corporations, than is the case in Russia.

The relative underdevelopment of the Russian banks may be explained, as noted above, first and foremost in terms of the constant outflow of liquid money-capital to foreign destinations. Another reason is the high degree of concentration of productive capacities within the real sector, a legacy of the socialist economic system. The commercial banks have had ten to fifteen years, at best, in which to become established, while the giant industrial companies took shape over decades. In addition, the size of the commercial banks has been limited by the peculiarities of banking-sector privatization.

The banking sector under socialism had four components. The most important part was Gosbank, the State Bank, which combined the functions of the Central Bank, emitting the national currency, and a huge commercial bank, which had a virtual monopoly on handling enterprises' disposable funds and on short-term lending to industry. The second component was the system of savings institutions, which was unified as Sberbank in the 1980s. It had a monopoly on accepting deposits of cash savings from individuals, but did not carry out other, independent operations. Instead, the savings banks put their deposits at the disposal of the state, to supplement national budgetary funds, which were otherwise inadequate. The third component was specialized long-term credit banks, which derived their resources from mandatory payments made by enterprises out of their depreciation funds. The fourth and last component was banks that serviced foreign economic operations.

Fragmentary data for 1988 give an approximate picture of the relative size of the first three components (in billions of rubles)[21]:

Short-term loans	302.3
Long-term loans	96.5
Sberbank deposits	296.7
Total	695.5

Since loans are assets and deposits are liabilities, the sum of these values is offered here for purposes of comparison only. Nonetheless, insofar as the total values of assets and liabilities balance out, these data give some indication of the scale of the banking system under socialism.

Compare those data with the assets of enterprises and organizations at that time, seen as the sum of fixed assets and working capital (in billions of rubles):

Fixed assets	2,699
Productive	1,808
Non-productive	891
Working capital	730.6
Total assets	3,429.6
Productive fixed assets + working capital	2,538.6

Comparison shows that at the end of the Soviet period, bank assets were equal to something on the order of 20 percent of enterprise assets, a level slightly higher than in 2000 (17 percent). Put differently, the relative development of Russia's banking system in today's market economy differs little from its condition under central planning.

What happened in the interim? During the reform of the banking system at the beginning of the 1990s, the Central Bank of Russia was stripped of the second of its two functions, commercial banking activity. The assets and liabilities associated with this activity were handed over, in part, to newly privatized banking organizations, but they were sharply devalued from the outset by rampant inflation. Although the other component of the banking system, Sberbank, survived, inflation drastically devalued its deposits as well. After the initial shock, they began to be rebuilt by personal savings deposits. The specialized long-term lending banks were privatized, and their assets devalued. The rate of devaluation was significantly less for the fixed assets of enterprises. Therefore, the ratio of banking assets to industrial business assets fell sharply, to a level of only 6 percent in 1996. In subsequent years it began to recover, but extremely slowly.

The banking reforms carried out in Eastern Europe were more successful than Russia's. Even under central planning, the commercial banks in those countries, though they were state-owned, did exist apart from the central banks, which dealt exclusively with currency emission. Since the main content of banking reforms there was privatization of the existing commercial banks, major losses from organizational chaos could be avoided. Inflation was also less severe in those countries, than in Russia. As a result, the banking system plays a substantially greater role in the economies of Eastern Europe. As of mid-2001, bank lending to the private sector in Russia was equal to only 14 percent of GDP, while in Eastern Europe it was as high as 60 percent.[22]

As already noted, the different degrees of concentration in industry and banking are a considerable factor in the relationship between banking and industrial capital in Russia. While commercial banks proliferated by the tens and hundreds in the 1990s, significantly decentralizing the banking system, the concentration of industry underwent few major changes from its configuration in the Soviet period.

2.5 The concentration of capital in the productive sector

We begin the next phase of our analysis with a few preliminary concepts. The term "concentration of production" usually refers to a share of total production, accounted for by sets of enterprises, grouped according to rank or absolute size.[23] Here the definition of "company" or "enterprise" is of importance. In Soviet statistics, "enterprises" included all production units having their own independent balance sheet, meaning they were being assigned fixed assets and working capital, operating accounts in banks, and other attributes of "full-set" profit and loss accounting. They may have belonged to production, or science and production, associations and combines, but they had a degree of independence within the larger organizations. Since they were state property, they also were subordinated to and managed by some sector or territorial administrative agency, such as a ministry, directorate, trust, etc. The independence of the enterprises under these command agencies was qualified. An enterprise might formally be endowed with capital, but its prerogative to deploy that capital was limited by the decisions of the superior agencies. Although the latter lacked their own balance sheets and were not organized as commercial concerns, in practice they played the role of major corporations in a modern market economy, dominating each of the main sectors of industrial production.

For this reason formal data on the concentration of production, based on enterprise data, are an inadequate representation of the real degree of concentration in Soviet industry. At the end of 1988, for example, Soviet industry officially had 46,400 enterprises, of which 10,500 (23 percent) accounted for 56 percent of national industrial output.[24] In actuality, there were only 200-300 national and republic-level ministries, to which all enterprises of any significance were subordinate. In other words, the real concentration of production in the Soviet period far exceeded what it was in the world's leading industrial nations. (To what extent such a high degree of centralization was economically justified is a separate question, which deserves more detailed study in connection with the market reforms of the 1990s.)

This is an important point, because privatization in the 1990s was done, with few exceptions, on the basis of individual enterprises. If a production unit had its own independent balance sheet, it was allowed to become owned by its employees, by holders of privatization vouchers, and so forth. This formal criterion was employed, even when it resulted in the senseless separation of enterprises that had been parts of larger combines or other organizations, integrated on the basis of their production activity. One side effect of this approach was the liquidation of many managerial, supply, sales, planning, and other organizations, needed for the enterprises to function smoothly. It was believed that the enterprises, upon becoming independent businesses, would establish market relations among themselves, on their own. But the organizations that were liquidated had been part of the infrastructure, without which a normal market cannot exist.

This process had two results: (1) production was, in effect, deconcentrated, and (2) a significant portion of the genuinely necessary and economically appropriate horizontal and vertical economic ties were broken. This deconcentration eliminated a significant part of the economy of scale in production, which theory defines as one of the most important positive aspects of concentration, and as an engine of technological progress.[25] As a result of the destruction of existing economic relationships, a large number of new commercial middlemen emerged. In most cases this development sharply increased not only distribution costs proper, but also transaction costs, which are the costs involved in seeking purchasers or sellers, and establishing ties with other economic agents.[26]

When this question was discussed in the Western literature, economists acknowledged the damage done to the economy by this type of decentralization, but they argued that no other option was available. In their view, there were only two possible pathways to the liquidation of the old hypercentralized system of management:

1. To create production associations from above (to some extent preserving the old system of directorates, trusts, combines, etc.);
2. To grant independence to the enterprises as such, leaving it to the market to decide, in the course of competition and natural selection, to what extent production should be concentrated and centralized in the future.

The first pathway might lead to arbitrary decision-making of yet another type. The second pathway was considered more natural.[27]

In practice, there was no such choice to be made. From the outset, the reigning idea was to privatize individual enterprises and transfer to their employees a significant portion of the ownership rights to their assets. The deconcentration of the firms and liquidation of their administrative "superstructures" was predetermined. Furthermore, privatization took place in a hurry. The reformers believed that the most important thing was to take down the old system, after which the market would sort things out. One of the people in charge of the privatization process explained to this author that their top priority was to tackle "the political task," and that they simply had no time to think about which solution would be best for the economy.

Thus, the process of concentration of production began as if from scratch, after privatization of the enterprises. But it began from the point at which industry had arrived, as a result of the enterprises' acquiring their independence. Formally, the process of privatization lasted throughout the 1990s and is not yet over. The great majority of enterprises, however, were privatized during the first two years, in 1993-1994. A total of 28,870 enterprises were privatized in the 1993-2002 period (21,652 in 1993-1999 and 7,118 in 2000-2002), of which 17,947, or 62 percent, underwent privatization during those first two years. Altogether, they constituted an overwhelming majority of the 30,000 state-owned enterprises that had existed in the Russian Socialist Federation of Soviet Republics (RSFSR, the Russian Federation within the Soviet Union) at the beginning of the market reforms, and had formed the industrial base of the country.[28] They are still its backbone, insofar as only a handful of new industrial enterprises have been created since that time.

In this same time period, a great number of new economic entities have been created in industry. At the beginning of 2000, there were 372,000 different companies and organizations in industry. One hundred fifty-eight thousand of them were operational productive-sector enterprises. Of those, 136,000 were small companies with fewer than 100 employees. The other 22,000 companies correspond approximately to the number of formerly state-owned enterprises. They account for 96 percent of total industrial output.[29] Smaller companies and small businesses will be discussed in a separate section of Chapter 3.

For a better understanding of the renewed concentration of production, Table 2.11 presents the composition of Russia's privatized enterprises by sector of industry.

Thus, a huge gap between the average size of fuels, energy and metals companies, and all other companies, was a peculiar feature of Russian industry from the outset. The fuel and energy sector and the metallurgical companies are an order of magnitude larger than the average size of all other industrial enterprises.[30] The companies making up the fuel and energy complex and metallurgy represent only 4.1 percent of the total number of companies in industry, but they account for 41.4 percent of all production. Of course the gap is partially due to the decline of machine-building and the consumer-goods industry, which are operating at only a small fraction of capacity. There are quite a number of large machine-building companies, which at full capacity would be comparable with the fuel and energy and metals giants. Nonetheless, the concentration of production clearly exhibited a significant initial bias toward the latter sectors.

Table 2.11 Distribution of enterprises by sector of industry, 2003

Sector	Number of enterprises	Shipped production (billions of rubles)	Average production per enterprise (millions of rubles)
1. Industry, total	145,000	8,498	58.6
2. Electric power industry	1,781	886	497.5
3. Fuels industry	1,716	1,407	819.9
4. Ferrous metallurgy	1,191	695	583.5
5. Non-ferrous metallurgy	1,825	530	548.0
6. Chemicals and petrochemicals	7,966	454	57.6
7. Machine-building and metal-working	46,818	1,483	31.7
8. Forestry, wood processing, pulp and paper	21,861	308	14.1
9. Construction materials	8,816	229	26.0
10. Light industry	14,552	102	7.0
11. Food industry	22,085	994	45.0

Source: RSY 2004, Tables 14.1, 14.22-14.79.

As it turned out, these sectors continued to occupy a special position after privatization was largely completed. One of them, the electric power sector, continues to function as a natural monopoly, almost entirely controlled by the holding company RAO UES (Russian Joint Stock Company Unified Energy Systems), in which the state remains the majority shareholder and controlling owner. The situation in the natural gas industry is similar. Despite repeated attempts to break it up, this industry retains the essential features of a natural monopoly, managed by Gazprom, which is under state control for all intents and purposes. Three other sectors in this group (the oil industry, steel, and non-ferrous metals), as well as the natural gas industry, are leading export-oriented sectors. As shown in Chapter 1, that means that they generate a significant amount of superprofit. For this reason alone, they drew the attention of the biggest capitalist groups and banks. In the process of tumultuous battles among these groups for control over the major sectors, they were reorganized on the basis of oligopoly, in which a few large companies dominate each of the sectors.

Data for 2003 showed that the eight largest oil companies accounted for 64 percent of all oil extraction and 57 percent of the oil-refining industry, while the top four accounted for 49 and 39 percent, respectively. In the steel industry, the first eight companies accounted for 53 percent of output in 2003, while the top four accounted for 40 percent. At first glance, the degree of concentration in non-ferrous metallurgy would seem to have been lower: 37 and 29 percent, respectively.[31] But these data are not conclusive. Unlike the oil and steel industries, various non-ferrous metals companies focused on different areas of production. Moreover, their domination of the aluminum or nickel markets is significantly higher than these data would suggest. Norilsk Nickel, for example, has practically no competitors in either nickel or platinum production. Russian Aluminum (Rusal) controls 70 percent of primary aluminum smelting. Neither the oil nor the steel industry has that high a degree of concentration of production.

Although the process of concentration of production had similar results across the export group of sectors, the specific pathways and methods of reconcentration differed. Initial preparations for privatization unfolded similarly in these sectors as in others (not counting the natural monopolies). Joint stock companies were established, each based on an individual enterprise. These companies were then supposed to undergo privatization in accordance with procedures set by law. But things turned out differently.

The deconcentration that occurred during the first years of the reforms had an extremely adverse impact on the oil and steel industries. Crude oil extraction fell from 452 million tons in 1992 to 310 million tons in 1994. Steel smelting declined from 77 to 49 million tons annually, during those years. While the overall economic crisis and curtailment of domestic demand were a major factor, the disruption of joint production operations and the supply and sales infrastructure also played no small part. The situation in the non-ferrous metals industries looked better by comparison. Primary aluminum production, for example, remained at roughly its pre-reform level.

Official attitudes toward the fate of these sectors have also varied. Oil has traditionally been seen as the country's chief export commodity. Even in the most difficult years, oil exports remained fairly high. In 1994 crude oil exports were 128 million tons, or 42 percent of production; counting other petroleum products, exports were 175 million tons, or 56 percent of the resources produced. In that year, oil exports to countries outside the former Soviet area alone brought in $12 billion, or one-fourth of all Russian export earnings. Although steel exports accounted for 10 percent of the total value of Russia's exports, and aluminum for 5 percent, government officials were relatively uninterested in these sectors.

2.6 Where the oil giants came from

It was in this same period, that Russian capitalist groups developed the particular interest in the gap between low domestic oil prices, and high oil prices on the world market, discussed in Chapter 1. The system of quotas and licenses for exporting oil lasted until 1995, as did the special list of authorized exporters, who were permitted to sell oil abroad in exchange for acquiring industrial products of ostensible interest to the state. That meant that the oil producers, most of which were state-owned joint stock companies, were not the only ones involved in exporting oil. Also in the business were numerous middlemen, including people who had not the slightest connection with the oil industry. The same went for other high-value exported commodities.

It all began with the scandalous story of one of the first millionaires of this era, Artyom Tarasov, who was granted the right to export a large shipment of fuel oil, in exchange for his promise to deliver imported products needed for Russian agriculture. The fuel oil was sold, and payment of $40 million was deposited in Tarasov's foreign bank account, but the promised imports remained abroad. This affair received wide publicity, but Tarasov used his connections to avoid criminal prosecution.

Another, less widely known affair involved an association of Russian textile factories, which obtained authorization to export a certain quota of oil to Uzbekistan in exchange for cotton, which was in short supply at the time. The textile company managers, however, decided it would be more profitable to re-export the cotton to the West than to use it at their own plants. Thanks to government connections, this affair, like many others, was hushed up.

In 1994, the Moscow-area company Balkar Trading, an automobile dealer, got permission to export an annual quota of 25 million tons of oil for five years at below world market prices. The purchaser was presumed to be Mobil, the American oil major. The quid pro quo was to be a loan from a Western bank to finance a federal program to modernize the Krasnoyarsk Combine Factory. The deal received high-level government approval. It fell apart, however, when the Presidential Administration instigated a criminal prosecution against acting Prosecutor General Valentin Ilyashenko, whose close relatives were behind Balkar Trading. After a long period of incarceration, Ilyashenko was acquitted of bribery charges. It is believed that he unwittingly became involved in the oil deal, which happened to impinge on the interests of some rival business group.

Detective stories like these graphically illustrate the situation around oil exports during the first reform years. Because the oil sector was so profitable, the government and the new private capitalist groups willy-nilly developed a certain mutual interest in reorganizing it on some relatively stable basis.

Vagit Alekperov, a former deputy minister of the Soviet oil industry, was a pioneer of the new tendency. In November 1991, just as the Soviet period came to an end, Alekperov had succeeded in creating the first unified state-owned concern, based on three major, formerly independent oil enterprises in West Siberia: Langepasneft, Urayneftegaz and Kogalymneftegaz. All three are situated in the Ob River floodplain between Surgut and Nizhnevartovsk. The first letters of the names of these three enterprises provided an acronym with which to name the new association—LUKoil, which was destined to become Russia's biggest oil corporation. In the years that followed, it expanded greatly, swallowing many other companies involved in the extraction, refining, marketing, and transport of oil and petroleum products. Lukoil operates in 40 regions of Russia and 25 foreign countries, although it remains based in West Siberia. In 2003, it accounted for 19 percent of Russian crude oil output and 10 percent of petroleum products. Privatized soon after its creation, Lukoil is controlled by a group of its top executives. Exactly how many shares they own is not known to the public, but press reports suggest that Alekperov, who still heads the company, owns at least 10 percent. *Forbes* magazine, in its annual list of the world's billionaires, put Alekperov's personal fortune at $1.3 billion in mid-2001.[32] If that fortune consisted chiefly of Lukoil shares, then his ownership of the company was in the area of 14 percent. Nearly five years later, estimates of his fortune had risen to $6.5 billion, equivalent to 9 percent of his company's market capitalization as of February 2006.[33]

Lukoil set a contagious example. In 1992 the government created three more major oil associations: Yukos, Surgutneftegaz, and Rosneft. At the end of 1992, when Victor Chernomyrdin was still minister of fuel and energy, Lukoil, Yukos, and Surgutneftgaz were sold at auction, with private investors being allowed to purchase up to 49 percent, and the state retaining 45 percent ownership (the remainder of the shares were distributed to company executives). All three are still in existence, though in dramatically different forms; about this more will be said below. Rosneft initially split into several other companies, spawning first Slavneft, Sidanco, the Eastern Petroleum Company, and Onaco, and subsequently, in 1995, also the Tyumen Petroleum Company (TNK) and Sibneft. Slavneft remained state-owned until December 2002, when it was sold to private interests (see below).[34] The story of five of these companies—Surgutneftegaz, Yukos, Sidanco, TNK, and Sibneft—is of greatest interest for understanding the concentration of production in the oil industry.

Outwardly, Surgutneftegaz looks like a smaller version of Lukoil. Created as an open joint stock company on the basis of an eponymous pre-existing production association, it initially incorporated the Kirishinefteorgsintez oil refinery in the Leningrad Region, which was one of the sector's five largest facilities, as well as four wholesale companies in northwest European Russia. The holding company subsequently acquired Surgutneftegazbank and Surgutneftestroy, which are banking and construction facilities, respectively. Thus, Surgutneftegaz from the outset has been a vertically integrated concern with well-defined production, refining, and marketing units. The company did not push to expand, but rather concentrated on mastering and making better use of its initial resources. That may be why its output and financial performance have remained comparatively high. Though holding only third place in oil extraction (13 percent in 2003) and refining (8 percent), Surgutneftegaz is second in market capitalization ($27.3 billion in March 2005, as against $28.9 billion for Lukoil and $15.9 billion for Sibneft).

As was the case at Lukoil, the Surgutneftegaz top management was able to keep the company under its own control. In mid-2001, *Forbes* estimated the value of Surgutneftegaz President Vladimir Bogdanov's shares at $1.6 billion, or 15 percent of the company. By

2005, his fortune was estimated at $5.35 billion, equal to 19.6 percent of the company's capitalization. Surgutneftegaz's 2000 annual report revealed that its other major shareholders are its subsidiary Surgutneftegaz Petroleum Company, and the Surgutneftegaz Pension Fund. Thus, the company is internally owned through these subsidiary organizations, in addition to the top executives' personal shares. Unlike Alekperov, whose name appears frequently in the media, Bogdanov remains largely in the shadows. In all of 2001, there appeared only a small amount of coverage of a visit he made to Belarus, where he received a high state award after concluding major deals with local companies. One French magazine, unable to obtain any detailed information about Bogdanov, called him "the most secretive billionaire in the world."

Until 2003, Yukos Oil was also one of the top three oil companies. Like that of Lukoil, its name derives from two of its original components: the Yuganskneftegaz oil extraction company (based in Nefteyugansk, near Surgut) and Kuybyshevnefteorgsintez, a major oil refinery and petrochemicals complex in the Samara Region. The name Yukos is decoded as Yu(gansk) + K(uybyshev) + O(rg) + S(intez). Unlike Lukoil, this new association was constructed as a vertical combination of crude oil extraction and refinery operations. Its two main components were located over 2,000 km apart. The presidential decree that created the company also gave it eight wholesale operations in European Russia. What was done in this case seems so appropriate and economically justified, in retrospect, that it is simply incomprehensible that the reformers were unable to reorganize all of Russian industry using these types of arrangements, rather than chopping it into dozens of weakly connected and unviable companies.

Before tracing the later history of Yukos, it makes sense to go back to certain dramatic events that accompanied its creation.

In May 1992, a private joint stock company called Neftesam was established as a 50-50 joint venture between the Russian state-owned trading company Samara Neft and a Belgian firm called Tetraplast. The owner of the latter was one Victor Masharin, a former Soviet citizen who had made his fortune in the old shadow economy. The head of the new company was Alexander Dybenko, a young engineer who had gone to work as an official in the Fuel and Energy Ministry and was well connected in Moscow's corridors of power.

Neftesam was included on the list of specially authorized exporters. The company would purchase oil in West Siberia, process it at the Samara refinery, and export petroleum products through the Port of Odessa. Until mid-1993, it was exporting 100,000 tons per month, unimpeded.

In mid-1993, the Samara refinery was transferred to Yukos. Various explanations have been offered for why Neftesam lost this asset. One of them is that the "Belgian" Masharin was connected with the criminal group of Otari Kyantrishvili, who had the ear of then-Vice-President Alexander Rutskoy. Rutskoy, by this time, was already out of Yeltsin's good graces, which may have affected the fate of Masharin. Be that as it may, the general director of the Samara Refinery was shot dead in the entryway of his apartment building that October. Then the Yukos people took over the refinery and informed Neftesam it could no longer make use of the refinery's services. After a conference held in Moscow to settle the conflict, Masharin's group was physically attacked, coming under automatic weapons fire. Masharin himself was wounded and evacuated to Belgium for surgery.

A government commission, formed to investigate the Neftesam affair, froze the company's bank accounts. Nonetheless, Neftesam managed to transfer its real estate to a new company it set up, called Svet. The new firm's head, one Vladimir Vasilyev, held talks with Yukos in Switzerland about reestablishing the previous relationship. He was invited to visit the Samara plant, but, upon his return to Moscow, Vasilyev was slain at the entrance of the Ministry of Fuel and Energy building. Yukos acquired uncontested ownership of the Samara refinery.[35]

Yukos was not a success during its first years of operation. Crude oil output fell sharply, and the company's debt to the government alone rose to $3.5 billion. Yukos was on the brink of bankruptcy. It is difficult to say if these problems resulted from tactics deliberately adopted by Yukos management in order to get the company privatized. In any event, in a series of tenders and auctions held in 1995-1996, the government did sell its shares in Yukos to a group of private investors headed by Mikhail Khodorkovsky, the president of Bank Menatep. The purchase price was substantially below the real value of Yukos' proven oil reserves. A short time later, in 1996, Khodorkovsky came to work at Yukos as its president. The company's affairs started looking up. In late 1997, Yukos acquired control of the Eastern Petroleum Company. This added another oilfield production unit, Tomskneft, to its property, along with the Achinsk oil refinery and a distribution network in the Tomsk and Novosibirsk Regions and in Khakasia. A 1998 attempt by Yukos to merge with Sibneft into a new concern called Yuksi, however, ended in failure. That was the year of the financial crisis, when world oil prices plunged. As the economy recovered, Yukos resumed its expansion. In 2001, it took over the East Siberian Oil and Gas Company (VSNK) and the Angara Petrochemicals Company. The company's share of total Russian crude oil production increased to 19.2% in 2003, up from 18.3% in 2002 and 16.7% in 2001. In 2003 it claimed to be the largest Russian oil company, though in crude output it was about equal to Lukoil.

It is striking that the Khodorkovsky group had been interested in oil as far back as 1992, when its company Menatep-Impex obtained government permission to barter Russian oil for Cuban sugar. The allotted quota of oil was loaded onto tankers, but only half of it reached the declared ports of destination. Angry Cuban officials sold the earmarked sugar to Western companies, which ultimately resold it to Russia at higher prices. An official investigation produced no indictments.

Until 2003, Yukos was completely controlled by the Khodorkovsky group, which held more than 60 percent of its shares through the Menatep financial group and direct ownership by individual leading group members. It gained popularity in the West as one of the best managed and transparent Russian corporations. Its capitalization reached a record $33.5 billion in September 2003, surpassing all other Russian corporations.

In October 2003, Khodorkovsky (together with Platon Lebedev, his partner and president of Menatep) was suddenly arrested and charged with conspiracy to defraud the government in the course of a number of privatization deals in the mid-1990s. Their trial carried on until June 2005, when they were convicted and each sentenced to nine years of imprisonment. As the case unfolded, Yukos was presented with large back tax bills, which it was unable to pay in full. In compensation, in 2004 the government seized and sold Yukos's largest production unit, Yuganskneftegaz, which accounted for 60 percent of the company's total crude oil capacity. Khodorkovsky's former subsidiary now belonged to Rosneft, a fully state-owned company. Yukos was effectively reduced to 40 percent of its former size. Its capitalization plunged to $1.4 billion in March 2005. We shall discuss the wider political and economic ramifications of Yukos's downfall later in this chapter and in Chapter 3.

The case of Sidanco, an oil company created by government decree in May 1994, was also dramatic. The government stakes in several firms were consolidated into Sidanco: Purneftegaz, Kondpetroleum, Chernogorneft, Varyeganneftegaz, Udmurtneft, Kreking (from English "cracking"; the Saratov oil refinery), the Angara Petrochemicals Company (ANKhK) and several wholesalers. The State Property Committee conducted a loans-for-shares auction of the state-owned 51 percent of Sidanco in December 1995. The winner was the International Finance Company (MFK), which was headed by Boris Jordan at the time and belonged to Vladimir Potanin's group. The nearest rival was the Alfa Group, which managed to take revenge later on, as we shall see. The controlling equity stake subsequently passed to the Interros holding company, which became the central institution of Potanin's group and was later headed by Potanin himself.

Potanin's managers, however, were unable to consolidate the Sidanco subsidiaries into a working unit. Crude oil production at the Sidanco fields began to drop off sharply. Hoping for assistance from the "Varangians" (as outside owners were dubbed, after the Norse invaders who were incorporated into the leadership of East Slavic cities in the eighth and ninth centuries), Interros sold 10 percent of Sidanco to one of the largest international oil majors, BP, and handed over another 10 percent of the shares to BP to manage. Nonetheless, the company's affairs did not get straightened out. The British co-owners were unable to fathom all the maneuvers, involving both finances and commodities, which the Russian executives of Sidanco's subsidiaries had employed. Some of the subsidiaries went into bankruptcy, not without assistance from the Alfa Group of Mikhail Fridman and Pyotr Aven, Potanin's rivals, who used their control over TNK to drive Interros out of the oil business.

TNK's key operation was to seize control, as authorized managers, of the Chernogorneft company, which belonged to Sidanco, but had entered bankruptcy in 1999. After a series of lawsuits, TNK offered to return Chernogorneft to Sidanco, in exchange for 25 percent ownership of Sidanco as a whole. Interros put up resistance for quite some time. In 2001, however, the George Soros-owned Cypriote firm Kantupan, a partner of Potanin, decided to sell its own, separate 40 percent share in Sidanco to Fridman's Alfa Group. The latter thereby acquired complete control over Sidanco, and joined Yukos as one of the major competitors of Lukoil and Surgutneftegaz for leading positions in the oil sector. This operation took place with the approval of BP, which had earlier opposed such a deal out of concern that it would lose its controlling position. But, given the opportunity to keep its men in top management positions at Sidanco, now headed by the Englishman Robert Shepherd, BP also crossed over into the camp of Potanin's enemies.

It is worth noting that at a certain stage of the battle for Sidanco, in March 2000, Ziya Bazhayev, who had headed the company in 1997-1998, died in a plane crash.[36] The incident was highly publicized because it also took the life of Artyom Borovik, head of the Sovershenno Sekretno (Top Secret) publishing house. The investigation established that carelessness by service personnel at the Tyumen Aviation Group was to blame for the accident. Whether or not there was criminal intent remains unknown.[37]

The Alfa Group exploited TNK in order to enter the oil business. This company had been founded in 1995 as a holding company uniting two West Siberian crude oil production companies: Nizhnevartovskneftegaz and Tyumenneftegaz. The latter included the famous Samotlor oil field, once the largest in Russia. Also incorporated into TNK were an oil refinery in Ryazan and five wholesale companies in the Tyumen Region and central European Russia. The state remained its biggest shareholder until 1997-1998, when a series of tenders and auctions resulted in control passing to New Holding, which belonged to the Alfa Group. The new owners used special pressure methods to make sure that TNK would not remain under previous management. Despite the Tyumen regional government's support for the previous executives, the bankers prevailed.

It soon became clear that those bankers had influential sponsors not only in Moscow, but also high up in U.S. business circles. Thanks to these connections, they were able to obtain a large loan from Chase Manhattan Bank, with U.S. Ex-Im Bank guarantees, to reconstruct the Ryazan refinery and upgrade production at Samotlor. This loan was not free of controversy. Then-Secretary of State

Madeleine Albright initially opposed it. Under pressure from the head of the influential Texas Halliburton Corporation, future Vice President of the United States Dick Cheney, Albright backed down.

Albright's initial objection arose from the fact that in 1999, TNK had forced through a decision to have Sidanco's subsidiary Chernogorneft declared bankrupt, and then put under TNK's control. During this process the rights of Sidanco's main foreign investor were ignored. That was BP, which had merged with the American oil major Amoco not long before. Angry investors pressured the State Department to take measures against TNK, and Albright acted accordingly. The American supporters of TNK, however, turned out to be stronger. Cheney was able to convince the State Department that blocking the loan would deprive Halliburton and other American firms of lucrative orders for equipment and construction projects at Ryazan and Samotlor. BP had to back off, although it did secure TNK's agreement to return Chernogorneft, albeit in exchange for the surrender of control over Sidanco by Potanin's Interros.

After Alfa's takeover of TNK, the oil company's new head was Simon Kukes, a Russian-born oilman who had emigrated to the United States at an early age and worked his way up to top managerial jobs at Philips Petroleum and Amoco. Under his leadership, TNK moved to acquire additional companies. In 2000, it bought control of Lisichanskiefteorgsintez in Ukraine and the Onaco petroleum company in Russia. Though it was not a top-ranked unit, the acquisition of Onaco boosted TNK's crude production by another 8 million tons per year, making it the fourth largest producer in the country. The purchase price of Onaco was over $1 billion. The fact that financing was provided in part by Sberbank and Vneshtorgbank indicates the group's strong influence in the Russian government.

Fridman said all along that his group wanted to boost TNK's market capitalization and then sell it profitably to a major multinational oil company. This indeed transpired in 2003, when BP bought half of TNK's shares and assumed the major executive positions in the combined TNK-BP. The other half belongs to three Russian investment groups: Alfa Group, Access Industries and Renova. In 2003-2004 TNK-BP also finalized the acquisition of close to 50% of Slavneft, which TNK had purchased at its privatization auction in December 2002. TNK-BP claims to be the second largest producer of crude in Russia. It is the only leading oil company that includes foreign capital in a big way. Additional details of this deal will be discussed in Chapter 6.

The owners of another Russian oil company, Sibneft, set their sights on a similar operation. There were reports that a deal of this type might come off, if the company could be sold for $3-4 billion.[38] This would have meant a substantial increase in its market capitalization, which stood at $2.5 billion in September 2001 (by early 2005, it was $15.9 billion). The story of how Sibneft had reached the top ranks of Russia's oil companies, facing such strong competition as there was in the sector, is of interest.

Like TNK, Sibneft was created by Presidential decree in 1995, on the basis of Noyabrskneftegaz in the Tyumen Region, the Omsk Petroleum Refinery, and several local geological prospecting and wholesale companies. In an auction of government-owned shares that had been mortgaged, the Petroleum Finance Company (NFK, a part of the Berezovsky-Abramovich group) acquired a controlling 51 percent stake. Later, Boris Berezovsky's company Sins bought another 19 percent in an investment tender, and 15 percent went to Refine Oil, owned by Roman Abramovich.[39] The company had little success at first. In 1998 its plan for a merger with Sidanco failed. But, as world oil prices shot up beginning in 1999, Sibneft's revenue soared and it began to expand. Unlike its competitors, Sibneft worked chiefly by obtaining licenses for new, as yet undeveloped oil fields.

Sources at Sibneft say that their aim was not so much to increase crude output, as to lower costs and make new investments profitable. This is not entirely accurate. First of all, Sibneft came on the scene comparatively late as an active contender for position within the oil sector. The most profitable assets had already been grabbed by its competitors. Secondly, Sibneft's attempt to expand through a merger with Yukos was one of several failures. In the fall of 2000, for example, Sibneft and Yukos tried to purchase the state-owned company Onaco in an investment tender, but lost out to TNK. This occurred even though Sibneft had earlier acquired 40 percent ownership in Orenburgneft, a subsidiary of Onaco, and continued to control that company even after the auction.

Crude oil output at Sibneft facilities fell from 25.5 million tons in 1993 to 17 million tons in 2000 (5 percent of total Russian production at that time), then rebounded to 35 million tons in 2004 (8 percent of total production). The company's production of refined petroleum products in 2000 was 12.5 million tons, or 7 percent of the sector total. Nonetheless, even though Lukoil's crude production was 4.5 times that of Sibneft, the number one oil company had only 3.5 times Sibneft's market capitalization. In the summer of 2001, Sibneft paid its shareholders a larger dividend than Lukoil and Yukos combined. This tactic certainly boosted the company's capitalization, which became the third highest in Russia.

In the course of such maneuvers by Sibneft, certain peculiar organizational features came to light. In addition to its core production companies, Sibneft is surrounded by a web of satellite oil traders that sell its output. Due to the spread between the price the traders pay Sibneft for the oil, and the final selling price, a significant portion of the company's profit is "diverted" to these formally independent agencies, which in reality belong either to Sibneft itself or to its main shareholders. Until 2002, 88 percent of Sibneft's shares were approximately evenly divided between Berezovsky and Abramovich. About the time of Berezovsky's forced emigration to London in 2000 (about which more will be said below), he apparently transferred his holding to Abramovich. The latter attempted to sell Sibneft to Yukos in mid-2003, but cancelled the deal after Khodorkovsky's arrest. It is believed that he was acting on orders from the Kremlin.

In 2001, the tax authorities opened a case against Sibneft for underpayment of taxes, committed in part by using the satellite oil traders to conceal a portion of its profit. Abramovich succeeded in quashing this case after meeting with President Putin, on condition that he incorporate at least some of his satellite firms into the main body of Sibneft. This was done. In the summer of 2001, two small companies registered in Kalmykia, called Vester and Olivest, were merged into Sibneft. Their profit substantially increased the parent firm's total reported profit, and higher taxes were paid. The following figures indicate the scale of this operation: the combined annual profit of these two middlemen was $300 million, whereas Sibneft's own pre-merger profit was $675 million. Some notion of the actual dimensions of the group's profit can be had if we realize that the two companies that merged represented only a small fraction of the entire Abramovich network of distributors.[40]

In mid-2005 it became known that Abramovich was moving to

sell Sibneft to Gazprom, with Putin's approval. The deal was finalized in October 2005, marking a substantial increase in the size of the government-controlled sector of the oil industry. The combined share of the expanded Rosneft and Sibneft is 25 percent of total oil production, greater than the output of any single oil producer in Russia.

The outcome of the battles for control over the oil sector can be seen in the listing of the top six crude producers, shown as a percentage of total output in 2004-2005:

Lukoil	19%
TNK-BP	17%
Rosneft	17%
Surgutneftegaz	13%
Sibneft (part of Gazprom)	8%
Yukos	8%
Rosneft + Sibneft	25%

These six leading companies account for 82 percent of crude oil production, a jump upwards since 1999, when their total share of output was 56 percent. In the space of those six years, some of the former Big Three (Lukoil, Yukos, Surgutneftegaz), notably Yukos, were pushed aside, while TNK-BP and Rosneft moved in. The government has emerged as a crucial factor in the partial nationalization of the industry, a shift from its 1990s role of helping to create private oil giants. And, for the first time, a foreign major (BP) has become a prominent producer, accounting for at least 9 percent of total crude output.

The reemergence of the government as a major participant in the oil market implies certain structural changes. The two government companies will now appropriate at least a quarter of the superprofit deriving from oil rent, and could, if the government so chose, channel most of it directly into the federal budget. Moreover, the government-controlled companies could follow non-monopolistic pricing practices in the domestic market, inducing other market players to exercise price restraint. Whether or not this happens will depend, of course, on the general direction of economic policy pursued by the government, and on the market strategy of the new, Kremlin-controlled oligarchical group of companies that is taking shape. The broader significance of the new group will be discussed in Chapter 3.

The development of concentration processes in the oil industry exhibits certain patterns in common with other sectors of the economy:

1. The major corporations were formed and have developed almost exclusively through mergers of state-owned production associations, as the government moved to give them away or sell them, at low cost, to private groups. It is not clear whether the partial renationalization of Yukos will remain an isolated case, or if it will spread to other companies.

2. All production units controlled by autonomous districts within the Russian Federation remained outside this battlefield. The largest of them, Tatneft, is one of the top eight companies traded on the Russian Trading System (RTS), as measured by capitalization. Since every such company is an important source of budget revenue for the local government of the area where it is based, the local authorities are in no hurry to transfer them to independent private ownership. Nonetheless, since each of these companies has been transformed into a joint stock company and their shares are theoretically available for purchase, it is not excluded that private groups will attempt to take them over. As we shall see, the posture of local authorities, rather than the federal government, plays a great role in how major corporations have been created and expanded in other sectors of the economy.

3. In the initial phases, there was some, often quite intense, involvement of organized crime in the fight for control over various companies. Gradually, however, either strong groups of company executives or groups of outside investors, not necessarily from the banking community, got the upper hand. We shall return, in Chapter 3, to the nature of managerial control in the Russian setting. For the moment, we may note that the staying power of such control depends to no small degree on what portion of a company's shares are the executives' own property or under their control. Conversely, outside investors have other means of taking over a company than by acquisition of a controlling ownership stake. The outside forces may act by effectively control-

ling the financial flows within a large corporation or having tight control over its subsidiaries. Since each corporation was formed as an association of previously independent enterprises, which often were separate joint stock companies, these can be seized by outside competitors, even if the subsidiary formally continues to belong to a given major corporation. Thus, for example, rivals of the Potanin group were able to wrest away its seemingly unassailable control over Sidanco.

4. The battle for control of the oil industry took place within certain limitations, in that it occurred at a relatively difficult time for the economy as a whole, when overall industrial production was declining or stagnating. Therefore, with few exceptions, the superprofit of the oil industry, large as it has been, did not lead to large investment programs, development of new oil deposits, or technological modernization. As the overall economic situation changes, one would expect renovation and oil exploration to resume on a large scale. This, however, has occurred only as the exception, rather than the rule. Favorable external conditions are more likely to give an impulse to a thorough-going transformation, than for it to emerge from the intrinsic viability of the corporations. We shall return in Chapter 6 to these manifestations of technological stagnation.

2.7 The battle for metals

Unlike the oil sector, which was accorded national strategic status, the government did not delay in allowing private interests to purchase assets in the steel and non-ferrous metals industries. As privatization proceeded, there was a long period of time during which major metallurgical combines, which became the property of their workforces, managers and outside investors, remained at least formally separate, without merging into larger firms. Even in some cases where production capacities and wholesaling operations came into the hands of the same investors or organizations, the units remained formally separate. This was the case in subsectors of the metals industry like aluminum or steel, where the Soviet-era structure involved a large number of distinct enterprises in different regions. Nickel production was different, in that a single company dominated this subsector from the outset, so that the only question was which group would control that company. We shall look at this comparatively simple case of nickel, before summarizing the developments in aluminum and steel.

Nickel: pre-existing concentration

In the early 1990s, nickel production in Russia was concentrated at the Norilsk Mining and Ore-enriching Combine in Taymyr and two enterprises in the Murmansk Region: Severonikel in Monchegorsk and Pechenganikel in Pechenga, formerly part of Finland. The Norilsk facility accounted for over 80 percent of their total output. In November 1989, not long before the end of the Soviet period, the state concern Norilsk Nickel had been created by government resolution, merging these three enterprises. Also attached to Norilsk Nickel were the Olenegorsk Machine Works in the Murmansk Region, the Krasnoyarsk Non-Ferrous Metals Processing Plant, and the Gipronikel Institute in St. Petersburg.[41] The only major nickel facility not included in the consolidated firm was the Yuzhuralnikel association, which processed solely imported ore from Cuba and was therefore not part of the unified production cycle of the big company's enterprises. The merger decision was an important one, which preserved the sector's high level of concentration and protected it from break-up in the course of privatization.

In June 1993, Norilsk Nickel became a joint stock company. Its component enterprises were sold at auction in 1994. The privatization procedure used was the most widespread scheme, under which about half of the shares were transferred to the company's work force. A portion was sold at voucher auctions, while 38 percent (but 51 percent of the voting shares) remained federal property. The enterprises were in sorry financial condition, despite the fact that Russia accounts for 20 percent of world nickel production, as well as the overwhelming majority of world palladium and platinum production (all of it by Norilsk Nickel), with most of the palladium and platinum being exported. The main battles here were for control of the financial flows associated with the company, and involved local governments, organized crime, the government of Krasnoyarsk Territory, and the federal government in Moscow. Little attention was paid to the production side of the business. Norilsk Nickel experienced an increase in wage arrears, alongside a catastrophic rise in its debt to the federal budget.

In these circumstances, the government decided on two steps in late 1995. First, a controlling stake in Norilsk Nickel passed to Potanin's Oneximbank at a loans-for-shares auction. A year and a half later, in August 1997, this same block of shares was bought for $270 million through an investment tender, by a subsidiary of Potanin's Interros holding company.

At the time, Potanin was accused of having bought Norilsk Nickel for far less than its fair price. The loans-for-shares auction at which he acquired his controlling stake was said to have been rigged. There was one other bidder, whose name remained secret. Matters reached the point that Prime Minister Chernomyrdin, taking a hint from Prosecutor General Yuri Skuratov, issued an order to postpone the auction. Only after the intervention of Anatoli Chubais, who was deputy premier and had designed major aspects of the overall privatization process, and head of the State Property Committee Alfred Kokh, was a final decision taken. Yeltsin fired Kokh soon afterwards, for his biased posture in disputes. Kokh and Chubais, among others, were later accused of taking an illegal book advance, allegedly financed by Potanin. In many people's eyes, the book scandal was the revenge of Berezovsky and Vladimir Gusinsky, in particular, for having lost the battle for Norilsk Nickel.

Later, when Putin was President, there was an official demand for Interros to make restitution of $140 million for underpayment at this auction. The matter was resolved without payment of this "fine," after Potanin acquiesced to a presidential request to invest a certain amount of money in completing a partially built nickel factory in Cuba.

Today the company accounts for 85 percent of the nickel Russia produces, 71 percent of the copper, 95 percent of the cobalt, and close to 100 percent of the platinum-group metals. Substantially more than half of this output is exported. Even in an environment of large price fluctuations, these exports made it possible to gradually stabilize the company's finances, catch up on wages and federal budget payments, make a certain level of profit, and even invest in updating the production capacities. The company's net profit rose from $328 million in 1993 to $1.3 billion in 1999, and over $2.5 billion in 2004. Nonetheless, even with its near-monopoly within Russia, storm clouds kept gathering over Norilsk Nickel.

In particular, its relations with the government of Krasnoyarsk Territory deteriorated. When Norilsk Nickel came under the wing of the Moscow-based oligarch, Potanin, the Krasnoyarsk government lost control over a part of its financial flows. A short time after the loans-for-shares auction, the Norilsk city prosecutor opened a case against the company's management for using the credits in ways other than those for which they were earmarked. Later, a spokesman for then-Governor of Krasnoyarsk Valeri Zubov threatened to bankrupt Norilsk Nickel. This spokesman subsequently turned up dead. In 1997, the State Duma passed a resolution, demanding that the controlling equity stake in Norilsk Nickel be returned to the government. But the resolution was ignored. These disputes between the authorities and the company were bad for business, giving rise to constant problems with tax agencies and the judiciary. In order to reduce the tension, Norilsk Nickel surrendered the Krasnoyarsk Non-Ferrous Metals Processing Plant to the territorial government. As a result of this deal, the governor effectively lost all control over Norilsk and the surrounding district. After Alexander Khloponin, the president of Norilsk Nickel, was elected head of the Taymyr Autonomous District in 2000 (later, in 2002, he won election as governor of Krasnoyarsk Territory as a whole), the company's administrative independence became even greater.

After the financial crisis of 1998, Norilsk Nickel was in danger of being sold. Interros got into financial difficulties and had to decide how to pay the debts of Oneximbank, which had gone bankrupt. The choice was to sacrifice either Sidanco or Norilsk Nickel. Potanin decided to retain the latter.

In 2000, the Federal Market and Securities Commission sued Norilsk Nickel for allegedly having obtained the company Norimet illegally. The lion's share of Norilsk's exports go through this firm.[42] This suit brought a halt to the restructuring of Norilsk Nickel. The concern had previously incorporated two subsidiaries: the Norilsk Mining Company and the Kola Mining and Smelting Company. The stock of these subsidiaries was listed on the stock exchange, alongside the stock of Norilsk Nickel proper, but as separate entities. The original idea here was to make these shares more attractive to investors.[43] But within a few years a new idea appeared: to get the shares listed on the New York Stock Exchange. For this purpose, a complicated operation was launched to make the Norilsk Mining Company into the parent company, while Norilsk Nickel and Norimet would be its subsidiaries. Only the Norilsk Mining Company's shares would be listed. As in the case of Sibneft's wholesalers, the integration of Norimet was designed to increase the group's profitability and capitalization. Norimet's share of Norilsk's total assets rose to 11 percent. With this addition, the company's overall capitalization climbed to just above $5 billion in the fall of 2001. Its directors talked about achieving the level of $8 billion by 2004. In the event, they did even better than that: Norilsk's capitalization in November 2004 was $13.3 billion.

From the standpoint of the concentration of production in the sector, the restructuring of Norilsk Nickel changed little. It is entirely possible, however, that this was only a first step towards bringing in strong foreign investors and, ultimately, handing control over to them. The probability of such a turn of events is enhanced by the fact that foreign investors acquired 24 percent of the shares back in 1999. These acquisitions chiefly represented portfolio investment by major investment funds that have no intention to control or participate in managing Norilsk Nickel. That situation could radically change, however, if the Potanin group decided to sell its 55 percent stake for a profit.

Aluminum: from disorder to monopolization

Russia inherited from the Soviet planned economy a highly developed aluminum industry, second only to the United States in production of this important metal. The take-off of the Soviet aluminum industry was almost entirely due to the requirements of the military-industrial complex (MIC). In the Soviet period, only a small fraction of Russian aluminum was used in the civilian economy or exported. The lion's share went into aircraft construction, primarily for the military. When the USSR came apart, aircraft production dropped off steeply, and with it went domestic demand for aluminum. Now, export took first place in the demand structure, rising sharply in the first years of reform. In 1992, Russian aluminum exports were 570,000 tons of primary metal (ingots), in 1993—810,000 tons, and in

1994—2.2 million tons. Aluminum exports continued to rise, reaching 2.7 million tons in 1997 and 3.1 million tons in 1999. Thereafter, exports oscillated around the peak level of 3 million tons per year. Thanks to high demand from abroad, primary aluminum production remained virtually untouched by the overall economic crisis. After a slight drop in 1991, output quickly achieved its previous levels and began to grow steadily from 1995 onward. The production of rolled aluminum, sold primarily to the domestic market, did not follow the same pattern. Output in this category initially fell by 50 percent, and did not begin to recover until 1999. Thus, aluminum production was sustained by export. The main sources of profit were the annually fluctuating gap between domestic and world prices, and the low cost of production thanks to low electricity rates. In the Soviet period, aluminum plants were built near major hydroelectric power plants, making aluminum production profitable even though the bauxite mainly had to be imported from Latin America and Africa.

Initially, almost all aluminum smelting was done at a dozen plants, of which the largest were in Krasnoyarsk, Bratsk, and Sayansk. A second tier of facilities, still major ones by world standards, included the Irkutsk, Novokuznetsk, Volgograd, and Kandalaksha plants. After the elimination of centralized planning in this sector, the government made no attempt to create large aluminum concerns. Each plant was privatized separately and acquired different new owners during the voucher auctions. The next stage of the process, as a rule, was a war over redividing the booty. Such conflicts, as we shall see, were not only acute, but sometimes dramatic and often bloody. By 2001, the outcome of the war was the effective monopolization of the sector by two groups, accounting for 70 and 20 percent of total output, respectively. This represents the second highest concentration of capital in any sector of Russian industry, after nickel.

One of the special features of the struggle for control of this industry was that, from the outset, foreign middlemen involved in selling aluminum on the world market played a significant part. The main venue for trading aluminum is the London Metals Exchange. Companies with experience in operating on that exchange became key players, first in monopolizing the trade in Russian aluminum, and then in attempts to take over the plants that produce it. They were the ones who introduced the idea of "tolling," which is the export of metal produced using only imported raw materials (bauxite), while the processors, the aluminum producers, are exempted from the value-added tax and import duties. This scheme was approved in March of 1992 for the Bratsk plant (BrAZ) by order of President Yeltsin, and subsequently extended to other aluminum producers. The result was a huge leap in the profitability of exporting aluminum.

At the same time, the position of the intermediary firms grew stronger, because they not only controlled the producer companies' access to the foreign market, but also had a grip on the bauxite supply lines. Any shortage of this raw material threatened to shut down the plants and cause serious material losses, since it would involve time and considerable cost to restart the continuous production process. Back in 1991, the Swiss firm Marc Rich & Co. gained a prominent place in the Russian aluminum trade. But it was quickly eclipsed by two other groups, which were also each other's rivals. They were the Aluminum International Organization Company (AIOC) and Trans-World Group (TWG). The latter was founded in 1992 by the brothers Mikhail and Lev Chernoy, emigres from Soviet Central Asia. At voucher auctions that year they managed to acquire large equity stakes in BrAZ and KrAZ (the Krasnoyarsk Aluminum Plant), and took them over.[44] The Chernoys' government connections also helped. Deputy Prime Minister Oleg Soskovets, who was in charge of the metals industries, personally introduced Lev Chernoy to a conference of aluminum plant directors as "a potential Western partner." With this kind of protection, TWG was able to sign a contract with the management of KrAZ at the end of 1993, under which the plant would supply 300,000 tons of aluminum annually for the next ten years, for sale through the Chernoys' company.

At the beginning of 1994, however, investigatory agencies opened a criminal case concerning the use of false payment orders for part of the TWG deal. The general director of KrAZ, Mikhail Turushev, who had discovered this abuse, was beaten half to death in the foyer of his apartment building and had to retire. His successor was the plant's commercial director, Yuri Kolpakov, who was considered the Chernoys' man. In 1994, meanwhile, TWG took advantage of an investment tender to increase its equity stake in BrAZ. Bids from competitors (the Victor Vekselberg and Vasili Boyko groups) were rejected without being considered.[45] The same year, a government commission headed by Soskovets beat back attempts by the Ministry of Nature and the Federal Currency and Export Control

Service to abolish the tolling system. Vladimir Sementsov, a Ministry of Internal Affairs (MVD) investigator who had rashly tried to open an investigation of Soskovets in connection with major embezzlement in the aluminum trade, was arrested. Sementsov spent a year and a half in prison, but was later completely exonerated.

Nonetheless, the tolling scandal seriously frightened both the deputy prime minister and the plant directors. In October 1994, KrAZ General Director Kolpakov struck TWG-controlled firms from the plant's shareholder list. In February 1995, the government took a decision to create the Transnational Aluminum Company (Tanaco) group, making KrAZ a part of it. At that moment, the later famous Anatoli Bykov showed up at KrAZ. He was a local organized crime kingpin, recruited to defend the plant against TWG and establish his own control. There was some attempt at an amicable resolution, but in April 1995 Kolpakov's deputy Vadim Yafyasov was killed in Moscow; he had just been appointed to that post, ostensibly to work towards the amicable settlement.

The person of Yafyasov deserves particular attention. It is believed that he was the one who in 1992 opened the door to the Chernoy brothers to gain control of BrAZ, which he could do because of his connections in the Russian Committee on Metallurgy (Roskommetallurgiya). He subsequently set up his own company and went into partnership with Mikhail Zhivilo, who had taken over the Novokuznetsk Aluminum Plant (NkAZ). A portion of NkAZ output was exported through TWG. In the summer of 1993, however, NkAZ management accused Yafyasov's company of presenting false payment orders. They broke their contract with the company, and Yafyasov himself went to work for Roskommetallurgiya, and then for Yugorsky Bank in Tyumen. He returned to the aluminum business almost two years later, in March 1995 becoming general director of KrAZ. According to one version of these events, the KrAZ management thought Yafyasov's close ties with TWG would be helpful in settling their dispute with the latter. Others say that Yafyasov not only failed to move matters toward a reconciliation, but pushed them in the opposite direction: he started talks on setting up long-term relations with AIOC, which at that time was the Chernoys' chief competitor in the Russian aluminum trade. In this version of events, Yafyasov's death was a revenge killing for his betrayal of TWG. Two months later came the murder of Oleg Kantor, owner and CEO of

Yugorsky Bank, where Yafyasov had worked before going to KrAZ. The view was that both were killed on orders from the Chernoys. A Ministry of Internal Affairs investigative committee looked into the case. In a letter to this committee, mailed from Venezuela, one of the brothers categorically denied this charge. The investigation was shelved. But in 2001 Zhivilo, who in the meantime had emigrated to the United States, formally renewed the accusation against the Chernoys by suing Siberian Aluminum (about which more below) in a New York court. This was not the end of the 1995 series of murders. In late August, it became known that the state-owned stake in KrAZ (37 percent) would be sold, and that AIOC, the Chernoys' rival, was going to bid for the tender. Exactly one week later, AIOC's Russian manager was found dead. At that point AIOC decided it were better to get out of the aluminum business in Russia. Meanwhile Krazpa Metals, a new wholesaler for KrAZ, joined the ranks of aluminum dealers. Krazpa Metals was jointly owned (50-50) by KrAZ itself and Glencore, formerly Marc Rich & Co., which had been renamed after its purchase by the Alfa Group (Fridman-Aven). In 1997 a new group secured a change of the top management at KrAZ, with the appointment of Igor Vishnevsky as general director. But not for long. Organized crime kingpin Bykov continued to build up his clout at KrAZ. Bykov acquired a 10 percent equity stake in the plant and gained control over other shareholders' stakes, including through the Russian Credit Bank, where he became a vice-president.[46]

Despite its temporary defeat in Krasnoyarsk, TWG remained among the top groups controlling the Russian aluminum business. In July 1996, it signed a protocol with the Sayansk, Bratsk and Pavlodar (Kazakstan) plants, as well as the TWG-controlled Zalog Bank, on establishing an industrial financial group (sometimes FPG, from the Russian acronym for this type of organization) called Siberian Aluminum, or Sibal. This initial joint statement of intent gave rise to what became one of the most powerful corporations in the aluminum industry. But first Sibal had to defend itself against the competition. Mikhail Chernoy was arrested in Switzerland in December 1996 on suspicion of involvement with organized crime. The MVD investigatory committee rushed to his defense, informing the Swiss authorities that they had no complaints against Chernoy. He was quickly released, but that turned out to be one of TWG's last successes. Just a year later, at the end of 1997, the Bratsk, Sayansk and

Novokuznetsk plants announced they were breaking relations with TWG. Another year after that, the Chernoys managed to acquire control over a 27 percent stake in KrAZ, and moved to take over the plant once again. Bykov, now chairman of the KrAZ board of directors, did everything he could to foil the attempt. But soon Bykov had a new foe to contend with: Krasnoyarsk Governor Alexander Lebed. Criminal proceedings were opened against Bykov, forcing him to emigrate in April 1999. He was arrested in Hungary in October of that year and promptly deported to Russia. Even in prison, Bykov stubbornly refused to sell anybody his shares in KrAZ. The removal of Bykov did not, however, lead to a restoration of TWG's influence. People who had been less prominent, notably Oleg Deripaska, began to play a greater role in the industry.

The base of this upstart oligarch was the Sayansk plant (SaAZ), which had begun operation in 1985 and was the most technologically modern of the Soviet-built aluminum-producing units. At privatization in 1993, the plant initially seemed to have no clear owner. One stake in SaAZ was acquired by the Al-Invest company, which showed little interest in actually running the plant. For a certain period of time SaAZ was effectively controlled by organized crime, particularly a local kingpin named Vladimir Tatarenkov. In early 1994, TWG moved to take control of the plant, managing to secure the appointment of Victor Tokaryov, a Chernoy loyalist, as its commercial director. Tatarenkov's attempts to consolidate his power at SaAZ were unsuccessful. TWG broke off talks with Tatarenkov and sicced the local authorities on him. The upshot was that Tokaryov and several other SaAZ executives died in contract killings. Tatarenkov later clashed with Bykov in Krasnoyarsk and was forced to flee abroad. He was arrested in Greece and deported to Russia, where his testimony (which he later recanted) would be used against Bykov. But he never managed to regain control over SaAZ.

In September 1994, companies controlled by the Chernoys won an investment tender, making them the largest shareholders in the plant. Vladimir Lisin, vice-president of a Chernoy company called Trans-CIS, became chairman of the board of directors, while the young oligarch-to-be Deripaska, who was 26 years old and generally unknown at the time, moved into the job of general director. Thus the Chernoys' patronage launched Deripaska's brilliant career. It is difficult to say why he was selected. But with his two university degrees (from the Physics

Department of Moscow State University and, in economics, from the Plekhanov Academy), Deripaska was a competent manager. SaAZ became the industry's most profitable plant, under his leadership. And, unlike the situations around the Krasnoyarsk or Bratsk plants, relative calm settled over Sayanogorsk with Deripaska's arrival, and the plant was rescued from the organized crime kingpins.[47]

The young manager set out to create a vertically integrated association of companies producing rolled aluminum and aluminum manufactured goods, in addition to primary aluminum. Even more important, Deripaska's alliance with the Chernoys made it possible for him to found Sibal, which was destined to become the aluminum industry's chief monopolist. As noted above, this took place in July 1996, with the signing by the Sayansk and Bratsk plants, as well as the Pavlodar factory in Kazakstan, Zalog Bank, and TWG (the latter two being Chernoy-controlled entities), of a protocol on the creation of Siberian Aluminum as an FPG. At the time, the written agreement represented more of a statement of intent, than any real integration, but, unlike some other consortiums of this sort, it did not fall apart. In June 1998 SaAZ issued additional shares, allowing Deripaska to acquire a major equity stake in the company. In October of that year he became the general director of Sibal. Subsequently, he also assumed the post of president.

Deripaska proved to have outstanding diplomatic skills. By making tactical alliances with competitors, he freed himself from TWG, even breaking his contracts with TWG for the mandatory supply of aluminum for export. The break was not complete, however, as the future would show. Mikhail Chernoy remained a major shareholder in SaAZ. A temporary rapprochement with Bykov set the stage for Deripaska to acquire the right to manage a controlling stake in the Samara Metallurgical Company (Sameco), the largest aluminum rolling mill in Europe. Through a temporary alliance with Chubais and RAO UES, Deripaska improved the situation for SaAZ in federal and regional government circles.

In early 2000, Deripaska moved to take over the Novokuznetsk plant (NkAZ), and the Nikolayevsk (Mikolayivsk) Alumina Plant (NGZ) in Ukraine. The case of Novokuznetsk unfolded with particular drama. Since 1993, NkAZ had been controlled by the Metallurgical Investment Company (Mikom), belonging to Zhivilo. But Zhivilo managed to clash with Governor Aman Tuleyev of the Kemerovo

Region, who decided to get rid of him. This made Governor Tuleyev a natural ally for Deripaska. The latter's connections with Chubais were also useful. The Kuzbassenergo power company, controlled by RAO UES, brought a court action against NkAZ for non-payment of debts, seeking to have the plant put into receivership, with a Siberian Aluminum representative to be appointed as its outside manager. Simultaneously, Deripaska opened negotiations with Zhivilo on the possibility of buying a major stake in NkAZ from him, but they did not reach agreement. Zhivilo stalled, in hopes of selling at a higher price to a different buyer—Berezovsky's LogoVAZ. The delay proved fatal. Charged with organizing an attempt on Tuleyev's life, Zhivilo was forced to emigrate. From abroad, he sold his stake in NkAZ to an American investor of Russian descent, who resold the shares to Deripaska's company. NkAZ came under Sibal's control.

In the same time period as the NkAZ saga, there took place a "historic" sale of the BrAZ and KrAZ shares belonging to TWG and to the Chernoys personally, to Abramovich, the owner of Sibneft. Both plants, along with NkAZ and Ukraine's NGZ, passed to the control of the newly established company Russian Aluminum (Rusal), which also included Sibal. The upshot was that this group controlled 70 percent of Russian primary aluminum production.[48]

While initially Sibneft seemed to have the upper hand among the owners of Rusal, Abramovich eventually, in 2003, sold Sibneft's stake to Deripaska, effectively making the latter the overall boss of Russia's largest aluminum concern, and the second richest man in the country after Abramovich. In early 2006, Deripaska's personal fortune was estimated at $12.7 billion. His principal company is now called Basic Element.

Deripaska's only major competitor is the Siberian-Ural Aluminum Company (SUAL), a holding company that includes two good-sized plants, the Ural and Irkutsk units, and three smaller ones—Bogoslovsk, Kandalaksha, and Nadvoytsk. This concern is able to supply its own raw materials, since it includes the Timan bauxite deposit, as well as mines in the northern and southern Ural region. SUAL is controlled by a company called Renova, which belongs to Victor Vekselberg. Renova initially worked in aluminum wholesaling, becoming one of the leading traders. Its attempts to acquire major equity stakes in any of the top aluminum plants were unsuccessful. Renova's bid for 19 percent of BrAZ in a 1994 tender was rejected without explanation, and when Vekselberg and a partner, Vasili Anisimov of Transconsult, acquired shares in KrAZ, they were squeezed out by stronger competitors. They had more success at the above-mentioned second-tier plants. SUAL was formally established only in 2000, at almost the same time as Rusal. A short while later, Anisimov's daughter was killed. He was forced to get out of the business and emigrate to the United States, leaving the company he had co-founded with Vekselberg under Renova's control.

SUAL would appear to be weakly positioned in the industry, since it does less than one-fourth the business Rusal does.[49] But Vekselberg has a strong ally, namely the Alfa Group, in collaboration with which he took part in the acquisition of TNK in 1997. Although Alfa itself has not penetrated the aluminum business, it is not to be excluded that this aggressive group will want to do so in the future.

In the course of his aluminum and oil adventures, Vekselberg substantially increased his personal fortune. It was estimated at $8.1 billion in early 2006, making him the fifth richest man in Russia.

In sum, the degree of concentration of capital in the aluminum industry is one of the greatest in Russia. Two corporations control 90 percent of the sector's output, with just one of them controlling more than 70 percent. They achieved this result, despite an initial privatization process in which the industry's enterprises were sold one by one and came under the control of a large number of groups, among which there was fierce competition. Some of these interests were groups of industry executives, while others consisted of outside investors, including those based abroad.

The aluminum sector differed from the oil industry, where in several cases groups of executives managed to keep dominant positions in the corporations they established, in that only one group of aluminum-industry managers, the group led by Deripaska, survived the struggle for control. Deripaska was able to persevere, thanks to alliances with and support from strong outside investors—first the Chernoys, and later the Sibneft shareholders.

The steel industry

The steel industry is one of the most complex sectors of Russian heavy industry, from the standpoint of organizational structure. This is due to its division into several clearly defined subsectors, for the production of raw steel and rolled steel, specialty steels, iron ore, coking coal, ferroalloys, standardized steel parts, and steel pipe. The number of major factories in each of these subsectors ranges from two or three, to eight or nine. The smallest number of plants for a subsector is two, in ferroalloy production, while the largest number, nine, produce raw steel and rolled steel. Two subsectors that process raw materials for supply to steel producers also have a large number of plants: there are eight in the iron ore subsector and six that produce coking coal. Seven factories produce steel pipe, an important final product in the steel industry. The ferrous metals sector has over 40 plants in all.

In the Soviet period, a single ministry managed all of them. As market reforms began, a few attempts were made to preserve the integrity of the industry. A company called the Corporation of Ferrous Metal Producers ("Roschermet"), created on the basis of the Soviet ministry, was supposed to become a state-owned monopoly. This late 1991-early 1992 first attempt, which was linked with the names of former minister Oleg Soskovets and Serafim Kolpakov, failed. In 1993, the government discussed a plan to organize coal and steel producers into vertically integrated holding companies. This scheme likewise went nowhere, due to strong opposition from producers and wholesalers alike, who had the support of State Property Committee Chairman Anatoli Chubais. In 1995, with the privatization of metallurgical enterprises in full swing, Soskovets—now a vice-premier, and close to President Yeltsin—proposed merging all the remaining state-owned equity stakes in steel plants into a single holding company. In September 1995, he secured a Presidential decree establishing the state-owned joint stock company Russian Metallurgy, which was supposed to comprise three major producers: the Magnitogorsk and Novolipetsk combines and Severstal. By this time, however, Chubais had already moved to launch loans-for-shares auctions, through which the state's equity stakes in a number of sectors, not only the steel industry, would be handed over to private banks. Chubais prevailed over Soskovets. The decree on the establishment of Russian Metallurgy remained a dead letter. At the end of 1997, the joint stock company bearing that name was liquidated by Presidential decree.[50]

So it came to pass that the steel sector, like most other branches of Russian industry, was privatized one enterprise at a time. Around them, as typically happened in this period, there unfolded a battle over carving up this valuable legacy of the state. For the sake of brevity, we shall look only at the redistribution of raw steel and rolled steel plants, which served as the focal points for the groups that gradually took shape and subsumed raw materials suppliers, as well as consumers of the finished product.

The three top enterprises out of the nine in this subsector were the same ones Soskovets had attempted to earmark for the state mega-holding company: Severstal and the Magnitogorsk (MMK) and Novolipetsk (NLMK) combines. Each of them produces nine to eleven million tons of steel a year. These three, plus the West Siberian Combine (ZSMK or Zapsib), which at five million tons annual production approaches them in size, account for around 70 percent of total Russian steel production.[51] The struggle for control revolved chiefly around these four units.

The most intense battle was the one for the biggest steel company (during the 1990s), Severstal, which had been established as a joint stock company in September 1993 on the base of the Cherepovets Metallurgical Combine. From the outset, its top managers invested in buying up shares in their company, and were able rapidly to acquire a controlling equity stake. As soon as shares in the Cherepovets combine were put on sale at a voucher auction in 1995, the company's finance director, Alexei Mordashov, at the request of then-General Director Yuri Lopukhin, set up a special company called Severstal-Invest for the purpose of buying up the shares. In October 1995, while loans-for-shares auctions of other steel enterprises were under way, a firm under Mordashov's de facto control bought a 15 percent stake from the government and arranged the transfer of another 5 percent to the plant's work force, i.e., to the executives. In April 1996, after gradual preparations, Mordashov secured Lopukhin's elevation to the position of chairman of the board of directors, and his own appointment as general director. Since then, he has run Severstal as virtually his own personal steel company. As of August 2001, Severstal's managers and its subsidiaries controlled over 70 percent of the shares in the company: the firm Severstal-Garant had 43.7 percent, Severstal-Invest had 18.2 percent, and Mordashov personally controlled 16.6 percent.[52] The market value of his personal equity stake was approximately $160 million in the fall of that year. That was far less than the fortunes of the top Russian oligarchs. By early 2006, however, Mordashov's fortune was estimated by *Finans (Finance)* magazine at the much larger sum of $6 billion, which implies that he now holds the majority of his company's shares personally, though the figure also includes his other assets, for instance in the automobile industry. (It must also be borne in mind that between 2001 and 2006, the personal fortunes of wealthy Russians increased sharply, due to the stock market boom, with its substantial rise in market capitalization. This aspect is discussed in more detail in Chapter 3.)

According to some reports, Mordashov had Chubais' patronage partly to thank for his swift rise. He had studied under Chubais at the Leningrad Institute of Economics and Engineering. But his capabilities as an executive and a financial manager are indisputable. A native of Cherepovets, and the son of a steelworker, Mordashov had to work his way up at the enterprise. His first job, after returning to Cherepovets from his studies, was the humble post of chief economist for one of the combine's shops. At the age of 24, he did a period of training at a steel plant in Austria. Soon after that he became the concern's financial director. Clearly ahead of his colleagues in his knowledge of finance, and certainly not behind them in technical expertise, he was able to stabilize the enterprise's economic condition, harness its financial flows, and get on top of the situation fairly quickly.[53]

Severstal became comparatively successful. The company penetrated the American market, where the low cost of production of Cherepovets hot-rolled steel made it possible to compete with U.S. producers. At the end of 1998 charges of dumping were filed in the United States against Russian steel producers. Quotas imposed on Russian steel imports effectively closed the American market to them. But exports to other foreign markets, in Europe and Asia, continued. Despite the attacks on Severstal in the United States, many Western specialists continue to rate the firm as a leading producer. In 2000, the European Bank for Reconstruction and Development (EBRD) made a loan to Severstal for modernization. Severstal is on the suppliers list of Philips, the major Dutch electronics company.

Severstal also has diversified its output for the domestic market. After purchasing a 5,000mm rolling mill from Izhora Works, Severstal became a leading producer of wide-diameter pipe for the natural gas industry. It went on to take over three other pipe factories, as a result of which one-third of Russian steel pipe production is concentrated in the Severstal group. At the end of 2000, the company acquired a 45 percent stake in the Ulyanovsk Auto Plant, and subsequently a substantial share in the Zavolzhsky Engine Plant, which supplies engines for cars and trucks, thus establishing itself as a major supplier to the domestic auto industry.

Despite these successes, however, Mordashov's group faced competition from an unexpected quarter. In mid-2001 a 35 percent stake in Severstal, consisting of shares either owned or managed by Mordashov, was frozen by a court decision in an alimony case brought by his ex-wife. Clearly the action had been instigated by a third party. It is believed that competitors were behind these actions, seeking to force Mordashov to yield to them his control over Severstal.

The largest such competitor is the Yevrazholding-UGMK (Ural Mining and Metals Company) group, an informal alliance formed in 1999. Its components are the West Siberian (Zapsib), Kuznetsk (KMK) and Nizhnetagil (NTMK) metallurgical combines, two specialty steel factories, the Kachkanar Mining and Ore-processing Combine (GOK), two major coking coal producers, and the Serov Ferroalloy Plant. The group came into being gradually, through a prolonged fight.

Privatization of these plants began in May 1993, when the government auctioned off a 35 percent equity stake in Zapsib and a 27 percent stake in NTMK. In November 1993, 35 percent of the shares in KMK went on the block. Loans-for-shares auctions began two years later, but the first such auction involving Zapsib did not attract investors, since the company was on the edge of bankruptcy at the time. In the summer of 1996 Kredobank, followed by the Alfa Group, attempted to initiate formal bankruptcy proceedings against Zapsib for debt-collection purposes, but the combine received an extension after government intervention. A year later, Alfa succeeded in getting Zapsib put into receivership, but a local banker was appointed to oversee the company, thanks to the efforts of local government authorities. Ultimately, Alfa had to give up its plan to take over Zapsib.

The first attempt in Russia to seize a company by force (courtesy of court bailiffs) took place in February 1996. The target was

KMK. Behind this action was a firm controlled by the Mikom group, dominated by the same Zhivilo who was to gain such notoriety later on. Mikom had initially been set up in 1991 by Zhivilo, when he was a broker at the Russian Commodities and Raw Materials Exchange, and his brother. Their plan was to use credits from the West to acquire steel plants. The group made no progress in those endeavors, however, and the attempt to take over KMK directly, without any large investment of capital, was their first major action that anybody noticed. It was rumored that Mikom enjoyed support from Aman Tuleyev, who at that time was chairman of the Kemerovo Region's legislature. Ultimately, the takeover attempt was stymied by the intervention of Kemerovo Governor Mikhail Kislyak, who supported KMK's existing management.[54]

A new phase of the fight over Zapsib and KMK began in 1998, with Tuleyev's election as governor of the Kemerovo Region. He decided to merge the two combines into a single concern. This time, his interests and those of Zhivilo diverged. Against the governor's wishes, Zhivilo's Mikom obtained a bankruptcy order against KMK and secured the appointment of one of their people as its temporary manager. Within a few months, Tuleyev, acting through regional prosecutors, opened a criminal case against Mikom for embezzlement of funds from KMK. The manager installed by the Zhivilo group was ousted. This was equivalent to a declaration of war. It was an uneven contest. At the end of 1999 Mikom lost control of the largest coal strip mine in the region. Then Zhivilo was forced to sell his other coal assets and get out of the steel industry. His ouster from the aluminum business was described above.

The next outside manager appointed for Zapsib was a representative of the up-and-coming copper magnate Iskander Makhmudov, who was to play an important role in the events to come, with repercussions far beyond the Kuzbass.[55] In 1999, new groups (Makhmudov's and the Alexander Abramov group) became interested in NTMK in the Urals, which was also on the brink of bankruptcy. This interest was occasioned by Sverdlovsk Governor Eduard Rossel's convocation of a national conference, which recommended that the government consider creating a large-diameter pipe manufacturing facility for Gazprom, at NTMK. Although this project in Nizhny Tagil did not come into being, the prospect of a large cash infusion enabled NTMK to reach a settlement with its creditors. At the same time, control over the plant passed to Yevrazholding, headed by Abramov. Makhmudov also laid claim to NTMK, but he and Abramov began to cooperate closely, rather than fighting each other.

Their alliance was based on the idea of unifying the Kemerovo and Ural steel plants into a single company. One of Makhmudov's men was put in charge of KMK, in addition to the one holding the reins at Zapsib. KMK then announced a cooperation arrangement with NTMK, where Abramov himself took charge. In August 2000, Yevrazholding reached agreement with the Alfa Group on taking over Zapsib, in exchange for paying the company's debts to Alfa.

Soon Makhmudov took over the Kachkanar GOK, which is located in the Urals not far from Nizhny Tagil and is the main supplier of iron ore to NTMK. In 1997, a businessman named Pavel Fedulov had purchased 19 percent of the shares in this combine, promising to resell them to a company controlled by Jalol Khaidarov, general director of the Kachkanar GOK. Fedulov broke his promise and was indicted for fraud. Even though he served a prison term, Fedulov retained control of his equity stake. After many twists and turns, in January 2000 the combine was physically taken over by the copper magnate Makhmudov's people, while Khaidarov and his partners were charged with having stolen their shares from the lawful owners. The takeover of the Kachkaransk GOK occasioned no quarrel with Abramov. He got NTMK, while Makhmudov got the iron ore deposits. Dealing with two different links in the technological process, they did not clash.

The Abramov-Makhmudov alliance now had control over close to 30 percent of the Russian steel industry, setting the stage for it to become, as of 2005, the largest steel producer in the country; at 12 million tons a year, it is ahead of Severstal. There is still no formal alliance between Yevrazholding and Makhmudov's UGMK. Because their partnership is largely based on personal connections and common interests, it is highly unstable by definition. Nonetheless, they represent a real and aggressive factor for competitors to contend with.[56] In the course of this expansion Abramov also made a nice fortune for himself, estimated in early 2006 at $4.61 billion, after Yevrazholding staged its IPO and he stepped down as chairman of the board and CEO, while retaining ownership.

Among other leading competitors, besides Severstal, is the Magnitogorsk Metallurgical Combine (MMK, also known as "Magnitka"). The Chernoy group (TWG) failed in attempts to take it over in the mid-1990s. Although TWG entered the winning bid at a 1995 auction of state-owned shares in MMK, the auction results were annulled. The Magnitogorsk Steel group, representing the plant's top management, made the winning bid at a second auction. Magnitogorsk Steel acquired a 30 percent equity stake in the plant, while TWG had to be satisfied with only 18 percent. The management-controlled equity stake later rose above the 50 percent level. A 25 percent equity stake in MMK allows its owner to block decisions by the board of directors. For a certain period of time, MMK management had to get approval from the Chernoys and from creditor banks for important personnel decisions. TWG later sold its stake to foreign investors. For self-protection, Magnitka's management purchased more of its own shares from minority shareholders.[57]

In 1997 Victor Rashnikov became general director of MMK, and effectively its proprietor, controlling at least 45 percent of the company's shares.[58] Besides running the plant, one of his chief concerns was to keep a sharp eye out for intrigues by competitors. Several criminal cases were launched against the Rashnikov team, any one of which, in Russian practice, could have meant a sudden loss of control. Rashnikov would regularly seek support from the central government in the person of Victor Khristenko, who served as deputy premier and then minister of industry, and had been vice-governor of the Chelyabinsk Region before assuming those posts in Moscow. In 2000, a major judo tournament just happened to be held in Magnitogorsk. President Putin, a judo enthusiast, attended. MMK, naturally, was the main organizer of the event, which provided an opportunity to lodge informal complaints with the President against the attempted incursions of Makhmudov and the Chernoy brothers. Using his customary vocabulary, Putin replied that everything should be done "according to the law." After that all criminal charges against the Rashnikov team were dropped, as if on command. Rashnikov easily consolidated his control over MMK. His personal worth stood at $2.66 billion in early 2006.

In 2001, MMK entered into an informal alliance with Severstal. Their first joint action was to purchase a controlling equity stake (51 percent) in Kuzbassugol, one of the nation's largest coking coal producers, outmaneuvering Yevrazholding and NLMK. Yevrazholding did acquire over 25 percent of the shares in Kuzbassugol, a blocking equity stake that forces the main owners to take its wishes into account. In addition, the Yevrazholding subsidiary NTMK established a new alliance with NLMK, the third largest steel producer in the country, under the name of Russian Steel.

NLMK, however, has largely remained aloof from other players in this market, although the battle for control over it was fairly intense. NLMK was run by the Chernoys' British-based TWG until 1994. Beginning in 1992, TWG's Russian director, Vladimir Lisin, had been the dominant figure at NLMK. TWG controlled 40 percent of the shares in NLMK, which it had acquired at its voucher auction. In 1994, Potanin's Interros group and Boris Jordan's Sputnik investment fund secretly acquired a 17 percent equity stake in NLMK. Lisin, with support from the local government, unsuccessfully attempted to have that deal annulled, when he found out about it. Potanin's offensive continued. In November 1995, another 15 percent of the shares in NLMK were mortgaged to the Potanin group. A year later, Interros acquired full ownership of these shares, bringing Potanin close to having a controlling equity stake in NLMK. Lisin then decided that the best defense was for NLMK itself to buy out TWG's 40 percent stake. Combined with the shares already owned by management, this would secure continued control of NLMK. But in August 1998, when this deal was about to be finalized, Russia's financial crisis upset the applecart. Thirty-four percent of the shares in NLMK were bought by Interros and Norilsk Nickel—the Potanin group once again. The stake belonging to Potanin's business partner Jordan was sold to the Russian Metallurgical Company (Rusmelko), which was under the control of NLMK management and Lisin personally. Lisin faced the Moscow oligarch Potanin in single combat, which he seemed destined to lose. But the outcome was a surprise.

By convincing TWG to sell its shares in NLMK, Lisin got rid of one of the two outside investors with whom he had been entangled for years. He was unable to dump the other, since Potanin had the capability to block any decision by the board of directors to dilute the shares. But Lisin quietly busied himself buying up shares in the combine, to the point that he controlled 64 percent. Potanin, who had been badly damaged during the 1998 crisis, still had his 34 percent. This was not the only setback Potanin experienced. As related above, his Interros was driven out of the oil business. In that instance, his competitors were powerful forces: the Alfa Group. In the case of NLMK, Lisin managed to outflank Potanin, acting almost alone, with support only from the local government.

Then, in 2001, Lisin convinced Potanin that it would be profitable for him to make a major investment in the modernization of NLMK, increasing its capitalization significantly. Potanin liked the idea and loaned $200 million to the combine for this purpose. Interros General Director Andrei Klishas explained that Interros was not seeking to control NLMK, but rather saw its equity stake in the combine as a portfolio asset that might be sold, for the right price.[59] So far, it appears that Lisin has managed to outmaneuver the Potanin interests, both by making use of their combined capital for his own benefit and by keeping control over his company. He also became a very rich man, whose personal wealth in early 2006 was estimated by *Finans* magazine at $9.35 billion.

It is readily apparent that the concentration of capital in the steel industry has basically followed the same tendencies observed in other export-oriented sectors. Moscow financial groups centered in the banking community, groups of managers with their roots in the regions, and local governments were the main players in the fight for control over companies in these sectors. In the case of steel, offshore traders also played a part. Another general pattern is that the concentration of capital took place by expanding beyond the boundaries of individual enterprises, to create new holding companies that combine horizontal alliances with vertical integration. These developments were the elements of new, broader industrial financial groups that began to replace the mid-1990s oligarchical "Reign of the Seven Bankers." Along the way, top manager-capitalists became a new layer of multimillionaires. We shall have more to say about these shifts.

2.8 Sectors producing for the domestic market

According to formal statistical criteria, where the unit of account is an individual industrial enterprise, the concentration of production is substantially less in sectors producing mainly for the domestic market, than in export-oriented sectors. Data for 2003 showed that the eight largest companies in each of the export sectors (oil, refined petroleum products, steel, and non-ferrous metals) accounted for between 37 and 64 percent of output. In other sectors of heavy industry, such as chemicals, machine-building, timber, and paper, the top eight producers accounted for only between 18 and 23 percent of output; and in the food industry, light industry, and the construction materials industry, the eight biggest enterprises produced only 10 to 13 percent of total output, respectively.[60]

A somewhat different picture emerges from data on the number of market-dominating companies. Companies are classified in this category in statistical reports if their market share for a given product is above 35 percent. The greatest number of such producers (123, or almost half the total number of such companies in all industries) were found in machine-building and metal-working. Next in rank were the chemicals and petrochemicals industries (39 companies), steel (29), non-ferrous metallurgy (23), the timber, wood-working, and pulp and paper industries (10), and fuels (only 6). There were seven such companies in the food industry and only one in light industry.[61]

The difference between these two sets of data reflects the relative complexity of how the output of various products is structured in the various sectors of industry. The output of the machine-building and metal-working industry, for example, is highly diverse, and the overwhelming majority of producer companies that dominate their specialized markets are not among the sector-wide top eight. At the same time, the great diversity of products made by the food industry or light industry means that the leading eight enterprises in those sectors do not necessarily dominate the market for any particular product.

Nonetheless, the actual concentration within sectors producing for the domestic market is substantially higher than what the formal statistics show. Data on a few representative subsectors of this segment of industry show this to be the case. To some extent, the development of concentration depended on the state of affairs within a sector. The establishment of holding companies and concerns depended, first and foremost, on interest from outside investors; and manufacturing companies that were less affected than others by the overall economic crisis attracted the attention of such investors. Conversely, enterprises in the most seriously crisis-afflicted sectors remained under the control either of their own management, or of the state.

The automobile industry

Despite a steep rise in imports, car production suffered least of all from the crisis. Its low point came in 1994, when 798,000 cars were produced, a 28 percent decline from the 1.103 million produced in 1990. The pre-crisis level was practically restored in the years that followed, with 1.012 million cars being produced in 2003. But not a single new auto plant was built (except for some semi-knocked-down assembly operations set up by foreign makers, beginning with the Ford Motor Company in 2002), so surpassing the peak production of the late 1980s was out of the question. Bus production also remained around its former level. But truck output had fallen by 1996 to a mere 20 percent of its pre-crisis level, and subsequently managed to recover only to 30 percent of the previous peak. Only 193,000 trucks were built in 2003, compared with 665,000 in 1990.[62]

The automobile industry comprises almost 3,000 manufacturing enterprises, most of which supply parts to car and truck assembly plants, of which there are a relative few. There are only eight assembly plants for cars: AvtoVAZ, GAZ, Moskvich, UAZ, Izhmash-Avto, RosLada, SeAZ, and an assembly plant in Kaliningrad.[63] Those eight plants came under the control of three groups. The largest group is AvtoVAZ, which, in addition to its eponymous lead plant, includes RosLada in Syzran, Izhmash-Avto in Izhevsk, and SeAZ in Serpukhov. The second-ranking group, which includes GAZ and a number of closely associated factories, is controlled by a holding company called Ruspromavto, which, in turn, is owned by aluminum tycoon Deripaska. The third major group centers on UAZ, in Ulyanovsk, which has been taken over by Severstal and is controlled by Mordashov.[64]

Thus, in the auto industry, as in the export-oriented industries, the concentration of production at the enterprise level has been superseded by the creation of larger concerns and holding companies. At first, control tended to be in the hands of a given enterprise's top management, which had acquired a large equity stake at the initial voucher auction.

The Gorky and Ulyanovsk plants were classic examples of this tendency. UAZ was one of the first to be privatized, in 1992. In addition to the 25 percent of its shares that were transferred to the work force, a firm called Kapital, established by the enterprise's general director and ten other top managers, acquired a significant number of shares. As for the Gorky plant, it underwent a scandalous voucher auction at the end of 1993, following which the GAZ management was accused of having used government funds to buy up shares in their own factory. Nonetheless, the company GAZ-Invest, controlled by top management, was confirmed as the owner of a large equity stake. These two plants remained under the control of their executives until 2000, when outside forces intruded.

Deripaska's Ruspromavto group began to buy up GAZ shares in September 2000, soon after its acquisition of 20 percent of the nearby Pavlovsk Bus Factory. By November of that year, Ruspromavto had increased its equity stake in GAZ to over 25 percent, at which point its man was named as the plant's new general director. Deripaska wanted to put together a larger machine-building complex, into which he had already incorporated the Likin, Golitsyn, and Kurgan bus factories, diesel equipment and fuel factories in Yaroslavl, the Kanashi Auto Parts Plant, and the Volga Motors company. Although Ruspromavto controlled no more than 20 percent of these companies, Rusal managers were installed to run them.

Mordashov's Severstal began to move into the automobile industry in October 2000, almost simultaneously with Deripaska. Severstal-Invest acquired 20 percent of the shares in UAZ and soon built up its equity stake enough to take control of the company. A short time later, it took over the Zavolzhsky Engine Plant.

With these takeovers, the independent management of GAZ and UAZ came to an end. Yet internal management's position grew stronger at Russia's largest automobile maker, AvtoVAZ, until very recently. Its ownership structure did not initially appear to be headed in that direction, since as of 1993 some of its shares had belonged to the All-Russian Automobile Alliance (AVVA), a joint project of AvtoVAZ itself (25 percent), Berezovsky's LogoVAZ (15 percent), Berezovsky's United Bank (10 percent), the Swiss company Forus, and several other organizations. AVVA had been set up for the purpose of financing construction of a new auto factory and production of a so-called "people's car." That project was not implemented, and what happened to the funds raised by AVVA remains a mystery to its investors and the public alike. AVVA continued to be co-owner of AvtoVAZ, holding 33.3 percent of its shares. But AvtoVAZ's own share in AVVA rose to 80 percent, because Berezovsky abandoned the project. Another large equity stake in AvtoVAZ belonged to the Automobile Finance Corporation (AFK), which, in turn, was 49 percent owned by AvtoVAZ, 10 percent by AVVA, and 26 percent by a company called Fitom, established by Vladimir Kadannikov, president of AvtoVAZ, and six of his close associates. With the departure of Berezovsky, control over AvtoVAZ thus passed entirely to its senior managers.

In late 2005, however, Kadannikov retired as CEO of AvtoVAZ. Soon afterwards, a controlling stake in the company, over 50 percent of its shares, was acquired by two state-owned institutions under the Kremlin group: the armaments exporter Rosoboronexport, and Vneshtorgbank. This new development was promoted as a step towards channelling investment funds into modernization of the Russian automobile industry. In any event, the days of inside management control at AvtoVAZ have come to an end.

The Moskvich plant has its own special story. Private investors showed little interest in this enterprise, which was unprofitable and constantly on the verge of bankruptcy. The company's top management continued to run the plant, while the government owned a controlling equity stake. In 1996, a promise was made to transfer that 59-percent state-owned stake to Moscow Mayor Yuri Luzhkov, who wanted to save the plant from bankruptcy. Lengthy negotiations about terms for this share transfer were fruitless. The broken promise put an end to Luzhkov's project to modernize the Moskvich plant in partnership with the French company Renault. In 2001, Deripaska began to express interest in taking over the plant, but to date it remains shut down and has not been producing for several years.

The "Millionaires and Managers" section of Chapter 3 will take up the question of which form of ownership is more promising—control by management, or by outside investors—from the standpoint of the Russian economy as a whole, and in comparison with Western prototypes. But it is appropriate to note here that a peculiar illegal system for the appropriation of surplus value by managers developed in the auto industry. AvtoVAZ and GAZ vehicles were shipped on the basis of barter and at understated prices, to dealers who were controlled or owned outright by the auto plants' executives. For a long time, organized crime groups also directly controlled a portion of AvtoVAZ's output. As control shifted to outside investors, these types of systems tended to be dismantled.

The sorry state of the Russian car industry as a whole is largely explained by two other factors. First, the low income level in the country does not support demand for even the current reduced output of the industry. Secondly, imports of foreign-made used cars have equalled the level of domestic production, and have constrained the possibilities for expanding domestic production of relatively inexpensive cars. The purchase of imported cars is limited exclusively to Russia's well-to-do minority. It is doubtful that a serious mass market for automobiles will appear, without a substantial increase in the real income of the majority of the population.

The food and allied industries

Based on overall performance indicators for the sector, it would appear that the food industry experienced a worse crisis than the auto industry did. By the 1996-1998 period, production in this industry had dropped by one-half from its 1990 level. Only after that point did it begin to show rapid growth, when the sharp devaluation of the ruble made imports more expensive. Even so, the 1990 level had still not been recovered as of 2004.

In some subsectors, however, the situation was not so bad. Production of cigarettes (included by Russian statistics under the "food and gustatory" heading), for example, fell by 20 percent by 1994, but then began to increase sharply, and in 2003 was at 3.5 times its pre-crisis peak. Vodka and liqueurs production grew even during the first post-reform years, and then, after declining slightly, rose again to surpass the old level. (Only legal alcoholic beverage production is considered here. If illegal alcohol production is counted, this subsector flourished throughout the period under consideration.) Beer production had fallen by one-third as of 1996, but then grew vigorously to more than double the 1990 level. With the exception of granulated sugar, however, output of all basic foodstuffs declined greatly.[65]

The boom in the tobacco industry attracted foreign capital,

which practically took over this entire subsector. The foreign investors shifted the product range to emphasize production chiefly of foreign-brand cigarettes. In the forefront were the British companies British American Tobacco (BAT) and Gallaher, which each acquired three Russian factories, and the American firms Philip Morris and RJR International, with two each. Later RJR (R.J. Reynolds) sold its Russian factories to the Japanese firm Japan Tobacco International. Foreign companies own 11 major Russian tobacco plants in all, making tobacco the only sector of the Russian economy that is effectively under the total control of foreign corporations. The acquisitions began in 1992 with the Uritsky Factory in Petersburg and Dukat in Moscow. Next were Moscow's Yava, Tabakprom in Krasnodar, and Prima in Saratov. New tobacco-processing factories went up as well. As the import of foreign cigarettes declined, domestic production rose sharply. By the beginning of the new millennium, Russia was able not only to satisfy domestic demand, but to export cigarettes to the Near Abroad. Although hundreds of small factories belonging to Russian owners still exist, it is difficult for them to survive in competition with the foreign giants.[66]

Unlike the tobacco industry, alcohol production (vodka and liqueurs) has remained primarily in the hands of domestically owned companies. The dominant firms in this market are Rosspirtprom, which groups six major factories and many smaller ones, the OST group, with three major factories, and Alfa-Eco, with a combine of two major producers. Sales of so-called elite alcohol, meaning imported spirits, are dominated by a handful of Russian companies. The largest of them, Rust, has 70 percent of this market. Several foreign companies, as well, are active in the alcoholic beverages market. The French firm Pernod Ricard bought the Zmeinogorsk Liqueur and Spirits Factory in Altay in 1992 and later acquired the Yerevan Cognac Factory, which sells a substantial part of its output in Russia.

The domination of the spirits market by domestic producers stems largely from the fact that the government held on to controlling equity stakes in many liqueur and spirits companies for a long period of time, evidently assuming that such ownership would bolster its right to collect the relevant excise taxes. At the same time, prolonged, contradictory, and not very successful efforts were made to push illegal vodka off the market. In reality, control over the producers and their financial flows remained in the hands of management at those factories, together with local authorities. In 2000, a government resolution created Rosspirtprom as a so-called Federal State-owned Unitary Enterprise (FGUP), assigning it equity stakes in over 120 factories. Struggles for real control of the major factories broke out between the old management and the new appointees from Rosspirtprom. The best known of these brawls unfolded over control of the Kristall Factory in Moscow, previously owned by the Moscow city government. After the city-owned shares were transferred to Rosspirtprom, competing groups of managers sought to get the upper hand with help from the courts and from OMON special police units. State ownership of a company does not exempt it from such turf wars. Rosspirtprom has other ways of exerting control than merely the formal ownership of shares. In particular, together with the Ministry of Agriculture, it sets spirits production quotas for all the companies in the industry. With something on the order of 600 legal producers of spirits in Russia, as against 200 in Soviet Russia, the alcoholic beverages market is oversaturated. Idle capacity averages around 70 percent. In these circumstances, the production quota assumes a key role. Lately, President Putin has voiced his intention to institute a state monopoly on vodka production.

The Alfa-Eco group first got into the alcoholic beverages business in 2000, when it bought half the shares in a company with the florid name Trading House of Supplier to the Court of His Imperial Majesty P.A. Smirnov and His Descendants in Moscow. This firm was founded in 1991 as the small state-owned company P.A. Smirnov and Descendants in Moscow, to produce the famous Smirnoff vodka using the original pre-Bolshevik Revolution recipe. When Alfa-Eko, seven years later, made its move by acquiring 50 percent of the shares in P.A. Smirnov et al. through offshore companies based in Cyprus, the firm's management resisted the new owners' attempts to take control. After fruitless negotiations, Alfa seized the main office and forced the company's founder, Boris Smirnov, into retirement. Earlier, the Alfa Group had absorbed another alcoholic beverage company, Vinoram.

Rust, the Russian domestic company that enjoys a monopoly in the elite alcoholic beverages market, also has an interesting background. When he was still a student, its founder, Rustam Tariko, started up a business selling small consignments of imported candies and beverages. In 1995, he obtained from several foreign companies the exclusive rights to sell Johnny Walker, the foreign-produced Smirnoff, and Bacardi rum in Russia; earlier he had acquired the rights to market Martini aperitifs and several other well-known brands.

There are three top groups in the beer business: Baltika, Ochakovo, and San-Interbrew. Foreign capital is prominent in two of them. The foreign element came in, starting in 1993, when the Scandinavian company Baltic Beverages Holding (BBH) purchased a 44 percent stake in the Baltika brewery in St. Petersburg. BBH's share soon grew to 75 percent, and Baltika became the biggest beer producer in Russia. In 1997, it gained control over the Donskoye Pivo (Don Beer) company in Rostov-on-Don, and later acquired the Taopin Brewery as well. Despite the foreign ownership, the Russian executive Taymuraz Bolloyev stayed on as general director of Baltika.

At the end of the 1990s, the Belgian company Interbrew became interested in the Russian beer industry. Starting with the acquisition of breweries in Omsk and Klin, it joined with the San Capital group in 1999 to form the joint venture San-Interbrew, which took over nine breweries in Russia and Ukraine. San Capital controls an additional three producers jointly with the Wimm-Bill-Dann industrial and commercial group, through their joint company TsEPKO.

The Ochakovo group remains owned by its Russian management. Besides the Ochakovo brewery in Moscow, it has facilities in Penza and Krasnodar.

Although the state of affairs in other subsectors of the food industry has been less than favorable, outside investors, including foreigners, have exhibited some interest there, as well. As in other sectors, there has been an intensive process of centralization of capital. In the confectionary industry the dominant companies are Red October, which groups together seven factories, and Babayev with six, as well as the foreign groups Nestlé, which controls three factories, Baring with three, Danone, which has a stake in Moscow's Bolshevik factory, and Mars, which has built two factories in Russia. Initially, Inkombank established control over the Babayev Confectionary Factory in 1995. A year later, it announced the formation of the Babayev Holding Company, which included five more factories, among them the famous Rot Front ("Rot" being from the German for "red," not the English for "decay"). Inkombank went bankrupt after the 1998 crisis. The fate of its 51 percent controlling stake in Babayev led to conflicts. The company's management sought permission for a supplemental share issue to dilute Inkombank's controlling stake. This attempt was disputed in court. At a shareholders meeting, convened by management, a brawl broke out in which several people were injured. The fate of the equity stake hung in the air. In early 2002, it was put up for auction. But the outcome was not accepted as legitimate by the German bankers who were among the major creditors of Inkombank. The Russian courts decided in favor of the domestic shareholders, but the battle continued. There were also acute conflicts, involving the arbitrage court, around control of the Babayev subsidiary Rot Front. By contrast, the largest company in this subsector, the Red October group, remains dominated by its management.

Ten groups can be identified in the oils and dairy products market, of which six are Russian. Wimm-Bill-Dann has nine companies, Petrosoyuz and EFKO have three companies each, Yug Rossii has two, and Rusargo and Razgulyay-Ukros jointly control two companies. The four foreign groups are Parmalat (four companies), Danone and Campina with two companies each, and Unilever.

There are major corporations in the meat-packing industry, such as APK Cherkizovsky with its six companies, and Kolibri with four. In the grain and sugar trade, Razgulyay and Rusargo are the leaders, with eleven companies each. Foreign capital is also active in this sector, in the form of the major American-based multinational corporation Cargill. The American giants Coca-Cola and PepsiCo dominate the soft drinks market. At one point, an estimated 60 percent of foreign investment in Russia was going into the food industry.

Light industry

Light industry went through a very difficult phase in the early 1990s. Many of its plants had been reequipped with Italian and German imported technology in the final years of the Soviet period. Yet the domestic market was flooded by imported goods, with which domestic manufacturers were unable to compete. As early as 1993, the output of Russian light industry had fallen to 49 percent of its 1990 level. By 1998, it had plunged to only 13 percent of that level. This sector of the Russian economy appeared to be on the brink of total ruin. After the devaluation of 1998, it began to revive, achieving a 50 percent increase in output by 2001, but it stagnated again after that partial recovery.[67] No more than one-fourth of domestic demand is satisfied by domestic production. The rest is covered by imports, both cheap Chinese and Turkish consumer goods, and expensive West European ones.[68]

Light industry managed to avoid acute struggles for control over its plants, in part thanks to the prolonged slump in the sector. An additional calming factor was the fact that the previous Ministry of Textiles and Ministry of Light Industry had been converted into state-owned concerns already in 1991. Two years later they became joint stock companies, still under government control. In cases where individual enterprises were privatized, as in the textile (Tryokhgornaya Manufaktura and others) or footwear industries, the absence of outside investors allowed management to take control.

At the same time, the old giants of this sector were joined by a large number of comparatively small private companies. In 1992, in Rostov-on-Don, for example, a businessman named Vladimir Melnikov founded the Gloria Jeans Company, producing denim garments for children. Over time this company, which now includes three factories, came to control 35 percent of that market.

In 1994, the British firm Illingworth Morris, in a rare exception to the pattern, attempted to take over the Bolshevichka garment factory, but management—after lengthy court proceedings and with support from the Moscow city government—was able to defend its control of the operation, acquiring a majority of the company's shares.

In 1995, the Rostextil holding company and the Sholk, Sobitex, and Paris Commune factories were acquired by Khodorkovsky's Rosprom.

In 1998, there was a fight for control of the Lomonosov Porcelain Factory in St. Petersburg, after 60 percent of its shares were bought up by two American investment funds. In this instance, the company's executives were unable to get the courts to declare the foreign takeover illegal, and control passed to the American managers.

In sum, the tendency toward concentration of production in sectors oriented to the domestic market mirrors, in many respects, what occurred in the export-oriented sectors. The main difference is the many small and medium-sized companies, existing outside of the major corporations and holding companies. Some of them remain from the Soviet period, but now belong to their management, while others have been created by private capitalists. The food industry and light industry are traditional small-business sectors in any capitalist country. Despite the underdevelopment of small business in Russia, its presence in these sectors does somewhat limit the sort of monopoly enjoyed by big business in the export-oriented sectors.[69]

2.9 The defense industry

Three special features distinguish the Russian defense industry from the other sectors considered thus far. The first is that it suffered more than any other from the crisis of the 1990s. Secondly, it was the only sector of manufacturing outside of the natural monopolies (electric power, natural gas, and the railroads),[70] where privatization was fairly strictly limited until recently: state ownership continued to prevail and the participation of private capital, including the leading oligarchical groups, was extremely weak. The third factor is that, as a result of peculiarities in how the government finances defense, this sector is of necessity export-oriented. Although factories in the defense complex (DC), as the military-industrial complex (MIC) is now often called, are major producers of certain consumer products, especially consumer durables (television sets, refrigerators, washing machines, etc.), in this section we shall deal only with the DC's defense-related output, which is categorized in statistical reports as "armaments and military equipment" (AME).

The defense industry was in a deep crisis throughout almost the entire 1990s. AME production in 1992 was at half the 1991 level. In 1997 it reached a low point of 8.8 percent of its pre-crisis peak. A turn for the better occurred only at the end of 1998, when the government of Yevgeni Primakov came to power, followed by that of Putin. By 2001, production had doubled since the low point, but was still only 18 percent of the 1991 level.[71] In subsequent years, DC output rose in line with GDP, still reaching only 22 percent of the 1991 level by 2004. Thus it is premature to talk about even a limited revival of this sector.

Defense industry growth rates continue to be held down by a low level of government financing. The Russian Federation Ministry of Defense accounts for less than half of all purchases of Russian-produced armaments. According to some estimates, the level is only 30 percent.[72] Thus, despite a sharp reduction of arms exports, compared with the Soviet period, the foreign market today is the main consumer of the Russian defense industry's products, and the main source of its earnings, to the extent that the government shares the relevant foreign currency revenue with the producers.[73]

Defense sector enterprises did undergo partial transformation into joint stock companies, and some of them were granted the right to be active in foreign markets, but the majority of them have gradually became more and more concentrated in the hands of the government, as has control over arms exports. Yegor Gaidar, who headed the first post-Soviet Russian government as acting premier, beginning in late 1991, attempted to launch the mass privatization of defense plants, but this was temporarily halted with the appointment of Chernomyrdin as prime minister in late 1992. A de facto ban on such privatizations lasted shortly over one year. In mid-1994, Kakha Bendukidze, better known for his acquisition of the heavy machinery giant Uralmash, purchased an equity stake of just over 10 percent in the Krasnoye Sormovo shipbuilding factory, which was privatized at a voucher auction in Nizhny Novgorod. Much later, in 1998, Bendukidze increased his stake to 30 percent and tried to install his people in the company's executive offices. But he was able to secure these management positions only in 2000, with help from then Vice-Premier Ilya Klebanov. At that point Bendukidze bought out the previous management's shares and became the owner of a controlling stake in the company. Upon emigrating to Georgia in 2004, Bendukidze sold all his properties in Russia.

In 1994, two investment companies bought up 29 percent of the shares in the Mil Helicopter Factor (MVZ) in Moscow. It was rumored that they were fronts for American corporations that wanted to quash this Russian competitor. Within six months, the government intervened, declaring a 25 percent stake in MVZ to be federal property for three years. Nonetheless, the American investors held 12 percent of the company's shares. By 1999, the government's ownership stake had grown to 40 percent, and Oneximbank held a small stake (8 percent), but the foreign investors had also increased their stake, to 42 percent. They then acted through a small creditor to initiate bankruptcy proceedings against MVZ. In 1999, the Interregional

Investment Bank (MIB) joined the battle for control over this producer, purchasing 58 percent of its debt and 7 percent of its shares. In 2000, however, the government-owned Gosinkor Corporation became the factory's main creditor, for all practical purposes placing the helicopter company back under government control. A new general manager, Andrei Shibitov, was appointed by the government in December 2004, and production, including new models, continued. Attempts to bankrupt and close the plant were thwarted.

In March 1995, the Interros Company, part of the Potanin group, bought 20 percent of the shares in the Leningrad Optical Instrument Association (LOMO), a DC firm. Management, however, which at that point meant LOMO General Director Ilya Klebanov and his colleagues, kept a controlling stake.

Soon Potanin's Oneximbank made its first attempts to acquire shares in the Sukhoy Experimental Design Bureau (OKB), whose Su-27 aircraft was already becoming popular among foreign buyers. Mikhail Simonov, head of Sukhoy, resisted these attempts, with backing from Inkombank. By the end of 1995, Inkombank had 25 percent of the shares in Sukhoy, and Oneximbank had 14 percent. Potanin's idea of including Sukhoy in the loans-for-shares program ended in failure. The government insisted on excluding the Sukhoy OKB from this list. But Potanin, who had secured a vice-premiership, did not give up. He managed to obtain a decree creating the Sukhoy Aviation Company, which incorporated the design bureau, as well as the Irkutsk Aircraft Production Association (IAPO) and the Taganrog Scientific-Technical Aviation Complex (TANTK). Potanin's close associate Alexei Fyodorov was named head of the company. Inkombank and Simonov, naturally, resisted the subordination of Sukhoy to Oneximbank. The Russian Credit Bank acquired a 40 percent equity stake in IAPO, casting doubt over that company's participation in Sukhoy. In early 1998, Simonov and his allies succeeded in ousting Fyodorov as head of Sukhoy and installed their man, designer Mikhail Pogosian, in his place. In the financial crisis, however, the Russian Credit Bank was forced to sell its IAPO shares, partly to the American and European investment companies Oppenheimer and Brunswick UBS Warburg (25 percent), and partly to Russian companies controlled by IAPO management, which already controlled 40 percent of the shares. In 2000, the plant obtained a $3 billion contract to produce the latest Su-30MKI fighter aircraft for

India, which effectively made the company financially independent. IAPO also acquired a controlling equity stake in the Avionika design bureau, which significantly reduced its dependence on the Sukhoy OKB. Nonetheless, the Irkutsk plant formally remained a part of the Sukhoy system.

In 1999, Pogosian replaced Simonov as head of Sukhoy. In 2001 Sukhoy became one of the main targets of the latest reform of the defense sector, which the government intended to get onto its feet by establishing several major holding companies. The Sukhoy Aviation Company, which by then was called the Sukhoy Aviation Military-Industrial Complex (AVPK), but really controlled only the Sukhoy design bureau (51 percent), was given 74.5 percent of each of two newly corporatized state-owned unitary enterprises, which had hitherto been part of the concern only formally: the Komsomolsk-on-Amur and Novosibirsk aircraft factories. The other 25.5 percent of the shares in each of them remained state property. The point of this reform was to give the holding company direct access to the revenue from these plants' multibillion-dollar contracts with China, while keeping the holding company under government control.

In mid-1995, a firm called Soyuzkontrakt, which at that time was one of the major importers of food products into Russia, purchased 33 percent of the shares in the St. Petersburg shipbuilding factory Severnaya Verf (Northern Shipyards). In 1997, after acquiring an additional 19 percent of its shares, Soyuzkontrakt attempted to change the management at Severnaya Verf. Failing in this effort, Soyuzkontrakt sold its 51 percent equity stake to Potanin's Interros. Severnaya Verf won a billion-dollar contract to build two destroyers for China.

At the end of 1995, the IST Group and the local Promstroybank became the largest outside shareholders in the Baltic Factory shipbuilding company in St. Petersburg. Two years later, IST's shares were acquired by Potanin's Oneximbank, which managed to piece together a 50.5 percent controlling equity stake. In this period of time the factory won a contract to build three frigates for the Indian Navy. After the 1998 crisis, however, Potanin's bank was forced to sell its shares to three firms controlled by the factory's management. The Interregional Investment Bank became part owner of Baltic Factory (with 17 percent of its shares), as IST later did (15 percent). Inkombank kept a small equity stake (9 percent), despite being in bankruptcy. In 2000, IST increased its ownership share to a controlling stake, pushing aside the other groups.

In early 1998, Interros sold all of its defense-industry equity stakes to the NPK (New Programs and Conceptions) holding company, headed by people from Oneximbank.

In 1999, Khodorkovsky's Rosprom group acquired a major stake in Kurganmashzavod, a leading producer of armored personnel carriers (APCs). A year later, however, when foreign orders for APCs had dropped off, Rosprom sold its stake to the Sibur petrochemicals company, which acquired 80 percent of the shares in Kurganmashzavod. Sibur's idea was to incorporate the plant into a new machine-building complex for the civilian sector, producing equipment for the petrochemicals and natural gas industries.

After Deripaska's Russian Aluminum group bought control over GAZ, it also acquired the Arzamas Machine-building Factory, another producer of APCs.

In 2000, the Siberian company Kaskol purchased a controlling stake in a Nizhny Novgorod factory called Sokol, producer of the MiG-29UB aircraft, which had secured a contract to modernize MiG-21 planes for India. Kaskol also acquired 15 percent of the Rostov helicopter company Rostvertol.

After two years of a relative free-for-all, during which over a dozen associations were authorized to export weapons, in November 1993 the state-owned company Rosvooruzheniye acquired a monopoly on AME exports. All enterprises wishing to deal in foreign markets had to obtain licenses from Rosvooruzheniye. Although less in total monetary volume than oil or gas, revenue from arms exports has fluctuated between $3 billion and $5 billion annually, which is no small sum in comparison with the state's other financial resources. Control over these financial flows has been an object of contention among various clans of government officials and defense plant directors. At the same time, competition for customers continued among the various enterprises, and the intermediaries who handle defense-sector products. Only under Putin were arms sales brought under the monopoly control of a single state-owned intermediary company, Rosoboronexport.

Also in the mid-1990s, the first state holding companies began to be established, bringing together enterprises involved in the development and production of related types of defense products. The first such association was Antey, created in December 1994, which specializes in the S-300v and Tor anti-aircraft defense systems.

In May 1995, a first step was taken towards merging the MiG aircraft complex with the Moscow Aircraft Production Complex (MAPO). Eleven enterprises were brought into this combine by Presidential decree at the beginning of 1996.

The year 1996 also saw the establishment of Oboronitelnyye sistemy (Defense Systems), a company that grouped together at first ten, and later 20, enterprises working on supplying S-300 PMU air defense complexes to China and Cyprus.

Despite the diversity presented here, the concentration of production and capital in the defense industry has reached a fairly high level. In 2001, the American journal *Defense News* even included six Russian companies on its list of the 100 largest arms producers in the world, ranked by sales. They are Rosvooruzheniye (now renamed Rosoboronexport, in 13th place, with $3.1 billion in sales), Sukhoy (35th place, $900 million), Severnaya Verf (52nd place, $532 million), Antey (62nd place, $350 million), MiG (88th place, $100 million) and the Tula Arms Factory (90th place, $90 million).[74]

Kommersant-vlast magazine characterized the structure of the defense industry in the following terms: "The structure of the military-industrial complex today is formally simple. Each enterprise is administratively subordinate to one of five defense agencies, depending on what it produces. Yet complete organizational chaos reigns in the MIC. This is caused by the fact that defense sector companies may be owned in three different ways: state-owned, mixed, or private. In effect, however, regardless of the form of ownership, the companies are controlled by their management, and their economic situation depends first and foremost upon export orders: whether or not they have them, and what size they are."[75]

The agencies mentioned by *Kommersant-vlast* were government institutions, created as independent organizations by Primakov's cabinet on the basis of the relevant departments of the Ministry of Economics. Their purpose at that time was to shift the overall management of the defense complex from then-Minister of Economics Yakov Urinson, who was close to Chubais, to a newly appointed vice-premier, Communist Party member Yuri Maslyukov. Subsequently, these agencies were put under the new Ministry of Industry, Science and Technologies, and then, in 2004, under the Ministry of

Industry and Energy headed by Khristenko.

There were five of these agencies: the Aviation and Space Agency (Aviakosmos, for short), the Control Systems Agency, the Conventional Weapons Agency, the Shipbuilding Agency, and the Ammunition Agency.

The Aviation and Space Agency included Sukhoy (five companies), MiG (eight companies), Saturn (six factories producing airplane engines), Aerospace Equipment (Aerokosmicheskoye oborudovaniye; 20 factories developing and producing airborne radio-electronic equipment—called BREO, from its Russian acronym—for the Su-27 and the MiG-29, including for Chinese and Indian customers), and Tekhnokomplex (12 companies, also producing BREO),[76] as well as over 300 other companies and enterprises, not belonging to any larger concern or group, among which are the above-mentioned Mil Helicopter Factory, Sokol, and Rostvertol.

The Control Systems Agency included Antey (10 companies), the leading producer of anti-aircraft defense systems; the Defense Systems FPG (20 companies), which has several major export contracts; the Almaz Science and Production Association, developer of the S-300 and S-400 surface-to-air missile systems; and around 300 other companies.

Under the Conventional Weapons Agency came Uralvagonzavod in Nizhny Tagil and Transmash in Omsk, which are tank producers; the above-mentioned Kurganmashzavod, producer of APCs for export, which has been partially retooled to produce heavy industrial equipment; the Splav Science and Production Enterprise; and over 250 other companies.

The Shipbuilding Agency was in charge of Baltic Factory, Krasnoye Sormovo, and Severnaya Verf, which were all discussed above, as well as Sevmash, Admiralty Shipyards, the Komsomolsk-on-Amur Shipbuilding Factory, the famous Rubin Design Bureau (the latter three are submarine designers and producers), the Medium- and Small-Tonnage Shipbuilding Concern (five companies),[77] and around 160 other factories.

The Ammunition Agency included 200 companies, which are not grouped into larger concerns.

Despite the concept that each company or concern, associated with one of these agencies on the basis of what it produces, ought to be subordinate to and managed by that agency, the agencies in reality had limited control over the companies, since they lacked financial resources and could not place orders with the producers. Nonetheless, the agencies played an important role. It was through them that the defense-sector companies accessed government authorities regarding numerous administrative and other issues. Domestic orders for defense-sector products generally come from the Ministry of Defense, which also finances military R&D and determines which companies will perform it.

All defense sector companies, with the exception of six that have special authorization, obtain their foreign orders with the mandatory participation of Rosoboronexport.

Under Putin in 2004, the defense industry as a whole was brought under the Ministry of Industry and Energy as a separate Federal Industry Agency (Rosprom). A new attempt to merge companies with a similar production profile into larger concerns did not succeed, due to rivalries within the sector, mainly associated with export orders and control over the revenue they generate. The main parties to these conflicts are the companies' management, private groups that have bought into certain key producers, clans of government officials who control the allocation of contracts ex officio, and, finally, regional elites who want to preserve the independence of companies, which the government is trying to place under the control of its centralized holding companies.

Therefore, although the attempted reform of the defense sector ought to have brought about the further concentration of military production, in reality it failed completely. In November 2005, Putin launched a further attempt to streamline MIC operations. He restored the Soviet practice of making the minister of defense (currently Sergei Ivanov) a vice-premier, in charge of coordinating the armed forces and the defense industry.

2.10 The oligarchy's industrial financial groups

The fusion of major banks with industrial concerns is typical of modern capitalism, at least since the end of the 19th century. Industrial financial groups came into being on this basis a long time ago, in all industrialized countries. These groups may be called oligarchical, in that in each country a few such groups control a significant part of banking, industry, transport, commerce, and other areas of the economy.

Initially this kind of group was created either by leading banks, which promoted the establishment of large industrial concerns as profitable areas for the long-term investment of their money, or by leading industrial companies, which took over banks in order to have guaranteed access to advantageous sources of credit. The Morgan, Rockefeller, Mellon, and other groups emerged this way in the United States.

Later, in the mid-20th century, as the founders of these empires and the first generation of their heirs died off, the industrial concerns became financially more independent, while the banks developed other profitable areas of lending, besides the direct financing of industry. These groups were then transformed into broad alliances of banks and non-financial companies, which coordinated their activity as they competed with other groups of the same type. Later still, in the process of globalization, the leading financial groups reached out beyond the borders of their home countries and turned into transnational empires and alliances.[78]

The new Russian capitalism naturally inherited the same tendencies, which proceeded in some respects even more rapidly toward the fusion of banks with industry, while preserving the particular features of the development of banking and of concentration in industry, described above.

The existence of such groups in Russia began to be discussed openly for the first time in early 1996, on the eve of the Presidential elections. At that time, thanks to Berezovsky, the term semibankirshchina (Reign of the Seven Bankers) gained currency. From approximately that time on, the leaders of those banks, followed by the leaders of major industrial concerns, came to be called "the oligarchs." Neither of these terms was accidental. The bankers were considered to be the leaders of the first groups, and since there were relatively few of them, initially only seven, and they enjoyed great economic and political influence, they were termed oligarchs.

By the end of 1996, the seven groups could be identified and characterized as follows[79]:

1. *The Alfa Group, headed by Mikhail Fridman and Pyotr Aven.*
   It included the trading company Alfa-Eco, the Tyumen Oil

Company (TNK), eight other firms in the chemicals industry, pharmaceuticals, the food and allied industries, and glass and cement production, as well as in construction, and a number of supermarkets. The group participated in a consortium of banks that controlled 38 percent of ORT television company (later called Channel One).

Fridman, the founder of the group, began his business career with a small apartment rental agency and a theater-ticket scalping operation. In the late 1980s, he also dealt in imported cigarettes, cosmetics, computers, and copy machines. The trading firm Alfa-Eco, which he set up in 1988, gradually accumulated enough starting capital to found Alfa Bank in 1991. A few months later he recruited Aven, the former minister of foreign economic ties in the Gaidar government, as a partner. Within two or three years, currency speculation and operations involving Russia's foreign debt had enabled the bank to put together several hundred million dollars in capital, which the partners began to invest in acquiring privatized companies. They learned earlier than others how to take over companies through bankruptcy proceedings. At the same time, Alfa-Eco, which specialized in exporting oil and importing sugar, turned into one of the leading intermediary companies in Russian foreign trade. Aven's connections came in handy. The group suffered only one major failure in its early period, namely losing out to Berezovsky and Abramovich in the battle for control over the privatized oil company Sibneft. Berezovsky was closer to the upper echelons of power in the country, and he prevailed.

2. *The Inkombank group, headed by Vladimir Vinogradov.* At that time, it included the Samara aluminum combine, the Babayev Candy Factory, the Magnitogorsk Metallurgical Combine, the Nosta Pipe Mill and the Sokol Aircraft Plant. Vinogradov had begun his business career in the late 1980s, when the Soviet authorities, including Mikhail Gorbachov personally, supported him in establishing the first private financial and construction organizations under the Komsomol. In 1988 Vinogradov received support from the Soviet Ministry of Finance and Gosbank, the state bank, to found Inkombank for this purpose. It later became the govern-

ment's authorized bank in Moscow, was included on the list of banks that could provide services to the State Customs Committee and in support of trade with the People's Republic of China, and established close ties with the Ministry of Defense and the Ministry of Internal Affairs, as well as with regional governments. It opened 68 offices in various regions to handle these relationships. Inkombank was able to use the money it made during those years to buy into a number of major industrial companies.

3. *Boris Berezovsky's group was centered on the LogoVAZ company*, which he set up in 1989 as the first private car dealership in the country, selling AvtoVAZ cars. Various schemes, such as selling cars inside Russia that had been earmarked for export, enabled LogoVAZ to put together a substantial sum of capital in a short period of time. This money was then invested in speculation through United Bank, which Berezovsky also controlled. Another highly profitable operation was the sale of shares in the AVVA investment company, created to accumulate funds for building a new auto plant. The factory was never built, and it is not known exactly what happened to the money raised for this purpose. Gradually the accumulated capital began to be used to take control of other companies. At the time, Berezovsky's group also included the Petroleum Finance Company, Sibneft, Aeroflot, part of ORT television, TV-6, *Nezavisimaya gazeta* newspaper, and *Ogonyok* magazine.

4. *Mikhail Khodorkovsky's group was initially based on Bank Menatep*, which came out of the Intersectoral Center for Scientific and Technological Programs, attached to the Frunze District Komsomol organization in Moscow. The bank's name, Menatep, is a Russian abbreviation of the name of this Center, and Khodorkovsky was a district Komsomol secretary. At first the Center dealt in imported computers. In 1988, it got registered as a private bank. As an authorized bank for the federal government, Menatep handled cash flows related to a number of federal budget programs, such as the sugar trade with Cuba and reconstruction in Chechnya. In 1993, Menatep became an authorized bank for the Moscow

city government, as well, and later for the city governments of St. Petersburg, Yaroslavl and Yekaterinburg.

Khodorkovsky established the Rosprom holding company to control the industrial and other companies he owned. Its components were Yukos Oil, firms in the food and allied, steel, chemicals, timber, paper, and light industries, part of ORT, and the English-language *Moscow Times*, as well as controlling stakes in *Literaturnaya Gazeta* weekly and a number of other publications. In the mid-1990s, one of the group's acquisitions was Apatit, a little-known but important producer of natural fertilizers. Ten years later, Khodorkovsky and his partner Lebedev would be found guilty of embezzling that state-owned property.

5. *Vladimir Gusinsky's group was also known as the Most group*, after the bank of that name, which was founded in 1989 to finance Gusinsky's office equipment sales and building repair cooperatives, which catered to new private companies. At the beginning of the 1990s, Most became the main authorized bank for the Moscow city government, and quickly got rich on real estate operations in the capital city's center. Later, it became an authorized bank for a number of regional governments, as well as the government of Azerbaijan. At the time, the Most holding company included Media-Most, NTV television, Ekho Moskvy radio, the Seven Days publishing house, *Segodnya* newspaper, *Itogi* weekly and part of *Obshchaya Gazeta* and *Novaya Gazeta* newspapers. The group also included companies inherited from the group's early days: Most Investment, Most Development and Most Engineering.

6. *Vladimir Potanin's group was centered on Oneximbank*, of which Potanin was president. A former employee of the Ministry of Foreign Trade, he founded his own company at the very beginning of the 1990s, naming it the International Finance and Investment Company (International Finance Company, for short, or MFK from its Russian acronym). Initially, it worked as a financial intermediary for ruble credits extended to state-owned enterprises. Oneximbank, created on this basis in 1993, became a payments agent for Ministry

of Finance bonds, and the main bank for servicing the city of Moscow's foreign economic relations. Until the end of 1997, a significant part of Russian customs payments went through Oneximbank. It was also the government's semiofficial bank for foreign trade operations.

It was Potanin's idea to mortgage large equity stakes in a number of state-owned industrial enterprises to a group of banks. These shares subsequently became the property of either the banks, or holding companies associated with them. The Potanin group's holding company was Interros, which at that time included over 30 industrial and other firms. Among them were the Renaissance Capital financial company, Norilsk Nickel, the Sidanco oil company, 26 percent of the ZIL truck plant in Moscow, 25 percent of the communications giant Svyazinvest, 15 percent of the Novolipetsk Metallurgical Combine, 40 percent of LOMO, 27 percent of Perm Motors, as well as *Izvestia*, *Komsomolskaya Pravda* and *Russky Telegraf* newspapers, and *Expert* magazine. *Business Week* estimated that in 1996, companies controlled by the Potanin group had total assets of $38 billion and an annual turnover of $16 billion.

7. *Alexander Smolensky's group originated with the Moskva-3 cooperative,* which dated from the late 1980s. The Stolichny Savings Bank (SBS, from its Russian acronym) was registered in that period, based on Moskva-3. In the early 1990s it was the only leading Moscow bank to create numerous branch offices in the regions to service small companies and the population at large. Using its government connections, especially with Chubais, SBS was able in 1996 to acquire a controlling equity stake in the formerly state-owned Agroprombank, with its approximately 1,500 branches in 68 regions. The bank was renamed SBS-Agro. Smolensky, unlike the other groups, did not get involved in acquiring shares of industrial companies. One exception was the publishing industry, where he purchased *Kommersant* newspaper and its associated weekly, and *Dengi* (*Money*), *Stolitsa* (*The Capital*), *Domovoy* (*House Fairy*), and *Avtopilot* (*Auto-pilot*) magazines.

This overview makes it clear that the oligarchical groups of that time varied in the extent to which they had penetrated industry. The least involved in industry were the groups of Gusinsky and Smolensky, which stayed almost entirely with publishing and media holding companies, apart from finance as such (ranging from banking to real estate). The industrial component of the Berezovsky group was also relatively weak, Sibneft being its only wholly owned concern. The most active in setting up industrial empires were the Alfa Group, Inkombank, and Potanin's and Khodorkovsky's groups. It is of interest that, with the exception of Inkombank and Khodorkovsky's empire (which disappeared quite recently), these industry-oriented groups still existed ten years later. They have been the most stable in the face of economic and political upheaval.

What all the groups of that period had in common, was domination by individuals who had made their fortunes in finance and came into industry via banking. Moreover, although in six of the groups (the exception was Berezovsky's relatively small United Bank), the main bank was one of the top dozen or so private commercial banks of that time, they were by no means the largest with respect to assets. The largest of them, Bank Menatep, ranked only seventh, Most was ninth and Alfa thirteenth. Their operations outside the financial sector were defined by their proximity to government circles, which facilitated their acquisition of privatized state-owned industrial companies, as well as by the profit-maximization strategies their leaders chose, and the means they used to achieve their objectives. Some were chiefly interested in banking as such. There were banks, besides SBS-Agro, that emphasized their role as payments and accounts settlement centers, considering forays into industry to be risky and less promising. For others, such as Menatep, Most, and Alfa, becoming a leader in the banking sector was never their main objective. Only Vinogradov at Inkombank and Potanin at Oneximbank combined major interests in both industry and banking.

By the beginning of 2005, less than a decade after the 1996 elections, the alignment of forces among these financial groups had changed substantially. Some of them practically ceased to exist. Others remained, but with an altered composition. Still others survived, but were allied with new, up-and-coming groups. These transformations, in the main, resulted from three interacting processes:

1. The above-described process of concentration of production, during which the correlation of forces among the existing rival groups changed, and new groups and alliances of groups arose.

2. The 1998 financial crisis, which hit the groups' banking component especially hard, but also affected the industrial companies.

3. Changes in the upper echelons of the political power structure, which greatly weakened the positions of some groups and strengthened others.

The concentration of capital and the formation of new, powerful concerns in virtually all sectors of industry significantly enhanced the industrial component of some of the oligarchical groups. Whereas in the earlier stage of development the top men of each group headed the groups' main banks, now, more often than not, they moved over to head up their holding companies or major industrial firms. For example, Potanin left his banks to head up the Interros investment holding company, which oversees all the component companies in his group. Khodorkovsky, before getting into trouble, left Bank Menatep and became president of the largest of his industrial concerns, Yukos Oil. Only Fridman and Aven continued to guide their group out of offices at Alfa Bank.

The financial crisis of 1998 also boosted the industrial side of these large holding companies, in that it led to the formal or de facto bankruptcy of all of their previous head banks, except for Alfa Bank. Vinogradov's Inkombank went bankrupt and vanished, as did Khodorkovsky's Menatep, Gusinsky's Most Bank and Smolensky's SBS-Agro, while Potanin's Oneximbank was completely reorganized and essentially ceased to exist. The only comparable event in the history of the world financial oligarchy was what happened in the United States during the Great Depression of the 1930s. The 1998 crisis in Russia caused the collapse of those oligarchical groups which had had a small and weak industrial component. By 2002 at the latest, the Inkombank and SBS-Agro groups had entirely ceased to exist, while the oligarchs who had headed them, Vinogradov and Smolensky, disappeared from the scene.

Although the 1998 crisis also hit industry, trouble at industrial companies was not what caused the banks to go under. There were two main factors: excessive involvement in short-term government bond (GKO) speculation and the banks' unsustainable level of indebtedness to foreign creditors, which had developed during the stock market and currency boom that preceded the crisis. Alfa Bank was able to emerge from the crisis in relatively good shape because it had been less involved in these operations than the others.

Changes at the top of the government affected the Gusinsky and Berezovsky groups first. These two oligarchs, Berezovsky especially, aspired to play a role in politics, using the newspapers and TV channels in their media empires to influence public opinion. They did not stop at that. Berezovsky occupied a special place in the immediate entourage of President Yeltsin. At one time he held high posts in Yeltsin's administration, and he extended financial assistance to Yeltsin himself and to members of his family. Gusinsky, besides his business operations, headed the Russian division of the World Jewish Congress and provided financial and other types of support to liberal and pro-Western elements of the opposition to Yeltsin.

In 1996, these two magnates, along with the other oligarchs, gave Yeltsin decisive support in his reelection campaign against the Communist Party candidate, Gennadi Zyuganov. In return, they received renewed support from the President and the government for a certain period of time. Gusinsky's relations with the authorities soured with the outbreak of the Second Chechen War, when he and his media outlets criticized Yeltsin and especially the new prime minister, Putin, and began openly to support Putin's rivals (the Luzhkov-Primakov bloc) for the Presidency in the 2000 election. Upon coming to power, the new President backed the initiation of criminal proceedings against Gusinsky in connection with an old privatization case, forcing him to emigrate. The authorities later used NTV's indebtedness to the government and Gazprom's leverage as a major creditor of and shareholder in the Media-Most holding company, to put Media-Most under the control of Gazprom, expelling Gusinsky as its main owner. Most Bank had gone bankrupt earlier. As a result, Gusinsky's empire in Russia essentially ceased to exist. The authorities were also helped in this conflict by the fact that the group's finances were in miserable shape. And when Most's finances had deteriorated, Gusinsky had not moved to sacrifice even a portion of his very considerable personal fortune in order to straighten out the affairs of the companies he owned. For all intents and purposes, they were abandoned to fate.

The Berezovsky group, unlike the other oligarchs, suffered little damage from the crisis, in part because it did not include a major bank. After the crisis, it became even more powerful, including through the acquisition of control over shares in ORT, which had belonged to a consortium of private banks that passed control of its shares to Berezovsky in a private deal, the details of which were never revealed. For a while, Berezovsky was virtually completely in charge of Russian TV's Channel 1, which significantly enhanced his influence. In addition, he bought the Kommersant publishing house, bringing *Kommersant* newspaper, and the associated influential weeklies *Kommersant-vlast* and *Dengi*, under his control, on top of *Nezavisimaya Gazeta* and *Novyye Izvestia*, which he already owned.

It was at that time, or slightly earlier, that Berezovsky formed close relations with Abramovich, a former successful oil trader who became his partner at Sibneft. As the oil company's Moscow representative, Abramovich also functioned as the cashier for Yeltsin and members of his immediate family in this period.

The first difficulties Berezovsky encountered came in a short episode in early 1999 when Primakov was premier. Primakov initiated criminal proceedings against Berezovsky in connection with his role in milking Aeroflot. But Primakov lost the first round of this battle, a defeat that became a factor in his forced resignation some weeks later. Later that year, Berezovsky provided a large amount of financial and other support to the newly created Yedinstvo (Unity) party, which brought Putin to power. Many people thought that after his inauguration, the new President would be under the total control of the "Family," the group of people close to Yeltsin, who were also associated with Berezovsky. In expectation of a new surge in their influence, Berezovsky and Abramovich even sought and won seats in the State Duma.

Their plans were not destined to succeed. Putin proclaimed his "equidistance" from the oligarchs, which turned out to mean not only his overt enemy, Gusinsky, but also Berezovsky, his recent ally and sponsor. The criminal prosecutions linked to Aeroflot gradually resumed. Under pressure from the Kremlin, the oligarch had to hand Abramovich control over his 49 percent stake in ORT. Berezovsky went over into open opposition to Putin, criticizing him publicly and making various accusations. Fearing arrest, he emigrated. But

Abramovich declined to take control of any part of central television, turning the proffered 49% stake over to the government. He quit the Duma and ran for the governorship of Chukotka on the Pacific coast, retreating far out of sight of the Kremlin's new ruler. The President, in return, promised not to prosecute him for his business activity.

On the surface it looked for a while as if Berezovsky's business alliances would be preserved. Those appearances did not last. Berezovsky intimated later, that Abramovich had talked him into selling his 44 percent share in Sibneft at a below-market price. This claim is supported by reports that Berezovsky's personal fortune was an estimated $1.6 billion in early 2005, a substantial decline from what it had been before he emigrated, while his former share of Sibneft was worth $6.3 billion in May 2005. Berezovsky also lost his de facto management and financial control position in Aeroflot and control over the television station TV-6, but kept control of most of his mass media holdings, including *Kommersant* and *Novyye Izvestia*. He has turned to expanding his media positions in Ukraine, but the larger oligarchical empire associated with Berezovsky in Russia has practically vanished.

In the first years of the new millennium, Abramovich, too, seemed to be interested in expanding his business interests in Russia. Before their separation, he and Berezovsky bought into Deripaska's Rusal. But subsequently Abramovich apparently first took over Berezovsky's shares and then, in 2003, sold them to Deripaska. Later that year he sold his stake in Sibneft to Yukos, in exchange for a large minority stake in the latter. Under pressure from the Kremlin, Abramovich soon canceled that deal, but then went looking for another buyer and found one, namely Gazprom. Thus, what looked like the beginnings of an Abramovich oligarchical group, allied with other groups, is in the process of disintegrating by the oil tycoon's own decision. Having accumulated a fortune of $18.7 billion (as of early 2006), Abramovich may be opting to leave unpredictable Russia and settle down in London, where his Millhouse Capital holding company is based, and attempt to enjoy his two luxury yachts, customized Boeing jet, and the Chelsea Soccer Club, which he bought in 2003. It would be an unusual finale for a man who is only 39 in 2006. Under pressure from Putin, however, Abramovich agreed to stay on for a second term as Governor of Chukotka. And his 2006 acquisition of a $3 billion stake in Yevrazholding and $300 million worth of Rosneft shares indicate that he still regards Russia as a place to invest profitably, even if he does not necessarily wish to build a new industrial empire.

At the same time, the relatively new industrial empire of Deripaska has expanded in recent years. After acquiring a solid position in aluminum, he moved into the auto industry, creating the Ruspromavto holding company, which controls a large number of automobile, bus, and related factories.

In 2000, Deripaska created his new holding company, Basic Element, which subsumed Ruspromavto and his long-term investments in various other companies. This quite diversified set includes Yevrosibenergo (two major hydroelectric stations in Siberia), Ingosstrakh (insurance), Soyuzmetalresurs (four mining and machine-building enterprises), a regional airline, and an aircraft building company, among others.

One essential component of an oligarchical group, which Deripaska lacks, is a wholly owned major private commercial bank or other credit institution, which would handle the financial side of the group's business. Soyuz Bank, owned through Basic Element, has assets of only 28.9 billion rubles (2004) and ranks 24th among private banks, so it can hardly serve as group leader. It may be that, rather than expand on a big scale into the banking business, which would be totally new for him, Deripaska has chosen to form an alliance with an existing independent large bank that is looking for a solid industrial base.

There is nothing unnatural in the emergence of new industrial financial groups as alliances of various industrial and banking groups. Recent decades have seen the majority of financial groups in the USA evolve in this way. It is also quite logical for Russia to be experiencing this phase of development at a higher level of concentration of capital.

For Deripaska, whose main interests have been concentrated in the highly profitable aluminum industry, the need for a head bank was secondary for a long time. Nonetheless, the rapidly growing MDM Bank, headed by Andrei Melnichenko, has become a natural ally in recent years. Overall, MDM Bank caters to relatively young industrial magnates from Siberia and the Urals, among them Deripaska (aluminum), Makhmudov (copper), and Abramov (founder of Yevrazholding in the steel industry). In 2004, it ranked fourth among major private commercial banks, with 121 billion rubles in assets. Among the head banks of other financial groups, it is surpassed in this respect only by Alfa Bank, and is about equal to Potanin's Rosbank.[80] Until recently, the chairman of MDM Bank was Alexander Mamut, head of the RUIE Commission on Banking Reform, who was rumored to have excellent access to the Kremlin. But the real head of the bank is Melnichenko, who, together with his partner, Sergei Popov, also controls a large coal, natural fertilizer, and steel pipe company. In the wake of the 1998 financial crisis, Melnichenko succeeded in making his bank a leader, creating, as he boasts, "more money than we need." Like Deripaska, Melnichenko is closely allied with Chubais and RAO UES, which is not surprising, considering their common interest in coal for the electricity-hungry aluminum industry and Chubais's power plants, respectively.[81] In 2006, at the age of 34, Melnichenko is personally worth $4.43 billion, as is his partner, Popov.

Assembling all the pieces, we have a picture of a broad new oligarchical financial alliance, taking shape gradually and, to date, fairly amorphously (Table 2.12). Its strength lies in the combination of a powerful industrial base in the eastern parts of the country, with access to at least one major Moscow bank.

Of the older groups, the ones that existed in 1996-1997, two survived essentially intact: Potanin's group and Alfa (the Fridman-Aven group), while Khodorkovsky's group, surviving and expanding until mid-2003, was largely demolished during the court case against him. Potanin and Khodorkovsky experienced major problems in connection with the de facto bankruptcy of their head banks, Oneximbank and Menatep, while Alfa Bank, as noted above, was able to ride out the 1998 financial crisis relatively unscathed. The political changes that took place had no substantial effect on these groups until mid-2003. They had not sought to play any particularly active political role earlier, so the new President had no complaints against them in that regard. Of these oligarchs, the one who got involved in politics earlier and more than the others was Potanin. He was a vice-premier in the Chernomyrdin cabinet for a time in 1996-1997, but limited his government activity to economic policy questions. Unlike Berezovsky, he did not meddle in politics at the top. The Potanin-controlled press, especially *Izvestia* and *Komsomolskaya Pravda,* took a neutral stance toward the new Putin regime, or even wrote favorably about it, though indulging in criticism on some specific issues. Potanin did not control

Table 2.12 Composition of the Deripaska-MDM financial group, 2004

Banks and companies	Capital (billions of rubles)	Share of control (1=100%)	Capital under management (billions of rubles)	Other parties sharing control
Banks and financial companies				
MDM Bank	121.2	1	121.2	
Soyuz Bank	28.9	1	28.9	
Basic Element (holding company)	5.0	1	5.0	
Total, banks and financial companies			155.1	
Real sector companies and enterprises				
Russian Aluminum	162.0	1	162.0	
Ruspromavto (15 enterprises)	84.0	1	84.0	
Yevrosibenergo (2 large hydroelectric power stations)	25.0	1	25.0	
Other businesses in Basic Element group	40.0	1	40.0	
MDM Group (3 companies)	105.0	1	105.0	
Real sector total			406.0	
Total for entire group			571.1 ($19.0 billion)	

any TV channels, while in the print media the critical tone of some of his journalists was not particularly eye-catching.

At first Putin gave Potanin something of a scare through the tax agencies, which indicated that they were going to review the legality of the privatization of Norilsk Nickel, as well as the company's tax-paying performance. As we saw in our brief history of the nickel industry, the oligarch was able to demonstrate his loyalty by readily agreeing to the President's request to invest a large sum in completing construction of the nickel-processing plant in Cuba. Putin was planning a visit to Havana, making it very timely for him to be able to promise Fidel Castro to resume work on the plant, which had been interrupted after the collapse of the Soviet Union. No further problems arose between Potanin and the President, and the tax matter was quietly forgotten.

The main setback suffered by the Potanin group was the de facto bankruptcy of Oneximbank. Although it continued to exist on paper, its role was reduced to the liquidation of prior debts. After the crisis, all of its solvent assets were transferred to Rosbank, which became the head bank for the Potanin group and successfully held on to a leading place in private commercial banking. Not counting directly or indirectly government-controlled banks like Gazprombank and the Bank of Moscow, Rosbank in late 2004 ranked third in private bank assets after Alfa Bank and MDM Bank. In 2005, after integrating a network of smaller provincial retail banks (OVK, or Mutual Credit Societies), Rosbank increased its assets by 30 percent, surpassing MDM Bank.

While Interros has a controlling stake in Rosbank (owning 36 percent of the shares outright and controlling another approximately 20 percent indirectly, through the personal holdings of Potanin and top management), an interesting detail is that Surgutneftegaz, one of Russia's top oil companies, which is controlled by its management under Vladimir Bogdanov, is a minority shareholder (7.6 percent) in Rosbank. Surgutneftegaz also owns 81 percent of its own Surgutneftegazbank. Nonetheless, its participation in Rosbank indicates that a financial partnership has developed between Potanin and Bogdanov. Thus the new Deripaska-MDM oligarchical alliance, considered above, is by no means exceptional.

Interros continues to serve as the investment center for the Potanin group. Potanin himself now heads the holding company, which owns controlling stakes in Norilsk Nickel, Silovyye Mashiny (Power Machines, a turbine producer), the agriculture project Agros, Soglasiye Insurance Company, and Prof-Media, which controls a number of newspapers and magazines. In recent years, however, Interros has sold its significant minority holdings in a number of industrial companies: Perm Motors, LOMO (20 percent), the Novolipetsk Metallurgical Combine (34 percent), Rusia Petroleum, the Sukhoy OKB, Severnaya Verf, and New Programs and Conceptions (defense industry). In 2005, its Prof-Media sold the important daily newspaper *Izvestia* to Gazprom, but retained control of the popular daily *Komsomolskaya Pravda, Expert* magazine, the Prime-TASS agency, and other media.

The Potanin group's biggest loss in industry was the Sidanco oil company, from which Alfa and BP drove it out. The story of this operation was told above, in the section of this chapter dealing with corporate concentration within the oil industry. The American financier George Soros played a certain role in it, when he went behind Potanin's back and sold some of his Sidanco shares to an ally of Alfa. Soros's partnership with Potanin had begun with their much publicized joint purchase of a large stake in Svyazinvest, the national telecommunications company, in which undertaking they had the support of then-vice-premiers Chubais and Boris Nemtsov. Potanin subsequently unloaded his Svyazinvest shares.

Interros diversified its investments in the years after the 1998 crisis. The above-mentioned Silovyye Mashiny, leading manufacturer of turbines for electric power plants, was a major acquisition. The largest Russian manufacturer of power equipment for hydroelectric, thermoelectric, gas and nuclear power plants, it had revenue of over $352 million in 2003.

Interros initially bought into the OVK group, which was later integrated into Rosbank. Agros, set up in 2001, became one of the biggest Russian companies in the agricultural and food industry sector; it includes more than 40 joint stock companies, with annual revenue of $311.9 million. Agros is a leading pasta producer and grain merchant both at home and abroad, while also being a frontrunner in grain storage capacity and poultry (broiler) production. The elevator network of RusElCo (a joint project of Agros Group and the Louis Dreyfus subsidiary Sungrain Holding) is the largest in Russia. Interros kept Soglasiye Insurance Company, one of its older assets, because it is so profitable, with over $550 million rubles of income from premiums in 2003.[82]

Potanin's change of strategy was related to his overall financial difficulties after the 1998 crisis, which forced him to concentrate on his main strategic interests (even as he diversified his portfolio positions, as noted above), and shed the "fat" the group had accumulated in the preceding period (Table 2.13). In a rare interview, Interros General Director Andrei Klishas described this financial and industrial strategy:

"We strictly differentiate the company's strategic assets from our portfolio investments. By direct, or strategic, investments, we mean the organizations in which we own a controlling stake, and are therefore responsible not only for the business results, but also for how the company functions overall, including with respect to ecological, social and other questions. ... In our portfolio investments, ... we are merely one of the investors, and the scope of our responsibility is defined by the size of our investment. ... We try to make our investments appreciate, to become capitalized. Portfolio investments require closer attention than direct investments. It often happens that portfolio investments yield the highest profit. ... These are sets of assets that we would, in principle, be prepared to sell if we got offers we liked. ... That depends on the condition of the market and the development of the particular company in which we have a stake. Our strategy also plays an important role: we may pull out of one sector of industry, but go back into another."[83] This statement dates from 2001, after which time Interros apparently sold most of its portfolio investments. They are not mentioned in its July 2005 corporate report.

In the course of this expansion, Potanin upped his personal fortune to $6.64 billion by early 2006. Equally wealthy is his close, but lesser known, partner Mikhail Prokhorov, who runs Norilsk Nickel. A graduate of the Moscow Financial Institute, he worked at a Soviet foreign trade bank, and then, together with Potanin, participated in taking one such bank, when they were liquidated, as the base for creating Oneximbank. His fortune was estimated at $6.7 billion in early 2006.

In the aftermath of the financial crisis of 1998, the chief loss suffered by the Khodorkovsky group was the bankruptcy of its head bank, Menatep. It did not entirely vanish, in that Group Menatep, where control over the group's companies was concentrated, survived. So did its subsidiary in St. Petersburg, becoming the independent entity Menatep-St. Petersburg, one of the top dozen commercial banks in the country. An even larger bank in the group was the Trust and Investment Bank (renamed simply "Trast"), which was controlled through a 19.9 percent equity stake belonging to Yukos Oil. But the latter, rather than any bank, became the kernel of the group for the next few years and was headed, until his arrest in October 2003, by Khodorkovsky himself, as if to emphasize that oil was chief among his interests.

The group's main industrial holding company, Rosprom, was closely linked with Bank Menatep, and followed it into bankruptcy. Rosprom had included dozens of companies in the steel, chemicals,

Table 2.13 Composition of the Potanin-Interros financial group, 2004

Banks and companies	Capital (billions of rubles)	Share of control (1=100%)	Capital under management (billions of rubles)	Other parties sharing control
Banks and financial companies				
Rosbank, including OVK	204.4	1	204.4	
Interros (holding company)	3.0	1	3.0	
Soglasiye Insurance	16.5	1	16.5	
Surgutneftegazbank	24.4	0.2	4.8	Surgutneftegaz
Total, banks and financial companies			228.7	
Real sector companies and enterprises				
Norilsk Nickel	388.5	1	388.5	
Silovyye Mashiny	10.6	1	10.6	
Agros	9.4	1	9.4	
Prof-Media	1.5	1	1.5	
Surgutneftegaz	816.0	0.1	81.6	Surgutneftegaz
Real sector total			491.6	
Total for entire group			720.3 ($24.0 billion)	

food, textile, timber, and paper industries. The situation leading to its collapse came about because Yukos was a loss-maker (at least on the books) during its first years of existence, and paid no dividends on its shares. At the same time, it came to light that Menatep had few profitable assets, so its debts had to be paid by liquidating Rosprom's property. One of the first assets to be sold was control over the Apatit Company (the later focus of the government's case against Khodorkovsky), which in the late 1990s had a virtual monopoly on the supply of phosphates to the chemicals industry.[84] Other companies and enterprises followed. One of the last ones sold was the Volga Pipe Factory, which the MDM group acquired in 2000. Khodorkovsky's industrial empire was essentially reduced to its largest component, Yukos Oil. As one analyst put it, the former financier turned into an oilman, whether he liked it or not.

Khodorkovsky fought for that last piece of his empire with all his might and means. He did not bow to foreign investors, who wanted to acquire property in the Russian oil industry. When the American billionaire Kenneth Dart purchased 12-14 percent of the shares in three Yukos subsidiaries—Samaraneftegaz, Tomskneft, and Yuganskneftegaz—Khodorkovsky pushed through a decision to issue new shares, diluting the American's holding. Dart and his representatives were not admitted to the shareholders' meeting where this decision was taken. Dart filed a number of lawsuits against Yukos, charging the company with concealing assets offshore. The Anglo-American oil major BP-Amoco then pulled out of its cooperation agreement with Yukos on long-term development of its oil operations. The American press made Khodorkovsky famous as a typical example of the pirates dominating Russia's new business scene. And when the scandal broke in the USA around covert transfers of billions of dollars from Russia to the Bank of New York (BONY), investigators put all the operations of the recently bankrupted Bank Menatep under surveillance. The press picked up the news that BONY employee Natalya Kagalovskaya, who was under investigation, was married to Konstantin Kagalovsky, a Menatep vice-president and partner of Khodorkovsky in the group.[85]

As much as one-third of the shares in Yukos did eventually end up in the possession of Western banks that were creditors of Menatep. In addition, Yukos had to agree for three foreign banks—one German, one Japanese, and one South African—to have one-third of the seats on the company's supervisory council.[86]

Nonetheless, Khodorkovsky managed to keep control of what was left of his banks, and of Yukos. After these scandals he hired an American PR firm to whitewash him in the eyes of foreign business circles and the media. Within two years after these events, an image of Khorodkovsky as a "reformed" businessman, guided by "honesty, openness and responsibility," had been established in the Western press. The *New York Times* wrote about this shift: "Mr. Khodorkovsky has concentrated on recasting Yukos to look more like a company that investors can trust. It paid $300 million in dividends for 2000, after years of paying little or nothing, and released three years' worth of financial results audited to international account-

Table 2.14 Personal worth of Khodorkovsky group partners, 2004-2005
(billions of $)

Person	2004	2005
Mikhail Khodorkovsky	15.0	0.21
Leonid Nevzlin	2.0	0.61
Mikhail Brudno	1.8	0.15
Vladimir Dubov	1.8	0.15
Platon Lebedev	1.8	0.15
Vasili Shakhnovsky	1.8	0.15
Total	24.2	1.42
Shrinkage (%)		94.1%

Sources: *Forbes* and *Finans* rankings, 2004 and 2005.

ing standards. Luckily for Mr. Khodorkovsky, markets have short memories. Analysts raved, and the stock price shot up."[87]

This was exactly what Khodorkovsky needed, since market capitalization is the most important indicator for investors of whether or not a company is creditworthy and their investments will be secure. Thus, despite a significant pullback after 1998, the Khodorkovsky group by mid-2003 still controlled assets worth around $33.5 billion, and was thus considered a leading force within the Russian industrial-financial oligarchy. Then government lightning struck, and within two years the group was in shambles. Yukos's main production unit, Yuganskneftegaz, was sold to the government-controlled Rosneft oil company in satisfaction of debts, while the market capitalization of Yukos fell by over 96 percent, to only $1.3 billion in May 2005. Khodorkovsky and Lebedev, the former head of Group Menatep holding company, are in jail. Most of their former partners and co-owners of Yukos are abroad, and are wanted by Russian law enforcement agencies on various charges. Many of Yukos's top managers, who are U.S. citizens, chose to stay abroad. The Khodorkovsky oligarchical group has ceased to exist, while Yukos, or what's left of it, continues to operate in physical and commercial terms.

With the group went the personal fortunes of its main owners, which mainly, though not exclusively, represented the market value of their Yukos shares. Their decomposition is summarized in Table 2.14.

The demise of the Khodorkovsky group was largely instigated

by political and economic interests centered around President Putin and members of his Presidential Administration. We shall consider their motives in Chapter 3, which deals with relations between the state and business. In a nutshell, Putin and his close associates are in the process of creating an oligarchical group of banks and companies of their own, much larger in size and power than any private oligarchical group could possibly be. In the process of creating such a group, the Kremlin oligarchs crushed Khodorkovsky and his partners, and expropriated their assets. The ethical aspect of this piracy is on a par with what Khodorkovsky et al. committed as they expropriated state-owned assets in the early 1990s. One might cynically contend that the two piracies cancel each other out. But whether or not that is truly the case, will depend on what the Kremlin oligarchs do: operate their newly acquired assets as genuine state property, or use them for their own personal enrichment.

We now return to the fate of the private oligarchical groups. The Alfa Group suffered the least from the financial crisis and political changes of the late 1990s and early 2000s. Moreover, it became the most aggressive in expanding its sphere of influence. Alfa is the most oriented toward striking up ties with Western business. Accordingly, it enjoys support from foreign capital.

Alfa's most successful operations in the immediate aftermath of the 1998 financial crisis were the preservation and further expansion of Alfa Bank, and the final takeover of TNK, the oil company. In the course of this battle, Alfa began to work with Vekselberg's Access/Renova group, which then became a regular ally. Vekselberg, like many others, started his business career in the computer trade in the late 1980s. His firm, Renova, accumulated enough capital to take over the Vladimir Tractor Factory in 1994 and install a Harvard Business School graduate as its managing director. Their efforts to revive this nearly bankrupt company failed. Vekselberg then began to build up his aluminum business. Since the late 1980s, Vekselberg has worked in close partnership with Len Blavatnik, who heads Access Industries and spends most of his time in the USA and Britain. Their alliance is known as Access/Renova.

Access/Renova came into the Alfa group with Russia's second largest aluminum company, SUAL. Joining forces and garnering support from the American financier George Soros, Alfa and Access/Renova succeeded in ousting the Potanin group from another

Table 2.15 Billionaires of the Alfa group
(billions of $, early 2006)

Person	Company and position	Personal fortune
Mikhail Fridman	Chairman, Alfa Bank	11.40
Victor Vekselberg	Chairman, Renova	8.10
Leonard Blavatnik	President, Access Industries	5.00
German Khan	Executive Director, Alfa Group	4.05
Alexei Kuzmichev	Chairman, Alfa Group	4.05
Pyotr Aven	President, Alfa Bank	1.41
Gleb Fetisov	Alfa Telecom	0.85
Total personal wealth		34.86

oil company, Sidanco, while also establishing partial control over the smaller, but very promising Rusia Petroleum.

In the next few years, Alfa went on to expand its operations in the food and allied industries, where it was already established; in particular, Alfa literally seized the Smirnov and Descendants Trading House. It also moved into a new area, telecommunications, acquiring control of Vympelcom, which had been the first Russian company to be listed on the New York Stock Exchange, and the Internet company Golden Telecom.

These acquisitions put Alfa on top of one of the largest industrial empires in Russia, as well as being a strong force in banking. Then, in 2003, it sold half of its crown jewel, TNK, to the giant oil multi BP. This effectively reduced the industrial sphere under direct Alfa control, but increased the personal wealth of the major TNK shareholders, who received payment partly in cash and partly in BP shares. Table 2.15 shows the billionaires associated with the Alfa group and estimates of their personal worth.

After the fall of Yukos and the relative pauperization of its owners, Alfa-Access/Renova has evidently become the largest group of associated billionaires and multimillionaires (Table 2.16).

Before summing up our review of the main Russian industrial financial groups, we should note that the other major oil and gas concerns have become independent groups with access to bank credit. Lukoil, for example, gained control of 59 percent of Petrokommerts Bank and 17 percent of Sobinbank, the latter in partnership with

Table 2.16 Composition of the Alfa-Access/Renova financial group, 2004

Banks and companies	Capital (billions of rubles)	Share of control (1=100%)	Capital under management (billions of rubles)	Other parties sharing control
Banks and financial companies				
Alfa Bank	210.0	1	210.0	
Alfa-Eco	5.0	1	5.0	
Access/Renova	2.0	1	2.0	
Total, financial			217.0	
Industrial companies				
TNK-BP	510.0	0.5	255.0	BP
Megionneftegaz	60.8	0.5	30.4	BP
Alfa Telecom	72.0	1	72.0	
Alfa Group companies	242.0	1	242	
SUAL	59.0	1	59.0	
Industry total			658.4	
Total for entire group			875.4 ($29.2 billion)	

the Energiya corporation. The combined capital of this group (in billions of rubles) in 2005 was:

Lukoil	819.0	
Petrokommerts Bank	45.9	
Sobinbank	19.1	
Total	884.0	($29.5 billion)

It is readily seen that this group's total capital surpasses all of the oligarchical groups that emerged from the Reign of the Seven Bankers period.

Gazprom constitutes an even bigger independent group, which, strictly speaking, counts as one of the state-owned monopolies discussed in more detail in the next chapter. Here we shall merely note, for purposes of comparison, the approximate composition and size of the total capital under Gazprom's control. Its foundation is the natural gas company itself, which owns 87 percent of Gazprombank, 20 percent of Olympic Bank and 37 percent of the National Reserve

Bank. The latter is co-owned by Tekhnosnabexport (14 percent), which also owns 19 percent of Konversbank. The concern's investment fund, Gazprominvestholding, also controls the Oskol Metallurgical Combine and the Lebedinsk GOK. Including the Itera gas company, which is affiliated with Gazprom, the group's capital looked like this (billions of rubles) in 2005:

Gazprom	2,940.0
Sibneft	410.0
Other companies	3.0
Total, companies	3,353.0
Gazprombank	286.7
National Reserve Bank	25.3
Konversbank	5.9
Total, banks	317.9
Total, group	3,670.9 ($123 billion)

The 2005 acquisition of Sibneft, with a market capitalization of $14.3 billion, substantially increased the Gazprom group's assets. Its total capital far exceeds the assets of all other groups.

Table 2.17 summarizes the industrial financial groups in descending order of assets.

Thus, in the years after the 1998 crisis, the number of leading oligarchical financial groups, run by private capital, fell from seven to four. Four groups disappeared: those of Gusinsky, Smolensky, Inkombank, and Khodorkovsky. A new private group emerged, namely the Lukoil group under Alekperov, which supplemented its leading position in the oil industry by taking control over two leading commercial banks. Elements of the Berezovsky-Abramovich alliance—with Berezovsky disappearing as a group leader and Abramovich selling major properties—blended into Deripaska's new alliance with MDM. Potanin's group and Alfa continued to expand and consolidate. In addition, a semi-public/private industrial financial group emerged under Gazprom, owning other industrial companies besides the gas giant itself, as well as three leading banks.

The Gazprom group far outstrips all the others in the size of assets under its control in both the banking and financial sector, and the real economy. Lukoil ranks first among the strictly private groups, based on its oil industry capital. Potanin's extremely diverse

Table 2.17 Comparison of financial oligarchical groups by assets, 2004
(billions of rubles)

Group	Banking and finance	Real sector	Total	Total, billions of $
Gazprom	317.9	3,353.0	3,259.9	123.0
Lukoil	65.0	819.0	884.0	29.5
Alfa	217.0	658.4	875.4	29.2
Potanin	228.7	491.6	720.3	24,0
Deripaska-MDM	155.1	406.0	571.1	19.0
Total, five groups	983.7	5,428.0	6,720.7	223.7
% of total national assets	16.4%	21.3%	20.4%	
Total, four groups (without Gazprom)	665.8	2,375.0	3,050.8	100.7
% of total national assets	11.1%	9.5%	9.8%	

empire lost its top rank due to being driven out of the oil sector. Conversely, the Alfa group managed almost to catch up with Lukoil by taking over TNK, selling half of it to BP, and going on the offensive in other sectors. The Deripaska-MDM alliance still lags substantially behind the others.

In 1996, Berezovsky openly boasted that those seven groups controlled practically half the Russian economy. That was a significant exaggeration. According to 2004 data on the mid-1990s, the five leading groups, combined, controlled only 20 percent, or one-fifth, of the total assets within Russia. If we exclude the Gazprom group, which was not part of the semibankirshchina in 1996, then the private oligarchical groups accounted for only 10 percent of the country's assets.

Admittedly, this is no small sum, considering that the five top groups represent only a fraction of what may be called monopoly capital in modern Russia. As we have seen, capital is highly concentrated in all sectors of industry. If the assets of the five groups in the real economy are compared with total assets in industry, where they are largely concentrated, their share increases to well over one-half (57 percent), while the share of the four private groups exceeds 25 percent. Thus, in order to establish oligopolistic control over the grain or potassium fertilizer market, the relevant companies did not need to come under the wing of one of the Moscow financiers. The assets of such companies, understandably, are not comparable with those of the oil giants. Even the giant steel plants do not come up to the oil concerns' level. The capital of the foremost steel company, Severstal, which has been in the process of transformation into an independent industrial financial group, is an order of magnitude smaller than that of Lukoil or Surgutneftegaz. The capital of the AvtoVAZ auto company or Aeroflot, the leading airline, is 30 times smaller than the oil giants' capital. All of the firms cited here are very large companies or groups. AvtoVAZ has a market capitalization of over $700 million, for example. Some steel and other company owners have become very wealthy individuals. For instance, Lisin, the owner of Novolipetsk Steel, was worth $9.3 billion in early 2006 and Mordashov, boss of Severstal—$6 billion, which puts them in a class with Potanin and Alekperov.

These patterns of concentration of capital were looked at from another standpoint in a report published by the World Bank in 2004, which studied the level of concentration in the Russian economy. Among other things, the report used 2001 data to trace the ultimate owners of industrial companies and banks, and thus to identify 23 industrial financial groups. Table 2.18 ranks these groups by total sales.[88]

Most of the groups and companies in this table have been already described or mentioned in this chapter. Those not discussed above include Tatneft, an oil company based in the Republic of Tatarstan; UGMK, producing iron ore; Mechel, a mining and metals company; Sistema, an electronics and IT group headed by Vladimir Yevtushenkov (personal worth $7.3 billion); IlimPulp, a paper and pulp concern in Siberia; and Metalloinvest, a metals company. Most of them are not closely associated with any particular large bank and therefore do not, strictly speaking, qualify under our definition of banking-industrial groups. Also, the World Bank study did not recognize alliances of groups. It therefore considers Alfa and Access/Renova, and the two components of Deripaska-MDM, as separate groups. Otherwise the results are fairly similar to ours.

The World Bank concluded that the 23 groups accounted for 17 percent of total commercial bank assets, and controlled 35 percent of total sales in Russian industry. The authors considered this degree

Table 2.18 Largest industrial financial groups according to the World Bank, 2001

Rank by sales	Sales, thousands of rubles	Managed by	Organization
1	384,100,000	Alekperov, Maganov, Kukura	Lukoil
2	183,600,000	Abramovich	Sibneft/Millhouse
3	154,700,000	Bogdanov	Surgutneftegaz
4	129,900,000	Potanin, Prokhorov	Interros
5	101,600,000	Khodorkovsky, Lebedev	Yukos
6	93,781,343	Fridman, Khan	Alfa
7	93,366,909	Kadannikov	AvtoVAZ
8	71,041,612	Mordashov	Severstal
9	62,487,413	Deripaska	Basic Element
10	52,937,720	Vekselberg, Balaeskul	Renova
11	52,937,720	Blavatnik	Access Industries
12	50,642,482	Abramov	Yevrazholding
13	48,244,538	Rashnikov	MMK
14	38,783,473	Lisin	NLMK
15	38,618,830	Popov, Melnichenko, Pumpyansky	MDM
16	31,741,691	Takhaudinov	Tatneft
17	29,705,884	Makhmudov, Kazitsin	UGMK
18	27,528,614	Zyuzin	Mechel
19	26,483,961	Yevtushenkov, Novitsky, Goncharuk	Sistema
20	20,046,203	Smushkin, Zingarevich	IlimPulp
21	12,779,973	Yakoboshvili, Plastinin, Dubinin	WimmBillDann
22	8,829,056	Bendukidze	OMZ
23	8,108,702	Yanovsky	Metalloinvest
Total	1,721,966,123		

Source: *From Transition to Development. A Country Economic Memorandum for the Russian Federation*, World Bank, April 2004, p. 96.

of concentration to be excessively high, leading to monopoly pricing practices and other market distortions. To quote: "For historical reasons, Russia's industry has large and excessively concentrated establishments (individual production facilities), but small firms. This induces economic pressure toward consolidation at the firm level. Horizontal integration has increased substantially over the last decade. This integration is often associated with expansion of financial-industrial groups. Since these groups, built mostly around natural-resource industries, have much larger means at their disposal than other Russian economic players, concerns have been raised about the threat of market dominance and monopolization."

The World Bank study broke down total industry sales into four categories:

Big business (23 groups)	35.0%
Government-controlled	25.0%
Foreign business	5.3%
All others (competitive sector)	34.7%

The importance of the state sector, which is comparable in size to big business, is apparent. More recently, its role has been on the rise, in connection with the Yukos case and other Kremlin-guided realignments in the energy, auto, and other industries. What is crucial, is that the combined share of big business and government-controlled industries is as high as 60 percent. Only somewhat more than one-third of industry is accounted for by medium and small business, the proper area of close-to-free competition. Actually, its share is even smaller. These issues will be further considered in Chapter 3.

NOTES

1. *Rossiiskii statisticheskii ezhegodnik (Russian Statistical Yearbook)*, 1998 (hereinafter RSY 1998), p. 375; RSY 2000, p. 301.

2. *The Russian Economic Barometer*, Moscow.

3. *Russian Economic Trends Quarterly* (hereinafter RET1), #4, 2000, p. 90.

4. Strictly speaking, a significant number of the privatized enterprises became the property of their workforce, but effective control passed either to company executives or to outside investors. This phenomenon is explored later in this chapter.

5. RSY 2000, p. 408.

6. RSY 1998, p. 524; RSY 2000, p. 271.

7. RSY 2000, p. 270.

8. This estimate is based on our calculation of the shadow economy's "invisible" revenue, in S. Menshikov, *Katastrofa i katarsis (Catastrophe and Catharsis)*, p. 112. For the entire 1975-1999 period, this revenue equalled 768 billion rubles. We assume that half that sum might have been accumulated in the form of monetary or other

capital, and that 10 percent of such accumulated capital was taken abroad at an average rate of 10 rubles to the dollar. This produces the figure of $3.8 billion.

9. In addition, official prosecutions are often instances of someone's using government agencies as a competitive tool. The criminally connected aluminum magnate Bykov, for example, fell victim to an attack by the upstart Deripaska, who enjoyed the support of local and federal authorities. Other cases of a similar nature are cited later in this chapter.

10. The level of the RTS on Sept. 1, 1995 is taken as a base.

11. For example, at the end of 1999 the charter capital of all insurance companies was only 11 billion rubles, or one twenty-seventh of total commercial bank capital. In the USA, the ratio of bank assets to those of insurance companies is 2.5 : 1.

12. RET1, #4, 2000, p. 83, 89; RET1, #10, 2002, Table 18.

13. Our calculation is based on data in RSY 2000, p. 509.

14. The share of long-term loans in the operations of major banks is significantly higher. As of June 1, 2001, 60 major banks had total loans outstanding that were worth 686 billion rubles, of which 182 billion, or 27 percent, were long-term. (*Profil*, July 30, 2001, p. 38.)

15. This was the case when the author visited Chase Manhattan Bank, three decades ago.

16. Interview with Alexander Mamut in *Izvestia*, July 5, 2001.

17. See, for example, Alina Gontmakher, Boris Grozovskii, "Bankovskaia oligolopoliia na starte, ili uskorennaia kapitalizatsia po Aleksandru Mamutu" ("A Banking Oligarchy in the Starting Blocks, or Alexander Mamut's Brand of Accelerated Capitalization"), Polit.ru, Aug. 8, 2001.

18. *Profil*, July 30, 2001, p. 38.

19. At the end of 2000, for example, Russia's largest industrial company, Gazprom, had 1.1809 trillion rubles in assets, while its market capitalization was only 365 billion rubles—less than one-third. But the assets of the national power company RAO UES on the same date stood at 173.9 billion rubles, only 23 percent higher than its market capitalization. Unfortunately, for many companies it is impossible to make this kind of comparison, due to a lack of data on their assets.

20. For reference, the U.S. totals are $525.2 billion for the banks, $1.286 trillion for the corporations, c/b ratio = 2.45; the totals for Great Britain are $317.6 billion for the banks, $771 9 billion for the corporations, c/b ratio = 2.43; the totals for Japan are $105 billion for the banks, $267.25 billion (average) for the companies, c/b ratio = 2.55; the totals for Germany are $96.16 billion for the banks, $175.35 billion (average) for the companies, c/b ratio = 1.83. The totals for 10 Russian institutions (in rubles) are R1.2782 trillion for the banks (including Sberbank), 536.7 billion for the commercial banks, 1.5808 trillion for the companies, c/b ratio 1 = 1.24, c/b ratio 2 = 2.95. The total for five Russian commercial banks is R368.3 billion, for five companies R1.3583 trillion, c/b ratio = 3.68.

21. *Narodnoe khoziaistvo SSSR v 1988 g.* (*The National Economy of the USSR in 1988*) (hereinafter NKh1988), p. 96, 623, 629. Data for the entire USSR are used, since the banking system was a single whole.

22. RET2, #7, 2001, pp. 9-10.

23. Sometimes enterprises may be grouped by criteria such as number of employees, size of functioning capital, etc. Strictly speaking, however, in such cases the subject is the concentration of the labor force or the concentration of capital. These aspects are also important, but in our analysis we shall deal only with the concentration of production in the stricter sense of the term.

24. NKh1988, pp. 331-332.

25. Economy of scale in production occurs when per unit costs of production are reduced at a company as output is increased. Such economies are achieved, as a rule, at large enterprises, where per unit costs may fall as very large output volumes are achieved.

26. According to the generally accepted Coase theorem, it makes economic sense to join enterprises into firms (through mergers) when the result will be a reduction of the total outlays they incur while existing separately. In particular, economies result from the creation of joint marketing, supply, design, research, and other agencies. Such economies are called economies of scale. In large organizations spending on such ancillary functions is relatively lower, as a rule, than in small organizations. Cf. S. Menshikov, *Novaia ekonomika (The New Economy)*, Moscow, 1999, p. 371.

27. See, in particular, the American economist Paul L. Joskow's work, *Privatization in Russia: What Should Be A Firm?* (Cambridge, Mass.: 1994).

28. RSY 2000, p. 295, 301; RSY 2004, Table 13.15.

29. RSY 2000, p. 277, 284, 301.

30. The gap appears somewhat smaller, upon analysis of the companies in terms of their number of employees. By this measure, companies in the four leading sectors surpass the industry-wide average by factors of 3 to 8. But the overall picture remains the same. For comparison's sake, the table below shows these data. The numbers in the top row refer to sectors of industry as listed and numbered in Table 2.11.

Average number of employees at one privatized enterprise:

1	2	3	4	5	6	7	8	9	10	11
604	5,091	1,800	3,539	2,659	1,592	865	552	478	163	411

The average figures will be much lower, if production and employment are taken for the total number of working enterprises, rather than privatized companies alone. The total number of working enterprises includes newly created small businesses, as well as intermediary companies, which do not directly produce goods; their inclusion significantly reduces the average size of the companies. But in no way does it change the significant gap between the sectors.

Average employment at one company, counting all working companies (1999):

1	2	3	4	5	6	7	8	9	10	11
83	583	444	457	255	121	83	51	73	46	63

31. Here and below, the data on the share of the top four or top eight companies in each sector are taken from RSY 2004, Table 14.5.

32. *Forbes*, July 2001.

33. Based on *Finans (Finance)* magazine, #6, Feb. 13-19, 2006 and RTS information, February 2006.

34. Anatoli Kuzmin, who initiated the creation of Slavneft, was shot while traveling in a corporate car soon after becoming head of the company.

35. There is some evidence that at the time of these events, in 1992-1993, Bank Menatep head Mikhail Khodorkovsky, who later gained control of Yukos, was simultaneously a deputy minister in the Ministry of Fuel and Energy, though not on the payroll (see *Kommersant-Vlast* [KV] of Oct. 23, 2001). It is not known if he was involved in the battle for the Samara refinery. Later, in 1994, one of the vice-presidents of Yukos was shot to death. His successor's car was blown to bits, though he was not in it. These may have been acts of revenge for Neftesam's failure.

36. Prior to holding that position, Ziya Bazhayev had been vice-president of Sidanco. In 1995, he also became president of the Southern Petroleum Company (Yunco), which the government established in order to restore the oil industry in Grozny, Chechnya. After leaving Sidanco, Bazhayev headed up the Alliance Group, which specialized in crisis management at petroleum industry companies.

37. This account is partially derived from the June 5, 2001 Strana.ru article by Pyotr Sergeyev, "Potanina vydavlivaiut iz neftianogo biznesa" ("Potanin Driven out of the Oil Business"), and from material published in *Business Week* in August 2001.

38. *Izvestia,* Aug. 18, 2001, "Sibneft khochet popast' v istoriiu" ("Sibneft Wants to Make History").

39. KV, Oct. 23, 2001.

40. *Izvestia,* Oct. 23, 2001, "Sibneft nashla khoroshii sposob uvelicheniia pribyli" ("Sibneft Finds A Good Way To Increase Profit"); Strana.ru, Aug. 17, 2001, S. Pletnev, "Poglotiv neftetreiderov, Sibneft stanet platit' bol'she nalogov" ("Swallowing Oil Traders, Sibneft Will Pay More Taxes").

41. These and several other details about the history of Norilsk Nickel are based on information on the company's web site, nornik.ru.

42. Norimet was initially chartered in Great Britain as a British joint stock company. In the United States, similar intermediary functions for the sale of Norilsk Nickel products are handled by Almaz USA.

43. In September 2001, the market capitalization of the parent company was $2.7 billion, while the larger of the subsidiaries had a market capitalization of $1.9 billion. It is believed that an additional reason for turning the [Norilsk] Mining Company into the parent company was to use this formal maneuver to protect Norilsk Nickel from the threat of repossession of its controlling equity stake by the government.

44. According to press reports at the time, the Chernoy brothers purchased 48 percent of BrAZ and 28 percent of KrAZ. The company Trans-CIS Commodities, established by the Chernoys, was registered in Monaco and then bought into Trans-World Metals, one of the biggest traders on the London Metals Exchange.

45. KV, #42, 2001.

46. Ibid.

47. Siberian Aluminum annual reports, KV, #42, 2001.

48. Russian Aluminum annual report for 2000.

49. In the first half of 2001, Rusal's financial turnover was $1.45 billion, while SUAL's was $360 million (*Dengi*, #43, 2001).

50. The story of this struggle is drawn from "Chernaia metallurgiia" ("Ferrous Metallurgy"), KV, #37, 2001.

51. According to company information and sector statistics.

52. "Dobyvaiushchaia promyshlennost' i metaly" ("The Mining Industry and Metals") *Biulleten Interfaksa*, #34, August 2001.

53. Mordashov's biography is taken from Severstal annual reports and the *Financial Times*, Oct. 19, 2000.

54. KV, #37, 2001, recounts the fight over the metallurgical combines in Kemerovo.

55. Born in Tashkent, Iskander Makhmudov graduated from the university in that city. In the 1980s, he worked as a translator from Arabic at Soviet trade representative offices in Libya and Iraq. In 1990, he began to work in Moscow as a coking coal and non-ferrous metals trader. In 1993, he founded his own company, which bought up copper plants. He got involved in the copper industry at a time when the aluminum market was overloaded with competitors and there was relatively little interest in copper. His Ural Mining and Metallurgical Company controls 19 plants in this sector. It did over $1.2 billion of business in 2000. (*Russia Journal*, Moscow, April 3, 2001.) In early 2006, his fortune was estimated at $5.85 billion.

56. It is difficult to fathom some of Yevrazholding's acquisitions. KMK, for example, was encumbered by large debts, which the combine's low rate of profit offered no possibility to pay off. A tricky maneuver involving the creation of several joint stock companies, based on KMK, was executed in hopes of raising enough cash through their stock offerings, to pay KMK's debts. It is not clear why Yevrazholding wanted to take over such a relatively uncompetitive plant. (Cf. *Izvestia*, Nov. 24, 2001.)

57. KV, May 18, 2000.

58. *Dengi*, #43, 2001.

59. *Izvestia*, Oct. 26, 2001.

60. RSY 2004, Table 14.5.

61. RSY 2003, Table 14.6.

62. RSY 2004, Table 14.61.

63. AZ stands for avtomobilny zavod, auto factory (or plant). AvtoVAZ, formally the Volga Auto Plant, is located in the southern city of Togliatti on the Volga River. GAZ, the Gorky Auto Plant, is in Nizhny Novgorod, Russia's third largest city. Moskvich is in Moscow, UAZ in the city of Ulyanovsk, and SeAZ is in Serpukhov.

64. For brevity's sake, we shall look here at light automobile production, leaving aside truck, bus, and related manufactures.

65. RSY 2004, Tables 14.79, 14.89, 14.87.

66. Data on food and gustatory industry enterprises: KV, #38, 2001.

67. RSY 2004, Table 14.74; RET2, 2001, p. 91.

68. Data on light industry companies: KV, #44, 2001.

69. See section 3.5 of Chapter 3 for a deeper look at the problems of small business in Russia.

70. On the natural monopolies, see Chapter 3.

71. The problems of the defense industry are laid out in more detail in the author's articles: "Stsenarii razvitiia VPK" ("Scenarios for the Development of the MIC"), in *Voprosy ekonomiki*, #7, 1999; "Sostoianie oboronnogo kompleksa Rossii" ("The Condition of Russia's Defense Sector"), in *Informatsionnyi biulleten' EKAAR-Rossiia*, #4, January 2001, http://www.ecaar-russia.org.

72. These and some other details on the defense industry are from KV, #48, 2001.

73. Chapter 3 deals in more detail with the battle for control over financial flows associated with the defense industry.

74. Radio Liberty news bulletin, Aug. 14, 2001.

75. KV, #48, 2001.

76. The Ramen Instrument-making Design Bureau, which effectively belongs to its general director Givi Janjgava, is considered the core of Tekhnokompleks.

77. The Interregional Investment Bank (MIB) has a strong position in this company.

78. These tendencies are analyzed in depth in our works, *Millionery i menedzhery* (op. cit.) and *Sovremennyi kapitalizm: ekonomika bez budushchego?* (*Modern Capitalism: An Economy without a Future?*) (Moscow: Mysl, 1986).

79. See, in particular, Donald Jensen, *The Big Seven—Russia's Financial Empires*, Radio Liberty Special Report, 1997.

80. *Bank,* supplement to *Izvestia*, Oct. 26, 2004.

81. *Banker,* Aug. 4, 2003, p. 26.

82. Interros site, http://www.interros.ru/eng/.

83. *Izvestia*, Oct. 26, 2001.

84. *Russian Journal,* Oct. 19-25, 2001.

85. *The New York Times*, Aug. 28, 1999.

86. *Russia/Central Europe Executive Guide*, New York, June 30, 2001.

87. Sabrina Tavernise, "Fortune in Hand, Russian Tries to Polish Image," *The New York Times,* Aug. 18, 2001.

88. *From Transition to Development. A Country Economic Memorandum for the Russian Federation,* World Bank, April 2004.

3 State Capital, Millionaires and Managers, Small Business

Chapter 2 dealt chiefly with the composition of private Russian capital, which was formed, in large part, on the basis of assets created by the Soviet state that passed into private ownership as a result of privatization. The new Russian state, of course, played an active role in this process. It set the rules for privatization, while receiving pitifully little compensation, only a small fraction of their real market value, for the privatized assets.

Thus the state was not merely a passive target of this de facto expropriation, but played an active role in it. Some officials promoted the creation of the new financial oligarchy, while making fortunes for themselves in the process. Some, like the family of former President Boris Yeltsin, received payoffs for their assistance from such oligarchs as Boris Berezovsky and Roman Abramovich. Others, upon leaving their ministerial posts, garnered appointments to leading positions in private and government concerns. Some of them even became the heads of such firms, or created their own. They were able to prosper by appropriating state assets and exploiting their old connections in the government. We have already seen how yet another group of officials, at the regional level, took an active part in setting up new private companies on the remains of pre-existing enterprises, and then became the de facto proprietors of those companies. The general rule was that serving in a high federal or local government post became one of the ways to acquire a large personal fortune, and join the elite capitalist class.

At the same time, privatization during the first ten years of the new Russian capitalism did not entirely liquidate state property or the part of the economy that formally (for the time being) remains under government control. Even that sector, however, is closely interconnected with the overall system of private capitalism, and to a certain extent serves private interests more than public. We now proceed to the analysis of the state sector.

3.1 The state sector and the natural monopolies

As of the beginning of 1995, state-owned fixed assets as a share of total fixed assets had fallen to 42 percent, compared with 91 percent at the beginning of 1992. They remained at that level for some time, standing at 40 percent as of 2004. Railroads and other transportation and communications companies accounted for slightly less than one-third of all state assets. Approximately the same amount was in housing and utilities, while the remainder came under the electricity and natural gas natural monopolies, and a part of the defense industry. The state sector also includes the largest diamond company in the country, a number of major banks, the oil pipeline system, and several other, less important enterprises.

Thus the role of the state sector in the economy remains large. We may provisionally divide it into three major parts, according to their functions. First come the natural monopolies, upon which the private sector, the population, and the state itself, with all its administrative institutions, depend almost completely for electricity, natural gas, and rail transportation. Secondly, there are state enterprises that compete with private companies in various areas of business (banking, communications, housing and utilities, raw materials for the jewelry industry and, more recently, oil). Finally, there are the defense plants, which are oriented primarily toward filling government orders and state-controlled export contracts. Of the three groups, the natural monopolies play the greatest macroeconomic role.

According to the IOT, 28.9 percent of all intermediary (current) inputs in the economy as a whole and 42.1 percent of such inputs in industry represent electricity, gas, freight transport, and the use of other industrial infrastructure (including the transport margin).[1] In 1999 spending for electric power alone accounted for 11 percent of all material costs in the economy, and 12 percent of spending in industry. In some years this level reached 16-18 percent.[2] The higher it is, other factors being equal, the greater are the costs of production in other sectors of the economy, and the less competitive these sectors become in both domestic and international markets. Excessive spending on products of the natural monopolies may contribute to an overall decline of production in the economy.

Fluctuations in the level of spending for those products depend on the relationship between the sales prices of goods and services, and the rates charged by the natural monopolies. While price formation for the majority of goods and services takes place in relatively free, even if somewhat oligopolistic, markets, the natural monopolies' rates are regulated by the government. This can produce contradictory situations. During the crisis and stagnation of the economy in the first half of the 1990s, for example, companies in most sectors had a relatively limited ability to pass on to the consumer the rising cost of electricity, natural gas, and railway shipments, insofar as the major firms in the various sectors were still in the process of being established, and they lacked adequate control over the markets for their output. The natural monopolies' rates, however, were relatively tightly controlled already at that time.

Table 3.1 shows that the ratios of electricity, gas, and freight rates to prices of industrial producers' output varied both over the long term (the decade of 1991-2001), and in specific segments of that period. During the initial period of generally high inflation, up until 1996-1997, electricity and freight rates rose more than twice as fast as the prices of industrial goods. At the same time, gas rates lagged substantially behind the overall rate of inflation. After 1997 a certain turning point in the overall tendency occurred. For about two years, rates in all three of these categories rose more slowly than the prices of industrial goods, on average. After 1999, however, there was a reversion to the previous pattern, in which the rates grew more rapidly than prices on produced goods.

These shifts had to do with changes in macroeconomic regulation policies. During the first half of the 1990s the central government did little to intervene into how the natural monopolies set prices. Formally, electric power rates had to be confirmed by the Federal Energy Commission and its regional subdivisions, but these agencies, with rare exceptions, merely rubber-stamped the local power companies' fee submissions. Rail freight rates were set by the Ministry of Railways (MPS, from the Russian acronym): in other

Table 3.1 Price ratios of industrial products, electricity and natural gas
(annual December figures, December 1991=1)

1 Producer price index for industrial goods
2 Producer price index for electricity
3 Index of the ratio of electricity price to the prices of all industrial goods
4 Producer price index for natural gas
5 Index of the ratio of gas prices to the prices of all industrial goods
6 Rates index for railway freight shipments
7 Index of the ratio of railway rates to the prices of industrial goods

	1992	1994	1996	1997	1998	1999	2000	2001	2002	2003
1	33.8	1,115	3,783	4,066	5,009	8,381	11,028	11,998	14,050	15,890
2	59.9	2,645	10,540	11,430	11,680	13,980	19,552	23,110	29,650	33,623
3	1.77	2.37	2.79	2.81	2.33	1.67	1.77	1.93	2.11	2.12
4	13.2	473	2,866	2,883	3,131	3,557	5,765	8,227	11,156	7,887
5	0.39	0.42	0.76	0.71	0.63	0.42	0.52	0.69	0.79	0.50
6	37.4	2,872	8,927	9,052	7,296	8,018	13,574	18,244	21,583	24,561
7	1.11	2.58	2.36	2.23	1.45	0.96	1.23	1.52	1.54	1.55

Sources: RSY 2000, pp. 567-568; RSY 2002, pp. 603-608; RSY 2004, Tables 24-19, 24-21, 24-30.

words, by the natural monopoly itself. Although the Ministry of Fuel and Energy set natural gas prices, the influence of the natural gas monopoly, Gazprom, was insignificant at that time. Unlike electricity and freight shipments, the cost of production of natural gas was small relative to its selling price. Moreover, the gas industry derived the main part of its profit from exports. For the time being, lagging domestic prices were of no great concern.

After the 1998 crisis, the state began for the first time to pursue a policy of restraining the rise of the natural monopolies' rates, seeing such restraint as an important factor in the recovery and growth of the economy. In 1999-2000, for example, relative electric power rates fell to the 1992 level, which considerably eased the situation for industrial consumers. Relative natural gas rates also dropped to the 1994 level. This policy helped to provide a practical solution to the non-payments crisis in the economy. In the preceding period rates, especially for electricity, had raced ahead, despite the fact that the majority of industrial consumers were unable to pay them. The industrial sectors accumulated huge debts to electricity suppliers, while all along the line, barter became the normal means of payment. As soon as the relative rates became more reasonable, and the financial situation in industry improved as the economy grew, barter again gave way to normal monetary payments.

The new wave of relative price hikes for services provided by the natural monopolies, in 2001-2002, was partly a reaction to the curbs on those rates in the preceding period, and partly resulted from the reforms that began to be launched in those sectors. For a better understanding of how the state-owned monopolies interact with the rest of the economy and with politics, let us now look at how these sectors developed in the post-Soviet period.

The electric power industry

That the electric power sector was not broken up early on, has to do with the June 1992 appointment of future Premier Victor Chernomyrdin to replace Vladimir Lopukhin as Minister of Fuel and Energy in the Gaidar government. Lopukhin had presented a plan for the electric power and natural gas industries each to be divided into a production component, and a transport and distribution component, followed by privatization of the production units. This plan was rejected, and Lopukhin was dismissed. Chernomyrdin put his deputy Anatoli Dyakov in charge of electric power, where he remained for more than five years, until 1997.[3]

In December 1992 a Presidential decree established the Russian Joint Stock Company (RAO) for Energy and Electrification, also known as Unified Energy Systems of Russia (UES), as a holding company for equity stakes in the majority of the regional power systems—which were simultaneously reorganized from state-owned entities into joint stock companies—as well as in the single nationwide transmission grid. Only nuclear power plants, accounting for over 10 percent of electric power generation, remained outside of UES.[4] Within a year, the holding company began to be privatized. Twenty percent of its shares were put up for sale at a voucher auction. A significant portion of this stake ended up in the hands of UES management.

Dyakov and his close associates gradually began to feel like the owners of the sector, not answerable to anybody, and moved to implement a series of abrupt rate hikes. Even very top government officials were unable to restrain the surge in rates. In early 1994, for example, Vice-Premier Oleg Soskovets, concerned about what would happen in the metals-producing industries, for which he was responsible, and alarmed at the latest doubling of rates, accused Dyakov of attempting to "establish communism in this entire sector," and demanded his removal. But Soskovets failed. Dyakov remained in his position.

In 1995, UES moved for the first time to cut power to industrial consumers for non-payment of bills. Many non-ferrous metals and steel factories were hit, as were defense plants. Average arrears reached as much as 300 days. The cut-offs were authorized by special government resolution. In response, many regional governments demanded that the state-owned stakes in local power companies be handed over to them for management, or even that the sector be nationalized. These counterattacks achieved nothing. Dyakov continued his offensive against electric power consumers, claiming that his company was not making any profit. This was partially true, due to the fact that the coal market had been deregulated, on top of unregulated oil prices.

Despite Dyakov's complaints about UES's lack of profit, foreign investors at this point began to be interested in acquiring the company's stock. By the end of 1996, they owned 22.5 percent of the total. Another 8.5 percent was sold to the National Reserve Bank. UES was increasingly transformed from its initial status as a fully state-owned concern, into a company with mixed ownership, including a solid portion of private capital.

With the arrival of Boris Nemtsov in the government as a vice-premier, a campaign was launched for the removal of Chernomyrdin's man Dyakov, and his replacement by somebody from the "young reformers" team. In April of 1997, they achieved the appointment of their candidate, Boris Brevnov, as president and CEO of UES, while Dyakov remained on as chairman of the board of directors. A months-long battle ensued between them for control over the utility's financial flows. Brevnov succeeded in banning all payments on the promissory notes, which, issued in the amount of billions of rubles, had been virtually the main source of income for the old management group. In response, Dyakov in early 1998 pushed through a board of directors decision to remove Brevnov. Chernomyrdin, whose dismissal as premier was practically a foregone conclusion, was powerless to help Dyakov. But the meteoric rise of Brevnov's career likewise came to an end, since a stronger "young reformer" was found for the job. At the end of April, former Vice-Premier Anatoli Chubais was confirmed as CEO of UES. His team soon acquired a majority on the board of directors. The "young reformers" had seized the electric power monopoly.

The Chubais era at UES has been marked by several radical changes. First of all, within two or three years, UES did away with barter payments, forcing practically 100 percent cash payment for its services. Secondly, the company became a personnel holding tank and reserve, not to mention a supplementary source of financing, for the Union of Right Forces (SPS) political party, which Chubais effectively heads. Thirdly, a program for the dismemberment and privatization of the sector, to be followed by the deregulation of electricity rates, was rammed through the government.

As noted above, the elimination of payment in kind was not exclusively the accomplishment of Chubais, with his tactics of shutting off power to customers. In 1999-2000, UES rates rose relatively slowly, lagging behind the rate of inflation, but this resulted more from the new regulatory policies, introduced by the Primakov and Putin cabinets, than from any restraint on the part of the power monopoly's management. Although Chubais insisted on payment in cash, rather than in-kind barter deals, he would not have been able to achieve the results he wanted, had the overall economy continued to stagnate. The incipient recovery improved the financial situation of most enterprises, making it possible for the first time for them to pay their electricity bills in cash. In any event, UES was able to emerge from the most acute phrase of the 1998 financial crisis. Chubais got what he wanted, namely control over the electric power monopoly's multibillion-ruble financial flows.

UES's corporate reports indicate the size of those flows. In 2004, the company's total cash revenue from all types of activity was 797 billion rubles.[5] By comparison, the budget of the Russian Federation Ministry of Defense for that year was 417 billion rubles. Thus, Chubais and his team had direct or indirect control over monetary resources, equal to 190 percent of the amount Russia could see its way to spending for defense needs. In financial terms, UES was larger than most federal government ministries. This total turnover figure includes sales by the numerous regional subsidiaries of UES.

Contrary to widespread belief, the electricity monopoly in this period was by no means a loss-making business, scarcely able to make ends meet. In 2000, for example, its costs of production were equal to only 36 percent of its total sales of goods and services, while its net profit, after payment of all current expenses and taxes, was 32 percent.[6] Detailed data on how these funds were spent are not available.

It is known, however, that after the arrival of Chubais, it became regular practice to spend UES resources for purposes falling outside of the electric power business. For example, UES at one time purchased Ren TV, evidently not so much for the company's own needs, as to provide a propaganda outlet for the SPS. In 2002, Chubais was involved in forming a consortium to bid for control of the TV-6 television station, which earlier had belonged to Berezovsky.

A number of prominent right-wing politicians, who lost their ministerial chairs, moved over to high posts at UES. For example, when Alexei Kudrin was removed as first deputy finance minister under Primakov, he became Chubais' first deputy at UES in a matter of weeks. Later, under Kasyanov, Kudrin returned to the government as finance minister and vice-premier. Another deputy of Chubais at UES was former Economics Minister Yakov Urinson.

At the same time, Chubais continued to blackmail the country with sometimes area-wide, and sometimes selective, power cutoffs, prompting widespread protests, since even consumers who paid their bills on time would be hit. The blackouts were frequently politically targeted. The resignation of Primorsky Territory Governor Yevgeni Nazdratenko, a long-standing foe of the rightists, was caused, in large measure, by UES-prompted power crises in the region. In January 2002, Chubais's henchmen, with support from Minister of Finance Kudrin, staged a provocation involving power cuts to military facilities in the Far East. There were press reports suggesting that the head of UES was deliberately using the "circuit-breaker war" to discredit the federal government and undermine President Putin's authority. Nonetheless, the President made no move to oust Chubais, who had the backing of forces with whom Putin preferred not to clash.

In parallel, Chubais undertook preparations for reform of the electric power sector. He calls it restructuring, but the content of these reforms is broader than that. We shall note their main features, without going into detail. The plan provides for hiving off the production aspects of UES, that is, all of its power generating plants, into independent joint stock companies, subsequently to be privatized. The mother concern would retain control over the unified power grid and the wholesale electricity market. It is proposed that, after some time, government regulation of electricity rates be abolished in favor of free price-formation, with competition among power producers and distributors. It is believed that this "liberalization" of the sector will lead to a doubling or even tripling of electricity rates. Chubais has asserted that rate hikes, along with stock issues by independent power producers, will attract foreign capital to the sector, making it possible to modernize it radically.

Although the UES plan received government support, a group of regional governors criticized it, as did members of the Academy of Sciences. They were backed up by Andrei Illarionov, then an adviser to Vladimir Putin on economics. At the end of 2000, the President established a commission of his new State Council, to work out a compromise. Tomsk Governor Victor Kress headed the panel. Its findings met with Presidential approval, but have been largely ignored by Chubais. Nonetheless, due to opposition in the State Duma and from Premier Mikhail Fradkov, the restructuring was still on hold as of mid-2006.

Besides principled disagreements about the impact of such a reform on the economy, this dispute involves a more mundane conflict among the interested parties, over who will acquire some very large pieces of state property, and at what price. The reform's critics assert that Chubais intends to transfer the physical assets of UES to local business clans at low prices, in exchange for hefty pay-offs to his team. The governors were objecting not to the new redistribution of state property, as such, but they were afraid of being cut out of the action. Foreign investors, chiefly American, who own substantial minority stakes in UES, are also concerned about being cut out. In July 2000, the foreign shareholders even demanded that an extraordinary shareholders' general meeting be convened for the purpose of ousting Chubais and blocking the reform of UES. Alexander Voloshin, the new chairman of the board (and also, at that time, chief of the Presidential Administration), managed to talk the foreign investors out of that idea. Most Kremlin officials continued to support Chubais.

Nonetheless, the story was not over. When it became clear, in 2001-2002, that excessive rate hikes by the natural monopolies were fuelling inflation, the Kremlin and the government insisted on tighter control over rates. The Presidential Administration also wanted to make sure that it could gain control over at least a portion of the relevant financial flows, as the sector was restructured. The practical issue was who would really control the Federal Grid Company, created at the beginning of 2002 to handle the main power transmission networks and associated infrastructure.

The state will eventually have to relinquish control over UES's production units. In early 2003 it emerged that major oligarchical financial groups, including companies belonging to Khodorkovsky, Abramovich, Potanin, Deripaska, and Vekselberg, had already bought up blocking equity stakes in many regional power companies. As for UES proper, the National Reserve Bank's ownership stake had fallen to 4 percent, while the portion directly or indirectly controlled by MDM Bank increased.[7] Foreign investors' ownership of these assets also rose. A 1997 law forbid non-residents from owning more than 25 percent of the shares in UES. De facto foreign ownership was already higher than that level at the time. In 2002, the government decided to eliminate this restriction altogether, and initiated the relevant legislation. According to early 2003 data, the foreign ownership share was estimated at approximately 30 percent. Down the road this may lead to the virtually total privatization of electric power generation. With time, the transmission grid monopoly could also come under private control.

Natural gas

The natural gas company Gazprom was established as a state-owned concern in 1991, before the breakup of the USSR. Upon coming to power, the Gaidar government attempted to hive off its gas-producing units, and transform them into independent joint stock companies that could then be privatized. Chernomyrdin blocked that plan, and it was not revived, despite repeated demands from the World Bank and the International Monetary Fund to break up the natural gas monopoly.

The issue was less the ideological differences between the reformers with their neo-liberal views and the advocates of state intervention in the economy, than the pragmatic question of control over a very lucrative key economic organization. Unlike most other state-owned concerns, Gazprom was an important foreign currency earner from the outset, because of its gas exports to Western Europe, and was one of the government's largest sources of tax revenue. It still is, today. In 1995, natural gas sales abroad accounted for 13.3 percent of Russia's total foreign currency receipts from foreign trade; as of 2003, this share had fallen to 10.3 percent. This level is only slightly less than the proceeds of crude oil exports, which accounted for 15.3 percent of the total in 1995 and 28.6 percent in 2004.[8]

Among major taxpayers, Gazprom remains the leader, despite the fact that other natural monopolies have also become profitable. In 2001, Gazprom paid 263 billion rubles in federal taxes and other collections, much more than UES (61.3 billion rubles). In 2004, Gazprom's tax bill on profit was 79.7 billion rubles, as against only 19.5 billion for UES.[9]

As noted in Chapter 2, over the years Gazprom turned into an independent industrial financial group, with its own banks and other financial institutions. As measured by assets, it was the largest such group, even before its later expansion into oil. This is also the case respecting control over income streams, which totaled 1.0556 trillion rubles in 2004. Gazprom's profit was 389 billion rubles that year. The natural gas monopoly was far ahead of UES in these terms.

It was not difficult for Chernomyrdin to prevail over Gaidar and convince Yeltsin that the natural gas sector should not be divided up. He sought and obtained special privileges for his favorite industry. In 1992, Gazprom received special dispensation to keep 38 percent of its earnings in foreign banks. To a significant extent, this protected its revenue from looting by Russian private banks.[10] That same year, Gazprom established its own bank, Imperial Bank, through which it purchased the East-West United Bank in Luxembourg, from the Bank of Russia (the Central Bank), to handle its accounts abroad.

By Presidential decree the company also acquired control over all participants in the gas sector, as well as licenses for the most promising natural gas deposits. It was granted exclusive rights to export natural gas under government-to-government agreements with other countries. It was exempted from paying duties on its foreign economic operations. The government also pledged to borrow $8.7 billion from foreign lenders to develop the natural gas sector. In November 1992, Gazprom was converted to an RAO, a Russian Joint Stock Company, while its extraction and distribution units became wholly owned subsidiaries. Upon moving to his government post, Chernomyrdin handed control of the monopoly to his close associate Rem Vyakhirev, who was to remain at the head of Gazprom for the next nine years, until 2001.

Soon Chernomyrdin and Vyakhirev conceived a scheme for the privatization of their baby. It made both of them multibillionaires. Under the new arrangement, 40 percent of the shares in Gazprom remained state property, 28.7 percent were sold for privatization vouchers, 15 percent ownership went to Gazprom employees, 5.2 percent to the population of the Yamal-Nenets Autonomous District, and 10 percent of the shares were kept in reserve for sale to foreign investors. The authors of the scheme also secured special directives from the State Property Committee, according to which the Gazprom voucher auctions would be closed and would be held in regions where company facilities were located, and only individuals with residence permits for the regions where the privatization was being conducted could purchase shares. This made it possible to exclude outside banks, companies and wealthy individuals from the auctions. Gazprom was able to maintain tight control over the privatization process. As a result of this operation, at least 40 percent of the shares in Gazprom wound up, directly or indirectly, in the hands of Chernomyrdin, Vyakhirev, and members of their team.

If we take market capitalization as roughly equivalent to total assets (2.3 trillion rubles in 2002), Gazprom management acquired on the order of $23 billion. In 2001, *Forbes* magazine estimated Rem Vyakhirev's personal fortune at $1.5 billion and Chernomyrdin's at $1.1 billion.[11] Earlier, the French daily *Le Monde*, citing CIA information, had suggested a higher figure for Chernomyrdin's wealth: $5 billion. More recent publications give much lower estimates. In early 2005, Vyakhirev's fortune was estimated at only $35 million, and Chernomyrdin did not quite make it onto the list of ruble billionaires.[12]

Fairly early on, de facto spheres of influence were carved out within Gazprom for the top members of Vyakhirev's team, whereby each of them acquired a certain part of the company as his personal fiefdom. Some time later, Gazprom shares began to be withdrawn into separate companies, established either as subsidiaries, or as independent firms.

The largest of these, Itera, was registered in the United States (in Florida) in 1992, as a company dealing in food supplies to Turkmenistan in exchange for exported Turkmen natural gas. The head of Itera, a former competitive cyclist named Igor Makarov, used personal connections in Turkmenistan to obtain the required license. In 1994, Itera contacted Gazprom's deputy CEO, Vyacheslav Sheremet, through whom it obtained permission to use a Gazprom pipeline to supply Turkmen gas to Ukraine. Ties between the two companies gradually expanded, with Gazprom transferring a number of its gas fields to Itera, making the latter the second largest natural gas company in Russia. These ties, which further enriched members of the Vyakhirev clan, came under investigation in 2000.

One of the shadier pages in Gazprom's business history is the creation of two parallel markets for its shares. The terms of Gazprom's privatization prohibited foreign individuals and entities from purchasing its shares inside Russia, where their price was relatively low. The 9-10 percent quota reserved for foreigners was sold through foreign investment banks at almost quadruple the domestic price. Ways around the prohibition were found fairly quickly. An unknown number of "domestic" shares were sold abroad through dummy companies, yielding a tidy profit for their owners and the intermediaries. Exactly who engaged in this business, and how many shares ended up abroad, remained largely unknown. According to some reports in the press, there are indications that Gazprom people were involved in these operations.

In early 1997, a firm called Regent Gaz Investment Company, registered in the Cayman Islands, issued $200 million worth of shares, announcing that they were guaranteed by shares in Gazprom. This was an attempt to resell at foreign prices, Gazprom shares that had been acquired at the domestic price. When the operation came under unwanted public scrutiny, Vyakhirev demanded that the company immediately self-liquidate, which it did, purchasing its own shares. If Gazprom management had not been behind this project, Vyakhirev's demand would not have been implemented with such dispatch.[13]

It was only in 2001-2002, after Vyakhirev's departure, that the issue of uniting the two markets was addressed. A special Gazprom committee took up the matter. It took another three years to resolve it.

In the first several years of its existence, Gazprom was subordinate to nobody, including the government. Premier Chernomyrdin's protection played a part in this state of affairs, as did various favors Gazprom performed for the regime. In June 1996, at the prime minister's request, Gazprom bailed out the Gusinsky (Most) group's NTV television company, which had gotten into financial trouble. Gazprom received an equity stake in NTV, as collateral for the foreign loan Gazprom took out to help NTV. Gusinsky had earned this aid by supporting Yeltsin during the 1996 electoral campaign.

The first attempt at an invasion of Vyakhirev's barony was made by Nemtsov after his appointment as first vice-premier in March 1997. He coaxed Yeltsin, while Chernomyrdin was out of town, into signing a decree abrogating the trust agreement, under which Vyakhirev had the right to manage 35 percent of Gazprom's shares, a part of the stake belonging to the state. But Chernomyrdin restored the status quo, as soon as he returned from leave. Vyakhirev's position remained fairly firm, even after Chernomyrdin's resignation as premier, since Nemtsov and Chubais left the government in March 1998 simultaneously with Vyakhirev's protector. No heavyweights prom. This arrangement was blocked by Igor Sechin of the Presidential Administration, who moved into the position of Rosneft's chairman of the board in July 2004. A new plan then emerged, for Gazprom to acquire the 72 percent of Sibneft's shares, controlled by Abramovich. Upon completion of this deal, which involved financing from a consortium headed by the Dutch bank ABN AMRO, the gas monopoly controls 8 percent of Russian oil production. Together with Rosneft's sharply rising share, the total government-controlled portion of oil production rose to 25 percent, making the state the leading proprietor in this industry. These are all important steps toward the creation of a new oligarchical industrial financial group, subordinate to the Kremlin (see Section 3.3).

Also in 2005, the government acted to increase the state-owned share of Gazprom's voting stock from 38 to 51 percent, thus obtaining absolute control. This also opened the door to proceeding with the long-awaited liberalization of trading in Gazprom shares, which will now be freely available to foreign investors. The concept here was to profit from the company's rising market capitalization, while retaining full control in the hands of the state.

The railroads

Eighty percent of freight shipments in Russia move by rail, and many sectors of the economy depend on the railroads. Rail is the only one of the three biggest natural monopolies that has, until quite recently, undergone only a very small degree of privatization. Essentially, the railroads continued to function as the state institution they used to be under the Soviet system: the Ministry of Railways (MPS). The MPS controlled 17 railroads, (organized primarily according to geographical regions), special freight service organizations, the railroad communications system, the Rosvagonmash production association (producer of rolling stock), the Chineysk ore and Elgin coal deposits (in the Baikal-Amur Mainline, or BAM, zone), Transkreditbank (ranking 32nd among Russian commercial banks in total net assets), the ZhASO insurance company, and several other organizations. The MPS was also given control of the federal government's equity stakes in locomotive production plants. The 17 railroad companies were formally listed as independent self-financing enterprises (and, subsequently, joint stock companies).[16]

For five years, from 1994 to 1999, the MPS had the right to set freight transport and loading/unloading rates. This prerogative was later transferred to a government commission. The rail monopoly's revenue steadily rose. In 2001, it had 304 billion rubles of revenue and 55 billion rubles of net profit from freight shipments alone. (True, around 20 billion rubles had to be spent to subsidize the passenger routes.) These resources, including a depreciation reserve, were enough to finance an 80-billion-ruble investment program in 2000.

For a long time this diversified economic unit was under the personal control of the Railways Minister: first Gennadi Fadeyev, then Nikolai Aksyonenko. Theoretically, MPS revenue was supposed to go directly into the federal budget, but in practice, a substantial part of it remained in the hands of the MPS and was spent for its needs.

The railroads had their share of corruption and violations of financial laws. One category that applies to all state-owned enterprises is officials' use of their positions for personal enrichment. In the case of the MPS, it was a regular practice for railway officials to work simultaneously in related private commercial organizations. Direct corrupt connections of this sort were discovered early on. The guilty parties were punished only lightly and, evidently, retreated "into the shadows."

Other cases of malfeasance had to do with the misappropriation of federal budget funds to subsidize dubious projects. Beginning in 1991, for example, a nationwide joint stock company called High-Speed Railways (or RAO VSM) operated within the MPS. It was supposed to build a high-speed line between St. Petersburg and Moscow. Alexei Bolshakov, who later became a vice-premier in the federal government, was in charge of the project. Ultimately the project was shut down, after costing the budget half a billion dollars, and enriching the subcontractors by the same amount. Among the subcontractors was the Baltic Construction Company, which was co-owned by a nephew of Railways Minister Aksyonenko. This nephew also owned (through a company called Yevrosib) a 24.5 percent stake in Baltic Bank (ranking 45th in net assets), another 49.7 percent of whose shares belonged to the MPS-controlled Oktyabrskaya Railroad. Yevrosib borrowed money from the bank for its purposes, but did not repay it. When Oktyabrskaya Railroad's boss, Anatoli Zaitsev, demanded repayment to the bank, he was fired by the minister.

Private wheeling and dealing of this sort is one thing, but using a ministerial chair to control multibillion-ruble financial flows for purposes of rewarding top management, and other unauthorized spending, takes things to a whole new level. Such behavior may be par for the course in any independent joint stock company, but it was not generally accepted in government institutions. Understanding the distinction, Aksyonenko tried to promote the privatization of the Russian railroads, in order to legalize the creation of essentially his own personal corporation. He failed, and was removed from office in 2002, before reform of the railroads could even get started.

The reform plan has begun to be implemented in the last few years, although private Russian oligarchical groups do not appear to be in a rush to privatize rail. Seizing more profitable sectors, like electric power generation and natural gas production, is higher-priority unfinished business for them.

A three-stage reform is envisioned. First of all, an RAO called Russian Railways has been incorporated, inheriting from the MPS its rail lines, stations, depots, and rolling stock. Up to 25 percent of all haulage is allowed to be done by private companies. In the second stage, passenger transport is to be split off from RAO Russian Railways and no longer subsidized by freight haulage fees. Rail construction and maintenance enterprises are slated for privatization. In a third stage, rail transport would be completely privatized, with RAO Russian Railways remaining responsible only for regulating the haulage market, and for track and right-of-way maintenance.

It is not entirely clear what portion of the national railway company's stock, under this scheme, will remain under government control, and for how long. This not unimportant detail has agitated certain representatives of private capital, such as the RUIE and the Association of Expediters, who complain that, in effect, one state monopoly is being replaced by another, no less tight. It is therefore quite probable that some part of the track and rolling stock will wind up in private hands, after some period of time. Major investment by private capital in the modernization and development of the railroads is unlikely, without transfer of the main fixed assets to private ownership.

Russian Railways remains 100 percent government-owned, but it is clear that its incorporation was only a first step. The company was initially headed by former Railways Minister Fadeyev, but he was replaced in 2005 by Vladimir Yakunin, an official hailing from St. Petersburg who is close to President Putin. Thus the Russian President has continued the practice of keeping the financial flows of major state-owned companies concentrated under his control, as will be discussed in Section 3.3.

3.2 The state and the defense industry

The organization of the defense industry, particularly its penetration by private capital groups, was discussed in Chapter 2. But the great majority of defense enterprises remain government-controlled. It appears that this situation will persist for some time. There are various reasons for this, some of them involving national strategic interests. Another factor is the above-mentioned desire of the federal authorities to retain control over the financial flows that run directly or indirectly through the Ministry of Defense and the defense industry.

Throughout most of the 1990s, the defense industry experienced a deep depression. This crisis was caused by two main factors: first, the overall downturn in the economy and reduction of the financial capabilities of the state; and, secondly, the Yeltsin regime's deliberate policy of reducing the armed forces and defense production. In those years, the federal authorities looked at the MIC as a heavy burden, which should be funded according to the "whatever's left over" principle. Table 3.2 documents what this meant.

As soon as it came to power, Yeltsin's government began to slash military spending. Expressed as a share of GDP, such spending fell from 7 percent in the Soviet Union's last year of existence, to 2.4 percent in 1998. The situation changed somewhat under Primakov and Putin, although not radically. Defense spending as a share of GDP rose only to 2.6 percent in 2001-2004. Because the economy as a whole grew, however, real defense spending approximately doubled. Nonetheless, it remained at only 29 percent of the 1991 level.

Table 3.2 also shows that defense industry output fell by a greater amount than defense spending, though it later recovered somewhat faster. In 2004, after a slight recovery, defense production was at only 33.5 percent of the 1991 level, whereas defense spending

Table 3.2 Defense spending and the defense industry, 1991-2004

	1991	1993	1994	1996	1997	1998	1999	2001	2003	2004
Real GDP, 1991=100	100	71	60	55.5	56.0	53.3	56.2	63.9	71.8	76.9
Defense spending as a portion of GDP, %	7.0%	4.2%	4.7%	3.0%	3.3%	2.4%	2.4%	2.6%	2.6%	2.6%
Real defense spending, 1991=100	100	43	40	24	26	18	19	24	27	29
Defense industry output, 1991=100	100	32.5	19.9	12.8	8.8	9.9	13.9	18.1	32.0	33.5

Sources: RSY, 1998 and 2004; MIC Teleinformation System (League of Defense Enterprises): http://ts.vpk.ru/index_c.htm. USSR data for 1991 have been adjusted for purposes of comparison with subsequent Russian Federation data.

stood at 29 percent of its early-1990s level. The difference was due to changes in the composition of defense spending. In 1990, 44 percent of the defense budget had been allocated for the procurement of weapons and equipment, 19 percent was spent on military R&D, and only 27 percent went for current expenses, including armed services personnel. By 1998, procurement's share had fallen to 19 percent, R&D got 13 percent, and 54 percent went for current expenses. In other words, the defense order had shrunk to 8 percent of its pre-reform level in real terms, deliveries of weapons to the armed forces were pitifully small, and, with a few exceptions, the military was receiving virtually no new-model weapons or military equipment.[17]

When a turnaround began, in 1998, there was some attempt to shift the composition of defense spending. The share of weapons and equipment procurement rose to 20 percent of defense spending in 2000, 24 percent in 2001, and 36 percent in 2004. Measures were taken to reduce the large debt the Ministry of Defense had accumulated to defense producers over the preceding years. Plans were announced to increase the combined share of equipment procurement and military R&D spending, from 30 percent of total defense spending in 2000, to 40 percent in 2005, and 50 percent in 2010.[18]

But that would still be less than the 1991 level of spending for these purposes, which was 62 percent of the total. It should be noted that a new factor here is the intention to transform the Armed Forces into professional organizations by the end of the decade, which implies a higher level of spending on service personnel salaries than in the past or at present.

Despite increases in the defense order during the last few years, the government continued to limit spending to equip the Armed Forces with new military technology. Until 2007-2008, the bulk of increased spending was slated to go into the development of new types of weaponry, with mass production of the new models and delivery of them to the Armed Forces kicking in only after that point. The assumption was that by that time, there would have been an improvement in the overall economic situation, and federal budget funding possibilities would be greater.

In the immediate years ahead, exports will remain a major source of orders for the defense industry.

Arms exports dropped sharply in comparison with the Soviet period (Table 3.3). In the record year of 1987, the Soviet Union had exported $29 billion worth of weapons and military equipment, much more than the United States. Of course, Soviet allies and other friendly countries were the recipients of the greater part of those exports, which by and large were provided free of charge or on credit, and did not earn much foreign currency revenue. Arms shipments abroad continued during the 1990s, and were now paid for in hard currency, but the total volume increased only slowly. After 1996, it fluctuated between $3.5 billion and $4.5 billion, representing 4-4.6 percent of total national export earnings. In 2004, it reached $5.2 billion.

Although selling weapons abroad yields much less foreign currency revenue than oil or gas exports do, the earnings are under more direct government control. This area of business became even more profitable after the devaluation of the ruble in 1998-1999. As of 2005, ruble-denominated arms exports were surpassed by Ministry of Defense procurement.

Exactly how arms export earnings are divided among defense enterprises, state agencies, and other middlemen is classified information. It is believed that, since Putin came to power, these financial streams have come under tighter control by persons directly subor-

Table 3.3 Arms exports compared with defense spending

	1994	1997	1998	1999	2000	2001	2004
Arms exports, billions of $	1.7	3.6	2.7	3.5	3.7	4.4	5.2
Arms exports, billions of rubles	3.7	20.8	26.9	86.9	104.2	128.7	150.8
Defense spending, billions of rubles	28.5	81.4	65.1	115.6	188.1	214.7	413.7
Domestic weapons procurement, billions of rubles	5.9	16.3	12.1	22.1	38.5	52.0	148.0
Exports as % of defense spending	13.0%	25.6%	41.3%	75.2%	55.4%	59.9%	36.5%
Exports as % of domestic procurement	62.7%	127.6%	222.3%	393.2%	270.6%	247.5%	101.9%

dinate to the Presidential Administration. Expressed in rubles, they are now equivalent to about 40 percent of the Ministry of Defense budget, but they are not part of it. Thus, they could serve as an important supplementary source of financing for the Armed Forces and the defense industry. Not surprisingly, the government is counting on their continued increase, to an annual level of at least $6 billion. To achieve this level will require developing the competitiveness of Russian weapons, especially military aircraft, ships, tanks and anti-aircraft systems, in comparison with the products of other exporters—the United States and Europe. New markets will have to be conquered, in addition to the two main ones, China and India. Russia will have to compete not only in prices, but also in qualitative military-technical parameters, which means the modernization of models produced for export. This, in turn, will divert limited available resources from the development of fundamentally new types of weapons for Russia's own Armed Forces.

Yet the latter task, the creation of new weapons systems, is a priority. This is the case not only due to the obsolescence of existing military equipment, which has essentially not been upgraded for more than a decade. It is also urgent because the United States, since the election of George W. Bush, has moved to build up its strategic strike power, and to construct a nationwide missile defense system of the type previously banned under the 1972 Soviet-American ABM Treaty. These developments have forced Russia to increase the production of weapons and military equipment, especially in key areas of strategic defense and the creation of new military technology.

In 1999-2002, for example, while the share of the Strategic Missile Corps (SMC) in the defense order fell from 40 percent to 18 percent,[19] spending for the SMC increased from 10 billion to 14 billion rubles in absolute terms. A significant portion of this spending goes to the space forces, which are responsible for servicing and developing the country's limited anti-missile systems, as well as, chiefly, the further modernization of the Global Orbital Satellite Navigation System (GLONASS), on which the development of more precise Russian nuclear and conventional weapons depends.[20] The continuing program to equip the SMC with land-based mobile Topol-M ICBMs also requires major spending, as does arming Russia's Tu-160 heavy bombers with new high-precision air-to-surface cruise missiles.[21]

But the need to upgrade Russia's strategic and space forces runs into competition for resources from the Ground Forces, the Navy, and the Air Force. Minister of Defense Sergei Ivanov has said, for example, that the transformation of just one Army division from its current conscript basis into a professional force (as called for in military reform plans) will cost 2-2.5 billion rubles.[22] Extended to the entire Armed Forces, the switch to a professional service would mean no less than 60-70 billion rubles. Ivanov has indicated that this spending will have to be stretched out over a good ten years.

Design and production of the "fifth generation" fighter aircraft that the Air Force needs will also be costly. The project is estimated at a minimum of 300 billion rubles,[23] more than the entire defense budget for 2002.

Under these circumstances, the limited resources allocated for defense and the defense industry are an extremely urgent issue. The Ministry of Defense does not control, for example, revenue from arms exports, although, as we have seen, their nominal value is greater than what the ministry is able to spend on the procurement of weapons and military equipment. Under existing law, it is prohibited to spend these resources to cover Ministry of Defense needs. They could become an important supplemental source of financing for the Armed Forces and the defense industry. But several obstacles would have to be overcome in order for this to happen.

First of all, it is not known exactly how these funds are allocated and used. Ivanov has said that the net annual income from arms exports, after deduction of the cost of production, and administrative and marketing overhead, was on the order of $500 million, or 15 billion rubles, as of 2002. If the same composition is assumed for 2004, that figure would increase to 20 billion rubles. Part goes into capital investment, but a substantial remainder is spent for non-military purposes. The defense minister believes that these funds should be used to augment spending on procurement of weapons and military equipment. With this additional margin, the government defense order could be substantially increased.

Moreover, arms exports are proportioned differently from the structure of procurement for the Russian Armed Forces, the latter being what military men consider optimal. The great majority of planes, naval ships, tanks, surface-to-air missile systems, and other types of armaments, delivered to China and India, are old models that have been in production for years. As a rule, they do not include the modern armaments that the Russian Armed Forces need for the years ahead. But it is more profitable for defense enterprises to produce the older models and sell them abroad, than to fulfill new weapons orders from the Ministry of Defense. As Ivanov put it, the defense industry "is not developing in the direction the state requires."[24]

Strategic weapons (both offensive and defensive) and space systems, for example, are produced only for use by Russia. It would make no sense to produce them for export. But they cannot compete, in profitability and financial attractiveness, with technically simpler and strategically less important weapons that are eagerly purchased abroad.

Lastly, the foreign currency earnings from arms exports are very unevenly divided among the enterprises working on export contracts and subcontracts. It frequently happens that scientific research institutes (NII) working on the development of important, sometimes even essential, components of state-of-the-art military technology do not receive adequate funding for their work, although these are top-priority military projects.

The scientific production association (NPO) Almaz, for example, has specialized for many years in the design and production of surface-to-air missiles (SAMs), which overlap the development of anti-missile systems. The S-300PMU system (designated SA-10 by the U.S./NATO), developed by Almaz, is considered one of the best in the world. Worldwide sales of this product have totalled around $1 billion. During seven years of such sales, the Almaz NPO received only $2 million, although as the system's developer it had been promised 3 percent of the sales revenue, or $30 million. At the same time, it was working on the Ministry of Defense order for the more advanced S-400 (SA-X-20) system. The new project was clearly underfunded, forcing Almaz to use its own resources to keep the work going. If the NPO had received the $30 million due it from the proceeds of S-300PMU exports, work on the new system would long since have been completed. Instead, this needed, top-priority state project was not finished on schedule.[25]

At defense enterprises that are less involved with export subcontracts than Almaz is, the financial situation is naturally even worse. The Applied Mechanics NII, for example, develops inertial guidance systems, used in practically all Russian ballistic missiles, satellites, and the International Space Station. These systems are also essential for the development and modernization of the GLONASS system, which the Ministry of Defense has made one of its top priorities. Yet the NII's director, Alexander Mezentsev, reports that this work is financed literally with crumbs: "Several research centers in the RF, including our institute, are working on the development of micromechanical inertial transducers, but unfortunately they are not only not coordinated through a federal program; they also receive practically no funding. If serious efforts are not made to correct this situation in the near future, Russia will fall hopelessly behind in technological progress, and will also be driven out of the inertial guidance systems market by cheap imports with integrated GPS systems (Global Positioning System, the American equivalent of GLONASS), built using microelectromechanical systems (MEMS). I hope that military readers will understand that these are the systems used in high-precision weapons, 'smart' bombs, etc., so nobody is going to sell us these systems. The manufacture of gyroscopic instruments is likewise a matter of national security."[26]

The irrational way in which export earnings are used also promotes fierce competition among state-owned enterprises for the role of general contractor when foreign orders are received. This competitive process involves high-ranking government officials, regional governors, who have an interest in tax revenue from enterprises in their areas, and under-the-table extra payments to local authorities. A conflict of this sort flared up between the Sukhoy OKB and the Komsomolsk-on-Amur Aircraft Factory, which formally is part of the holding company headed by Sukhoy, but wanted to act as the lead enterprise on a contract to supply China with fighter planes for $1.5 billion. The matter was initially settled by the government in favor of the Komsomolsk-on-Amur Aircraft Factory. In March 2002, however, Prime Minister Kasyanov changed his mind and gave the deal to Sukhoy. Khabarovsk Territory Governor Victor Ishayev lodged a protest. In another case, the government rewarded a contract to sell destroyers to China for $1.5 billion, shifting it from one St. Petersburg company to another: first Baltic Factory, then Severnaya Verf.[27]

The upper echelons of the executive branch of government have consistently gotten involved in the battles over the assignment of defense orders. Under Yeltsin, Prime Minister Chernomyrdin locked up control over this process. When Primakov was prime minister, Vice-Premier Maslyukov became involved. Upon Putin's assuming office, the entire arms-export bureaucracy was reformed, with officials personally loyal to the President assuming the top positions. Former Prime Minister Kasyanov, who had initially been effectively barred from involvement in these matters, was able to take revenge by demoting Ilya Klebanov, who was in charge of the defense sector, from vice-premier to mere minister, while Kasyanov took over his defense industry duties. Later the area was put under control of the newly created Federal Industry Agency, under Minister of Industry and Energy Khristenko. But Putin loyalists in Rosoboronexport (the government monopoly for arms exports, formerly Rosvooruzheniye) effectively have a larger say on such matters.

It is understandable, why so many people have staked out an interest in trying to control the foreign currency cash flows of defense industry enterprises. Regardless of whether these enterprises are state-owned, semi-state-owned, or private, they all are independent entities for accounting purposes, meaning that their flows of funds, except for tax payments, are outside of the state budget. In other words, there is no direct government supervision of how they are spent. God Himself has commanded, as the saying goes, that people fight for pieces of that pie.

3.3 The state sector: the Kremlin oligarchical group, and some conclusions

The traditional role of the state sector in a capitalist economy is to promote the development of areas of the economy that are beyond the capability of the private sector to handle efficiently. At the same time, the state may assume responsibility for low-profit or loss-making industries, if it would be against the national interest to abandon them altogether. In either case, the state sector's role is seen as temporary, preparatory to the transfer of the relevant enterprises to private hands, as soon as is feasible.

Late 20th-century capitalism in Russia was heir to a system, in which the state sector dominated the entire economy, and in many branches of industry was the only game in town. Therefore, one of the top priorities for the capitalist state that came into existence along with this economic system, was to transfer the state sector to private ownership: privatization. In most industries this objective was achieved by handing state property to new owners at far below its true value. Exceptions were the natural monopolies, the defense industry, to some extent, and several other relatively small segments of the economy.

As we have seen, the vector for the natural monopolies has been pointed in the same direction: toward their eventual conversion to private property. At the same time, the creation of a "free market" was supposed to be on the agenda for these sectors. That would mean releasing prices from government regulation. The final outcome of such changes would be that prices of the goods and services provided by the natural monopolies would rise to levels comparable with world prices. The gap between domestic and world prices would be eliminated.

In the defense industry these processes were camouflaged, but they were essentially the same. The objective was to hand the most profitable niches over to the private sector, leaving the government encumbered only with things that were of no direct interest to private capital.

From the standpoint of political economy, this means far-reaching changes in the formation and distribution of total surplus value. If means of production are transferred to private control on a huge scale, this substantially expands the area in which surplus value is produced. At the same time, changes occur in how this surplus value is distributed and appropriated.

As discussed in Chapter 1, superprofit from export-oriented sectors comprises a significant part of total surplus value. In the extractive industries this surplus value is called natural rent. It is appropriated through a certain niche, formed as a result of the discrepancy between domestic and world prices.

Now, imagine that as a result of reforming the natural monopolies and closely associated sectors, such as the oil industry, the gap between domestic and world prices were minimized and, taking transport fees, export duties, and other charges into account, essentially disappeared. Would this mean that today's superprofit would also disappear?

To simplify the analysis, we shall assume that, at current price levels, the export-oriented sectors derive superprofit only from sales abroad, whereas the profit they earn inside the country is at the general, "normal," or average level. From the standpoint of foreign countries, this means that the Russian economy is largely subsidized by its export sectors, enjoying a certain advantage over foreign competitors due to artificially low costs of production. If the price gap were to be eliminated, the superprofit deriving from that difference in prices would disappear, as would this covert form of support for other domestic producers.

In reality, however, surplus value—including superprofit—is created not on the basis of a gap between domestic and world prices, but rather, with transport and marketing overhead taken into account, from the difference between the domestic costs of production, and the prices of sale. If selling prices inside Russia draw level with world prices, the superprofit will not only not decline, but will rise, since domestic purchasers will be forced to pay the ruble equivalent of export prices. We assume that the costs of production will not rise to the same extent as sales prices, since the costs of production are determined by prices for the output of other domestic sectors, which will inevitably grow more slowly than prices for the output of export-oriented sectors.

Gazprom, for example, calculates that natural gas prices should rise at an annual rate of 35-40 percent, if the overall rate of inflation is 10-15 percent. This means that if, hypothetically, the domestic price, being roughly equivalent to the cost of production, were initially $15 for 1,000 cubic meters of gas, then in, say, four years the price of gas would rise to $45, while the cost of producing it would reach only $22. In other words, profit on total domestic gas sales would grow at the rate of $23 per 1,000 cubic meters, or over $9 billion (almost 300 billion rubles).[28] For comparison, official data for 2003 showed the entire sector's net profit as 25 billion rubles,[29] or far, far less than its anticipated growth in the event of price "equalization." The total growth of superprofit, as a result of a chain reaction of price levelling on products of the export-oriented sectors, would be measured in tens of billions of dollars, or over 1 trillion rubles, which was on the order of 6 percent of Russia's GDP in 2004. (As of early 2006, global inflationary processes have driven the actual export prices charged by Gazprom for natural gas to levels an order of magnitude above the prices used in this example, but the principle holds.)

Such a shift could not fail to have a substantial impact on the national economy. Obviously, the increased natural rent would have to be paid by energy-consuming sectors (that is, by the economy as a whole) and the population, so it could be seen as an enormous tax increase, in favor of the fuel and energy complex, on the profit of all other sectors of the economy, plus an additional direct deduction from the personal disposable funds of the population. The economy and the population would be able to pay these two "taxes," only if the total profit of the energy-consuming sectors and the disposable income of the population were to increase by at least the magnitude of these "taxes."

This latter condition could only become possible, if there were a fairly high rate of economic growth, and if energy prices were raised fairly slowly. Yet, more expensive fuel and electricity in and of themselves will retard economic growth, for the following reasons: (1) profit in the energy-consuming sectors will fall, reducing the resources they have available for capital investment; (2) the real income of the population will decline, reducing demand for personal consumption goods and services. Moreover, increased superprofit in the energy sector does not guarantee a higher rate of capital investment, even in that sector. On the contrary, one of the fundamental disproportions within the Russian economy will be amplified, namely, the capital accumulation glut in the fuel and energy complex and other extractive industries, as a whole, and the deficit of resources for capital investment in other sectors of the economy. We shall explore this problem in more depth in subsequent chapters.

Another important shift that took place in recent years is the expansion of the state sector into the oil industry. First, the state-owned company Rosneft took over Yuganskneftegaz, which had belonged to Yukos. Then the state-controlled Gazprom acquired a controlling stake in Sibneft, previously owned by Abramovich. As a result of these acquisitions, the weight of the state sector in the oil industry rose in 2005-2006 from 5 percent, to 25 percent.

At the same time, a group of companies from the oil and natural gas industries, as well as several institutions and companies in other sectors of the economy, were placed under direct control of the Presidential Administration, through the appointment of persons who are either directly subordinate to Putin, or personally loyal to him. At Gazprom, for example, besides CEO Alexei Miller, there is Dmitri Medvedev as chairman of the board of directors, with his simultaneous top posts in first the Presidential Administration and then the government. Presidential Administration Deputy Chief Igor Sechin became chairman of the board of directors of Rosneft in 2004. Even earlier, close Putin loyalists assumed the top executive positions at Rosoboronexport. Another deputy chief of the Presidential Administration, Victor Ivanov, became chairman of the board of directors of the major missile producer Almaz-Antey. Two other top Kremlin operatives, Vladislav Surkov and Sergei Prikhodko, moved into this same post at Aeroflot (earlier controlled by Berezovsky) and Transneft (owner of the entire Russian oil pipeline network), respectively.

Vneshtorgbank, the second largest state-owned commercial bank, met the same fate, with Putin loyalists from the Bank of Russia coming onto its board. Vneshtorgbank helped to finance Rosneft's purchase of Yuganskneftegaz. In 2004, Vneshtorgbank bought up the nearly bankrupt Guta Bank, one of Russia's 20 largest private banks.

Through Gazprom, Putin was able to maximize Kremlin control over the country's three main TV channels, ORT-Channel 1, RTR, and NTV, as well as to acquire from Potanin control over the prominent daily newspaper *Izvestia*.

Also in 2005, Rosoboronexport and Vneshtorgbank acquired a controlling stake in Russia's top automobile company, AvtoVAZ.

Thus a special, Kremlin group of major state-owned companies is taking shape. They are controlled by the President and officials close to him. This group is quite distinct from certain other state-owned companies, which might be called "the Chubais group" (RAO UES), as well as from state-owned companies led by other clans within the bureaucracy.

Summing up the sales of Gazprom, Rosneft, Yuganskneftegaz and Sibneft, plus AvtoVAZ, arms and diamonds exports, we obtain total financial flows of $76 billion. The combined assets of Vneshtorgbank, Gazprombank, and Guta Bank total $29 billion. Combined, these two amounts represent around one-fifth of Russia's GDP.

For such incalculable political and enormous economic power to be concentrated in the hands of so few people, runs counter to hopes for the democratization of the country and any fair redistribution of the national wealth. Of course, control over financial flows is not the same thing as controlling one's own personal property. Nonetheless, this is certainly a step toward the personal enrichment of yet another group of highly placed officials, led by the President, and their transformation into multimillionaires.

3.4 Millionaires and managers

The traditional division of the ruling capitalist elite into two categories, millionaires and managers, developed when free competition capitalism turned into monopoly capitalism. As large monopolies and banks emerged, an elite layer of the very wealthiest property owners emerged within the capitalist class. It was comprised of those who controlled these concerns, banks and financial groups. At the same time, a layer of elite professional managers was formed. They were the people, without whom it would be impossible for the wealthy to manage and control these empires profitably. Partly for natural reasons (the founders of the empires, who were both owners and managers, gradually died off), but for other reasons as well, such as the necessity of giving the managers some property of their own, top-level managers were gradually integrated into the wealthiest elite layer of the capitalist class. The managers became partners and co-owners with their previous bosses, and their income reached levels comparable to that of the wealthiest families. This happened in the United States, in Europe, and in Japan, with slight variations in the pattern in each country. In some instances a category of high-ranking government officials and military officers was also co-opted into the ruling elite. Elsewhere, wealthy families may have achieved their status not exclusively through capitalist accumulation, but sometimes by expanding fortunes inherited from the old landed aristocracy.[30]

In the new capitalist countries that arose during the second half of the 20th century, such as in Southeast Asia, the capitalist elite was based on state-owned concerns, which functioned as monopolies. As these concerns were privatized, an elite layer of former state officials, associated with them, became wealthy managers and property owners. The evolution of South Korea's chaebols (industrial-banking conglomerates) is a classic example of this type of transformation.

The Russian capitalist elite differs from these two types, in that it developed almost exclusively by appropriating state property. The wealthiest property owners emerged from the ranks of former shadow economy kingpins, who initially accumulated a certain amount of capital within the Soviet planned economy, and from among the managers of state-owned enterprises, who, as we have seen, were able to grab controlling stakes in those companies as they were privatized, thus becoming their owners.

The new Russian capitalism is too young, historically, for large hereditary fortunes to play a prominent role. In the old capitalist countries, the holders of these family fortunes more often than not have abandoned direct control over their empires and exert control only through a layer of trusted managers. Insofar as there are instances of absentee ownership in Russia, they take the form of individual oligarchs (like Berezovsky), who have been forced to take up residence abroad for political reasons.

In order to determine the division of the Russian business elite by type, we shall use a list of 100 individuals, categorized by *Dengi* (*Money*) weekly as upper-echelon managers in late 2001.[31] It should be noted from the outset, that the list includes both managers proper, and multimillionaire property owners who serve as executives of their own companies. The criterion for inclusion on the list was the size of the financial flows under the person's control (company earnings), based on expert estimates of the portion of the company's revenue, controlled by that particular person. Such estimates can be imprecise, but what is of interest to us here is not so much the size of the funds involved, as the list itself, which is a fairly representative sample of the upper-echelon business elite. This list is restricted to the non-financial sectors of the economy and does not include bank managers.

Without reproducing the entire list, we may divide it into three groupings within the Russian business elite: (1) primarily multimillionaire property owners, who serve as executives at the same time as they exert overall control over their companies; (2) managers who hold top executive positions in a company and are on a par with the millionaire property owners with respect to status and influence, but do not have comparable personal fortunes (Category 1 managers); (3) managers who play a significant role in their companies, but are clearly subordinate to individuals in the first two groupings (Category 2 managers).

Of course, lists of this sort become outdated, since people move from one company to another, or lose their key positions. What interests us here is not the individuals, but their approximate distribution among the three groups. This type of distribution, as a rule, changes slowly, over years, though abrupt exceptions, caused by events like the Yukos case, are possible. In several instances *Dengi's* estimates of the absolute size and the portion of financial flows controlled by various people in 2001 were debatable. The roles of Khodorkovsky, Abramovich, Deripaska, Potanin, Fridman, Mordashov, Vekselberg, and several other oligarchs were clearly understated in these data. Nonetheless, it is possible to distinguish and compare the groups. These particular financial statistics should be considered in the broader context of all the available data about the oligarchical groups at that point in time, what the position was of the various people on the list, what their personal fortunes were, and so forth.

The list of the 100 influential people in Russia's non-banking business elite included 37 property owners, 43 Category 1 managers, and 20 Category 2 managers.

The first conclusion we can draw is that Russian property owners, as a rule, prefer to manage their own companies. Looking specifically at the multimillionaires on the list, we find, first of all, that many of them were from the industrial financial groups, the oligarchical groups, discussed above in this chapter and in Chapter 2: Vagit Alekperov, Mikhail Khodorkovsky, Vladimir Bogdanov, Alexei Mordashov, Roman Abramovich, Vladimir Potanin, Mikhail Fridman, Oleg Deripaska, Vladimir Lisin, Iskander Makhmudov, Victor Vekselberg, Alexander Abramov. Secondly, there were leaders or co-owners of other major groups and conglomerates, which did not rank among the handful of very top oligarchical groups: Kakha Bendukidze (OMZ), Valeri Otchertsev (Itera), Alexander Fain (Alfa-Eco), Vladimir Yevtushenkov (Sistema), Alisher Usmanov (Gazprominvestholding), David Yakobashvili (Wimm-Bill-Dann). The category was filled out by some smaller multimillionaires, who control their own companies, but those companies are of regional, rather than national significance, though their annual turnover approaches that of the larger conglomerates.

The Category 1 managers were fairly diverse. Particularly prominent in 2001—and this remains the case—were leaders of the natural monopolies, as well as of smaller state-controlled companies that play a role in natural monopoly-dominated sectors. Notable among them were Alexei Miller (Gazprom), Anatoli Chubais (UES), Sergei Bogdanchikov (Rosneft), Mikhail Gutseriyev (then-President of Slavneft), Vyacheslav Shtyrov (top manager at the Alrosa diamonds company at the time), Alexei Ogaryov (Rosvooruzheniye), Semyon Vainshtok (Transneft), Mikhail Pogosian (Sukhoy), Valeri Benkov (Severnaya Verf), Vladimir Simonov (Antey), Yuri Semyonov (Energiya), Alexander Medvedev (Khrunichev State Research and Production Space Center), Vladimir Alexandrov (Admiralty Shipyards), Oleg Shulyakovsky (Baltic Factory), and Konstantin Ernst (ORT). These "state managers" form one of the largest groups among Category 1 managers.

The degree of independence "state managers" enjoy from the government that appointed them depends on the specific circumstances. Formally they are all elected by their boards of directors, on which government representatives do not always constitute a majority. Even when they do, the incorporation papers of a given joint stock company may require a three-fourths majority vote to oust the company president. That is what happened with Vyakhirev, whom Putin's government was unable to dismiss from Gazprom right away. Chubais initially managed to institute a similar rule at

UES. Although the three-fourths requirement was later lifted, Chubais was able to keep his job by skillful maneuvering, despite opposition to him in the upper echelons of the regime, and complaints from foreign shareholders in UES.

Miller, appointed to replace Vyakhirev at the helm of Gazprom, encountered stiff resistance from the previous team of top executives, and had to expend much time and effort to consolidate his control over the company. The chief factor in Miller's favor was his close association with Putin, who personally moved him into this job, from the less significant post of deputy minister of fuel and energy.

Putin also called the shots in the appointment of a new team of top managers at Rosvooruzheniye, as the key agency for MIC exports was called at the time. The creation of new holding companies and appointment of their executives are done within the MIC by Presidential decree, often against the will of the government agencies directly responsible for the sector. It also took the intervention of the Presidential Administration, to establish government control over the leading television company, ORT-Channel 1.

In most cases, the independence of the "state managers" extends only to day-to-day decisions, and they serve at the pleasure of the country's top leadership. With rare exceptions, their subordinate status is quite apparent. In that respect, they are quite different from the millionaire property owners, whom it is extremely difficult for the government to dislodge, and attempts to do so are made only in extremis. In the case of Berezovsky, even exile abroad did not immediately end his control of a number of leading newspapers and publishing houses. The regime was more successful in depriving him of control over TV-6, as it also was in essentially liquidating Gusinsky's media holding company. In the case of Yukos and Khodorkovsky, the state took extreme measures, jailing the oligarch and his top partner, and effectively bankrupting his main company with disproportionately large demands for back tax payments. But the removal of "state managers" who do not suit the highest state authorities is relatively easy.

Yakov Goldovsky, for example, was president of Sibur petrochemicals company, a subsidiary of Gazprom, when Vyakhirev still headed the latter. Taking advantage of his close personal ties to people in the Gazprom leadership, Goldovsky obtained credits from Gazprom and associated banks, which he then used to buy shares in

Sibur. When Miller replaced Vyakhirev, he found that Sibur's assets had effectively been removed from Gazprom's control. But since Sibur's debts to Gazprom and the other creditors had not been paid, Miller was able to reassert control over the would-be breakaway subsidiary, and secure the arrest and dismissal of Goldovsky for his attempted swindle. It should be noted that Goldovsky ranks high on the *Dengi* list, in 25th place, since at the time the list was compiled, he was viewed as essentially the owner of Sibur, controlling 65 percent of its financial flows. But even with this degree of control, it proved not very difficult to oust him. Although the formal criteria of cash flow volume placed him above, say, the de facto owner of the Novolipetsk Metallurgical Combine Vladimir Lisin, who ranked 28th, we would classify Goldovsky as having been a "state manager," since he was part of the state-controlled Gazprom empire.

The removal of "state managers" frequently involves a collision of interests among various clans in and around the government. In 2002, for example, there was an effort to remove Gutseriyev as president of Slavneft. It would seem to have been a straightforward matter, since the Russian government owned 75 percent of the shares in Slavneft, as against Gutseriyev's 4 percent.[32] Premier Kasyanov ordered the appointment of a new president for Slavneft: Yuri Sukhanov, who was rumored to be close to Sibneft's owner, Abramovich. At that point, however, Sukhanov found himself the target of a criminal prosecution for embezzlement. The case involved the systematic understatement of the sale price of exported oil, creating a margin of "gray" profit, part of which was appropriated by a group within the company's management. Then one Anatoli Baranovsky turned up as acting president of Slavneft; Baranovsky had the support of the government of Belarus, which held an 11 percent stake in Slavneft, as well as that of an even more important patron, Mezhprombank, in which the principals were siloviki (uniformed service men, in this case mainly former FSB officers), hailing from St. Petersburg and close to President Putin, and the banker Sergei Pugachov. They temporarily took over the company, rumors of Kasyanov's imminent resignation began to circulate, and the appointment of a new head of Slavneft was left hanging. Pavel Borodin, executive secretary of the Russia-Belarus union, weighed in on Baranovsky's side.[33] Ultimately, Kasyanov and his allies prevailed. In late 2002, the company was sold to Sibneft, which was allied with TNK.

At stake in the case of Slavneft was a company capitalized at $500 million, with an annual financial turnover of $1.3 billion. Mezhprombank, for its part, was Russia's fifth-ranking bank in assets at the beginning of 2003, and ranked third among the private commercial banks.

As we saw in our look at the concentration of capital in various branches of industry, competitors frequently succeeded in driving out even the legal owners of major companies. Anatoli Bykov, the biggest shareholder in the KrAZ, ended up behind bars, while another aluminum magnate, Mikhail Zhivilo, was forced to emigrate (see Chapter 2).

Nonetheless, as long as such managers keep their jobs, the economic power inherent in their control of monetary flows can be comparable to, or even exceed, the economic power of the millionaire property owners. And their influence is not measured in the size of the relevant income streams alone. The real role of Chubais, for example, extends far beyond his position as head of one of the natural monopolies, because of his political connections. The role electricity plays throughout the economy is also relevant. On the basis of this economic fact, it has been possible for him to build networks of influence in various regions, as well as in the upper echelons of power in Moscow.

Another layer of Category 1 managers is made up of executives of companies that belong to the private-sector oligarchs. Simon Kukes, the former president of TNK, is one example. Others include Sibneft president Yevgeni Shvidler; Boris Kuzyk, general director of New Programs and Conceptions; Taymuraz Bolloyev, president of Baltika Breweries; and Maxim Boyko, president of Video International. There were only six such managers in the *Dengi* top 100 for 2001. The simple reason for this is that, for the time being, the oligarch property owners prefer to run their own major companies. Exceptions occur when one of them has several such companies, making it difficult to serve as chief executive in several places at once, or when an owner prefers to recruit a highly skilled professional in the relevant industry as his top manager.

As a rule, hired managers of this type rarely speak as public personalities in their own right, deferring to the oligarch owners of the companies they manage. In a few cases, however, they have begun to play an independent role. Oilmen Kukes and Shvidler, for instance, took part from time to time in meetings with Kasyanov when he was prime minister, on the matter of joint actions with OPEC to restrict oil exports. Khodorkovsky, when he was head of Yukos, and Bogdanov of Surgutneftegaz preferred to take part in such high-level meetings in person, whereas the bosses of Kukes and Shvidler (Fridman and Abramovich, at the time) stayed away from them.

Another group of managers consists of the leaders of companies that are not part of any major oligarchic group, but function as relative independents. Though these executives do own shares in their companies, their stakes tend to be insufficiently large for them to control the company or step up into the category of property owner. This is a fairly uncommon category, since in the majority of companies where managers dominate, they have long since become the owners.

Members of this category who figured in the *Dengi* 100 included Vladimir Kadannikov, chairman of the board of AvtoVAZ, and the general director of the Magnitogorsk Metallurgical Combine (MMK), Victor Rashnikov. Although we have identified MMK as a component of the Yevrazholding FPG (Alexander Abramov), the relationship is really more of an alliance or partnership, than one of control. In the most recent period, Rashnikov has been identified as belonging to the category of billionaire property owners. As for AvtoVAZ, we noted in Chapter 2 that its independence resulted from successfully balancing between various attempts by outside forces to take it over. The basis for preserving this independence was the large equity stake controlled by top management. They maintained this control not so much through direct shareholding, as by a system of overlapping ownership in AvtoVAZ, AVVA, and AFK. In 2001, top management owned only 10 percent of AvtoVAZ's common stock, with a total value of $70 million. In early 2005, not long before he retired from AvtoVAZ, Kadannikov's personal fortune was estimated at $190 million. In other words, although Kadannikov and his close associates became very wealthy, their personal fortunes were substantially smaller than those of the oil company managers.

Finally, the third category includes people who were either second-rank managers in large corporations, but subordinates of Category 1 managers or owners, or managers of relatively small companies, in which they were not the most prominent personalities. In this category were Leonid Melamed and Vitali Savelyev, the second-ranking executives at UES and Gazprom, respectively; Ravil Maganov, number two at Lukoil; Alexander Bulygin, the first deputy general director of Russian Aluminum; and others of this type.

These Category 2 managers undoubtedly play a great role in their companies. They also have no small influence on other firms they deal with, as well as on regional and local governments. But it is also beyond any doubt that they are subordinate to owners and to Category 1 managers. They occupy a lower rung in the hierarchy of the Russian business elite.

Unfortunately, it is not yet accepted practice in Russia to publish data on the salaries and other personal income of top managers, which is a mandatory requirement, for example, for companies listed on U.S. stock exchanges. Their income from their basic salaries, bonuses, and stock options can only be guessed. Chubais refused to reveal the compensation he receives, even when the question came from UES shareholders. But it did come out in the press that his annual salary as head of UES was on the order of $350,000.[34]

The theory we put forward in *Millionaires and Managers* about executive income, based on U.S. data, was that upper-echelon managers' income should be approximately equal to that of an independent capitalist who heads a corporation of approximately the same size. The idea is that managerial skills, combined with capital from an outside investor, are equivalent to the additional capital that an investor would have needed, to earn a comparable rate of profit. In other words, a senior executive's income is equal to the potential profit from the capitalization, so to speak, of his management abilities. A hired executive has to be paid as much as he would be able to earn, if he established his own business.

This pattern is borne out, of course, only if there is a fairly well-developed market of executive talent, relative freedom to move from one company to another, and the possibility of raising outside capital to found one's own business. This market is underdeveloped in Russia, but the pattern shows up in its own way.

First of all, the managers who ended up in charge of privatized enterprises in Russia themselves became the controlling owners, expropriating power over the companies from the broader shareholder base. Secondly, there have been cases of managers becoming owners, and vice versa. Boris Jordan, who began his business career in Russia as the representative of a foreign bank, subsequently founded his own financial and investment company (in partnership with other owners), then became a top executive of Gazprom-media, and, finally, joined a group of investors who attempted to acquire NTV television.

The transformation of managers into private shareholders through the acquisition of stock options, a widespread practice in the West, has barely begun in Russia. The options system gives a company's executives the right to buy its shares at a fixed, usually discounted price. The difference between the market price and the discounted price represents extra income for the manager, on top of his regular salary and bonuses.

UES was a pioneer of stock options in Russia. In the spring of 2002, UES developed a program for awarding stock shares to several thousand managers at its subsidiaries, the regional and local electric power utilities, which are supposed to become independent in the course of reform. These managers received the right to purchase shares in their companies, as two- to three-year options. Five percent of the shares in each subsidiary were reserved for this program. The total value of the regional company shares involved was $240 million, or approximately $3-5 million for each subsidiary. In addition, a decision was announced to distribute 1 percent of the shares in the UES parent company to 400 of its executives. Each manager was to receive an equity stake worth approximately $250,000, for a total of $100 million. This program was initiated by Chubais, whose idea was to give the managers a personal stake in reforming UES in such a way, that the market capital value of the head company and regional subsidiaries alike would rise substantially.[35]

This scheme is of interest not only in and of itself, but also as an illustration of current pay levels for top executives at one of the country's major corporations. In order to acquire a $250,000 equity stake in the course of three years, a manager would have to have at least $83,000 available out of his annual income. If we assume that he would purchase the shares for cash, not on credit, and that around one-third of an executive's annual income would be available for this purpose, the average annual after-tax salary and bonuses of such an executive totalled at least $250,000 in 2002.

If we go by the practice of corporations in the West, where options are a form of supplementary compensation for executives and are offered at discounted prices, it somewhat changes the picture, but not drastically. Suppose the total net income of the monopoly's top 400 managers is $100 million, or over 3 billion rubles. Is that a lot, or a little? The head company had estimated profit of 15 billion rubles in 2001, with net profit of 9 billion, and 14 billion in costs of production.[36] These data suggest that the managers' compensation, as calculated, was overstated. It is unlikely that their average annual income in 2001-2002 was more than $150,000. The UES stock option was likely calculated for use in the future, in anticipation of a substantial hike of electricity rates and, consequently, of the generation of surplus value in this sector. In addition, it was evidently assumed that the shares would be purchased in installments and at a discount.

Official statistical publications do not provide even approximate data on the income of Russia's multimillionaires and leading managers. Various estimates by non-governmental agencies have appeared in the press. Many of them are no more than guesses, but some of them deserve our attention. For example, as a very wealthy upper grouping within the capitalist class took shape, banks became interested in providing special services to such VIP customers. Besides ordinary services involving accounts and credit cards, this means trust management and investment support, financial consulting, tax planning, funds transfers to banks abroad, etc. This sort of business is highly profitable for banks, comprising as much as 15-20 percent of their business. Every one of the leading private banks has a group of specialists working on this area of services.

The banks have also undertaken research on this potential set of clients. Specialists at one of the banks estimated in 2002 that this potential client base had $60-80 billion at its disposal. Another major commercial bank estimated that there were on the order of 10,000 individuals in Russia with personal fortunes of $1 million or more (averaging in the range of $6 to $8 million). All of them are of particular interest to the banks as prospective clients. Also of great interest is the larger category of some 80,000 people whose annual income exceeded $120,000 as of 2002. Estimates were that this second layer had $40,000-60,000 annually in available funds, which the banks would like to attract.[37]

We shall use these estimates to make a few very approximate calculations of the wealth and income of the upper echelon of the

Table 3.4 Personal wealth of individual financial oligarchs in 2002
(billions of $)

Mikhail Khodorkovsky	3.7
Roman Abramovich	3.0
Mikhail Fridman	2.2
Vladimir Potanin	1.8
Vladimir Bogdanov	1.6
Rem Vyakhirev	1.5
Vagit Alekperov	1.4
Victor Chernomyrdin	1.1
Oleg Deripaska	1.1
Total for nine billionaires	17.4

Russian capitalist class.

If there were 10,000 millionaires, in dollar terms, in 2002, and their average fortune was $5 million, their total capital was $50 billion. Compare this figure with the personal wealth of the leading financial oligarchs, as estimated by *Forbes* magazine at the time.[38]

Table 3.4 shows that the nine wealthiest property owners had one-third of the total capital belonging to all Russian millionaires. At first glance, it would seem that the total capital of the millionaires must have been understated. But if so, it was not by much.

Compare the 2002 figures with the market capitalization of Russian companies listed on the country's leading stock exchange, the RTS. At the beginning of 2003 the total market value of companies listed on the RTS was $90 billion. This did not include Gazprom, which was worth almost $40 billion at the time, or the majority of the commercial banks, representing another $20 billion. If these entities were counted in, total market capitalization in Russia was on the order of $150 billion.

Looked at from this standpoint, the estimated total fortunes of all the millionaires in Russia do not seem to have been understated. For them to be holding $50 billion, approximately one-third of all market capital in 2002, is reasonable in light of the value of the equity stakes belonging to the government and to small shareholders. Expressed in rubles, their capital was 1.5 trillion, or more than the total household property of the rest of the population, which was valued at 1.4 trillion rubles in 2000,[39] and substantially more than total personal bank deposits, which stood at 650 billion rubles at the end of 2001.[40]

But the millionaires hold only a small fraction of their money in Russian bank accounts. The larger part of their fortunes is invested in Russian and foreign securities, in which form it circulates. It should be kept in mind that Russia millionaires are first-generation wealthy people. Unlike many foreign millionaires, they are working businessmen, rather than rentier capitalists who live by clipping coupons. Experts estimate that they earn an average of 20 percent per annum on their capital. That means that those $50 billion in 2002 yielded $10 billion, or more than 300 billion rubles.

These 10,000 wealthiest people in Russia, less than seven hundredths of a percent of the population, accounted for 6 percent of total personal income.[41]

More recent estimates, published in the Russian journal *Finans* in early 2006, indicate a substantial increase in the wealth of the billionaires.[42]

According to the same 2006 *Finans* report, 450 individuals, whose per capita personal wealth was $60 million or more, had assets totalling $273 billion. The total wealth of all millionaires and billionaires (in dollar terms) may be projected as approximately $300 billion, of which the billionaires alone accounted for the nearly $200 billion shown in Table 3.5. This would appear to be grossly overstated. But it should be kept in mind that, according to these data, there were only nine such billionaires in Russia in 2002, whereas in 2006 there were 51. Such rapid growth as an eleven-fold increase in the wealth of the billionaires alone, and a six-fold increase in the wealth of the billionaires and millionaires combined, in the space of just four years, is entirely possible, in view of the growth of the economy and the stock-market boom during those years. The total market capitalization of Russian companies, adjusted in all appropriate ways for the beginning of 2006, had risen into the range of $800 billion. And many companies, owned by billionaires and millionaires, are not listed on the stock exchange.

Moreover, comparison with the national wealth figures reveals that the personal wealth of this category of the capitalist class in 2005 equalled 5.7 percent of all privately owned property. This corresponds to our data on this category's share of total personal

Table 3.5 Wealth of individual financial oligarchs in 2006
(billions of $)

Roman Abramovich	18.600
Oleg Deripaska	12.700
Mikhail Fridman	11.400
Vladimir Lisin	9.350
Viktor Vekselberg	8.100
Vagit Alekperov	8.000
Vladimir Yevtushenkov	7.315
Mikhail Prokhorov	6.715
Alexei Mordashov	6.700
Vladimir Potanin	6.640
Vladimir Bogdanov	5.350
40 other individuals with personal worth of $1 billion or more	98.605
Total for 51 billionaires	199.475

income on a national level.

The second category of VIP customers identified by banking specialists included people with annual incomes above $120,000, which came chiefly from various types of business activity, as well as from employment as corporate or bank executives. The same source estimated that there were around 80,000 such people.

We are unable to break out managers as a subcategory of this group. We may provisionally assume that they make up at least half of it, or on the order of 40,000 people. If we assume that their average annual income was double the threshold level for this group, or $250,000, then their total income in 2002 would have been as much as $10 billion, or over 300 billion rubles. It is thus comparable with the total income of the millionaires, but is distributed among a greater number of people. Their income and that of the millionaires, combined, was equal to 600 billion rubles at that time ($20 billion), or 12 percent of total personal income in Russia. That level also represented over 40 percent of total personal income from business activity and property ownership (adjusted for understatement in official statistics).[43] The comparable figure for 2004 was 1.39 trillion rubles ($48 billion), still 12 percent of total personal income.

The shares of different segments of the capitalist class in total personal income are summarized in Table 3.6.

Table 3.6 Income of different segments of the capitalist class as percentage of total personal income, 2003

Property owners with personal fortunes of over $1 million	6%
Top corporate and bank managers	6%
Businessmen with annual incomes above $120,000	6%
Other business executives	10%
Total, capitalist class	28%

It is purely coincidental that the first three categories each have the same percentage. These figures represent orders of magnitude, not precise proportions.

The important thing here is that over 40 percent of the total income of the capitalist class goes to the top layer of property owners and managers. Other property owners and managers represent well-established enterprises, some of which may be quite large, but which are outside the major concerns and FPGs. A significant number of them are associated with medium-sized and small businesses, which will be discussed in the next section.

3.5 Small business and its prospects

Small business has been a topic of discussion in recent years at the highest levels of government: the Parliament, the cabinet of ministers, and the President. The reason is that small business is underdeveloped, compared with other forms of enterprise. The common view is that small business in Russia is lagging far behind its status in the leading industrial countries, necessitating special government action to spur its development. Before getting into the theoretical, practical, and political economy aspects of this problem, let us review the situation.

Russian statistics define small businesses as commercial organizations (juridical entities) with an average number of employees not exceeding:

- 100 people in industry, construction, and transport;
- 60 people in agriculture, science, and technology;
- 30 people in retail trade and consumer services;
- 50 people in wholesale trade and other categories.

Table 3.7 Small businesses and their role in total production

	1997	1999	2000	2003
Number of small businesses	861,100	890,600	879,300	882,300
Total number of enterprises (millions)	2.727	3.106	3.346	3.845
Total number of private enterprises (millions)	2.014	2.312	2.510	2.957
Small businesses as % of all businesses	31.6%	28.7%	26.3%	22.9%
Small businesses as % of all private businesses	42.8%	38.5%	35.0%	29.8%
Percentage of production from small businesses	8.0%	6.2%	5.9%	6.0%
Small business employees as % of total employed	12.0%	12.8%	13.6%	12.4%

Sources: RSY 2000; RSY 2001; RSY 2004; *Malye predpriiatiia—2001 (Small Businesses—2001)*, Goskomstat publication, hereinafter MP2001.

Investors in a small business, who are not directly involved in it, should own no more than 25 percent of such a firm. Consumer cooperatives are not considered small businesses, regardless of their number of employees.[44] This is important to bear in mind, since small businesses are treated quite differently, with more restrictions, as a rule, in tax regulations. This pattern will be discussed below.

The data in Table 3.7 confirm the common belief that small business is stagnant in Russia. The great majority of these businesses were established in the initial years of the market reforms, but beginning in the mid-1990s their number increased very slowly, by only 20,000-30,000 annually, at most. After 1999 the number of small businesses dropped. The percentage of small businesses among all enterprises, as well as among all private businesses, began to decline in 1997. In that year small businesses made up almost one-third of all enterprises and over 40 percent of all private businesses, but by 2003 these percentages had dropped to 23 percent and 30 percent, respectively, which was a steep decline in such a short period of time.

Although the share of small business in total employment remained stable at around 12-13 percent, its contribution to the total national output of goods and services fell from 8 percent in 1997 to

Table 3.8 Distribution of small businesses by sector and size, 2000

Sector	Number of businesses Thousands	% of total	Number of employees Millions	% of total	Sales Millions of rubles	% of total	Average number of employees per business Persons	Average output, thousands of rubles Per business	Per employee
Industry	134.2	15.3%	1.433	21.7%	168,098	27.4%	10.7	1,253	117.3
Construction	126.8	14.4%	1.350	20.5%	131,117	21.4%	10.6	1,034	97.1
Retail and public dining	407.5	46.3%	2.320	35.2%	158,701	25.9%	5.7	389	68.5
Three-sector subtotal	668.5	76.0%	5.103	77.4%	457,916	74.6%	7.6	665	89.7
Total, all sectors	879.3	100%	6.597	100%	613,651	100%	7.5	698	93.0

Source: Our calculations, based on MP2001.

6 percent in 2003.

A special study conducted by Goskomstat in 2000 showed that small businesses employed an even smaller portion of the labor force: 10.2 percent of total employment in the Russian economy. At the same time, small business accounted for only 2 percent of all fixed assets and 4.6 percent (other data indicate 2.6 percent) of capital investment. According to the same Goskomstat study, small businesses handled one-fourth of total retail trade and almost half of wholesale trade turnover. Some industries had a fairly high percentage of small businesses (in number): 26 percent in printing and 11 percent in the forest products industry.

Table 3.8 shows that over three-fourths of all small businesses are in three sectors: industry, construction and retail trade (including public dining establishments). Almost 80 percent of small business workers are employed in these sectors, which account for 75 percent of small business sales. No other sector of the economy employs more than 4 percent of the total number of small business workers.

Most small businesses are small, indeed. In industry and construction, they employ 10-11 workers on average, and there are only five or six workers in each retail trade establishment. Average sales per small business in 2000 were 1.3 million rubles in industry, 1 million rubles in construction, and only 389,000 rubles in retail. Thus, output per worker was a relatively small 117,000 rubles in industry, 97,000 rubles in construction, and 69,000 rubles in retail. By comparison, the average wage in that year was 33,000 rubles in industry, and 27,000 rubles across the whole economy. Even with the low level of sales, the owner of a small business could receive some amount of surplus value, albeit small. If we assume a 100-percent rate of surplus value, the average annual profit of a small business establishment in 2000 was around 350,000 rubles ($12,600). Since such results would hardly be worth the effort of generating them, we may assume that a significant portion of small businesses' actual income passed under the counter.

The average figures, of course, obscure significant differences among different-sized businesses. It is estimated, for example, that a great majority of small industrial enterprises—110,000-120,000 of them (80-90 percent)—are small workshops with three to five employees, while a small minority of them, some 10,000-20,000, are full-scale shops with 50-60 workers. Such businesses may even have an officially reported annual turnover of 5-10 million rubles ($200,000-400,000) and $50,000-100,000 in profit. That is a level of economic activity that merits attention, if only as a first step toward encouraging it in the future.

Table 3.9 summarizes the place of small businesses in the U.S. economy, for comparison with the data on their Russian counterparts, shown in Tables 3.7 and 3.8. U.S. statistics classify as small businesses production or commercial establishments employing fewer than 20 people.

In order to adapt the American data for comparison with the Russian, Table 3.9 shows not only all businesses employing fewer than 20 people, but also industrial enterprises with 20-99 employees and retail establishments with 20-29 employees. In our comparison years, small businesses made up two-thirds of the total number of businesses in the United States, as against only 30 percent in Russia. In the USA, they accounted for 23 percent of all employees and 17 percent of total economic output, while Russia was far behind, at 10 and 6 percent, respectively, for these levels.

In the United States only 6 percent of small businesses were in industry. In Russia, this share was 15 percent. Average-sized American industrial enterprises with fewer than 100 employees had an average of 13.5 employees (10.7 in Russia). But they included a layer with 20-99 employees, averaging 38.7. The average output of an American small business was $1.7 million annually, as against only $45,000 in Russia. These figures really are incommensurable. We calculated that a relatively successful small enterprise in Russian industry might generate $200,000-400,000 annually. In the United States, the average turnover of industrial enterprises with 20-99 employees was in the range of $4.8 million. This was tenfold higher than in Russia.

The service sector dominates small business in the USA, accounting for 56 percent of all small businesses in the comparison years (a higher percentage than in retail, where the share of small business was 35 percent). Almost one-third of all small business employees worked in services, with an average of 4.4 employees per establishment. The average sales of a small business in the service sector were $300,000. The United States has a high density of small shops, gas stations, etc.

Table 3.9 Small business in the USA, 1997

Sectors and classes of business	Number of businesses	Number of employees	Sales	Average number of employees per business	Average sales per business
	Millions	Millions	Billions of $	Persons	Millions of $
All sectors					
All businesses	6.895	105.299	18,243	15.3	2.6
Small businesses	4.593	24.282	3,087	4.5	0.6
Percentage small businesses	66.6%	23.1%	16.9%		
Manufacturing					
All businesses	.394	18.633	3,991	47.3	10.1
Small (≤ 99 employees)	.288	4.164	491	14.5	1.7
Percentage small businesses	73.1%	22.3%	12.3%		
Retail					
All businesses	1.592	22.004	2,578	13.8	1.6
Small (≤ 29 employees)	.872	4.986	527	5.7	0.6
Percentage small businesses	54.8%	22.7%	20.4%		
Services					
All businesses	2.554	37.385	2,657	14.6	1.0
Small	1.764	7.831	603	4.4	0.3
Percentage small businesses	69.1%	20.9%	22.7%		

Source: Our calculations, based on *Statistical Abstract of the United States*, 2000, p. 45. We have included businesses with 1-19 employees, with the exception of manufacturing, where companies with 1-99 workers were counted, and retail, in which case we counted businesses with 1-29 employees.

We may draw several general conclusions from this comparison with the USA.

1. Russia is behind the United States in the number of small businesses in relative, as well as absolute terms.

2. The majority of small businesses in America are in the service sector and retail, both of which are underdeveloped in Russia.

3. Russian small business output of goods and services is far below American levels, as is its productivity.

In discussions of the reasons for the underdevelopment of small business in Russia, there is a general consensus. The most frequently cited factor is exorbitant taxes, followed by excessive bureaucratic reporting requirements, and the need to bribe officials in the course of registering a business and running it. While fleecing small business in these ways, the government machine does practically nothing to defend it against organized crime, which exacts its own additional tribute.

Living within these strictures, small business encounters other problems, as well. For example, its low level of development in industry is due to the stranglehold imported goods have had on the Russian market, including relatively cheap imports from China, South Korea and Taiwan, especially in the period before the 1998 crisis, but also afterwards, as the real exchange rate of the ruble rose. Another problem is that bank credits are even less accessible for small businesses than for major enterprises and corporations.[45]

The press and Russian politicians have often taken up the fact that small business will not be able to get on its feet, without special support from the government. For a while during Yeltsin's Presidency, there was even a special government committee on small business issues, headed by Irina Khakamada, but despite her apparently honest desire to improve the situation, the committee had nothing to show for its efforts and was disbanded. At the local level, many regional governors and mayors of large cities have also made a show of protecting small business, but it hasn't helped.

In the fall of 2001, President Putin decided to tackle the problem in earnest. A congress of the Delovaya Rossiya (Business Russia) association, created by representatives of small and medium-sized businesses, took place in October of that year. Its leaders met with Putin. For some reason, he made a point of praising the achievements of small business, declaring that it "was working effectively in sectors of the economy that were loss-making under the [Soviet] planned system"—trade, the food industry, and tourism.[46] Although it is true that these sectors were poorly developed under the planned economy, they were by no means loss-making. Indeed, they provided fairly substantial tax revenue to the state. The President soon understood that what was wanted of him was not so much praise, as help in finding a way out of the dismal situation small business was in.

Putin ordered the formation of a special commission to work up a concept for small business development, for review by the State Council. This commission proposed to simplify the tax code for small businesses, create conditions whereby banks would be eager to lend to them, make it easier for them to rent federal government-owned or municipal premises, and block unfair competitive practices from being used against them by big business.[47]

However the relevant tax policy issues may be decided, the future of small business only indirectly depends on them. The most important problem is lack of clarity in the government's overall approach to this policy area. The President proclaims his great concern for small business, depicting it as practically the top-priority area of the government's economic and social policies for the creation of a broad middle class in the country, which would be a social base for the upper middle class and the financial oligarchy. At the same time, however, the same government—this time, the cabinet of ministers, and especially the financial agencies—tries in every way possible to cut corners at the expense of small business, slashing to a bare minimum any fiscal incentives that might have been contemplated for this segment of business.

The roots of this ambiguity reach beyond subjective barriers like the narrow-mindedness of financial policy bureaucrats. If that were all there was to it, it would not be very difficult to remove such barriers, since tax abatement for small enterprises would represent a tiny fraction of total government revenue. Various data show that taxation of small businesses provides between 1 and 1.7 percent of all federal tax revenue, or between 0.4 and 1 percent of consolidated budget taxes (federal plus local budgets). Consequently, even if the institution of tax incentives for small business would mean a temporary loss for the Treasury, it would be miniscule, relative to the budget and to the economy as a whole.

The impact of the program would look even less like a loss, if we consider that one of the main announced goals of the proposed reform is to bring a significant part of small business out of the shadow sector of the economy. This would mean an actual increase of tax revenue, though it is hard to say by how much. That margin depends both on what portion of total small business output has been off-the-books, and on the nature of the tax abatement. It is estimated that institution of the flat personal income tax nearly doubled revenue from this category. If something on the order of half of small business activity is off-the-books, the increased tax revenue could be quite substantial.

If that is the case, other questions follow. The first one is whether, if the share of the shadow sector in small business is so large, the statistics presented at the beginning of this section did not grossly understate the size of small business as a whole. If the share of small business in Russia's total output of goods and services were 11-12 percent (rather than 5.5-6 percent, as shown above), then this would be only slightly less than the share of small business in the United States, which is 16 percent.

Secondly, the problems of understating and evading taxes are just as severe, if not worse, in the case of big business, which has a much greater ability to falsify accounts, bribe officials, and maintain its own independent defenses against organized crime than small business does. Even if the government managed to collect 50 billion rubles in taxes on small business, rather than just 25 billion, this increment would not begin to compare with the multibillion ruble sums of natural rent that go unpaid to the state by large companies.

Once again, it proves impossible to avoid the problem of the shadow sector in the Russian economy, if we want to look at how things really work.

3.6 The shadow economy, organized crime, and corruption

The Russian scholarly literature and the mass media, even more so, give widely varying estimates of the dimensions of off-the-books business in Russia, ranging from 20 to 50 percent of GDP. Most of the people who write about this phenomenon do not define "shadow economy" with any precision, and do not reveal the methodology behind their computations. The only more or less consistent, systematic approach is the one used by Goskomstat, which each year has to incorporate, in its official reports on GDP and other leading indicators, substantiated estimates of unreported production and income, which are concealed from data-collection agencies. We shall now review the basic principles of Goskomstat's methodology and consider the extent to which it is acceptable and adequate for the processes it attempts to analyze.

First of all, the approach distinguishes between types of economic activity not reported in official statistics, and criminal activity (not properly economic activity) taking place in the economy. The first area includes unregistered production of goods and services, as well as concealed income. Unreported production has to be added to the GDP shown in the statistics and, minus current material costs of production, should correspond to total concealed income.

In contrast, criminal activity taking place in the economy—larceny, robbery, fraud, extortion, etc.—does not create any additional value, but brings about a redistribution of the national product, income, and wealth.[48]

Computations that include organized crime in estimates of the shadow economy do not accurately reflect the weight of the latter. We saw above, for example, that a significant part of the output, and therefore also of the income, of small enterprises is missed by official statistics; it is "in the shadows," or off-the-books. A certain portion of this concealed income is appropriated by criminal groups, who extort the money by various techniques.

It would obviously be incorrect to sum together the concealed income of small businesses with the income of organized crime groups, since that would mean double-counting the same output and the same income. Some exaggerated estimates of the shadow economy result from that methodological error, and therefore cannot be accepted as sound. Of course, the unjustified summing of shadow and criminal incomes applies not only to small business, but also to large enterprises and corporations, which also conceal a portion of their output and income.

Next, Goskomstat divides unreported economic activity into three categories: concealed, informal, and illegal. The first two categories cover activity that is legal in and of itself, but does not get reported in official statistics for various reasons. *Illegal economic activity* means the production of goods and services prohibited by law. This category includes narcotics production and trafficking, prostitution, the illegal arms trade, and smuggling.

Concealed economic activity is entirely legal activity, carried out by duly registered enterprises and organizations, but the people doing it conceal or understate its scale, chiefly for the purpose of avoiding taxes and mandatory contributions to fund social programs. Activity of this type may occur in almost any sector or area of the economy. It generates concealed business income and profit, as well as off-the-books labor income.

Informal economic activity is defined as the activity of individuals or groups, who have not properly registered what they are doing, and produce goods and services either for their own household consumption, or for sale to a small circle of purchasers outside of any organized market. This type of activity generates income from informal activity, which is often classified as "mixed income." For this type of income the boundary between wages and business income is not clearly defined.

Goskomstat accounting, which includes estimates of the shadow economy's share in GDP, industrial output, trade, and income, concentrates almost exclusively on concealed and informal economic activity, deliberately excluding illegal production. Nor does Goskomstat estimate the scale of the income redistribution that results from organized crime activity.

How complete a picture of concealed and informal economic activity does the Goskomstat method produce? Unfortunately Goskomstat does not publish the results of its calculations in any detail, providing only individual examples, which it terms "provisional." These illustrative examples show, for instance, that for industrial output, the mark-up for the shadow sector is 4.4 percent overall, of which only 2.5 percent is accounted for by output at duly registered industrial enterprises. The remainder is comprised of goods produced by households, and industry-related services provided to the population by individuals.

Unreported production by duly registered enterprises is calculated on the basis of spot checks of proper payment of the VAT. The results of these checks are extrapolated to all existing enterprises, on the assumption that the unpaid VAT is approximately equal to the level of off-the-books production.

The striking thing about these data is their divergence from estimates, also issued by Goskomstat, of the total size of concealed and informal economic activity. During the second half of the 1990s, these estimates fluctuated in the range of 20-22 percent of GDP, but the figure for 2001 was lower: 18 percent.[49] This change was associated with the introduction of the flat income tax rate, which resulted in some business activity beginning to "emerge from the shadows." Kasyanov, who was prime minister at the time, explained that this phenomenon occurred on such a large scale, that it even affected official GDP data for 2001. A reduction in the amount of output being added for the shadow economy resulted in a decline of GDP growth from 5 percent to 4 percent. In the 1990s the opposite had occurred. The statistics for 1997 showed a slight growth of GDP, instead of yet another year of decline, due to the fact that Goskomstat had increased its estimate of the shadow economy's weight within the economy as a whole.

Despite the lack of published systematic data on this account, such figures can be derived indirectly, using the available statistics on concealed income. As noted above, the concealed portion of value added in the economy (i.e., that portion of GDP) should correspond to concealed income. The latter is represented in official statistics by only two components: "concealed compensation of employees" and "mixed income" of the population. The first component is off-the-books payments to workers, on which businesses do not pay the mandatory social tax, while the second expresses the population's income from informal economic activity. These data are summarized in Table 3.10.

Concealed labor income fluctuated in the range of 21 to 28 percent of total compensation of hired labor, while mixed income ranged between 19 and 22 percent of household income. As the table shows, these two types of off-the-books income have made up 20-24 percent of GDP, stabilizing in recent years at about 20 percent. It is difficult to say how accurate these estimates are, since the methodology behind them is only partially revealed in the statistical publications. We do know that the population's total money income is established only indirectly, as the sum of all money spent and saved by the population, plus changes in the population's cash on hand. While the latter two components of this total, savings and cash, can be obtained from bank records, total money spending is defined as the sum of goods and services

Table 3.10 Concealed income compared with GDP
(billions of rubles and %)

	1995	1997	1998	1999	2000	2001	2003
1. GDP	1,540	2,479	2,741	4,757	7,063	9,041	13,285
2. Concealed compensation of employees	160	290	277	525	782	1,003	1,488
3. Concealed compensation of employees as % of GDP	10.4%	11.7%	10.1%	11.0%	11.1%	11.1%	11.2%
4. Mixed income	189	296	348	575	692	864	(1,228)
5. Mixed income as % of GDP	12.3%	11.9%	12.9%	12.6%	9.8%	9.6%	(9.2%)
6. 2 + 4	349	586	617	1,066	1,474	1,867	2,716
7. 2 + 4 as % of GDP	22.6%	23.6%	22.9%	23.4%	20.9%	20.7%	(20.4%)
8. Total compensation of employees	696	1,239	1,293	1,948	2,821	4,069	6,132
9. Total compensation of employees concealed, %	23.0%	23.4%	21.4%	27.0%	27.7%	24.6%	24.3%

Sources: RSY 2000, RSY 2001, RSY 2002, RSY 2004. Figures in parentheses are our estimates.

purchased by the population. And that indicator, as we have seen, is based on indirect estimates. Using this approach, it is possible to determine only a total for concealed labor income and mixed income, as the difference between reported wage and personal income data, combined, and total estimated income. These values cannot be calculated separately.

It is possible to arrive at a certain approximation of total mixed income, using estimates of business income. In previous chapters we treated business income, as well as income from property, as part of the income of the capitalist class. In reality, it makes up a very small portion of the income of this layer, since in income statistics business activity includes only the provision of goods and services to the population by individuals, such as the production—in individual part-time operations—of food or non-food goods to be sold, services in the areas of housing construction and repair, private transport, tutoring, private practice of doctors, veterinarians and lawyers, shoe and garment repair, etc. This type of activity accounts for 72 percent of all mixed income; the provenance of the remainder is not indicated.

This circumstance has several not unimportant consequences:

1. The off-the-books income listed in Table 3.10 does not include the concealed income of most major entrepreneurs, except for what they pay out in the form of "compensation of employees";
2. Also not included is the margin by which the profit of duly registered businesses is understated by overstating costs;
3. Also not included is the margin by which the value of exported goods is understated, which is another source of concealed profit for export-sector corporations;
4. Also omitted is another source of concealed profit—ghost imports.

The concealed and informal income shown in Table 3.10 totalled 20-23 percent of Russia's GDP in the 1990s and early 2000s. This level coincides with Goskomstat's general estimate of concealed and unreported informal economic activity. But to this total must be added the four above-indicated categories, insofar as they express unreported primary income. We shall now attempt to quantify them.

Concealed income of major enterprises. In Section 3.4 we presented an estimate of the total personal income of major businessmen as 18 percent of total personal income nationally, or on the order of 900 billion rubles at the end of 2001 (we shall use that year as a benchmark for later-period estimates). Included as "major businessmen" were property owners with a personal fortune in excess of $1 million, upper-level executives in companies and banks, and businessmen with an annual income greater than $120,000. Not all of this income, however, may be defined as primary income. For example, income from commodities, securities and currency speculation, and the appreciation of assets, including real estate, is not primary income. A portion of the income of upper-level executives figures in the statistics under "concealed compensation of employees," and must be excluded from primary income in order to avoid double-counting. The income of the wealthy segment of the population also includes, in one way or another, the "take" of the upper echelons of organized crime, which lives off the redistribution of income, both primary and secondary, rather than by producing any output of its own. Finally, we have to reduce the total by that part of legal personal income from business and property, accounted for by major businessmen. These subtractions can be made as follows (in billions of rubles, for 2001):

1. Estimated total personal income of major businessmen: 900 billion rubles;
2. *Minus* income from speculation and asset appreciation (assumed to be one-fourth of the total personal income of major businessmen): 225 billion rubles;
3. *Minus* half the income of executives, assumed to be counted under "concealed compensation of employees": 150 billion rubles;
4. *Minus* personal income of the upper echelons of organized crime, assumed to be one-fourth of the total personal income of the wealthy class: 225 billion rubles;
5. *Minus* legal income of major businessmen (half of total personal income from business and property): 50 billion rubles;
6. On balance, the concealed primary income of major businessmen was 250 billion rubles, or 5.5 percent of GDP, in 2001.

This concealed income takes many forms. Most numerous are the various ways in which proprietors or managers of companies spend company funds for personal purposes (over and above their legal wages, bonuses, health benefits, vacations, travel and entertainment, etc.). Big businessmen use company cars, planes, and helicopters. Company funds pay for their housing and personal services, including dining. There is nothing out of the ordinary in this. The Russian capitalist class is merely following the example of the USA and other centers of capitalism. Another form of income within this category is the income streams generated by private companies, owned by their managers, who essentially place orders with themselves.

Concealed profit resulting from overstating current material costs. Overstating current material costs is a long-established practice in Russian industry. In the planned economy this was one of the methods used to obtain additional raw materials, fuels, and semi-manufactures, to be used in making off-the-books products. With the transition to a market economy, the old scheme no longer worked in the same way, but overstating costs was still a method of understating profit in official accounts, and thus reducing taxable earnings.

A comparatively modest overstatement of current material costs, by only a few percentage points, translates into very large sums on the scale of the national economy. If, for example, the reported intermediate consumption of semi-manufactures were to have been overstated by just 5 percent, in 2003 that would have meant concealing 569 billion rubles of gross profit as primary income, or 4 percent of GDP; and GDP would have been reduced by that amount.[50]

Such overstated material costs are reflected in an overstated value of the output, produced by supplier sectors and purchased by the relevant other sectors. The total market value of produced output on the scale of the whole economy does not change, but there is a redistribution between value added and value transferred. The volume of physical production remains the same.

Understating the value of exports. This technique can be illustrated by an example that Accounting Chamber investigators uncovered. Criminal charges were filed against executives of the state-owned company Slavneft for systematically understating the value of the oil they exported. Slavneft would sell crude to its subsidiary Slavneft-Belgium at below market price. Slavneft-Belgium then sold the same oil to a foreign intermediary called Sibneft Oil Trade, with a slight mark-up. Sibneft Oil Trade sold it to Shell, BP, and other multis at full market price. Most of the profit accrued to the Sibneft subsidiary, which then shared it with the top management of all the participating companies. The Russian government, as the main shareholder (75-percent owner) of Slavneft, missed receiving 370 million rubles in dividends in 1999, as a result of this scheme.[51]

The suppressed dividends represented only a part of the unreported profit. Slavneft's net profit for 1999, shown on its books, was 10.5 billion rubles. It paid 4.3 billion rubles into government budgets at all levels (federal and local), and 435 million rubles in dividends to the government as shareholder.[52] Thus, the Russian state received in dividends around 4 percent of Slavneft's declared net profit. If we extrapolate the 46 percent underpayment of dividends to the company's entire net profit, its concealed profit can be estimated at 8.9 billion rubles. Slavneft's earnings from the export of oil and petroleum products in 1999, meanwhile, according to reported data on the physical volume exported (3.2 million tons) and the average export price for Russian oil ($105.80/ton), should have been $338 million, or 8.3 billion rubles. Given the $80/ton gap between the export price and the domestic price, the superprofit from exporting the oil should have been $256 million, or 6.3 billion rubles. If this sum had been shown as part of the company's reported gross before-tax profit, it would have accounted for 42.6 percent of it. Understating the export price by $10.60 per exported ton of oil cost Slavneft $32 million, or 840 million rubles, and shorted the Russian Treasury by the 370 million rubles mentioned above.

Other available data show that the Treasury missed receiving 150 million rubles, or $6 million at the 1999 exchange rate, just on the sale of two million tons of diesel fuel.[53] That was equivalent to discounting the market price by $6.9/ton.

Let us allow that the case of Slavneft was out of the ordinary, and that the average rate of understatement of export prices is substantially lower. If it averages 5 percent, a figure cited in the literature, that would mean that the value of exported goods and services was understated by $5.8 billion in 2001, or 168.9 billion rubles, which was 1.9 percent of GDP.

Ghost imports. These may occur in two ways: (1) prices are overstated for goods that really were imported, with the difference between the declared and the actual price being divvied up between the importer and the foreign seller or intermediary; (2) money is paid for undelivered goods or for services that are not provided. The latter method is one of the most widely used ways of illegally exporting capital or transferring funds (usually, concealed income). If ghost imports rise to the level of even 5 percent of official imports, the total overstatement of imported goods and services was $3.7 billion in 2001, which was 107.8 billion rubles, or 1.2 percent of GDP.

Summarizing these categories of concealed primary income,

we have the following (billions of rubles and percent of GDP in 2003, using proportions extrapolated from 2001):

1. Concealed income of major businessmen	730	5.5%
2. Overstated current material costs	569	4.3%
3. Understated export prices	252	1.9%
4. Ghost imports	159	1.2%
5. Total additional concealed income	1,710	12.9%
6. Concealed income according to Goskomstat	3,108	23.4%
7. Total concealed income	4,818	36.3%

Thus, the level of concealed income indicates that the shadow economy accounted for approximately one-third of GDP in 2003. That is far below some extreme estimates, which include all of organized crime's revenue, but it is significantly higher than Goskomstat's calculations. We stress that a substantial upward correction of the Goskomstat figure does not mean that the output of goods and services was higher by that proportion. The source of the additional concealed income should be accounted for either by correcting estimates of foreign economic operations to produce a more complete value expression of GDP, or by redistributing the value of total output in such a way as to reduce the share associated with costs of production, and increase the share associated with newly created value.

Now, we shall look at criminal business as such: the operations of organized crime. Estimates of its "turnover," or total revenue, in money terms ranged between $40 billion and $60 billion, or 1.2-1.8 trillion rubles, in 2000.[54] The average of these extreme estimates coincides with Goskomstat's estimate of the size of the shadow economy in 2001. How realistic are these figures?

According to the Russian Prosecutor General's Office, as many as 60 percent of the enterprises and organizations in the country are controlled by organized criminal groups. Usually this control takes the form of "protection," called *krysha* ("the roof") in Russian; the regular payment of protection money is the chief source of income for these groups. Only very large corporations (and not even all of them) are free from this type of control, because they have the resources to maintain or legally hire their own security force. Most companies are forced to accept "services" from the mob. In addition, organized crime groups may have their own commercial organizations, which are difficult to distinguish from legal companies. There are practically no statistical data on their operations. We shall therefore limit ourselves to looking at protection operations, and consider how they mesh with data on the shadow economy.

We shall assume that protection money (and other payments to criminal organizations) cannot be paid legally. Therefore the source of such payments has to be the concealed income of businesses and entrepreneurs—not all of it, but only the portion not earmarked for normal business operations. It is unlikely that more than 10 percent of "concealed compensation of employees," and 40 percent of concealed profit, is spent for this purpose. As we saw above, Goskomstat estimates the total of these two categories as 6 percent of GDP, a figure corrected by us to 11 percent of GDP, or on the order of 950 billion rubles in 2001. The low range of estimates of organized crime's revenue, 1.2 trillion rubles, is substantially greater. But if we assume that the "roof" takes up to another 40 percent of the personal income of major businessmen from speculation and the concealed income of executives, we reach the level of 1.1 trillion rubles, not much below the lower estimate of organized crime revenue. These proportions can be considered more or less accurate within an inevitable margin of error.

Thus, we project that around 40 percent of the total concealed income of the capitalist class goes to pay for the "services" of organized crime. It is substantially higher than the 13 percent personal income tax rate, or the reduced 24 percent tax rate on profit (previously 36 percent). If such an estimate of the rate of extortion is unjustifiably high, then the above-cited estimates of organized crime's revenue must also be quite exaggerated. If we assume that the capitalist class spends no more than one-fourth of its income for these purposes, the estimated revenue of organized crime would have to be lowered to 600 billion rubles in the benchmark year, or 6.5 percent of GDP.

How do the shadow economy and organized crime affect Russia's economic development? The main detrimental factors are obvious.

1. By concealing income, the private sector underpays taxes due the government by an amount equal to at least 10 percent of GDP, creating a permanent sense that funds are short

for centralized deployment into the social services sector, defense, and economic infrastructure. If the private sector were to emerge further from the shadows, it would be possible to lower taxes more, which would encourage economic growth.

2. The shadow economy serves as the main nutrient medium for organized crime, which because of its far-flung organizations and huge levels of extortion blocks any normal development of investment and all other economic operations. If we take 25-40 percent of concealed profit as the average level paid out in protection money, it becomes clear why most enterprises are forced to conceal income, and why the total fees, exacted by the government as taxes and by organized crime as protection money, seem to be so inordinately high. Freeing businesses from paying even half the cost of their *krysha* would palpably alleviate the tax burden.

3. The existence of the shadow "octopus" helps promote capital flight, thus depriving the economy of adequate resources for capital investment. First of all, things are calmer for capital abroad, far away from the all-seeing eyes of organized crime. This consideration may carry greater weight than businessmen's fear of expropriation by the government. Criminal organizations are capable of cleaning out capitalists who are not firmly enough anchored, more thoroughly than any government. Secondly, the disincentives for declaring capital in full include not only fear of the official tax agencies, but also the fact that doing so makes an enterprise more attractive a target for criminal kingpins.

The shadow economy has positive aspects, too.

The Sociology Center at the Russian State Service Academy has found that the shadow sector makes life easier for the population by supplying goods and services at prices considerably lower than what the products of legally registered businesses cost. It is no secret that middle-class Russians, not only the poorest layers of the population, frequently patronize informal businesses for this reason. Goods imported by the so-called "shuttle traders," individuals who bring in small quantities of consumer goods from neighboring countries like Turkey or China, are unquestionably cheaper than similar products sold at ordinary retail outlets. It is cheaper to hire immigrants off-the-books to perform household services, than to order such services from duly registered commercial providers. There are many other examples.[55]

These considerations, however, have to do chiefly with small-scale informal businesses, not with the bulk of the shadow economy. Having to pay protection money to organized crime does nothing to lower the prices charged for goods, but has rather the opposite effect. And the overstatement of costs in order to conceal profit fuels inflation.

How may the shadow economy be overcome? It is probably impossible to defeat it completely. Even developed industrial nations have a shadow economy, although it is relatively smaller than in Russia. But it is absolutely necessary to hold it to a minimum. The main obstacle to this would appear to be that the only agency capable of doing it is the government, but the government itself is corrupt; the bureaucracy collects kick-backs from both the informal economy and organized crime, and thus relies on them for sustenance.

We shall not explore in any depth the problem of corruption in Russia, since other studies have treated its basic aspects in detail. The INDEM (Information Science for Democracy) Foundation, headed by former Presidential aide Georgi Satarov, has published detailed sociological studies of corruption. INDEM's comprehensive study *Russia and Corruption: Who Will Win?* (1998)[56] was followed by the methodologically innovative work *Diagnostics of Russian Corruption* (2002), containing the first attempt to estimate the size of the "corruption services" market in Russia.[57] An INDEM study with new estimates appeared in 2005 under the title *Corruption Process in Russia: Level, Structure, Trends. Diagnostics of Corruption in Russia.*[58]

In May 2002, Satarov said on Vladimir Pozner's Vremena TV program, that officials in the executive branch of the Russian government, including the Presidential Administration, had shown very little interest in these reports. He saw this lack of response as typical of the disinclination, and inability, of the government to wage any effective fight against corruption, despite public pronouncements made by President Yeltsin and then President Putin. The inadequacy of federal budget resources to fund a special agency to combat corruption has been cited, but Satarov believes that the economic losses from corruption are so great, that reducing them even par-

Table 3.11 Income from corruption compared with income from the shadow economy and organized crime

(2001, except rows 2a and 3a, which represent INDEM estimates for 2004)

	Income, billions of $	Income, billions of rubles	Income as % of GDP
1. Corruption, total	36.3	1,058.8	11.7%
2. "Household" corruption	2.8	81.6	0.9%
2a. Same in 2004	3.0	87.0	0.5%
3. "Business" corruption	33.5	977.3	10.8%
3a. Same in 2004	316	9,164.0	56.2%
Of which:			
4. Non-financial oversight agencies	11.6	338.1	3.7%
5. Licensing agencies	11.5	334.2	3.7%
6. Fiscal and tax oversight agencies	7.4	215.0	2.4%
Level of government:			
7. Municipal	25.1	732.9	8.1%
8. Regional	6.7	195.5	2.2%
9. Central	1.7	48.9	0.5%
10. Shadow economy	94.8	2,764.2	30.5%
11. Organized crime—high estimate	37.7	1,100.0	12.3%
12. Same—low estimate	19.9	580.0	6.5%

tially would more than compensate for whatever the government might spend for this purpose. His opinion is indirectly supported by estimates of how much money the bureaucracy receives from graft.

We shall use chiefly the 2002 INDEM report, since specialists consider it the most trustworthy and realistic. Its authors divided this market into two parts: the "household" segment, used by private individuals, and the "business" segment for enterprises and business organizations. We may compare the quantitative estimates in the report with our estimates of the size of the shadow economy and organized crime.

Regarding the INDEM estimates for 2004, shown in rows 2a and 3a of Table 3.11, it should be noted that, while the estimate of "household" corruption may be accepted, with certain qualifications, the estimate of "business" corruption does not stand up to criticism at all. This estimate is equal to 56 percent of GDP, and is one and a half times greater than actual gross profit in the economy, which is simply beyond belief. Bear in mind that these bribes are paid out of the revenue of the shadow economy, which no set of data puts at greater than 30-36 percent of GDP.

INDEM's error, which many Russian and foreign analysts noticed immediately, stems from excessive reliance on polling of businessmen, according to which the average size of a bribe in business increased by a factor of 12 between 2001 and 2004. Even taking into account inflation and rising business receipts (nominal GDP almost doubled in this period), such an estimate of the growth of business bribes is exaggerated beyond all proportion. Even if business corruption did increase during these years, perhaps doubling in money terms, it is unlikely that it rose substantially—say, more than from 11 to 13 percent—as a share of GDP.

In any event, we cannot use INDEM's new estimates, so we shall continue to rely on the 2001 estimates, as a more reliable base from which to make calculations respecting later periods (see Table 3.12, below).

Obviously the dimensions of "household" corruption are far smaller than those of "business" corruption. In the case of the former, the payer is the population, for whom paying bribes even to the tune of 2 percent of their disposable income is fairly burdensome. Income generated by "business" corruption, however, is estimated at 10.8 percent of GDP, only slightly less than the high estimates of organized crime income. The authors of the report on corruption believe that their figures understate the case.

There is a problem of commensurability in making this comparison. It is clear that businesses use the same source to pay both bribes and protection money: their own shadow income. Our high estimate of organized crime income assumed that the shadow economy cannot spend over 40 percent of its concealed income on services provided by organized crime. If payments of approximately the same dimensions, for bribery of officials, are added, then total spending on such fees would reach 75-80 percent of the shadow economy's concealed income. Either the estimates of concealed profit must be significantly understated, or the estimates of organized crime and bribe-takers' "services" must be overstated.

Most likely a certain correction needs to be made for the double-counting that inevitably occurs when income streams from various types of activity are simply added together. The above-mentioned report on corruption, for instance, includes a special section that explores the so-called "seizure of the state" by business, whereby business takes the initiative to feed government officials under the table, and derives greater ongoing benefit from doing that, than it spends on the bribes (otherwise the whole operation would make no sense for business). Hence bribes paid to officials at fiscal oversight agencies become a way to evade taxes. If 215 billion rubles is spent on that type of bribe, as the authors of the report estimate, then the amount of taxes not paid ought to be significantly greater than that figure. Total taxes paid into the consolidated state budget were 2.332 trillion rubles in 2001, or an order of magnitude more than total bribes paid to tax-collectors. If we presume that "legalized" tax evasion is at least double the level of this type of corruption, then the state budget has failed to receive at least 430 billion rubles, or 5 percent of GDP. But since tax evasion is one of the sources of concealed business income, it is problematic to be sure this calculation is correct.

Presumably Goskomstat does not include, within concealed profit, the total of evaded taxes, 430 billion rubles, because tax officials do not show these violations in their records of business activity. It might seem excessive for bribes to equal 50 percent of this total (i.e., 215 billion rubles), but those bribes could be considered the unavoidable costs of a financial operation to maximize net profit. In macroeconomic calculations, that entire 215 billion would have to be added to the estimate of concealed income of the shadow economy, since we have not yet counted this source of income under any other heading.

Bribes to non-financial oversight and licensing agencies, however, unlike bribes to tax-collectors, do not add anything directly to concealed profit, although the very existence of enterprises, and of their shadow turnover, not infrequently depends on them.

The INDEM Foundation authors include an important disclaimer, to the effect that their estimates of corruption at the federal government level are probably understated, since they included only *everyday business corruption*, chiefly at the local and regional levels, without *"bringing in serious corruption in the upper echelons of power."* It is difficult to say why this element was excluded from the study. Indeed, there have been plentiful examples in the press of the direct melding of big business and the federal government bureaucracy. There even used to be a special web site dedicated to high-level Russian corruption: www.corruption.ru, which posted compromising material (not always accurate) about top Russian government officials. Among them were several former Russian premiers, deputy premiers, ministers, an ex-Central Bank chairman, deputy ministers, etc. After coming under pressure from top level authorities, the site went dormant.

One of the targets of such exposes was Kasyanov, known at one time as "Misha two percent," for the bribery rate he allegedly exacted from businesses he assisted from his position as a high-ranking Ministry of Finance official. Andrei Vavilov, as deputy minister of finance, managed to become a multimillionaire and buy control of an oil company. When he came under suspicion, he quickly sold his company and secured an appointment to the Federation Council, Russia's upper house of Parliament, which provided immunity from prosecution. In January 2004, the FBI forced an airplane carrying Vavilov to land in California, in order to interrogate him in a case of embezzlement of Russian Ministry of Defense funds, also involving former Ukrainian Premier Pavlo Lazarenko. This incident tarnished Vavilov's reputation even more. In early 2005 his personal fortune was estimated at $350 million.

If upper-echelon corruption has equalled something in the range of 2 percent of GDP, that means it was almost 180 billion rubles ($6 billion) in 2001. Of course this sum did not accrue to just one or two bribe-takers, but was divided among all the members of the bureaucratic elite, not equally, of course, but according to the place of each person in the upper-echelon corruption marketplace.

Other sources of income associated with corruption in the upper ranks of government include financial speculation, based on access to classified insider information, the acquisition of state-owned assets at deliberately suppressed prices, the ability to handle state property and financial flows because of connections with high-ranking state officials, and more. It is impossible to make even an approximate estimate of the dimensions of wealth acquired through such operations. If we were to sum up the market value of all assets under the control of oligarchical groups inside and outside the country that were acquired chiefly through corrupt connections, it would amount to hundreds of billions of dollars. The value of this wealth

Table 3.12 Distribution of gross profit among business, the state, corruption, and organized crime

	Revenue (billions of rubles)	% of GDP	Revenue (billions of rubles)	% of GDP
	2001		2004	
Gross domestic product	8,943.6	100%	16 751.5	100%
Gross profit (official)	3,692.6	41.8%	6,267.4	37.4%
Gross profit (including concealed)	4,832.6	54.7%	8,763.4	52.3%
Taxes on profit	1,070.4	12.0%	1,907.6	11.4%
Business corruption	965.9	10.8%	2,177.7	13.0%
Payments to organized crime	580.0	6.5%	1,088.8	6.5%
Total deductions	2,806.6	31.3%	5,174.1	30.9%
Profit after deductions	2,026.0	23.4%	3,589.3	21.4%
Gross investment in fixed capital	1,689.3	18.9%	3,002.9	17.9%
Available remainder	336.7	4.5%	585.4	3.5%
Capital flight (minimum estimate)	341.9	3.8%	303.6	1.8%

far exceeds the annual GDP of Russia.

In conclusion, we offer Table 3.12, which summarizes our calculation of the distribution of effective gross economic profit among the entrepreneurial class, the state, corruption, and organized crime. Our estimates for 2004 differ substantially from the INDEM data, which exaggerated business corruption revenue out of all proportion.

It is clear that after the distribution of profit among all of its legitimate recipients and the covert spongers, little remains for consumption by the wealthy. And yet Russian television and the press constantly show us pictures of our "elite's" parasitical consumption. Rarely is such an orgy of conspicuous consumption on display anywhere in the developed capitalist countries. And there are remarkably many revellers at this feast in the time of the plague—people who believe they have earned their money fairly, and that to cast doubt on that belief is a crime.

This is not a novel phenomenon. All of the developed countries experienced this phase, as America did in the late 19th and early 20th centuries. Thorstein Veblen, the theoretician of the "leisure class," wrote about the phenomenon a hundred years ago, as did the prominent economist John Kenneth Galbraith in the mid-20th century. Rereading their books, however, one sees that not even America in those periods experienced conspicuous consumption by the nouveaux riches on such a scale, as exists in Russia today.

The source of this frenzy of consumption is the gross profit, mentioned above, which flows in wide rivers and smaller streams throughout the large bureaucracy and the criminal world. But that is not the whole of it.

A significant part of this revenue is concealed in official statistics as "business revenue" and "income from property." These two sources combined, accounted for almost 1.8 trillion rubles ($60 billion), or 12.8 percent of GDP, in 2003.

Our official statistics include no figures on dividends. Each company has its own way of paying dividends. Until quite recently, the tax on dividends was only 4 percent; it was raised to 9 percent only in 2004. For some reason our wealthy individuals pay substantially less on their earnings from shares, than any laborer does on his wages, which are assessed at the 13 percent flat income tax rate.

The income of the wealthy is also hidden under the "compensation of employees" heading, which accounts for around 40 percent of GDP. This category groups together quite diverse types of wages: those of ordinary state-sector workers (at or below the subsistence minimum), the relatively highly paid oil and gas industry workers, government officials and private company managers at various levels, and, of course, top-ranking executives like Anatoli Chubais or Alexei Miller, with their numerous deputies and their hundreds-of-thousands, if not multimillion-dollar salaries. In this category, too, go the wages and bonuses received by Vekselberg, Deripaska, Fridman, and the other oligarchs, and their entourages, for running their companies. The income of the wealthy class is also hidden in company overhead costs, which include much of their personal spending for transport, legal representation, and many other purely personal expenses.

All in all, as much as 30 percent of all personal income goes to the wealthy class. They consume at least 10 percent of Russia's GDP.

Several conclusions follow from what has been presented here. First and foremost, contemporary Russian capitalism is a fusion, or a merger, of oligarchical capital with a corrupt bureaucracy and organized crime. Since each of these groups is interested in maximizing its own share, the system cannot exist without concealing from the government a significant portion of it income, relying on a large shadow sector. The unfavorable investment climate in the country is largely due to the entrepreneurial class's having to pay exorbitant tribute to government officials and criminal mafias. The government claims to be committed to combatting corruption and crime. Its successes in these endeavors are few, since the government, to some extent, is composed of the selfsame corrupt individuals, or sometimes even of mafia chieftains.

It is in the process of dividing up gross profit, related property, and financial flows, that conflicts between the government and the oligarchy have unfolded. The smashing of Khodorkovsky and Yukos, in parallel with the formation of a "Kremlin" oligarchical group, is the clearest example of this redistribution, which is not yet over.

When personal enrichment occurs on the scale Russia has experienced in recent years, it begins to have a substantial and extremely detrimental impact on the composition and growth rate of the national economy. In the next two chapters, we shall trace these effects, first as they are manifested in the distribution of the national product and national income, and then as they appear in economic dynamics.

NOTES

1. These calculations are based on the input-output tables for 1995 in the electronic database of the Institute for Scientific Economic Research at the Russian Federation Ministry of Economics. In subsequent publications of the IOT (for 1998, 1999 and 2001), unfortunately, data for the natural gas sector and freight transport were not broken out.

2. RSY 2000, p. 528.

3. The account of events in the electric power sector is based in part on the article "Komu prinadlezhit Rossiia. Energetika" ("Who Owns Russia. The Power Industry") in KV, #45, 2001.

4. In 1990, nuclear power plants produced 118 billion kWh of electric power, or 11 percent of total power generation of 1,082 billion kWh. In 1999, nuclear power generation was 150 billion kWh, while total electricity generation had declined to 916 billion kWh. Thus, the share of nuclear power in the total had risen to 16 percent (RSY 2004, table 14.25).

5. Report of RAO UES of Russia to 2004 annual general meeting of shareholders.

6. Calculated from the RAO UES of Russia Profit and Loss Report for 2000.

7. *Izvestia,* Feb. 8, 2003.

8. RSY 2004, Tables 25.2, 25.16; RET2, #10, 2002, Tables 13-14; additional calculations.

9. *Finansovye Izvestiia,* March 5, 2002. Financial accounts of both companies for 2004.

10. This account of Gazprom's history is largely based on the article "Komu prinadlezhit Rossiia. Gazovaia promyshlennost'" ("Who Owns Russia. The Gas Industry"), in KV, #47, 2001.

11. *Forbes,* July 2001.

12. *Finans,* Feb. 13, 2005, http://www.finansmag.ru//12390.

13. These details, and more, were laid out in KV, #47, 2001.

14. Strana.ru, March 11, 2002.

15. Strana.ru, Jan. 10, 2002.

16. This section uses material published in "Komu prinadlezhit Rossiia. Zheleznodorozhnyi transport" ("Who owns Russia. Rail transport"), in KV, #2, 2002.

17. A. Sokolov, "VPK na dne" ("MIC Hits Bottom"), in the Forum section of ECAAR-Russia's web site: http://www.fastcenter.ru/ecaar/sokolov.htm.

18. MIC Teleinformation System, http://www.ts.vpk.ru/index_c.htm (see sources for Table 3.2).

19. "Armiia: odin god s Sergeem Ivanovym" ("The Army: One Year with Sergei Ivanov"), Strana.ru, March 28, 2002.

20. GLONASS is described on the web site of the Russian Federation Ministry of Defense's Coordinating Center for Scientific Information, http://www.rssi.ru/SFCSIC.

21. "Armiia u Rossii est'" ("Russia Has An Army"), *Krasnaia Zvezda,* March 30, 2002; "Rossiia moderniziruet strategicheskuiu aviatsiiu" ("Russia Modernizes Its Strategic Air Forces"), Strana.ru, March 28, 2002.

22. See source in Note 20.

23. "Novye 'stapeli' dlia samoleta piatogo pokoleniia" ("New 'Assembly Jigs' for Fifth-generation Aircraft"), *Krasnaia Zvezda,* March 29, 2002.

24. *Krasnaia Zvezda,* March 30, 2002.

25. "Mify i legendy oboronki" ("Myths and Legends of the Defense Sector"). Interview with NPO Almaz General Director Igor Ashurbeili, *Nezavisimoe voennoe obozrenie (Independent Military Review),* March 29, 2002.

26. "Khabblu by nashi pribory" ("If Only the Hubble Had Our Instruments"). Interview with Alexander Mezentsev, director of the Applied Mechanics NII, *Krasnaia Zvezda,* March 30, 2002.

27. RFE/RL, March 20, 2002.

28. Our calculations are based on data in "Gazprom predlagaet poetapnyi otkaz ot regulirovaniia gazovykh tsen" ("Gazprom proposes a gradual move away from gas price regulation"), Strana.ru, April 19, 2002.

29. RSY 2004, Table 14.37, p. 322.

30. S. Menshikov, *Millionery i menedzhery* (op. cit.) describes these processes in detail.

31. *Dengi,* #43, 2001. We have corrected two obvious errors. First, Alexei Miller, who the authors say controls 50 percent of Gazprom's cash turnover, is erroneously shown as controlling an amount equal to only 5 percent of that turnover in 2001. Second, Rosenergoatom Executive Director Yuri Yakovlev is listed twice.

32. "Zakhvat, plavno perekhodyashchii v minirovanie" ("A seizure that morphed into minelaying"), Gazeta.ru, May 25, 2002.

33. "Mezhprombank vzial Slavneft'" ("Mezhprombank has seized Slavneft"), Gazeta.ru, May 1, 2002.

34. RFE/RL, May 16, 2002.

35. "Menedzheram RAO EES nuzhno naiti po $250 tys. na pokupku aktsii svoei kompanii" ("UES managers must come up with $250 thousand each to buy shares in their own company"), Strana.ru, April 27, 2002.

36. Our calculation, based on data from the UES web site, http://www.rao-ees.ru.

37. "Vazhnyi klient. Banki otrabatyvaiut tekhnologii po obsluzhivaniiu VIP-person" ("The important client. Banks develop approaches to servicing VIPs"), *Izvestia,* March 27, 2002.

38. "Amerikanskii Forbs naschityvaet v Rossii sem' milliarderov" ("America's *Forbes* counts seven billionaires in Russia"), Strana.ru, March 1, 2002. Our list includes two billionaires, Rem Vyakhirev and Victor Chernomyrdin, who were on the *Forbes* list for 2001, but not 2002.

39. RSY 2000, p. 266.

40. RET2, #2, 2002, p. 34.

41. Our calculation, based on RET2, #2, 2002, p. 16.

42. *Finans,* #6, 2006 and #5, 2005. Since Vladimir Bogdanov inexplicably disappeared from the 2006 *Finans* list, the 2005 estimate of his fortune is shown.

43. Our calculation, based on RSY 2000, p. 149. Officially business and property income represented around 20 percent of total personal income before the adoption of the single flat income tax rate. After the institution of the flat tax (which represented a tax cut for higher income-earners) and the emergence of a certain portion of income "out of the shadows," the share of business and property income rose to 28 percent. Some estimates indicate that, even after the tax change, personal income on the whole is 40 to 50 percent higher than reported. Cf. *Finansovye Izvestiia,* April 25, 2002.

44. RSY 2000, p. 297.

45. "Izmenenie povedeniia ekonomicheski aktivnogo naseleniia v usloviiakh krizisa. Na primere melkikh predprinimatelei i samozaniatykh" ("Changes in behavior of the economically active population during the crisis. The example of small

businessmen and the self-employed"), Moscow Public Science Foundation, *Nauchnye doklady*, #119, Moscow, 2000.

46. "Vladimir Putin: srednii biznes effektivno rabotaet v kogda-to upadochnykh sektorakh sovetskoi ekonomiki" ("Vladimir Putin: medium-sized business is working effectively in previously depressed sectors of the Soviet economy"), Strana.ru, Oct. 16, 2001.

47. "Gosudarstvo opredelilo 8 uslovii protsvetaniia malogo biznesa" ("The state has defined 8 conditions for small business to thrive"), Strana.ru, Dec. 17, 2001.

48. Here and below, Goskomstat's methodology for analysis and accounting of the shadow economy is presented on the basis of *Metodologicheskie polozheniia po statistike. Vypusk vtoroy* (*Methodological Principles of Statistics, 2nd edition*) (Moscow: Goskomstat of Russia, 1998), pp. 11-130.

49. "Nevidimyi sprut. Razmakh tenevoi ekonomiki Rossii otsenivaetsia v 90-110 milliardov dollarov" ("An invisible octopus. Russia's shadow economy is valued at $90-110 billion"), *Trud*, Jan. 10, 2001.

50. Our calculations are based on productivity statistics in the National Accounting System, RSY 2004, Table 12.3.

51. "NTV soobshchilo o spekuliatsiiakh 'Slavnefti'" ("NTV reports Slavneft speculation"), SMI.ru, May 5, 2002.

52. Data on Slavneft are taken from its web site, http://www.slavneft.ru/newsdump/169.1.html.

53. "'Slavneft' kak tochka sborki" ("Slavneft as assembly point"), SMI.ru, May 17, 2002.

54. *Trud*, Jan. 10. 2002, op. cit. (Note 51).

55. "Tenevaia ekonomika v Rossii protsvetaet" ("The shadow economy is flourishing in Russia"), *Argumenty i fakty*, #18-19, May 2002.

56. *Rossiia i korruptsiia: kto kogo. Analiticheskii doklad* (Russia and Corruption: Who Will Win? Analytical Report), Regional public foundation Information for Democracy (INDEM Foundation), Moscow, 1998, http://www.indem.ru/ic/.

57. *Diagnostika rossiiskoi korruptsii: Sotsiologicheskii analiz* (Diagnostics of Russian Corruption: A Sociological Analysis), Moscow, 2002, http://www.anti-corr.ru/.

58. Preliminary report, http://www.indem.ru/en/Publicat/corr5720.htm.

4 How Our Economy Works: Production and Income Distribution

Analysis of how any economy works has to proceed from two standpoints. One of them is an investigation of who and what the economic agents are, and what determines their behavior. The previous chapters of this book dealt with this aspect. The other aspect is macroeconomics: the behavior of many thousands of agents (tens of millions of them, if individual consumers are included), taken as a whole, is presented as an integrated summary. The statistical expression of this summary picture is the gross domestic product (GDP). We have mentioned GDP several times in the foregoing discussion, presuming that the reader is familiar with this concept. Since we are now going to look more closely at this summary category, it may be useful to review a few relevant definitions.

GDP is simultaneously the total of all primary incomes, meaning income created in the real economy, and the total of all types of end use of output. In the middle of the 19th century, economists asserted that these two values were equal, which was confirmed using statistics in the middle of the 20th century. In other words, total primary income, being the sum of wages, gross profit, and business income (pre-tax in all cases, but including depreciation of fixed assets) is always equal to the sum of personal consumption, gross investment (including net inventory growth), government consumption and net exports of goods and services (exports minus imports).

The first total is the final product of the economy in terms of the sources of value added (or new value produced), while the second total represents the final product in terms of its utilization. It is called the "final product" because it does not include current material outlays for the production of output, corresponding to intermediate

Table 4.1 GDP distribution by source of income
(% of total)

	1991	1992	1993	1994	1995	1996	1997	1998	1999	2000	2001	2002	2003	1992-2003 average
GDP	100	100	100	100	100	100	100	100	100	100	100	100	100	100
Components:														
Compensation of employees	43.7	36.7	44.5	49.3	45.2	49.6	50.0	47.2	40.9	39.9	45.0	46.6	46.2	45.5
Including off-the-books compensation of employees	–	–	5.3	8.5	10.4	11.7	11.7	11.1	11.0	11.1	11.0	11.5	11.2	10.0
On-the-books compensation of employees	43.7	36.7	39.2	40.8	34.8	37.9	38.3	36.1	29.9	28.8	34.0	35.1	35.0	35.5
Adjusted compensation of employees	43.7	36.7	41.8	45.0	40.0	43.7	44.1	41.6	36.4	34.3	39.5	40.8	40.6	40.3
Net taxes on production and imports	4.5	3.4	10.6	9.5	7.8	13.5	14.4	15.2	15.9	17.0	15.6	14.1	13.3	12.5
Gross economic profit and gross mixed income	51.9	59.9	44.9	41.2	43.0	36.9	35.5	37.8	43.1	42.9	39.6	39.3	40.5	42.1
Mixed income	2.6	7.0	8.7	8.9	12.3	11.8	11.9	12.7	12.1	10.7	9.7	9.5	(10.1)	10.5
Gross economic profit	49.3	52.9	36.2	32.3	30.7	25.1	23.6	25.1	31.0	32.2	29.9	29.8	(30.4)	31.6

Sources: RSY 2000, p. 142, 250; RSY 2002, p. 280; RSY 2004, Tables 12.5, 7.2; NAS 1993-2000, Table 2.3, Goskomstat, 2001 (hereinafter NAS2001). Amounts shown in parentheses are our estimates.

products, which are goods and services supplied from one sector to another and consumed in the second sector during the time period under consideration.

GDP data may appear to be simply a static impression of the economy—its summary result for one year, or one quarter, or some other period of time. But they may also be considered as a totality of interconnected elements, each of which determines what happens with the others and, consequently, in the economy as a whole. Wages and non-labor income, for example, determine current and, to some extent, future demand for household and personal consumption products. Gross profit determines the volume of capital investment, or demand for capital goods, in future periods of time, as well as the current period. Taxes, which are more or less proportional to the above-mentioned types of income, determine the volume of current government demand. Total final demand, in turn, determines the dimensions of total national output and its distribution by sector. And the volume of output determines the demand for labor, and hence the number of persons employed and the size of labor income. Gross profit (as defined above) is the remainder when wages are subtracted from value added.

Thus, GDP statistics reflect the complex circulation of output and income, upon which the economic process is based. With that brief introduction, we shall now proceed to explore the composition of GDP in capitalist Russia.

4.1 The composition of national income: the relationship of labor income to gross profit

Table 4.1 compares GDP distribution in the period of reforms with the base year of 1991 (the last year of the Soviet period).

Comparing the average figures for 1992-2003 with the base year, we first notice that compensation paid to hired workers, or wages (plus payments by employers for social security), changed little, if so-called "concealed" (off-the-books) labor income is included. It increased by only 1.6 percent, from 43.7 percent to 45.3 percent of GDP. But the category of off-the-books labor income is not well-defined. First of all, it is a rough estimate, given by Goskomstat with a 1 billion ruble margin of error, whereas all other types of income are measured by official accounting data with only a 1 million ruble margin of error. Here are the off-the-books hired labor compensation figures by year (millions of rubles)[1]:

1994	52,000
1995	160,000
1996	250,000
1997	290,000
1998	277,000
1999	525,000
2000	782,000
2001	993,500
2002	1,249,000
2003	1,488,000

The method by which these estimates were derived is also highly dubious. Furthermore, off-the-books labor income here includes not only so-called "black cash," extra payments that employers hand to ordinary workers on the sly, in order to avoid paying the mandatory social tax, but also compensation paid to the capitalists themselves and to senior executives, which really should come under the category of types of distribution of profit, rather than under labor income. If we assume that these components of off-the-books compensation are approximately equal, we can derive an adjusted (not overstated) estimate of labor income.

Goskomstat's IOT, it should be noted, make no attempt to relate off-the-books labor income to specific sectors of the economy. Such off-the-books payments are counted not under "compensation of employees," but under "gross profit and gross mixed income."[2] Strictly speaking, this approach is not the same as classifying it as non-labor income. What happens is that Goskomstat calculates gross profit and gross mixed income by sector, by subtracting labor income from value added. But that means that the statistics do not break out the labor component of "off-the-books compensation of employees."

It should also be noted that the statistical category of reported compensation of employees includes employers' social insurance contributions, thus exaggerating the amount actually paid as wages to workers. These components can be distinguished on the basis of

Table 4.2 Two measures of components of compensation of employees, 1995
(billions of redenominated rubles)

1995 IOT	
Compensation of employees	358.9
Social insurance deductions	139.9
Total compensation of employees	498.9
1995 NAS	
Compensation of employees paid to hired workers	695.8
Off-the-books compensation of employees component	160.0
On-the-books compensation of employees	535.8

the unpublished IOT for 1995, but the publicly available IOT for subsequent years conceal their relative shares. Table 4.2 compares, for example, the totals for the national economy as a whole in the draft version of the 1995 IOT, with the NAS data for that year, published later.

Here it can be seen that the share of labor income, in the strict sense of the term, equaled 71.9 percent of total reported compensation of employees. If that percentage is assumed to be approximately the same for the entire post-Soviet period, the share of wages will have fallen to 25.8 percent of its 1991 level. Such a low level is unprecedented for a country with developed large-scale industry and an employed workforce numbering in the millions.

Unfortunately, we are unable to cite these data for each year of the reform period. According to the IOT data for 1990, wages made up 89 percent of total labor income at that time, meaning that social insurance deductions were substantially less. Wages as such accounted for 40.5 percent of GDP at that time, as against only 25.8 percent on average for the reform period.

If we take total reported on-the-books compensation of employees, including social insurance deductions, its share in GDP fell abruptly and by a large amount, nearly 20 percent, from 43.7 percent in 1991 to 35.5 percent on average for the subsequent decade. Although the figures for individual years fluctuated around that average (in a range between 28.8 and 40.8 percent), in no year did the share of wages in GDP exceed its Soviet-era level. The underlying causes of this pattern were the decline of real wages, which will be

Table 4.3 Ratio of non-labor income to labor income (%)

	1991	1992	1993	1994	1995	1996	1997	1998	1999	2000	2001	2002	2003	1992-2003 average
Ratio of gross economic profit and mixed income to compensation of employees	119	163	101	84	95	74	71	80	105	108	88	84	88	96
The same, including off-the-books unearned income	119	179	111	92	105	81	78	88	116	119	97	96	100	106
Ratio of total non-labor income to reported compensation of employees	119	163	115	101	124	97	93	105	144	149	120	121	121	121
Ratio of adjusted non-labor income to on-the-books compensation of employees	119	179	127	111	136	107	102	116	158	164	132	128	132	132

discussed in more detail in Section 4.2, and their relative lag behind overall GDP growth.

Adjusted labor income (including, as noted above, one-half of off-the-books compensation of employees) improves the picture somewhat. Average annual adjusted labor income fell from 43.7 to 40.3 percent, by only 3.4 percentage points. Nonetheless, the general trend is the same as for the unadjusted figures.

The share of non-labor income (gross profit and mixed income) also fell, on average, from 51.9 to 42.5 percent. To a significant degree, this comparison is misleading, because the share of net indirect taxes, which are measured in market prices and included in GDP statistics, rose significantly. If we exclude the impact of this factor, the share of non-labor income rises to 48.5 percent, as against 54.3 percent in 1991. Moreover, the relative weight of gross profit and mixed income within total non-labor income underwent a marked shift in favor of mixed income. In 1991, the private sector's share was negligibly small. Despite the absence of any surge in small business development during Russia's capitalist period, the average share of mixed income for that period rose to 10.6 percent. This is also reflected in the relative weight of gross profit as such, which averaged 32 percent, as against 49 percent in 1991.

All of these data, however, need to be adjusted. We showed in Chapter 3 that official GDP statistics are understated by at least 10 percent. Practically all of the understatement is associated with gross profit. Taking this factor into account and adjusting for the share of net indirect taxes, the average share of non-labor income during the capitalist period ought to be at least 53.7 percent, rather than 42.1 percent, and the share of gross profit should be 42.9 percent, rather than 31.9 percent. Adding the portion of off-the-books labor income that actually constitutes payments to the capitalists and senior executives, the average share of unearned income rises to 64 percent, which is substantially higher than the corresponding figure of 53.4 percent for 1991.

The same trends are evident from a direct comparison of non-labor and labor income (Table 4.3). This figure coincides with the rate of surplus product for society as a whole.

If we use only the official data for gross profit and mixed income, and look at the relationship of their sum to total labor income, we find that the average rate of surplus product declined in comparison to the base year. Adjusting for off-the-books profit slightly increases this indicator, but not by a lot. Looking at the ratio of all non-labor income (but without counting off-the-books profit) to only the reported portion of labor income, the average rate of surplus product in the reform period is only very slightly higher than the 1991 level. These estimates ignore our 50-50 division of off-the-books compensation of employees into non-labor and labor components, since the ratio would remain approximately the same, if equal coefficients were applied to the numerator and the denominator. Finally, when off-the-books profit and the portion of off-the-books labor compensation that actually goes to the capitalist class are added in, the rate of surplus product rises to 132 percent, compared with 119 percent in 1991.

It should be noted, of course, that the figures being compared for these years differ in a fundamental way. In the Soviet period the greater part of gross economic profit was at the disposal of the government or of state-owned enterprises, while in the years that followed, a growing portion of the after-tax surplus product has been at the disposal of private companies or individual private property owners, and is used by them as they see fit. This fact substantially changes the way in which the composition of GDP, in terms of income categories, affects its composition in terms of utilization, and thus affects the economic process as a whole. These changes will be discussed in detail in later sections of this chapter.

Let us compare the composition of Russia's GDP by types of income, with the analogous data for the USA (Table 4.4). To what extent does the state of affairs in our country differ from the situation in modern capitalism's benchmark country?

U.S. statistics on types of income are broken down in more detail than ours. Consumption of fixed assets is broken out of gross economic profit for each year, whereas Goskomstat publishes these data only in the IOT, and not for every year. U.S. mixed income is broken down into its three main components: business income, rent, and interest.

Table 4.4 shows that the share of gross economic profit in GDP is lower by one-third in the USA than in Russia, while the share of labor income is 27 percent higher. The share of mixed income is also substantially higher in the USA, because small and medium-

Table 4.4 GDP by types of income—comparison with USA

	USA: 1989-1998 average, billions of $	USA: % share of total	Russia: 1992-2001 average, % share of total
GDP	6,956.8	100%	100%
Consumption of fixed assets	856.4		
Corporate profit	587.2		
Gross economic profit, total	1,443.6	20.8%	31.9%
Business income	472.8		
Rent	92.5		
Interest	410.5		
Mixed income, total	975.8	14.0%	10.8%
Non-labor income, total	2,419.4	34.8%	42.5%
Labor compensation paid to hired workers	3,971.8	57.1%	44.8%
Net indirect taxes	565.6	8.1%	12.3%
Rate of surplus product, %	–	61%	97% (133%*)

* Including off-the-books profit.

Source for U.S. data: *Economic Report of the President of the United States*, 2000.

sized business is more developed there. On the whole, even if we take the official data and do not adjust them for off-the-books profit, the rate of surplus product in Russia averages 60 percent higher than in the leading capitalist country. If the off-the-books income of the capitalist class were counted, the rate would be 2.2 times higher than the U.S. rate.

To some extent this tilt results from the "pirate" nature of Russian capitalism, which has practically no regulatory limitations of the sort that bourgeois reformers introduced in the USA (and other leading industrial nations of the West) beginning in the 1930s and 1940s. But that is not the only cause of the discrepancy. Capitalism in Russia inherited from our socialism low levels of labor income, together with relatively low, government-subsidized consumer spending for utilities and social services. In addition to state property, Russian capitalism appropriated a disproportionately high share of the surplus product, which the state had previously received, but now redounded to private capital.

In all of these respects, Russian capitalism lags behind the more

Table 4.5 Distribution of the population's total income by groups

(% of total, unless noted otherwise)

	1970	1991	1992	1994	1998	2000	2002	2003
Quintiles of the population								
First — lowest incomes	7.8%	11.9%	6.0%	5.3%	6.0%	6.0%	5.6%	5.6%
Second	14.8%	15.8%	11.6%	10.2%	10.4%	10.4%	10.4%	10.3%
Third	18.0%	18.8%	17.6%	15.2%	14.8%	14.8%	15.4%	15.3%
Fourth	22.6%	22.8%	26.5%	23.0%	21.2%	21.2%	22.8%	22.7%
Fifth — highest incomes	36.8%	30.7%	38.3%	46.3%	47.6%	47.6%	45.8%	46.1%
Ratio of fifth to first quintile	4.7	2.6	6.4	8.7	7.9	7.9	8.2	8.2
Ratio of tenth to first decile	–	–	8.0	15.1	13.8	13.8	14.0	14.3
Gini coefficient	–	0.260	0.289	0.409	0.399	0.399	0.398	0.400

Sources: RSY 2000, RSY 2001.

developed models, prevalent in the industrialized countries of the West. Whether or not it will begin to converge with them depends on many factors, which we shall explore below.

4.2 Income distribution inequality, social stratification, and the middle class

The course of capitalist development in Russia, compounded by the nearly total absence of organized resistance on the part of workers, or palpable signs of social-democratic or other social reformism, has produced a significant increase of inequality in the distribution of income and of the national wealth. Government statistics from recent decades show this to be the case (Table 4.5).

Inequality in personal income distribution was steadily declining in the Soviet period. During the two decades prior to the collapse of the Soviet Union (1970-1991), the gap between the average income of people in the upper and lower quintiles shrank significantly, from a factor of 4.7 to a factor of 2.6. Of course, Soviet statistics did not count off-the-books income in the illegal sector of the economy, and the income of the top Party and government nomenklatura was only partially reflected in official statistics. Nonetheless it is undeniable that this period witnessed a strong tendency toward the equalization of income in various sectors of the economy and regions of the country. It should be remembered that these data are for the Russian Federation, where income distribution was more uniform than in the USSR as a whole, which contained the very substantial gap between income in the Baltic republics and in Central Asia.

In 1991, Russia's Gini coefficient, which measures the concentration of income, was one of the lowest in the world: 0.26. It was on approximately the same level as in the socialist countries of Eastern Europe, and much lower than in the social reformist countries of Western Europe, such as Sweden, not to mention leading developed capitalist countries, or the even more extreme cases in the Third World, with their immense gaps between rich and poor.

These conditions were also reflected in the nature of the consumer goods market, which was oriented primarily toward the prevalence of relatively low- and middle-income groups. Thus, in 1991, 70 percent of total effective demand was accounted for by the

Table 4.6 Composition of personal monetary income
(% of total)

	1970	1990	1992	1994	1998	2000	2003
Business income	2.5	3.7	8.4	16.0	14.5	15.9	12.0
Labor compensation	83.3	76.4	73.6	64.5	64.8	61.4	63.9
Social entitlements	12.6	14.7	14.3	13.5	13.4	14.4	14.1
Income from property	0.6	2.5	1.0	4.5	5.5	7.1	7.8
Other income	1.0	2.7	2.7	1.5	1.8	1.2	2.2

Sources: RSY 2000, RSY 2001, RSY 2004.

lower 80 percent of the population with respect to income.

This egalitarian quality of income distribution was disrupted in the very first years of the transition to capitalism. By 1994, the Gini coefficient had reached its highest mark (0.409), from which it has barely wavered in the years that followed. The gap between the top and bottom quintiles rose to a factor of 8.2 in 2003, more than triple what it had been in the base year, 1991. The gap between the top and bottom deciles rose to a factor of 14.3. The 80 percent of the population with low and middle-level income now accounted for only 52 percent of total monetary consumer demand, far less than in the last year of Soviet power. The consumer-goods market split into the elite and ordinary sectors that are typical of capitalist countries.

The growth of income inequality can be explained by two sorts of reasons: first, by changes in the social composition of income as such, and, secondly, by the influence of the country's entry into the world market, bringing greatly increased exposure to the processes of globalization.

Before the reforms, labor income (compensation of employees and social entitlements) was essentially the only type of personal monetary income in Russia, accounting for 96 percent of the total in 1970 and 91 percent in 1990 (Table 4.6). In reality, business income hidden in the shadow sector had become a significant phenomenon toward the end of the Soviet period; we estimate it at 10 percent of GDP. But for the sake of comparison with subsequent years, we shall stay within the bounds of official statistics, which made certain minimal adjustments for the illegal economy.

The rise of business income from its 3.7 percent share of total income in 1990 to 15.9 percent in 2000, and of income from property

Table 4.7   Concealed income
(as % of GDP)

Goskomstat estimate of concealed income, included in GDP	23.4
Other concealed income of the capitalist class	12.6
Bribes to government officials	11.7
Income of organized crime	13.2

from 2.5 to 7.1 percent in the same period, increased the degree of inequality in income distribution, for the simple reason that these types of income tend to be significantly higher than average labor compensation.

Official data understate the degree of inequality, for at least two reasons. First of all, a portion of the sums counted under the "compensation of employees" heading are actually salaries and bonuses received by senior executives, who in effect belong to the capitalist class. Secondly, as we saw in Chapter 3, a significant portion of non-labor income is concealed for the purpose of tax evasion, or fails to be counted in personal monetary income statistics for other reasons. Let us review our approximate estimates of these amounts (Table 4.7).

We have already indicated why these sums cannot be totalled, due to double counting. Business has to buy off government officials, as well as organized crime. Furthermore, not all of these concealed sums represent personal income for members of the capitalist class. Nonetheless, it may be assumed that in reality, the share of such income is at least double what the official statistics show. If this is the case, then the data for income of the upper quintiles and deciles of the population need to be adjusted substantially upwards. With these assumptions, the gap between the average income of the highest and lowest deciles rises to a factor of 25 in 2000, while the Gini coefficient approaches 0.5 or even higher. Interestingly enough, the World Bank in one of its annual reports offered an estimate of the Gini coefficient very close to this: 0.48.[3]

Over and above the transition to capitalism, which in any case presumes a significant gap between a wealthy minority and the less well-off majority, the growth of inequality was compounded by Russia's integration into the world economy and greater exposure

Table 4.8 Changes in nominal wages, retail prices and real wages

	1991	1992	1993	1994	1995	1996	1997	1998	1999	2000	2001	2002	2003
Nominal wages (growth, multiple)	1.81	10.9	9.8	3.8	2.1	1.7	1.2	1.1	1.45	1.46	1.48	1.34	1.26
Retail prices of goods and services (growth, multiple)	1.87	16.3	9.8	4.1	2.9	1.5	1.15	1.28	1.81	1.22	1.22	1.16	1.14
Real wages (growth, multiple)	0.97	0.67	1.0	0.92	0.72	1.14	1.04	0.86	0.8	1.2	1.21	1.16	1.11
Real wages (1990=100)	97	65	65	60	43	49	51	44	35	42	51	59	65

Sources: RSY 2000, RSY 2001, RSY 2004.

to the influence of the world market.

The impact of globalization on the standard of living can be traced, above all, in the difference between the growth rates of retail prices and nominal wages. In the very first phase of market reforms, the domestic market became more dependent on imports of consumer goods: foodstuffs, and both non-durables and durables. In this situation, retail prices overall began to orient toward the prices of imported goods, to a large extent, especially since as much as half of total demand was accounted for by well-to-do layers of the population, who could afford those high prices.

At the same time, nominal wages were determined by entirely different criteria. The base level was the Soviet one, which allowed for socialism's traditional low-cost housing, utilities, transportation, and healthcare services, and virtually free education. Under the new conditions, the cost of these services gradually rose, though remaining comparatively low for a long time, thus defining a likewise low average wage level. The overall economic situation, of course, also played its part: economic crisis and stagnation lasted until 1998, with significant unemployment. Hired labor was poorly organized and lacked experience in fighting for its rights.

The data in Table 4.8 show that the growth of monetary wages in 1992-1995 consistently lagged behind the rise of retail prices, resulting in a decline of real wages (according to official data) to 43 percent of their 1990 level. In subsequent years the economic slump stopped worsening, while inflation abated. Wage growth, albeit weak, did catch up to the rise of prices, without achieving pre-reform levels.

The 1998 crisis, accompanied by an explosion of inflation, once again drove the standard of living downwards. By 1999, real wages had fallen to 35 percent of their 1990 level. The subsequent economic recovery brought jobs growth, falling unemployment, and a substantial increase in average wages. Real wages, however, rose very modestly. As of 2001, real wages had regained only their pre-crisis "peak" of 1997, when real wages were at 51 percent of the 1990 level. Later the gap was reduced, but real wages are still below the 1990 peak.

Lowering real wages intensifies social inequality, since the employee compensation paid to an absolute majority of workers can be categorized as average or low income. The great majority

Table 4.9 Ratio of average wage for industrial sector to average wage in all industry
(multiple)

	1970	1991	2000	2003
Sectors with improvement of wage levels				
Fuels industries	1.43	1.65	2.42	2.35
Non-ferrous metallurgy	1.52	1.60	2.26	1.80
Finance, banking	0.86	1.63	1.99	2.31
Electric power industry	1.07	1.51	1.47	1.41
Steel industry	1.15	1.15	1.29	1.23
Transport	1.05	1.08	1.22	1.19
Communications	0.74	0.82	1.05	1.14
Unchanged				
Management	0.96	0.89	0.89	1.07
Sectors with deterioration of wage levels				
Construction	1.14	1.15	1.02	1.02
Machine-building and metal-working	1.00	0.97	0.77	0.83
Light industry	0.76	0.95	0.44	0.43
Food industry	0.93	1.08	0.87	0.82
Trade	0.72	0.78	0.58	0.61
Health care	0.70	0.69	0.50	0.58
Education	0.80	0.64	0.45	0.53
Culture and art	0.67	0.61	0.45	0.54
Agriculture	0.66	0.76	0.33	0.33

of pensioners also fall into this group. Persistent mass poverty is steadily generated from these groups of the population; they are the segments of our population whose income is consistently below the official minimum subsistence level.

The average pension, which in Soviet times was above the poverty line, under capitalism tended toward the subsistence minimum, falling far below it after the crisis of 1998. Despite a substantial increase in pensions under Vladimir Putin, this lag has not been erased. At least two-thirds of Russia's pensioners, or 25 million people, are firmly in the category of chronic poverty, without any real prospects of getting out of this situation in the years ahead.

It is telling, that hired workers' average wages have also experienced a sustained decline in relationship to the subsistence minimum. While in 1992 the average wage level was triple the poverty level, by 2001 it was only 2.2 times higher. Among the sectors of the economy where average wages are either equal to or below the subsistence minimum are light industry (especially textiles and garments), agriculture, health care, education, and culture. These sectors employ a total of more than 20 million blue-collar and office workers. Combined with the impoverished pensioners, that makes 45 million people. Add the non-working members of their families, and the army of the chronically poor reaches 55-60 million people, or 38-41 percent of the population of Russia.

As the years pass, the gap between wages in a number of select sectors which are closely tied to the world market, and in sectors oriented primarily to the domestic market, has steadily increased.

Table 4.9 shows the ratio of the average wage in each sector to the average wage in industry as a whole. In 1991-2003, workers in the export-oriented sectors (fuels, non-ferrous metals, and steel), the natural monopolies (electric power, transport, and communications), and finance and banking experienced improvement in their wages.

The wage situation deteriorated, relatively speaking, in practically all of the sectors producing for the domestic market (construction, machine-building and metal-working, light industry, the food industry, trade, health care, education, culture and art, and agriculture).

The powerful impact of globalization on wage inequality is also

Table 4.10 Average per capita income in various regions

Average per capita monthly income (rubles)

	1994	2000	2003
Russian Federation	206.3	2,192.9	5,162
Moscow	691.1	9,291.3	16,819
St. Petersburg	223.2	2,589.6	6,851
Moscow Region	186.6	1,908.3	4,425
Ryazan Region	140.3	1,200.4	3,309
Ivanovo Region	113.9	912.3	2,293
Voronezh Region	128.3	1,239.0	3,391
Leningrad Region	156.5	1,357.1	3,037
Nizhny Novgorod Region	163.8	1,561.6	4,022
Ulyanovsk Region	147.0	1,212.3	3,063
Tyumen Region	409.4	4,905.3	10,555
Siberian Federal District	–	1,765.6	4,355
Far East Federal District	–	2,227.5	5,788

Moscow compared with others (multiple)

Moscow/Russia	3.3	4.2	3.3
Moscow/Moscow Region	3.7	4.9	3.8
Moscow/Voronezh Region	5.4	7.5	5.0
Moscow/Ryazan Region	4.9	7.7	5.1
Moscow/Ulyanovsk Region	4.7	7.7	5.5
Moscow/St. Petersburg	3.1	3.6	2.5

evident from data on average income by geographical area (Table 4.10).

In only two of the constituent territories of the Russian Federation is the average income substantially higher than the nationwide average. They are Moscow, where practically all of the country's major exporting companies, most of the leading banks, and the representative offices of foreign corporations are headquartered, and the Tyumen Region, center of the West Siberian oil and gas fields. In two others, St. Petersburg and the Far East, incomes are slightly higher than the national average.

Moscow especially stands out as a comparatively wealthy oasis in the surrounding provincial "desert." The gap between Moscow and the rest of the country, with respect to average income, steadily widened during the 1990s. In 1994, Moscow incomes were already

3.3 times greater than the average national per capita income. In 2000, Moscow incomes were 4.2 times the national average. By 2003, the difference had narrowed, but incomes in the capital were still more than triple the level prevalent elsewhere in Russia. The gap is especially large between Moscow and some of the old cities of central European Russia: the average Muscovite's income was 7.5 times the average in Voronezh Region and 7.7 times the average income in Ryazan and Ulyanovsk Regions. Gaps of that magnitude are typical of Third World countries that have been caught in the net of the globalized economy: they have parasitical cities against a backdrop of general desolation and poverty.

The steep increase of inequality has serious socioeconomic consequences. The polarization of society creates an environment for social and political instability. Mass poverty fuels the growth of extremist political opposition groups. Contrary to the claim that a large new middle class is emerging in Russia, with adequate income and the ability to serve as a natural foundation for social stability, the middle layer remains relatively small.

Natalya Rimashevskaya, head of the Russian Academy of Sciences Institute for Socioeconomic Population Studies, believes that this growing inequality has split society into "two Russias, which speak different languages and do not understand each other. ... They are opposed to each other, and the distance between them is growing, with respect to behavior, preferences, and orientation. They have two different standards of living, and two consumer goods markets, which are quite distinct both in prices and in the availability of products. A particularly dangerous aspect of this split is that the political elite is drawn from the Russia of the wealthy and the super-wealthy."[4]

The growth of economic inequality is visible in the segmentation of the domestic market into one group of products, and their producers, which are oriented almost exclusively to wealthy, elite layers of society, while another group has to provide products to the impoverished majority and the far-from-wealthy middle layers, who have limited effective demand. The first category of producers gets by with producing relatively small output, but setting very high prices. The second category cannot break out of the bounds defined by the relatively low-quality products that the average consumer can afford.

The middle class

There has been considerable discussion in the literature about the emergence of a middle class, which would not belong to the extreme categories described above, and would partially mitigate the polarization of Russian society. There is little agreement on the definition of this middle class, or on indications that it is developing. The widely differing criteria, proposed for defining the middle class, make it extremely difficult to give even an approximate estimate of the size of this social group.

A 2002 Carnegie Foundation study, using a combination of three factors—education and professional qualification, having one's material needs satisfied, and self-identification—found that 7 percent of the population of Russia is in the middle class. For an additional 12 percent, according to the study, there are some indications of their belonging to the middle class.[5]

Professor Akos Rona-Tas of the University of California at San Diego astutely observed in his article, "Post Communist Transition and the Absent Middle Class": "A middle class that is in the minority is an oxymoron. In democracies the middle class is the nation proper. The typical member of a national community is a member of the middle class. ... The middle class is not everyone, but it is the majority and it represents what everyone else can become." Sam Vaknin, citing that article, concludes, " ... Russia has a long way to go to achieve this ubiquity. Its middle class, far from representing the consensus, reifies the growing abyss between haves and have-nots. Its members' conspicuous consumption, mostly of imports, does little to support the local economy. ... The Russian middle class is at a ... primordial stage. ... [It is] viewed with suspicion and envy by ... the overwhelming majority of Russia's destitute population."[6]

Indeed, if the Russian middle class (plus the numerically small rich upper layer) comprises only 20 percent of the population, that really is a small minority, as against the 30 percent of the population living below the poverty line, and fully one-half of the population, occupying a place between the very poorest and the middle class, and categorized by sociologists in the West as "lower class." This "lower class" group includes the great majority of ordinary workers and other employees, whose monthly per capita income ranges between $60 and $150 (1,800-4,500 rubles at the 2002 exchange rate).

Ultimately, theirs is the income level that determines the growth rate of personal consumption in Russia.

This state of affairs likewise determines the tight straits in which domestic manufacturing finds itself. This question will be analyzed in detail in the next section.

4.3 The composition of GDP: personal consumption, investment, and government consumption

The distribution of the national income, described above, naturally determines the composition of aggregate final demand, or GDP viewed from the standpoint of how it is consumed and otherwise utilized.

The first striking feature shown in Table 4.11 is the extremely low share of personal consumption (compared with the industrialized nations of the West), represented by the line "household final consumption." It averaged 46.9 percent of GDP in 1992-2001. By comparison, the share of personal consumption in U.S. GDP is stable at a level of around 67 percent.

It would appear that Russian capitalism has managed to turn to its own advantage the low share of personal consumption in GDP inherited from the Soviet period. Under the centrally planned economy, limitation of personal consumption made it possible to allocate significant resources for capital investment and military purposes. For capitalist society, it became a way to suppress labor income and increase surplus value.

In analyzing Table 4.11, it should be kept in mind that the significant jumps in the share of net exports in GDP greatly influence the data for the period of reforms. Discounting this factor, we obtain quite an interesting picture of the changes in the share of personal consumption in aggregate domestic demand or, in other words, its place in the domestic market. Two sub-periods emerge: 1992-1997, when the share of personal consumption was 40-50 percent, and 1998-2003, when it rose to 57-62 percent. This is a substantial difference, which had an impact on overall economic growth, as we shall see in detail in the next section.

In order to obtain a better understanding of how income affects

Table 4.11 Composition of GDP by utilization
(current prices, % of total)

	1991	1992	1993	1994	1995	1996	1997	1998	1999	2000	2001	2003
GDP in market prices	100	100	100	100	100	100	100	100	100	100	100	100
Spending on final consumption	62.6	49.9	64.2	69.6	71.2	71.4	74.8	76.6	68.2	62.5	65.1	67.7
Households	41.4	33.7	40.9	44.1	49.3	48.8	50.0	54.6	51.6	46.1	49.6	49.6
Government institutions	16.9	14.3	17.9	22.5	19.5	20.2	21.3	18.7	14.4	14.9	16.3	16.9
Gross accumulation	37.1	35.7	27.8	25.8	25.3	24.5	22.3	16.2	15.0	18.6	21.9	20.8
Gross accumulation of fixed capital	23.8	24.7	21.0	22.0	21.2	21.1	19.0	17.7	15.8	17.8	18.8	18.4
Change in inventories of physical working assets	13.3	11.0	6.8	3.8	4.1	3.4	3.3	−1.5	−0.8	−0.7	3.2	2.4
Net exports of goods and services	0.3	14.4	8.0	4.6	3.5	4.1	2.9	7.2	16.8	20.4	12.6	11.5

Sources: RSY 2000, RSY 2001, RSY 2004.

the growth of aggregate demand, however, we shall first compare the share of labor income in GDP with the share of household consumption (Table 4.12).

This direct comparison of income with personal consumption is not entirely valid, since direct taxes need to be subtracted from income. The relative growth of these two categories, over time, is nonetheless meaningful, since the share of taxes changed little during the period under consideration. The following conclusions may be drawn. First of all, total labor income, including off-the-books payments, was roughly equal to total personal consumption until 1998, at which point income regularly began to lag behind consumption by 10-15 percent. Secondly, reported labor income lags behind personal consumption for the entire period after 1993, and in the most recent years corresponds to only 60-65 percent of the personal consumption level, and only 50-60 percent of total personal consumption, when the share of domestic demand in GDP is taken into account.

These figures confirm the observation of many authors, including our own in previous works, that the Russian personal consumption goods and services market is less and less aimed at people with ordinary workers' income levels, but rather targets people with other sources of income. But since the latter, primarily elite group of consumers is comparatively small in numbers, the low share of labor remuneration in GDP severely restricts the overall capacity of the consumer goods market.

Another important feature of the composition of GDP is that gross profit substantially exceeds gross accumulation of capital (Table 4.13).

Back in the Soviet period, gross accumulation also lagged behind gross profit and mixed income, but that was because a significant part of the surplus product was consumed by the state, including for military purposes. During the reform period, military spending and government consumption as a whole shrank considerably, but accumulation failed to fill the resulting vacuum. Thus, accumulation as a share of the surplus product fell from 72 percent in the Soviet period to 60 percent, on average, in the first half of the 1990s, and 40-45 percent after 1998.

The share of fixed capital accumulation in gross profit in the economy does not follow this growth pattern. Quite the contrary,

Table 4.12 Labor income and household personal consumption
(% share of GDP)

	1991	1992	1993	1994	1995	1996	1997	1998	1999	2000	2001	2003
Compensation of employees	43.7	36.7	44.5	49.3	45.2	49.6	50.0	47.2	40.9	39.9	45.0	46.2
Off-the-books component of compensation of employees	–	–	5.3	8.5	10.4	11.7	11.7	10.1	11.0	11.1	11.0	11.2
Reported compensation of employees	43.7	36.7	39.2	40.8	34.8	37.9	38.3	36.1	29.9	28.8	34.0	35.0
Adjusted compensation of employees	43.7	36.7	41.8	45.0	40.0	43.7	44.1	41.6	36.4	34.3	39.0	40.6
Household consumption	41.4	33.7	40.9	44.1	49.3	48.8	50.0	54.4	50.4	45.5	49.6	49.6
Household consumption as % of domestic demand	41.5	39.4	44.5	46.2	51.1	50.9	51.5	58.8	61.8	57.9	56.9	56.0
Ratio of compensation of employees to household consumption	105.6	108.9	108.8	111.8	91.7	101.6	100.0	86.8	81.2	87.7	90.4	93.1
Ratio of reported compensation of employees to household consumption	105.6	108.9	95.8	92.5	69.9	77.7	76.6	66.4	59.3	63.3	66.5	70.6
Ratio of reported compensation of employees to household consumption, adjusted for share of domestic demand in GDP	105.6	93.1	88.1	88.3	68.1	74.5	74.4	61.4	48.4	48.7	57.8	62.5

Sources: NAS 1993-2004, RSY 2000, p. 265.

Table 4.13 Gross profit in the economy and the accumulation of capital
(% share of GDP)

	1991	1992	1993	1994	1995	1996	1997	1998	1999	2000	2001	2003
Gross profit in the economy and gross mixed income	51.9	59.9	44.9	41.2	43.0	36.9	35.5	37.8	43.1	42.9	39.5	40.5
Mixed income	2.6	7.0	8.7	8.9	12.3	11.8	11.9	12.7	12.1	10.7	9.7	10.1
Gross profit in the economy	49.3	52.9	36.2	32.3	30.7	25.1	23.6	25.1	31.0	32.2	29.9	30.4
Gross accumulation	37.1	35.7	27.8	25.8	25.3	24.5	22.3	16.2	15.0	18.6	21.9	20.8
Gross accumulation of fixed assets	23.8	24.7	21.0	22.0	21.2	21.1	19.0	17.7	15.8	17.8	18.8	18.4
Ratio of gross accumulation to gross profit in the economy and mixed income	0.72	0.60	0.62	0.63	0.58	0.66	0.63	0.44	0.35	0.40	0.46	0.45
Ratio of accumulation of fixed assets to gross profit in the economy	0.46	0.47	0.58	0.68	0.69	0.84	0.81	0.65	0.51	0.55	0.62	0.60
Consumption by state institutions	16.9	14.3	17.9	22.5	19.5	20.2	21.3	18.7	14.4	14.4	16.9	16.9
Net indirect taxes on production and imports	4.5	3.4	10.6	9.5	7.8	13.5	14.4	15.2	15.9	17.0	15.6	13.3
Government consumption minus net indirect taxes	12.4	10.9	7.3	13.0	11.7	6.7	6.9	3.5	−1.5	−2.6	1.3	3.6
Gross accumulation plus consumption by government institutions minus net indirect taxes	49.5	46.6	35.1	38.8	37.0	31.2	29.2	19.7	13.5	14.5	23.2	24.4
Ratio of the previous line to gross profit in the economy and mixed income	0.95	0.78	0.78	0.94	0.86	0.85	0.82	0.52	0.31	0.32	0.59	0.60

Table 4.14 Gross profit and taxes on profit
(billions of rubles)

	1996	1997	1998	1999	2000	2003
Gross profit in the economy	537	585	696	1,493	2,237	3,481
Taxes on profit	97	105	99	221	399	526
Taxes on profit as % of gross profit	18.0%	18.0%	14.2%	14.8%	17.8%	15.1%

Sources: RET #3, 2002; RSY 2000, RSY 2001, RSY 2004.

Russian big business has spent, on average, even a larger portion of its profit on capital investment, than Soviet enterprises used to. Obviously, one major reason for this, is that enterprises under the planned economy faced administrative restrictions on how they could spend their profit, whereas private companies enjoy more discretion. Nonetheless, the latter spend an average of no more than 50-60 percent of gross profit (including depreciation) on capital investment, to replace or expand their fixed assets.

The statistical record does not support the common belief that the reason for low capital investment is high taxes on profit.

Taxes collected on profit (Table 4.14) actually range between 15 and 18 percent of gross profit (much less than the official tax rate, which was 35 percent in 2001), not counting investment tax credits, or 23 percent, adjusted for investment tax credits; in 2002 the unadjusted rate was 24 percent, and could not in practice present any substantial obstacle to the use of profit for purposes of investment. According to some estimates, less than half of gross investment by large and medium-sized companies is financed out of profit: 20-21 percent, or 27-28 percent including depreciation.[7]

Lastly, we shall look at changes in the share of government consumption (Table 4.15).

Our division of government consumption into individual and collective goods and services is somewhat provisional. The first category includes free healthcare, educational, and cultural services for the population, i.e., government-provided discounts and subsidies in this area. This represents only a part of government spending on social needs, and equals about half the cost of in-kind social entitlements. In 1991, total in-kind entitlements were equal

Table 4.15 Share of government institutions' consumption in GDP
(%)

	1991	1992	1993	1994	1995	1996	1997	1998	1999	2000	2001	2003
Government institutions' consumption	16.9	14.3	17.9	22.5	19.5	20.2	21.3	18.7	14.4	16.3	17.6	16.9
For individual goods and services	6.5	7.2	8.3	9.9	9.5	9.5	9.6	8.1	6.1	6.6	7.2	7.6
For collective services	10.4	7.1	9.6	12.6	10.0	10.7	11.7	10.6	8.3	9.7	10.4	9.3

Sources: RSY 2000, RSY 2001, RSY 2004.

Table 4.16 Direct military spending as percentage of GDP

1991	1992	1993	1994	1995	1996	1997	1998	1999	2000	2001	2003
7.0	4.7	4.2	4.7	3.2	3.0	3.3	2.4	2.4	2.66	2.6	2.67

to approximately 10 percent of GDP; in 1998, they had reached 12 percent, but they declined to 9 percent in 2003.

The statistical reports categorize as collective services all spending on defense, government administration, and non-commercial spending on science. It is striking that right up until 1998, the share of spending for these purposes averaged about what it had been in 1991, although military spending was sharply reduced starting in 1992. Some official data show the share of military spending (Ministry of Defense budget) in GDP for these years as shown in Table 4.16.

These data are clearly inconsistent with the NAS, which does not show military spending in the way U.S. and other Western statistics do. Goskomstat does not reveal its methodology in detail (as is also the case for social transfers), but certain insights may be gained from the composition of the government consumption column in the annual IOT.

Let us look at the data for 1999. In that year a total of 410.1 billion rubles was spent by government institutions for collective services. According to the IOT, 393.7 billion rubles, or 96 percent, went to purchase products listed under "Services of financial, insurance, management, and public organizations" (sector #21 in the IOT). It is not difficult to guess that this vague category grouped banks and insurance companies together with the Ministry of Defense, the Ministry of Internal Affairs, and certain other government administrative agencies, in order to conceal the real picture. Thus, the military spending bill was moved from final consumption to intermediate, which is of course contrary to generally accepted national accounting rules. Such artistic finesse was not applied even in classified input-output reports during the Soviet period; military consumption by the state was reported where it ought to be, namely, as part of final consumption.

Government purchases are relatively minor as a portion of the output of individual sectors of the Russian economy. According to the IOT data, for example, only 32 billion (3.7 percent) of the total 863.2 billion ruble output of machine-building and metal-working was purchased by the state in 1998-1999. That was far less than went to exports (21.6 percent), fixed asset accumulation (21.6 percent), household consumption (12.8 percent), or intermediate consumption (38.3 percent).[8] In 1991, the state's share had been 5.6 percent, while exports accounted for 15.9 percent, fixed capital accumulation for 27 percent, households for 9.9 percent, and intermediate consumption for 49.3 percent.[9]

The IOT for 1991, however, substantially understated the data on military equipment deliveries. With defense spending assumed to be 7 percent of GDP at that time, military equipment deliveries were estimated at 97.9 billion rubles, while weapons and military equipment procurement was an estimated 39.3 billion.[10] That is 3.4 times the state purchases from the machine-building and metal-working sectors, shown in the 1991 IOT. Evidently, those authors are correct, who argue that a significant part of arms deliveries to the state is routinely hidden as intermediate consumption. But, if the 39.3 billion rubles figure is correct, then the government's share in purchases from these sectors in 1991 was more than four times greater than shown in the IOT: 22.4 percent, not 5.6 percent.

The 1999 data show weapons and military equipment purchases of 22.1 billion rubles, significantly less than what the IOT report. This figure represents only 2.6 percent of the sector's output. Thus, the real share of the national defense market in the output of Russian machine-building fell from 22.4 percent in 1991 to 2.6 in 1999, by a factor of almost nine. This decline is practically not reflected in the NAS.

But the decline did play an important, dual role in how the economy developed. First of all, it contributed to the development of a huge deficit of aggregate demand during the first half of the 1990s, thus indirectly aggravating the overall economic crisis. Secondly, a significant portion of the burden on domestic machine-building, namely its forced work for the DC, was removed. The positive potential of that shift, however, was not utilized for the benefit of the economy, since the machine-building sector's freed-up capacities were not used to upgrade or expand fixed assets. Instead, a vacuum formed; this vacuum also contributed to the prolonged depression in the economy as a whole.

Table 4.17 Growth or decline of GDP and its main components in comparative prices
(the first figure of each pair is an index based on 1991=100; the second figure is year-on-year % growth or decline)

	1992	1993	1994	1995	1996	1997	1998	1999	2000	2001	2002	2003	2004
Gross domestic product	85.5 −14.5%	78.1 −8.7%	68.1 −12.7%	65.3 −4.1%	60.9 −6.7%	61.5 +0.9%	58.9 −4.3%	61.3 +4.7%	67.0 +8.7%	70.1 +4.9%	73.4 +4.7%	78.7 +7.3%	84.3 +7.1%
Household consumption	69.6 −30.4%	70.4 +1.2%	71.3 +1.2%	69.3 −2.8%	66.0 −4.7%	69.6 +5.4%	67.9 −2.4%	65.6 −3.4%	71.4 8.9%	77.7 +8.7%	84.3 +8.5%	90.6 +7.5%	100.8 +11.3%
Consumption by state institutions	72.3 −27.7%	67.7 −6.4%	65.7 −2.9%	66.4 +1.1%	66.9 +0.8%	65.3 −2.4%	65.7 +0.6%	66.1 +3.0%	67.2 +1.6%	66.6 −0.9%	68.3 +2.6%	69.8 +2.2%	71.4 +2.3%
Gross accumulation	82.3 −17.7%	58.1 −29.4%	39.9 −31.2%	35.6 −10.8%	28.3 −20.6%	27.3 −3.6%	19.4 −28.7%	21.1 +8.5%	24.7 +17.3%	28.8 +16.7%	28.1 −2.6%	31.8 +13.2%	36.2 +13.9%
Gross accumulation of fixed capital	88.7 −11.3%	65.8 −25.8%	48.7 −26.0%	45.0 −7.5%	36.4 −19.3%	34.3 −5.7%	30.9 −9.8%	32.4 +4.7%	37.4 +15.5%	41.7 +11.4%	42.9 +2.8%	48.4 +12.8%	53.6 +10.8%
Net exports of goods and services	4,075 +3,975%	3,024 −25.8%	2,717 −10.2%	2,805 +3.2%	3,399 +21.2%	3,100 −8.8%	6,541 +111.0%	11,271 +72.3%	11,542 +2.4%	10,377 −10.1%	10,709 +10.1%	11,030 +3.0%	10,004 −9.3%

Sources: NAS 1993-2004, RSY 2000, p. 265.

Thus, the Russian economy functioned under the influence of several damaging structural factors:

- low personal income and insufficient consumer demand;
- excessive surplus value, without any possibility to realize it in the form of adequate investment in the renewal and replacement of fixed assets in the productive sector;
- an acute shortage of aggregate demand on the part of the government.

All of these factors, in combination with monetary ones (which will be discussed separately) and with a wrongheaded economic policy, had a huge adverse impact on the course the economy took.

4.4 GDP dynamics

From the standpoint of Russian economic dynamics, two periods may be clearly distinguished:

- the overall decline of production in 1992-1998, with a short pause in the stagnation year of 1997;
- the overall growth of production, starting in 1999.

The specific features of these two periods are evident from the data tabulated above in this chapter, and in Table 4.17.

The crisis and stagnation of 1992-1998

The cumulative collapse of GDP during the seven years of the first period was 41.1 percent, or 7 percent annually on average. The greatest rates of decline were experienced in the initial reform period (1992-1994), after which the rate of shrinkage became comparatively moderate. The composition of the collapse varied from year to year. In 1992, for example, every single domestic component of GDP fell sharply: personal consumption by 30 percent, government consumption by 28 percent, and the accumulation of fixed capital by 11 percent. The domestic market essentially collapsed, and only a forty-fold increase of net exports (achieved through the contraction of imports) held the officially reported total decline of GDP in 1992 to 14.5 percent. In reality, domestic demand shrank by 22.5 percent, with the greatest part of the contraction (almost 60 percent) coming in personal consumption, more than a fifth (22 percent) in government consumption, and another fifth (19.5 percent) in gross accumulation.

The main factor in the acute crisis experienced by the economy was shock therapy, in the form of the instantaneous decontrol, without proper preparation, of the vast majority of prices, especially the prices of consumer goods and services. In the resulting inflationary spiral, personal income lagged behind the rising prices. In a single year, the real disposable income of the population fell by 47.4 percent.[11] Inflation also devalued enterprises' working capital, so much so that the enterprises were forced to make drastic cutbacks in production and investment in fixed assets. But the scale of collapse of capital investment during that first year, large as it was, still lagged behind the rate of decline of personal consumption. Some capital construction or new equipment programs continued by the force of inertia, carried forward from previous years.

Unlike those spontaneous processes, government consumption was slashed deliberately and with forethought. Gaidar, the acting prime minister in that initial period, relates in his memoirs how, in 1991, he convened the executive board of Gosplan, the state planning authority, and ordered steep reductions in weapons and military equipment production targets. In 1992 alone, real defense spending shrank by 46 percent, while the output of military equipment and weapons fell by 50.5 percent. The NAS expressed these changes as a reduction of government consumption in the category of collective services by 41.6 percent. On a macroeconomic scale, this was equivalent to a 20 percent contraction of aggregate domestic demand. But the actual destructive impact was at least twice that, since the collapse of defense production was followed by a steep reduction of demand for the output of related sectors of the economy.

The crisis shock of 1992 resulted practically entirely from the economic and financial policies of the Gaidar government. Had it not been for the inflationary take-off of prices, caused by those policies, and the administrative reduction of defense spending, the decline of production would have been much less.

In this section we concentrate on an analysis of each component of the decline of GDP, without going into the accompanying institutional changes, which played a destructive role of their own. By institutional changes, we mean the collapse of the previous system

Table 4.18 Composition of the decline of final demand in 1992-1998

	% share, 1991	% share, 1992-1998	% share of decline
Domestic final demand	100.0	48.9	100.0
Household consumption	41.4	32.1	27.0
Government consumption	16.9	34.3	11.8
Individual goods and services	6.5	3.3	0.4
Collective services	10.4	52.2	11.4
Gross accumulation	37.1	80.6	61.2
Fixed capital accumulation	23.8	69.1	33.6

of central planning and distribution of output, the liquidation of centralized planning and financing of capital investment, the destruction of Russia's economic ties with the former Union republics, the destruction of cooperation in the framework of the Comecon, etc. All of these processes did play an enormous role, but our objective in this section is to present a quantitative estimate of the composition of the shrinkage of the final product at each stage of our capitalist transformation. This review is most efficiently accomplished through a part-by-part analysis of GDP.

Let us sum up our analysis of the components of GDP for the entire 1992-1998 period (Table 4.18), concentrating on the main cause, which was the absence during this time of real conditions for overcoming the crisis and restarting growth.

The predominant factors in decline and stagnation in this period as a whole were gross accumulation, which accounts for over 60 percent of the absolute shrinkage of domestic final demand, and household consumption, which accounts for over a quarter of the shrinkage. These two factors, combined, are responsible for 88 percent of the overall decline. Within gross accumulation, the greatest role belonged to the decline of fixed capital investment, which accounted for 40 percent of the total reduction of domestic demand. This factor was at least one and a half times more important than the shrinkage of personal consumption. Another 11 percent is attributable to the reduction of government consumption categorized as collective, which denotes chiefly defense spending.

The differences in the dynamics of these various components

are of fundamental importance. Both personal and government consumption plunged practically right away, in 1992-1993, after which time they remained depressed at a low level. The decline of gross accumulation and investment in fixed assets, however, continued throughout the entire period, making it inevitable that the crisis would continue and would be followed by stagnation, despite the stabilization of personal and government consumption.

Since total final consumption remained essentially unchanged after 1994, the subsequent significant and persistent decline of capital investment cannot have been due solely to the continuing contraction of the domestic market. To some extent, this decline became independent and autonomous. Accumulation turned from a factor that depended primarily on the volume of output, into an independent factor in the overall decline.

Several additional observations are in order at this point. The overall level of consumer demand remained too low during these years to inspire new investment. Moreover, the share of imports in domestic sales was steadily rising, which set the stage for a further reduction of domestic consumer goods production. This was also reflected in the stagnating level of heavy industry output, which consisted chiefly of products for intermediate consumption. Output continued to decline in the overwhelming majority of industrial sectors, especially machine-building, light industry, and even the food industry. In 1996-1997, productive capacity utilization in industry stood at only 54 percent of the level considered normal by the enterprises.[12] Not even large companies were in any position to undertake new investment.

Payments within the economy were regularly and increasingly disrupted during these same years. In 1998 the average share of barter in industrial companies' sales rose to 51 percent (not counting other forms of non-monetary settling of accounts, such as promissory notes), as against 42 percent in 1997, 35 percent in 1996, and 22 percent in 1995.[13] Under these conditions, the prospects for new capital investment in the economy appeared unfavorable. Total capital investment was below even the level, necessary for the replacement of fixed assets that were retired due to obsolescence.

Another not insignificant factor was that the basic composition of banking and industrial monopoly capital was only just taking shape. Oligarchical organizations focussed their attention on accumulating capital in money form, most often at the expense of productive capital. During a period of stagnation, it was deemed more profitable to invest in financial instruments, than in fixed assets.

All of these additional factors notwithstanding, the main reason for economic stagnation in the period under consideration was the distorted composition of GDP: the excessive share of gross profit (surplus value) and the extremely low share of labor income. With such a high share of surplus value in the economy (to which depreciation must be added), any capitalist country would experience difficulties in selling its output on the domestic market. This is the famous "realization crisis," around which Marxist theoretical debates often revolved. If surplus value is not fully utilized within a given country for accumulation, consumption by the capitalist class, and other purposes, such as redistribution through government financial mechanisms, a problem arises regarding the realization of that part of the domestic product.

During the hundred years since those early 20th-century discussions, developed industrial capitalism discovered two additional ways to solve the problem: (1) government interference in the redistribution of income, and the use of government consumption to compensate for insufficient private investment; (2) the expansion of the service sector, making it possible to realize in this area of the economy, a growing share of the surplus value, created in the productive sector. Both methods lead to increased employment in the service sector and government institutions. The share of hired workers rises, while the share of surplus value, distributed directly in the form of profit, declines.

It took decades to effect these transformations, but freshly minted Russian capitalism was not nearly mature enough to assimilate them. It encountered the same problem that had preoccupied Marxists at the outset of the 20th century: the system is unable to sell its entire product on the domestic market, if the system itself claims an excessive share of the surplus value.

The data presented above indicate that Russia had enormous internal sources for growth, surpassing U.S. growth rates, because the Russian economy could spend a larger share of its product on expanding production and providing for the social needs of its citizens. But "youthful" Russian capitalism does not behave that way. To date, it has spent only a negligible portion of surplus value and depreciation on capital investment. The greater part of this sum, after taxes, was used for "financial investment" (buying other companies) and investment in government securities (with 60 percent yields, up until August 1998), or transferred abroad for safekeeping in banks, Western securities, and real estate.

Due to the excessively high share of surplus value in Russia during 1992-1998, the national savings rate consistently surpassed domestic investment. This occurred, despite a significant government budget deficit. The excessive domestic accumulation was spent on financial speculation inside the country, as well as capital flight. It is striking that the size of the surplus, expressed in dollars, is roughly equal to the illegal export of capital from Russia.

Two circumstances should be borne in mind during analysis of the official statistics. First of all, capital goods price indices rose more rapidly than the average rate for all prices. Therefore, the share of capital investment in GDP, in current prices, was regularly overstated. Adjusting for this factor, we obtain an entirely different figure for capital investment: 9-10 percent of GDP. New capital investment, at fairly low levels, went only into housing and office building construction (including bank and oil company headquarters). At the same time, the share of equipment in Russian capital investment was only 3-4 percent of GDP, compared with 7-7.5 percent in the United States. Over half of investment went into the oil and gas industry, chiefly for laying pipelines.

Secondly, even the inflation-exaggerated investment figures were less than depreciation, meaning that net investment was negative. Consequently, productive fixed assets shrank at an alarming rate. Since the new capitalism arrived in Russia, essentially not one single new major production facility has been funded by private capital. The system that has taken shape is absolutely sterile with respect to the processes by which material values are produced.

A period of growth (after 1999)

At the height of the 1998 crisis, few people expected that the economy would be able to turn around quickly and resume even moderate growth. But that is what happened. Over the next five years (1999-2004), real GDP grew by 37.5 percent (an annual average rate of 6.5 percent). And though national output in 2004 re-

Table 4.19   Imports, 1997-2003

	1997	1998	1999	2000	2001	2002	2003
Billions of $	72.0	58.0	39.5	44.9	53.8	60.9	75.4
1997=100	100	80.6	54.9	62.4	74.7	84.5	104.7

mained substantially lower than the pre-reform level (by almost 16 percent, compared with 1991), it presented a decisive contrast to the preceding period.

Two main factors are usually mentioned in analyses of this turnaround:

- The nearly 85 percent devaluation of the ruble, which made many domestic products price-competitive with imports and produced a strong import-substitution effect; and,
- The sharp increase of prices on exported oil and natural gas, which significantly increased the resources available for economic growth.

The first hypothesis is largely substantiated in fact. Imports did begin a steep decline in 1998, both due to declining demand and as a result of financial paralysis and a sharp increase of prices on imports. The result was a reduction of imports by 20 percent that year. But the steepest decline occurred in 1999, when imports were 45 percent lower than in 1997, and 32 percent below the 1998 level (Table 4.19).

Imports made a gradual comeback in subsequent years, but the 1997 pre-crisis level was achieved only six years later, in 2003. By that time import-substitution had been used up, as a growth factor.

Oil and natural gas export prices were able to spur nominal GDP, but they affected real GDP growth only indirectly, and only under certain circumstances. They could bring about an increase in real output, only if rising prices led to increased oil and gas production. Indeed, the oil industry produced 37.5 percent more in 2003 than in 1997, while the natural gas industry was at output levels 8.6 percent higher than in 1997, after having stagnated for three years. The point here is that the petroleum products industry represented only 13 percent of total industrial output and 6.5 percent of GDP

Table 4.20 Composition of GDP, 1999-2004

	Composition of GDP in 1998, %	1999-2002 increase, %	Composition of growth, %
Total GDP	100.0	+43.1	100.0
Personal consumption	54.6	+48.4	60.7
State consumption	18.7	+ 8.7	3.1
Gross accumulation	16.2	+86.6	27.5
Total domestic demand	89.5	+46.1	91.4
Net exports	7.2	+52.9	8.6

(value added in the economy as a whole).[14] Consequently, this sector directly accounted for only 3.8 percentage points out of the 37.5 percent increase of GDP in 1998-2004. In other words, without the physical increase of oil and gas output, overall GDP growth would have been 33.7 percent rather than 37.5 percent, which is not a very striking difference.

An additional indirect impact of higher oil and gas export prices on real GDP growth could also be observed, (1) through the use of this sector's gross profit to finance capital investment in the fuels industry, as well as in other sectors; (2) through the redistribution of this profit by means of tax measures; (3) through the oil and gas sector's increased intermediate consumption and higher spending on labor compensation. Further analysis of the components of GDP growth will help sort out this question and its significance for overall economic growth.

Let us now estimate the components of the overall 1999-2004 recovery (Table 4.20). According to our calculations, domestic demand accounted for 91.4 percent of total GDP growth, while only 8.6 percent was attributable to net external demand (real growth of exports plus the import-substitution effect). Nearly one-third of the increased domestic demand was accounted for by capital investment, while personal consumption accounted for two-thirds.

The results shown in Table 4.20 are important in several respects. As noted above, personal consumption fell sharply in 1999, before rebounding in the years that followed. The relative weight of household consumption increased significantly, becoming the principal growth factor and replacing capital investment in its initial role

Table 4.21 Statistical gap between real income and personal consumption

	1995	1996	1997	1998	1999	2000	2001	2002	2003
Per capita real income, index	100	101.3	108.2	91.4	78.5	87.6	95.0	105.5	121.2
Population (millions)	147.9	147.6	147.1	146.7	146.3	145.6	145.4	145.2	145.0
Population, index	100	99.8	99.5	99.2	98.9	98.4	98.3	98.2	98.0
Population's real income, index	100	101.1	107.7	90.7	77.6	86.2	93.4	103.5	118.7
Household consumption, index	100	95.3	100.4	98.0	93.7	102.5	111.4	120.8	129.9
Ratio of consumption to income	1.00	0.94	0.93	1.08	1.21	1.19	1.20	1.17	1.09

as the major demand factor. Sustained economic growth at fairly high rates is impossible, without capital investment in the lead as a supply factor. And, indeed, capital investment previously grew at rates that were twice as high, on average, as GDP growth.

It is only possible to explain the economic growth of 1999-2004 fully, however, after we answer the question of why official statistics show such a divergence between the growth rates of real income and of personal consumption. Table 4.21 shows these data.

According to Goskomstat data, per capita real income regained its pre-crisis level only in 2002, and this was seen as quite an achievement. In the interim, since Russia's population continued to shrink, total real income growth was even slower. But if we allow that real income did surpass the 1997 level in 2003 by 10 percent, why did real personal consumption in 2003 exceed the 1997 level by 30 percent (again, according to Goskomstat figures)?

The ratio of personal consumption to real income rose steadily. Until 1998, consumption lagged behind income, but after that year it was consistently higher. This can only happen if the population is either saving more than normal, or, on the contrary, spending for consumption what it would normally be saving.

Table 4.22 The savings factor in personal consumption
(% of total population monetary income; % change)

	1995	1996	1997	1998	1999	2000	2001	2002	2003
Personal income, total	100	100	100	100	100	100	100	100	100
Personal income taxes	5.6	5.8	6.3	6.2	6.6	7.8	8.9	8.6	8.3
Disposable income	94.4	94.2	93.7	93.8	93.4	92.2	91.1	91.4	91.7
Purchases of goods and services	70.5	69.3	68.7	77.7	78.5	75.5	74.6	73.2	69.0
Savings, total	23.9	24.9	25.0	16.1	14.9	16.7	16.5	18.2	22.7
Of which: Real estate purchases	0.1	0.1	0.8	1.3	1.3	1.2	1.4	1.8	2.0
Change in financial assets (% change)	23.8	24.8	24.2	14.8	13.6	15.5	15.1	16.4	20.7
Net increase of cash on hand (%)	3.6	1.4	1.6	1.7	1.8	2.8	2.0	1.7	2.7

Indeed, Table 4.22 shows that the savings factor played a very important role in the recovery of 1999-2003.

With the steep decrease in real income in 1998, the population began to compensate by reducing the savings rate, resulting in a relative rise in purchases of goods and services. At the bottom of the trough, in 1999, real income was 18 percent less than in 1997, but real spending fell by only 6 percent in those two years. Spending on purchases of goods and services as a ratio to total personal monetary income, which had been 68-70 percent before the crisis, rose to 78-79 percent, by fully 9 or 10 points, during the crisis and immediately afterwards. This helped boost personal consumption, which accounted, as we have seen, for almost half of the overall increase of aggregate demand in 1999-2002. The rising ratio of consumption to income (showing a marked tendency toward consumption) continued to increase in 2002, and played a decisive role in promoting overall economic growth.

This could not have happened, of course, without a substantial shift in the direction of savings. Of the main components of personal savings, namely, financial assets (bank deposits, securities purchases, etc.), the population's increased cash on hand (salted away in the piggy-bank), and purchases of foreign currency, the greatest reduction occurred in the latter category. Before the 1998 crisis, 15 to 21 percent of all personal income was spent on net foreign currency purchases (gross purchases minus sales), but after the crisis this component dropped off rapidly, and it was only 7-8 percent in the critical years of 1999-2003. Changes in foreign currency purchases are not shown separately in Table 4.22, but they are included in purchases of financial assets.

The population always bought foreign currency as a hedge against inflation. Even relatively poor layers of the population used this method. The reduced interest in this form of savings might have been influenced by lower rates of inflation, especially in 2001-2002, when consumer price rises were quite moderate. But the steepest drop in foreign-currency savings occurred in 1998-1999, when inflation was higher.

A more plausible explanation is that, during the year of the crisis and immediately thereafter, a portion of the population spent their savings, accumulated in prior years, on consumption, in order to maintain at least a certain subsistence living standard. The new composition of spending was maintained into the years that followed, as real income began to rise again. Spending on goods and services grew in parallel with the overall rise of income.

The considerations above apply, of course, to those parts of the population whose income is above the subsistence minimum, and who therefore have some ability to save money.

Thus, the ratio of consumer spending to income rose sharply in this period, both from middle-income people's efforts to maintain their accustomed level of consumption, and as a result of the practically total loss of the savings of those with the lowest income.

Fluctuations in the rate of personal savings may continue to play a substantial role in determining economic growth rates. For example, a return to the savings patterns typical of the pre-crisis period, such as occurred in 2003-2004, helps to slow GDP growth. Conversely, a further reduction of hard currency purchases, as a

Table 4.23 Composition of capital investment in 1995-2003, compared with earlier periods
(% of total)

	1975	1980	1985	1991	1995	1996	1997	1998	1999	2000	2001	2002	2003
Industry, total	36.1	35.6	37.0	34.7	34.4	34.8	36.4	33.3	37.2	38.3	38.7	37.2	42.5
Electric power	3.4	3.3	3.9	2.7	5.2	6.0	6.9	6.1	4.5	3.7	3.6	4.2	5.2
Fuels	6.6	8.6	11.5	11.1	14.4	14.9	15.4	12.1	13.9	18.5	19.2	16.8	20.5
Oil	3.8	6.0	8.3*	8.0	8.4	8.0	8.5	7.3	8.7	12.0	12.7	10.6	13.3
Refined petroleum products				0.2	1.4	1.2	0.9	1.1	0.8	1.5	1.7	1.5	1.5
Natural gas	1.6	1.3	2.1	1.5	2.9	4.0	4.3	2.5	3.4	4.3	3.9	3.7	4.9
Coal	1.1	1.2	1.0	1.4	1.7	1.7	1.6	1.2	1.0	0.8	0.9	0.8	0.7
Ferrous metallurgy	–	–	1.6	1.6	2.0	1.8	1.6	1.9	2.0	2.0	2.3	1.6	1.9
Non-ferrous metallurgy	–	–	–	1.6	1.9	1.6	1.9	1.6	2.4	2.7	3.2	2.7	3.0
Chemicals and petrochemicals	3.3	2.6	2.0	1.7	1.6	1.7	1.7	1.6	1.6	1.6	1.8	1.6	1.8
Machine-building and metal-working	9.5	8.4	8.3	6.9	3.1	3.4	3.1	3.2	3.6	3.0	3.0	3.1	3.3
Light industry	1.2	1.0	0.9	1.2	0.3	0.3	0.2	0.2	0.3	0.2	0.2	0.2	0.2
Food industry	2.2	2.2	1.9	3.1	2.7	2.7	3.1	4.1	5.8	3.4	3.2	3.8	3.6
Agriculture	16.9	17.0	15.1	17.8	3.5	2.9	2.5	3.0	2.9	2.6	3.9	4.4	2.9
Transport	11.3	12.8	12.9	8.5	13.2	13.5	15.2	14.1	18.5	21.5	20.7	17.2	18.0
Communications	0.8	0.8	0.8	0.9	1.4	1.8	2.8	3.5	3.2	2.6	3.0	3.4	5.4
Retail and public dining, wholesale trade	1.9	2.1	2.4	1.7	2.0	2.2	2.2	2.5	2.4	2.3	3.0	3.7	2.8
Housing	15.8	14.6	16.0	18.2	22.8	20.3	16.7	16.1	14.0	11.6	11.1	13.7	8.1
Utilities	–	–	–	4.3	6.7	6.3	7.0	8.6	6.7	6.4	5.4	5.0	6.2

* Entries for 1975, 1980, and 1985 represent combined investment in the oil and refined petroleum products industries.

Source: RSY 2004, Table 22.4.

result of the ruble's stabilization against the dollar, could help to sustain moderate economic growth.

The 1999-2002 recovery took place during a period in which the middle class, with its consumerist inclinations, did begin to grow rapidly, while the initial impulse toward accumulating money practically came to an end. It may be presumed, therefore, that the new composition of personal income utilization more likely represents the emergence of a long-term pattern, than some kind of short-term deviation. And, if that is the case, the growth of personal consumption by the middle class may become one of the drivers for sustained economic growth.

As noted above, capital investment accounted for a significant part of GDP growth in 1999-2004. We shall now look at the distribution of this growth across various sectors of the economy (Table 4.23).

The first thing to note is that the share of capital investment in goods-producing sectors (industry and agriculture) fell from 56-59 percent in the Soviet period, to 41-44 percent in the reform period as a whole. While industry's share changed little, remaining in the 34-38 percent range, the share of agriculture shrank markedly, even catastrophically: from 15-18 percent in the Soviet period, to 2-4 percent after reforms began. In the service sectors, the share of investment in housing (though it fell in absolute terms) and in construction of office buildings for new corporations and banks rose in the years before the 1998 crisis. In industry, the share of the fuels industries, above all oil and gas, climbed markedly, and the share of investment in the electric power industry rose somewhat, while the share of investment in the metals industries, chemicals, light industry and, especially, machine-building and metal-working fell from 8-9 percent in the Soviet period, to 3 percent under the reforms. It should be kept in mind that these shifts occurred in the setting of an overall steep collapse of capital investment as a whole.

The resumption of capital investment growth in 1999-2002, at the good clip of 5 percent in 1999, 17 percent in 2000 and 7 percent in 2001, immediately posed the question of the extent to which it would spur growth in the economy and industry as a whole. Table 4.23 shows that the shares of the fuel industry, non-ferrous metals, transportation, and communications in total investment rose during this period. But the table does not reveal what these sectors' share

Table 4.24 Distribution of 1999-2003 capital investment growth by sectors of the economy
(% of total, except first line)

	1999–2003
Real growth of capital investment (%)	50
Industry	86.4
Fuels	44.1
Steel	13.2
Non-ferrous metallurgy	13.6
Machine-building	8.2
Food industry	2.3
Other industries	5.1
Electric power	–22.2
Transport	–2.7
Communication	18.2
All other sectors	–4.6

in total investment growth was for these years. With total investment taking off, other sectors could have been party to the overall boom, even if their portion of the total remained unchanged or slightly declined. Table 4.24 summarizes the results of calculations designed to show this distribution.

In 1999-2003 practically the entire real growth of capital investment went to the oil and natural gas industries, ferrous and non-ferrous metallurgy, and communications. Machine-building received only 8 percent of the increase. In other sectors of industry, capital investment growth in this period was very low. In the critical electric power industry, real investment even fell.

The limited range of areas receiving capital investment was due to the great difference in profitability levels between the main export sectors, and sectors producing primarily for the domestic market. Because of superprofit in the oil and gas industries, as well as steel and non-ferrous metals, which were due to favorable external economic conditions, significant investment growth became possible in those sectors. Machine-building experienced some indirect benefit because of orders from the export-oriented industries. In most other sectors, however, the temporary restoration of competitiveness through the devaluation of the ruble did not create sufficient incentives for the renovation of fixed assets. Growth of output in these sectors was achieved almost exclusively by making use of idle capacities. The food industry was a partial exception, and only for a short period of time.

This uneven development resulted in a situation where, even in years of significantly increased total capital investment, the greater part of the economy's potential to finance capital investment went unrealized. The surplus profit received in the export sectors, due to natural and export rent, continued to go abroad, rather than being used in capital-deficit sectors.

To some extent the underdevelopment of Russia's lending and finance infrastructure was to blame, in that it was unable to channel capital from the export sectors into sectors producing for the domestic market. Given the known gap between the rates of profit in these two groups of sectors of the economy, however, it was not realistic to have expected market forces spontaneously to eliminate the tilt.

Thus a dilemma arose: without elimination of that structural imbalance between the rates of profit in these two most important areas of the economy, there would be no renovation of fixed assets. Therefore, modernization of the economy as a whole would be blocked, as would the creation of preconditions for rapid economic growth to develop on its own.

Lastly, there was the problem of reduced consumer demand, discussed above, which had to do with the extremely unequal distribution of the national income. During the recovery of 1999-2003, the increase of intractable poverty among a large segment of the population of Russia was partially offset, but by no means eliminated, by the growth of the middle class and a lower savings rate. The fundamental problem of chronically insufficient consumer demand will be with us until a substantial redistribution of the national income takes place, and a healthier relationship between labor compensation and gross profit is established.

Future Russian economic growth depends decisively on overcoming these two main structural imbalances:

- the bias in favor of gross profit at the expense of inadequate labor income;
- the bias in favor of the export sectors, sustained by an incorrect distribution of natural and export rent.

It is not difficult to see that these two problems are closely interconnected. Expanding labor's share in the distribution of the national income will automatically increase domestic demand from the population and will help soak up the surfeit of money in the economy.

It is unlikely to become possible to solve these problems, without serious changes in the government's economic policy principles. These questions of national economic policy will be explored in detail in Chapter 5.

NOTES

1. NAS2001, Table 2.3.

2. The relevant Goskomstat publication says the following: "In accordance with NAS [National Accounting System–S.M.] methodology, labor compensation paid to hired workers includes employers' deductions for social insurance. Off-the-books labor compensation by sector is counted as part of gross profit and gross mixed income." IOT for 1998-1999. *Statisticheskii sbornik* (*Statistics Handbook*) (Moscow: Goskomstat, 2002), p. 3.

3. *From Plan to Market. World Development Report 1996*, p. 89.

4. *Vek* magazine, #30, Sept. 6, 2002, interview with N. Rimashevskaya.

5. *Novye izvestiia,* Nov. 14, 2002, interview with Yelena Avraamova.

6. Quoted from UPI analytical review, "The Russian Middle Class," Dec. 18, 2002.

7. RET #3, 2002, p. 63.

8. Calculated from *Zatraty-vypusk Rossii* (Russian IOT), 1998-1999, pp. 159-161.

9. Calculated from the 1991 IOT.

10. Calculated from RSY 2000 and *Ekonomika i zhizn'* (*Economy and Life*), #30, 1998.

11. RSY 2000, p. 141.

12. RET1, #3, 2002, p. 126.

13. Ibid.

14. Calculated on the basis of RSY 2001 and the IOT for 1998-1999.

5 Economic Policy

Capitalism's latest phase developed in Russia to the almost constant accompaniment of discussion about the role of the state, and government intervention in the economy. At one pole were the advocates of reducing such intervention, along with the overall role of the state, to a minimum. The opposite pole attracted those who see an active government economic policy as an important instrument for overcoming the crisis and structural contradictions. The first tendency is represented by so-called neo-liberalism, while the various currents within the second group range from Keynesians to communists.

With the exception of the short-lived Primakov government (September 1998–April 1999), all of Russia's governments, under Gaidar, Chernomyrdin, Kiriyenko, Putin, Kasyanov, and Fradkov, have implemented, or at least declared, a neo-liberal policy. The advocates of active state intervention have had to function mainly as opposition forces.

There were several reasons for the prevalence of neo-liberalism in Russian economic policy. *First of all,* soon after the election of Boris Yeltsin as president, he handed the reins of economic leadership to a group of economists (Gaidar, Chubais, et al.), who had already begun to preach neo-liberal theories during the last years of the Soviet regime. They were strongly influenced by the partisans of this tendency in the West, where neo-liberalism has dominated economic policy since the early 1980s, when Ronald Reagan came to power in the USA and Margaret Thatcher in Great Britain. The International Monetary Fund and the World Bank, institutions from which all of the post-Soviet Russian governments tried to obtain financial support, pushed the same line.

Secondly, the notion of holding the state's role in the economy to a minimum suited the Russian financial oligarchy as it emerged. That oligarchy viewed the state as its instrument, rather than as a master to whom it should listen or submit. The victory of these ideas within the Western elite was associated with the onset of the era of transnational capitalism, for which government regulation in any one country represents an obstacle to unlimited domination of the world market. Russian companies and banks rapidly subscribed to the transnational ideology.

This was the basis of the alliance between the neo-liberal ideologues whom Yeltsin recruited to his government in order to build capitalism, and the direct representatives of the incipient monopolistic bourgeoisie. For some time (1993-1997), this alliance was personified by Prime Minister Victor Chernomyrdin, who represented the former Soviet economic bureaucracy, which had merged with the new multimillionaires, and his first deputy Anatoli Chubais, who handed over the most valuable assets of the state to those billionaires, and functioned as an unofficial Gauleiter for the Western financial elite within the Russian government. The greatest "successes" in building capitalism, while destroying the Russian economy, occurred during the period when these two reigned, enjoying Yeltsin's protection. Picking up the baton from Gaidar, who had provoked the first steep plunge of the economy in 1992, they presided over its further disintegration, capped off by the 1998 crisis.

The Putin and Kasyanov governments did not flaunt such a blatant symbiosis of the political elite with the domestic and foreign financial oligarchy. To the extent Putin was suspected of having such connections, it was with second-level groups, which did not even always prevail over their competitors, despite their proximity to the President. Though Kasyanov was considered a representative and protégé of the so-called Yeltsin "Family," which included people from several of the longer-standing oligarchical groups, his cabinet was dominated by a new generation of neo-liberal ideologues, who had replaced Gaidar and Chubais. Unlike their predecessors, they could boast that on their watch, at least the economy was growing. They saw this as vindication of their liberal principles. Is this true?

After Kasyanov's replacement by Fradkov as prime minister in early 2004, three important changes occurred. First, despite the continuing prevalence of neo-liberals in the economic policy ministries (German Gref as minister of economic development and trade, Alexei Kudrin as minister of finance, and Mikhail Zurabov as minister of social affairs), Fradkov, supported by the ministers in charge of certain sectors of the economy (agriculture, industry, transportation), insisted on a more active role for the state, to the point of introducing elements of government indicative planning. The cabinet remained split, with Putin refusing to take sides with either faction. Secondly, Putin initiated a devastating attack on Khodorkovsky's financial group and thus asserted a more aggressive stance toward the financial oligarchy in general. Thirdly, Putin proceeded to create his own, Kremlin oligarchical group, under the guise of reestablishing partial state control over key industries. The neo-liberals' influence was weakened.

One of Putin's potentially important moves was his pledge to double Russia's GDP by 2010. Previously, he had urged Kasyanov and his ministers to accelerate economic growth, but had met with resistance from the neo-liberal ministers, particularly Gref. Putin's new demand implied sustaining an average annual growth rate of 7.2 percent. The goal was supported by the new premier, but Gref criticized it as too ambitious. Putin kept insisting, but did not suggest any specific changes in economic policy that would help reach their target. The neo-liberal policy remained in place by default, making acceleration impossible. Actual growth remained around 6-6.5 percent, a full percentage point below the target. Even the additional petrodollars earned in recent years have not been utilized to bolster growth.

The fundamental contradiction within neo-liberalism is that, while declaring its main goal to be minimization of the state's role in the economy, it nonetheless counts on that very state to achieve this objective. The result is something resembling one of the fundamental theoretical principles of scientific communism, whereby the proclaimed goal of the withering away of the state was to be achieved through the development of the state's function of guiding society. It may be objected, of course, that this paradox of neo-liberalism was a temporary phenomenon, and that after completion of an initial phase of structural reforms the role of the state would shrink of its own accord. Secondly, it might be said that no institutional changes are possible, without the active participation of the state, being the only institution capable of codifying in law its own non-participation in the economic process.

The point is that, in the course of the thorough-going destruction of the institutions and ties that had characterized socialist society and the planned economy, phenomena emerged that impeded economic growth. Initially it was supposed that these negative processes would be short-lived, and that it would be possible to correct them through macroeconomic policies. In any event, after construction of the basis for a capitalist economy and modern market infrastructure, economic growth was supposed to assume natural patterns, following capitalism's typical tendency toward expanded reproduction. In Russia, however, this did not happen. The institutional changes, which we shall refer to here as structural reforms, were destructive at the onset of the changes, and then continued to put a brake on economic progress long afterwards. What's more, there are a number of instances in which macroeconomic policy not only proved unable to counteract these negatives, but even enhanced their effect. We shall now examine these cases in more detail.

5.1 Structural reforms

Following the rules of neo-liberalism, the initial market transformations were focused on two main points:

- freeing enterprises from administrative control by planning organs, and introduction of freedom in price-formation;
- privatization.

It was believed that these two reforms would suffice to get a market economy to work.

We shall not go into the limitations of this approach, which ignored important components such as the need to create a market infrastructure to replace the dismantled planning system. Nor shall we discuss the speed of the reforms or the related dilemma of "shock vs. gradualism." We shall not repeat our own critique of privatization, which became in practice the looting of state property (see Chapter 2). Even without going into these aspects, it can be stated that the two above-mentioned reforms plunged the Russian economy into crisis.

During preparations for the decontrol of prices, the Gaidar government did not take into account the inflation it would unleash. Their calculations suggested that a doubling of retail prices ought to be enough to erase the consumer goods shortages existing at that time. In reality, prices soared six-fold just in January 1992, the first month after the deregulation of prices, and by the end of the year (December 1991–December 1992) prices had increased 26 times over. It would be a long time before inflation abated, never mind coming to an end. In 1993 consumer prices rose by another 940 percent, followed by 320 percent in 1994.[1] These were not the results the authors of the price decontrol policy had expected.

What was their miscalculation? First of all, upon being released from their plan targets and given the freedom to set their own prices, enterprises and trade organizations made little effort to maintain their previous levels of output and sales. If anything, they moved to reduce them. They reckoned on making the same or greater profit as before, with higher prices on a lower volume of output. During the initial period of shortages, this was quite possible.[2]

In relatively highly monopolized sectors, the typical capitalist mechanism of maximizing profit while reducing output kicked in. In other sectors, however, the new entrepreneurs copied the pattern of maximizing profit, by taking advantage of the artificially created deficit. As shown in Chapter 4 (Table 4.1), it was in 1992 that the share of gross profit in the economy reached a record height, despite the steep decline of GDP. The crisis of production was aggravated by the acute shortage of working capital, which had been devalued by inflation and the collapse of traditional economic ties. There was also increased competition from foreign goods, which gained free access to the Russian market for the first time. The influx of imports compensated, to some extent, for the domestic supply shortage, but the prices, including profit taken by middlemen, rose just as rapidly as prices on domestic products. And the overriding impact of the inflation, occurring on an unanticipated scale, was to slash the buying power of the population and enterprises alike, thus bringing more chaos and disorganization to the entire economy.

Privatization played no small role in aggravating the crisis. Especially in its first phase, privatization destroyed economic ties and specific forms of cooperation that had existed within sectors of industry. The most detrimental effect of privatization was that it enabled new owners to appropriate the capital of formerly state-owned enterprises, which the new owners then used not for productive purposes, but for their personal enrichment, taking a portion of their money abroad. The psychology of this looting process was described in Chapter 2.

After the 1998 crisis, the intensity of the structural reform process let up somewhat. It resumed only in 2000 under Putin, when "next-generation" neo-liberals Gref and Kudrin were put in charge of the government economic ministries, and an economist from the same school, Andrei Illarionov, became an adviser to the new President. At that point a long-term economic program was formulated, defining the further reduction of the role of the state in the economy as its central goal. In particular, reform of the natural monopolies and a comprehensive package of social sector reforms, including housing and utilities, were put on the agenda.

We discussed the natural monopolies (electric power, natural gas, railroads) in Chapter 3. Reforms planned for this area involved, first of all, privatizing what had not already been privatized and, secondly, creating a free market for their products: that is, practically total price deregulation. It was to be a miniature version of the original Gaidar-Chubais reforms. Unlike the reforms of 1992-1994, though, the new series of changes would occur not as a shock, but gradually, with a prolonged process of discussion at various levels of government. But the essence of the matter remained the same, despite corrections to the implementation process.

Past experience shows—and the initiators of these reforms do not deny it—that they will result in higher rates for electricity, gas, and rail travel. These are obviously inflationary measures. Official estimates are that power rates will triple, at the very least. That will automatically increase per-unit costs in all sectors of the economy and, consequently, cause an overall surge of prices.

The extent of the detrimental impact of such a new phase of privatization is hard to predict, but it follows from the discussion of how private companies would function in the electric power sector, that they would shut down a portion of the capacity they acquired, on grounds of insufficient profitability. This perspective promises neither increased electricity output, technological updating of the sector, nor the creation of conditions for free competition.

Now we turn to the reforms proposed for the social services sector: health care, education, pensions, housing, and utilities.

Without going into the details and specifics of each, it can be said that the general direction of these reforms is a shift to the market principle of for-fee services. The ideologues of neo-liberalism view all of these social services as commodities, which should be paid for at full value.

We shall not discuss here the relative merits of a market versus a free or discount (socialist) system of social services. The shortcomings of the latter in the USSR do not alter the fact that they have worked fairly well and efficiently in several developed countries in the West. Free health care in Sweden and Canada, and free primary and secondary education in many Western European countries and the United States, are examples. It is just as clear, that for-fee healthcare systems in other developed Western countries do not automatically ensure that the care will be of good quality and readily available. This author can testify to the latter fact on the basis of personal experience, since a system of this type has been in effect in the Netherlands (where he lives) for more than a decade. These questions can be debated ad infinitum.

The main question before us is a different one: has the economic environment, currently existing in Russia, prepared the way for such reforms? Charging fees for social services presumes that the majority of the population is able to pay them in full, meaning that people must have a sufficiently high income level to handle the fees. Since the majority of the population earns a living mainly by working for pay, the assumption is that wages will include outlays for the full cost of social services. The wage structure we inherited from socialism, however, excluded such costs, and still does. Consequently the best way to implement the above-mentioned reforms would be in parallel with the transition of the majority of the population into the "middle class" category. People will need to have income substantially above the subsistence minimum, thus enabling them to pay for all the social services they need, at market prices.

In Western European countries, which are by no means socialist, the need for free or discount social services, provided in full or in part by the state, arose during the first half of the 20th century, when the prevailing wage levels did not cover such services. For understandable reasons, employers did not want to raise wages, but the lack of social protection had a negative impact on workers' physical and psychological condition, aggravated the inevitable social conflicts, and suppressed profit. Therefore, the introduction of state-subsidized social services suited workers and employers alike, at that stage of things, and was the result of a social contract between them.

Wage levels ultimately depend on labor productivity. As labor productivity grew in the West, wages also rose, allowing workers to purchase social services in addition to the ones available free of charge. At a certain point, the need for state-supported services partially or entirely faded away for the majority of the population.

The problem of for-fee services is above all a question of labor productivity and the population's prevailing income levels. If productivity is too low, government subsidies are inevitable. In the case of Russia, it should be noted that there are presently no grounds to anticipate any surge in the growth of wages. Public-sector employment (at state-owned and municipal companies and organizations) accounts for less than 40 percent of total employment. Wage increases for so-called budget-sector employees are subject to financial austerity. As for the private sector, it is virtually out of the question for there to be any voluntary increase in the portion of available funds allocated to paying wages (i.e., any increase in real wages at rates faster than the rise of labor productivity).

The inverse relationship of economic growth rates to the introduction of for-fee social services must also be considered. If they are introduced too soon, it is equivalent to cutting the real purchasing power of the population for all goods and services. It is like the imposition of an extra tax, without a wage increase to compensate for it. Since personal consumption accounts for around half of Russia's GDP, any limitation of the growth of solvent demand curbs overall growth rates.

It follows that steady overall economic growth is a precondition for social reforms to succeed. The experience of foreign countries shows that, although it is during periods of economic difficulty that major structural reforms are needed, it is only really possible to implement them during economic upswings, when the necessary financial and other resources are available.

Russia's economic growth during 1999-2005 proved to be an inadequate base on which even to start transforming the social sector in the direction of for-fee services. The absence of objective preconditions notwithstanding, the government, some local authorities, and, of course, the private sector began to campaign for such measures. But protests, including mass demonstrations in some cities, forced this series of reforms to be sidelined.

Prospects for the implementation of structural reforms depend, to a significant extent, on the prevailing outlook within the ruling elite, which in turn reflects the interests of monopoly capital. There are two tendencies at play. One of them seeks chiefly to keep profit at a high level as a portion of total income, while the other cares more about steadily expanding the domestic market and improving the conditions for economic activity. In the long term, an emphasis on stable growth also allows the greatest possible increase of profit. In the short term, however, these two tendencies may conflict, since the redistribution of the national income in favor of profit acts to reduce labor compensation and other income, thus contracting the market, slowing growth, and, ultimately, worsening conditions for the maximization of profit in the long term.

This conflict provokes periodic shifts in the thinking of the ruling elite, from concentration on reforms that enrich the elite and keep social spending to a minimum, to prioritizing a break-out from economic stagnation, and the achievement of higher growth rates. Besides certain political factors, a shift to the latter outlook is what led to the appointment of Primakov as prime minister in the fall of 1998 and to the practical abandonment of structural reforms for a two-year period, which made it possible for the economy to overcome the crisis rapidly and start to grow. In the spring of 2002 an analogous situation, the slowing of economic growth, made Putin order his own neo-liberal government to step up growth rates, setting reforms aside for the time being.

During Putin's second term there was another twist of the same sort. In January 2005, the long-planned monetization of in-kind benefits for pensioners, disabled persons and veterans—the replacement of free services by cash payments—was put into effect, substantially cutting the real income of millions of elderly people. Protest demonstrations followed in many parts of the country. The government was forced to restore a large part of the subsidized in-kind benefits.

In the same time period, three "revolutions" took place, in Ukraine, Georgia, and Kyrgyzstan. The threat of their spilling over into Russia induced Putin in late 2005 to announce four National

Projects, dealing with health care, education, housing, and agriculture. These were widely publicized as a breakthrough toward the improvement of socio-economic conditions. The effects of this reform are yet to be seen, but the planned budget appropriations for all four programs amount to only 0.7 percent of annual GDP, which is considered too small to improve conditions significantly in those sectors. With petrodollars pouring into government coffers at a record rate, much more should have been budgeted for these purposes.

Growth rates are not determined by structural reforms alone, but primarily by macroeconomic instruments such as budget, tax, credit, and monetary policy. These areas will be analyzed in the next sections.

5.2 Budget and tax policy

State budget policy has two fundamentally different aspects, which involve both the raising and spending of budget funds. One of them, which we may provisionally call *passive*, has to do with raising sufficient revenue to cover expenditures that follow from the various functions of government. Here the main goal is to balance the budget, preferably with a surplus of revenue over expenditures, or, in extremis, with as small a deficit as possible. The second, *active* approach involves maneuvering with respect to budget spending and revenue in order to influence the economy and its rate of growth. Here the fiscal outcome—balancing the budget—is not the decisive consideration. Rather, the main task is defined as dealing with situations like a slump in production, or excessive inflation.

Even though the passive approach does not set out to influence the condition of the economy, there is always a two-way interconnection between business activity and the budget. The spending side of the budget consists largely of government purchases of goods and services, either in the form of financing for a part of domestic capital investment, or in monetary transfers to individuals and organizations. In all such cases, the government directly or indirectly augments domestic demand for the economy's output, thus helping to expand the domestic market. At the same time, through the revenue side of the budget, the government lays claim to a part of the funds that private individuals and organizations might have spent on acquiring goods and services produced by the economy. Thus, the budget process also causes some contraction of the domestic market.

If the government spends more than the revenue it takes in, the net result of government economic activity is to inject additional money demand into the economy. If, on the other hand, government spending is less than budget revenue, there is a net reduction of money demand in the economy. It follows that a budget deficit spurs economic growth, when productive capacities are not being fully utilized. Conversely, a budget surplus acts as a curb on economic growth, preventing the full productive potential of the economy from being realized.

The reverse effect also occurs. If the government finances a budget deficit by borrowing from private-sector lenders, this reduces the resources available for private capital investment. Again, conversely, a budget surplus in principle expands the possibilities for such private capital investment. Everything depends, however, on how these resources are used: whether by the government, or in the private sector. If the government spends the surplus on current consumption, this diverts funds from private capital investment, and the inevitable result is slower economic growth. The same thing happens if the private sector fails to make full use of the resources at its disposal, sending capital surpluses abroad or using them to finance speculative activity.

In any event, government revenue depends directly on the condition of the economy. An economic crisis automatically reduces budget revenue, while an economic upswing increases it. Meanwhile, insofar as budget spending, as a rule, does not depend directly on the economic situation, economic downturns inevitably breed budget deficits, while economic upswings produce surpluses. And since deficits stimulate the economy during crises and surpluses restrain it during upswings, the budget mechanism provides a certain degree of cyclical stabilization.

In the last few years, the budget revenue deriving from extraordinarily high world oil prices has been an additional factor in Russia. This influx tends to create budget surpluses of a different nature, which provide extra funds that could be used to finance overall economic growth. The utilization of these surpluses has become a hot political issue. It will be discussed later in this section.

1992-1997 budget policy

The situation in the Russian economy after 1992 only formally resembled the stagflation that had appeared 20 years earlier in the industrially developed countries. It was of entirely different origin, stemming from the unjustified deregulation of prices in a setting of goods shortages, the sudden abandonment of planning before any market infrastructure existed, and the abrupt curtailment of government financing. The consequences of Russia's stagflation, however, were the same as in the West, except many times more intense, because the collapse of output was deeper and the price rises became hyperinflationary.[3]

The health of the budget rapidly deteriorated, while budget policy became extremely contradictory and turned into a source of tension.

GDP declined by 15.5 percent in 1992, while the share of government revenue in GDP fell from 50 percent to 28 percent. Overall real government revenue fell by more than one-half in a single year. The disproportionately great decline in government revenue was caused not only by the crisis in the economy, but also by changes in the composition of tax payments. In the final years of the Soviet period, 75-77 percent of all revenue came from three types of payment: the turnover tax, deductions from the profit of state-owned enterprises, and deductions from revenue deriving from foreign economic activity (customs duties, export revenue, etc.). This revenue averaged around 35 percent of GDP. Only 8-9 percent of budget revenue (4 percent of GDP) came from direct taxation and other collections from the population.

In 1992, the turnover tax was replaced by the VAT and excise taxes, while payments by state-owned enterprises gave way to a tax on profit. Together with the revenue generated by foreign economic activity, these taxes accounted for 79.7 percent of all payments into the budget, although they fell to 22.3 percent of GDP. The share of personal income taxes in budget revenue remained at 8 percent, but now this was only 2.2 percent of GDP.

This shift in the composition of budget revenue was of fundamental significance, especially the tax on profit. During the Soviet period profit, above a certain level that the enterprises were allowed to keep, had simply been taken by the government as budget revenue. Now, the enterprises were required only to pay a fixed tax rate. In 1992, this meant that the budget received 1.567 trillion rubles from the tax on profit, while total profit in the economy (after subtracting losses) was 5.623 trillion rubles. In other words, the tax on profit was effectively no greater than 28 percent, while in the last years of the Soviet period, after the partial market reforms carried out by Gorbachov, 50 percent or more of profit had been collected for use in the budget.

One would think that the reduced tax burden would have alleviated the economic crisis. But with the economic mechanism disrupted and having partially disintegrated, the tax relief was not enough of an incentive for enterprises either to maintain the previous level of output, or to undertake new capital investment.

With tax collections at less than half their previous level in real terms, the government was forced to cut its spending sharply, as well. The need to fight hyperinflation dictated the same course of action. Nonetheless, despite the further decline of GDP and the subsequent drop-off of real budget revenue, the spending cuts imposed in 1992-1994 did not come fast enough to prevent the rapid growth of a budget deficit. From 3.4 percent of GDP in 1992, the deficit rose to 9.5 percent of GDP in 1994. Theoretically this should have mitigated the crisis, but in reality it merely drove inflation even harder. During this initial post-Soviet period, the government had no clear anti-inflation program and was more following the inertia of stagflation, than attempting to combat the crisis and stabilize prices.

A turning point in budget policy arrived in 1995. In part it was connected with the influence of the International Monetary Fund (IMF), which began to lend money to Russia that year, accompanied by conditionalities respecting budget policy. But the changes also had to do with the financial reform, pushed through the State Duma by the government at that time. They chiefly affected how the budget deficit was to be financed.

From 1992 through 1994, two-thirds of the federal budget deficit had been covered by direct borrowings from the Bank of Russia, the central bank, while the rest was handled by the issuance of a modest quantity of government bonds and by borrowing abroad on a relatively small scale. The central bank issued its credits to the government in the form of newly minted cash, a measure that promoted inflation.

In 1995, the State Duma prohibited this procedure, forcing a radical shift in how the budget deficit was financed. That year nearly half the federal deficit was covered by government securities (mainly short-term, three- and six-month government bonds, the so-called GKOs), while the remaining part was covered by IMF credits.[4] The proportions of these two sources changed little in the years that followed. In 1995, 46 percent of the federal deficit was financed from domestic sources, mainly GKOs; in 1996, this level was 55 percent, and in 1997 it was 43 percent. The rest was covered from foreign sources, mainly IMF loans.[5]

It can be argued that the measures adopted in 1995-1996 to reduce government spending in real terms, which cut the budget deficit as a share of GDP in those years, had a greater effect on reducing aggregate money demand, than it had on this shift in how the deficit was financed. Moreover, the practice of budget sequestration (mandatory cuts of already allocated funds), which was begun in those years, prolonged the economy's stagnation. Influenced by IMF monetarists to concentrate on the battle against inflation, the government postponed the end of the production crisis by several years.

The shift to financing the budget deficit by issuing GKOs also turned out to be a poorly conceived policy, which ultimately helped to bring on the financial crash of 1998. The federal government had to pay very high interest rates on its bonds, due to the condition of the credit market at the time. In 1995, the average market yield of a GKO was 162 percent; in 1996 it was 85.8 percent. The average yield fell to 26 percent in 1997, but exploded again in 1998, reaching 135 percent in August, just before the crisis.[6] This meant that the government regularly had to borrow funds, not only to cover part of the budget deficit, but also to pay the interest on GKOs issued earlier. Over time, the interest payments substantially exceeded the amounts borrowed.

One result of this process was a steady increase in the volume of GKOs issued. The total face value of bonds issued (minus bonds that had been redeemed) had reached 74 billion rubles at the end of 1995, 237 billion in 1996, 385 billion in 1997, and 436 billion in June 1998, not long before the default.[7] At the same time, the amount of GKO interest that had to be paid, out of the same budget, also rose. Interest payments accounted for 19 percent of total federal budget spending in 1995, 29 percent in 1996, 24 percent in 1997, and 34 percent for the first seven months of 1998.[8] This meant that less and less of budget resources could be spent for primary, non-interest purposes. This process was leading inexorably toward state bankruptcy, which struck at the end of August 1998, when the government terminated all payments on GKOs, including both interest payments and redemption of outstanding bonds.

Many have asked why the government continued to issue GKOs up to the very last moment, although the inevitability of the default was clear long before it happened. The only explanation is that the GKO pyramid operation benefitted financial magnates, who were speculating in the government bond market and making money on the enormous interest rates. It is impossible to calculate the total profit taken from this operation, but the interest alone, paid out on GKOs in 1995-1998 (until the default), was 372 billion rubles, or $69 billion at the exchange rate of that time. The fact that this sum is approximately equal to Russia's earnings from oil and petroleum product exports during those years gives an idea of the enormous amount of money involved.[9]

The economy sustained direct damage. As noted, government spending represents a direct addition to GDP, but only if it is spent on purchasing domestically produced goods and services. Spending to pay interest on the national debt does not come under this category. The greater the share of debt service in government spending, the more resources are sucked out of GDP.

The rising GKO interest payments were responsible for a steady decline in the real level of non-interest federal budget spending during these years (Table 5.1). In 1998 such spending plummeted, adding yet another factor to aggravate the financial and economic crisis.

Analysis of budget policy in the 1992-1998 period shows that it contributed to deepening the prolonged economic crisis and dragging out the period of stagnation.

Budget policy in 1999-2005

The budget situation changed substantially after the 1998 financial crisis. Now, federal budget revenue grew more rapidly in real terms than GDP did. Accordingly budget revenue as a share of GDP was 11.9 percent in 1997 and 9.8 in 1998, subsequently rising to 12.9

Table 5.1 Nominal and real federal budget spending, 1995-1998

	1995	1996	1997	1998
Federal budget spending (billions of rubles)	286.2	427.1	494.8	407.2
Minus: interest payments on government debt (billions of rubles)	54.6	124.5	117.8	106.8
Non-interest spending (billions of rubles)	231.6	302.6	377.0	300.4
Non-interest spending (in 1995 prices)	231.6	217.9	208.6	142.1
Non-interest spending as index, 1995=100	100	94.1	90.1	61.4

Source: RET2, #2, 2000, calculated on the basis of Tables 1, 11.

percent in 1999, 16 percent in 2000, 17.6 percent in 2001, and 20.3 percent in 2002 (Table 5.2).

Since tax rates not only did not increase in this period, but in some cases were even reduced, the main reason for the growth of budget revenue was an expansion of the tax base through economic growth, and a relatively higher growth rate of personal income, profit, and turnover in the private sector. In 2000, a substantial additional source of revenue emerged, namely the growth of taxes and export duties on the production and export of oil and petroleum products.

The government did not, however, use the increased budget revenue to make more resources available to the economy. The share of federal spending in GDP remained practically unchanged in 1999-2001 at around 14 percent, considerably lower than its 19.2 percent level in 1997. Only in 2002-2003 did it recover to 19 and 18 percent, respectively. These levels were facilitated by the government's refusal to service the greater part of its domestically circulating state debt, after the 1998 default. Moreover, in 1999 the habitual primary budget deficit was replaced, for the first time, by a small surplus. Beginning in 2000, the surplus became large enough to handle all foreign debt obligations. A positive balance of payments also helped, making it possible to accumulate foreign currency reserves on a regular basis. In the upper echelons of power, the prevailing viewpoint was that debt repayment to foreign creditors took priority over providing incentives for

Table 5.2 The federal budget, 1997-2003
(billions of rubles and % of GDP)

	1997	1998	1999	2000	2001	2002	2003
GDP	2,479	2,741	4,757	7,063	9,063	10,834	13,285
Revenue	293.9	269.9	608.0	1,127.6	1,590.7	2,204.7	2,586.2
% of GDP	11.9%	9.8%	12.8%	16.0%	17.6%	20.3%	19.5%
Expenditures	475.6	384.3	664.7	954.1	1,325.7	2,054.2	2,358.6
% of GDP	19.2%	14.0%	14.0%	13.5%	14.6%	19.0%	17.8%
Deficit (–) or surplus (+)	–181.7	–114.4	–56.6	+173.5	+265.0	+155.5	+227.6
% of GDP	–7.3%	–4.2%	–1.2%	+2.5%	+2.9%	+1.4%	+1.7%
Interest payments	117.8	106.6	162.5	172.2	231.1	229.6	220.9
% of GDP	4.8%	3.9%	3.4%	2.4%	2.5%	2.1%	1.7%
Non-interest spending	357.8	277.7	502.2	781.9	1,094.6	1,824.6	2,137.7
% of GDP	14.4%	10.1%	10.6%	11.1%	12.1%	16.8%	16.1%
Primary deficit or surplus	–63.9	–7.8	+105.9	+345.7	+496.1	+385.1	+448.5
% of GDP	–2.6%	–0.3%	+2.2%	+4.9%	+5.5%	+3.6%	+3.4%

Sources: Calculated on the basis of RET2, #10, 2002, Tables 14, 15; RSY 2001, Table 21.3.

domestic development. In 2000-2003, interest payments stabilized at 1.7-2.5 percent of GDP (in 1997, when the government was also paying interest on the GKOs, these payments were double that level). While interest payments on the foreign debt were technically included in the expenditure side of the budget, repayment of the core debt now began to be done out of the overall budget surplus.

A belief took hold in the government and in circles close to the President, that economic growth needed to be stimulated by economizing on any non-interest budget spending, thus making it possible to reduce the tax burden on the private sector. The opposing view, according to which increased government spending ought to be directed toward the country's urgent social and defense needs, was rejected.

Nonetheless, Putin initiated well-advertised pension and wage hikes for the so-called budget-sector workers during those years. These are the low-paid employees of state institutions: doctors and

Table 5.3 Comparison of personal consumption and individual income, 1997–2003
(current prices, billions of rubles)

	1997	1998	1999	2000	2001	2002	2003
GDP	2,478.6	2,741.1	4,757.2	7,063.4	9,063.0	10,834.0	13,285.0
Year-on-year increase		262.5	2,016.1	2,306.2	1,999.6	1,771.0	2,451.0
Household consumption	1,265	1,499	2,520	3,337	4,496	5,418	6,561
Year-on-year increase		234	1,021	817	1,159	922	1,143
Compensation of employees	1,238.9	1,292.7	1,947.8	2,821.5	4,069.1	5,047.5	6,132.2
Compensation of employees as % of GDP	50.0%	47.1%	40.9%	39.9%	45.0%	46.6%	46.2%
Share of concealed labor income	290.0	277.0	525.0	782.0	993.5	1,249.0	1,488.0
Reported (on-the-books) labor income	948.9	1,015.7	1,422.8	2,039.5	3,075.6	3,798.5	4,642.0
Average monthly wage (rubles)	950	1,052	1,523	2,223	3,240	4,360	5,499
Number employed (millions)	60.0	58.4	63.1	64.5	64.7	66.1	65.8
Accrued wages	684.0	737.2	1,153.2	1,720.6	2,515.5	3,458.3	4,342.0
Accrued wages as % of GDP	27.6%	26.9%	24.2%	24.4%	27.8%	31.9%	32.7%
Accrued wages as % of labor income	55.2%	57.0%	59.2%	61.0%	61.8%	68.5%	70.8%
Money income of population	1,653.9	1,767.1	2,847.9	3,814.7	5,385.0	6,829.3	8,885.6
Income minus accrued wages	969.9	1,029.9	1,694.7	2,094.1	2,869.5	3,371.0	4,543.6
Pensions paid	150.3	183.9	206.8	320.0	491.2	661.7	776.4
Year-on-year growth		33.6	22.9	113.2	151.9	170.5	114.7
Pensions paid as % of household consumption		14.4%	2.2%	13.8%	13.1%	12.2%	11.8%
Income minus wages and pensions	819.6	846	1,488.4	1,774	2,397.6	2,709.3	3,767.2
Year-on-year growth		26.4	642.4	285.6	623.6	311.7	1,057.9

Sources: Calculated on the basis of RSY 2001, Table 2.3; RET2, #10, 2002, Tables 8, 9, 10; *Osnovnye pokazateli natsional'nykh schetov (Basic National Accounting Indicators)*, 2001, 2002; *Metodologicheskie polozheniia po statistike, vypusk vtoroi (Methodological Principles of Statistics, second edition)* (Moscow: 1998), pp. 196-198.

other healthcare personnel, teachers and other school staff. An impression was created that, first of all, the government was spending significant amounts of money for these purposes, and, secondly, this would promote the growth of effective demand and, consequently, overall economic growth. We shall now attempt to evaluate the extent to which this assertion was true.

As shown in earlier chapters, official wage statistics contain a number of mysteries. Let us look at them once again, using the data in Table 5.3. The broadest category, "Compensation of employees," includes the salaries of middle-level and top managers, who, strictly speaking, are not workers. But even if we ignore that fact and exclude so-called "Concealed labor income," the remainder, "Reported (on-the-books) labor income" exceeds accrued wages by a large margin. This is because "Labor income" includes the deductions made by enterprises for social insurance, which do not figure directly in employees' income, although from the employers' standpoint they are part of the outlays for labor compensation and represent a tax on their hiring of labor. Nonetheless, it would be incorrect to count these deductions as a part of the money that workers can spend to buy goods and services. The dynamics of these resources are reflected in the category "Accrued wages," after the subtraction of taxes and other collections, as well as wage arrears. Accrued wages before those subtractions accounted for only 55 percent of "Labor income" in Russia as a whole in 1997, and 60-62 percent in 2000-2001. They represented 73 and 84 percent, in the two time-frames respectively, of "Reported (on-the-books) labor income." The share of social deductions dropped substantially in this period, from 27 to 16 percent.

It is evident that the relative growth of wages during these years helped to promote economic growth. Comparison of the annual growth of accrued wages with the growth of household consumption shows that rising wages correlate with the rate of economic growth. The more quickly GDP grew, the more increased personal consumption was paid for by rising wages. For example, 68-70 percent of the increase in individual consumption in 2000 and 2001, when GDP grew by 8.7 and 4.9 percent annually, was accounted for by rising wages. Such consumption rose by over 50 percent in 2002, when GDP growth was 4 percent, but by only 23 percent in the crisis year of 1998.

Table 5.4 Pension payments compared with previous periods

	1995	1996	1997	1998	1999	2000	2001	2002	2003
Number of pensioners, millions	37.1	37.8	38.2	38.4	38.4	38.4	38.4	38.4	38.2
Average monthly pension, rubles	188	302	328	399	449	694	1,024	1,379	1,637
Pensions paid, billions of rubles	83.7	137.2	150.3	183.9	206.8	320.0	471.9	661.7	776.4
As % of GDP	5.4%	6.3%	5.9%	6.7%	4.3%	4.4%	5.2%	6.1%	5.8%
Real size of pensions as % of the previous year's payments	80.5%	108.7%	94.6%	95.2%	60.6%	128.0%	122.2%	117.0%	106.0%
As index, 1995=100	100	108.7	102.8	97.9	59.3	75.9	92.7	108.5	114.9
Average pension as % of subsistence minimum for a pensioner	101%	116%	113%	115%	70%	76%	91%	100%	102%

Source: Calculated on the basis of RSY 2000, 2001, Tables 6.6, 7.38. Official statistics give two series of average monthly pension figures, one of them substantially higher than the other. We have chosen the lower of the series, which, multiplied by the total number of pensioners, approximately coincides with Pension Fund reports on actual pension payments.

Thus, it would appear that the increase of wages during these years was not so much due to government policy, as it was a spontaneous feature of the economy's upturn. Turnover and profit were increasing rapidly in the private sector, necessitating the hiring of additional workers and making it possible to pay them more. In addition, unemployment was cut from 13.2 in 1998 to 8.1 percent in 2003. Real wages, which had fallen by 13 percent in 1998 and 22 percent in 1999, compared with the 1997 level, regained their pre-crisis level only in 2002. The economy's growth was nourished, to a significant extent, by the low starting level of wages and the availability of a large pool of unemployed labor.

To what extent did the measures adopted to raise the compensation paid to government employees promote economic growth?

Over 85 percent of the total increase in wages was accounted for by sectors of the economy that are not under the direct control of the government: industry, agriculture, construction, transportation and communications, and trade. The majority of "budget-sector" workers are employed in health care, education, and administration. Only 8 percent of the increase in wages was associated with the healthcare and education sectors, where average earnings barely exceed the subsistence minimum. That is less than the growth of labor compensation in four selected industries, where wages are substantially above the average for the economy as a whole: the electrical power industry, the fuels industry, non-ferrous metals, and steel. These industries, which employ less than one-fifth of all industrial workers, accounted for half the increase of wages in industry.

Another of Putin's initiatives, besides the announced pay raises for state-sector employees, was to raise the average pension level. The macroeconomic effect of this measure was shown above in Table 5.3, which makes clear that pensions paid in 2000-2003 increased by an amount equal to 13-15 percent of the total growth of personal consumption in those years. The impact of this component of budget policy—pension and public-sector wage increases, combined—on the growth of consumer demand can be estimated at 20 percent.

There is, however, another side to pension policy.

Table 5.4 shows that pensions paid during these years of economic growth totalled no more, or even less as a percentage of GDP, than in 1995-1998. Nominal pension growth was significant, quadrupling in the 1997-2002 period. The average pension's real increase, however, looked big only in comparison with 1999, when there was a 40 percent drop in one year, due to inflation. As a result, the average real pension in 2003 barely exceeded the 1996 level. It is also telling that the average pension was regularly below a pensioner's subsistence minimum, which is calculated by Goskomstat at a special reduced level for this category of the population, throughout these economic growth years, whereas the average pension had exceeded the subsistence minimum in the earlier period, 1995-1998. Pensioners had it substantially worse under Putin, than even under Yeltsin.

It is evident that in 1999-2003 budget spending was used virtually not at all to create growth incentives, while increases in pensions and public-sector wages served more to make up for the losses of the 1998 crisis, than to advance any real improvements in the standard of living.

The liberal Kasyanov government also made some attempts to use tax policy as an economic stimulus. Chief among these measures were:

- reform of the personal income tax, under which the progressive rate structure, with higher rates for higher personal income, was abolished in favor of a flat 13 percent rate for all income categories;
- reform of the tax on profit, which was reduced to 22 percent, accompanied by the elimination of a number of privileges, particularly the right of enterprises to deduct from their taxable profit, half of what they spent on capital investment.

The income tax reform was intended more to address fiscal concerns, than to work directly as a stimulus. The theory was that an end to progressive taxation would prompt high-income individuals to "come out of the shadows," that is, to stop concealing and understating their income, and thus to pay more in taxes.

The reform did have a certain fiscal impact. Personal income taxes collected during the first year after introduction of the flat tax (2001) showed a noticeable rise. A certain portion of higher-income individuals did decide to "come out of the shadows." It is fairly difficult to identify this effect in the statistics, since nominal wages grew substantially in 2001, and personal income taxes for employees of enterprises and organizations are collected automatically on the basis of wages. Moreover, the tax rate for the majority of individuals with comparatively lower income rose, since they had to pay 13 percent, instead of the 12 percent that had been their maximum rate under the previous system.

Data on taxes and contributions by households bear out this pattern. The average level of taxation per household, having fluctuated in a stable range of 6-6.5 percent during 1995-1999, rose sharply to 8 percent in 2000, even before the changes in the tax scale. It continued to increase in subsequent years, to 9.2 percent in 2001 and 10 percent in 2002.[10]

According to economic theory, the reduction of the tax on profit, beginning in 2002, was supposed to have a direct stimulatory impact. The government expected it to be an incentive for companies to increase their capital investment, thus supporting economic growth rates, which, in turn, would increase total revenue from the tax on profit, compensating for any potential fiscal losses. The actual outcome was quite different.

The abolition of the investment deduction, in the opinion of big business's organizations, not only failed to reduce the effective taxation rate on profit, but actually increased it from 18 percent to 22 percent. This caused companies, first of all, to curtail their investment plans sharply (capital investment growth in 2002 was only 2.4 percent, as against 7 percent the previous year) and, secondly, to show lower profit, while increasing their tax-exempt allowances for depreciation. The macroeconomic effect was clearly negative. But fiscal damage was done, as well. Revenue from the tax on profit fell from 6 percent of consolidated budget revenue in 2001 to 4.7 percent in 2002, and from 2.6 to 1.7 percent of federal budget revenue.[11]

These tax reform failures prompted Putin in the spring of 2002 to criticize the government publicly for passivity, and to demand measures to accelerate economic growth. Violating their usual practice of verbally agreeing with the President, yet sabotaging his demands in practice, this time both Prime Minister Kasyanov and Minister of Economics Gref publicly refused to resort to any additional stimulatory measures, maintaining that such actions could lead to economic collapse. Putin had to swallow that pill.

Similar criticisms began to be heard among the oligarchs, particularly from the RUIE. With support from Presidential adviser Illarionov, they demanded even larger tax cuts. Under this pressure, the government began in late 2002 to consider the possibility of reducing the unified social tax (UST) from 41.5 percent to 39 percent or lower, and the VAT from 20 percent to 18 percent, or even 15 percent. Any significant reduction of the UST would directly hit pensions and other social spending, since the UST is paid by businessmen, but is spent exclusively to bolster the Pension Fund, cover medical insurance, and so forth. The Expert Institute, a research organization attached to the RUIE, even proposed to raise the pension age for both men and women to 65 (from 60 for men and 55 for women). To its credit, the government resisted this extreme demand. Yet it is typical of the situation that developed around tax policy.

In 2003, the government agreed for the first time to take a differentiated approach to taxation of the extractive and the manufacturing industries, in order to provide incentives for the development of the latter. The idea was to compensate for lower tax revenue from manufacturing, with higher taxes on the extractive industries, especially those that are export-oriented. It goes without saying that the slightest hint about reshaping tax policy along those lines brought a hostile response from the elite oligarchs, who are nourished primarily by superprofit from the export of fuels and metals. For that reason the planned reform in this area went nowhere. This question will be considered in more detail in Chapter 6, when we analyze ways to free the Russian economy from its fuels bias.

In Putin's second term, the government finally did reduce the average UST rate to 32 percent and the VAT to 18 percent. The official explanation was that the savings to business would be used to raise capital investment and restrict price inflation. The actual effect was quite different. Business swallowed the additional revenue, but did not respond with either price restraint or more active capital investment. The new tax reform did reduce revenue for the government Pension Fund, which ended up with a large fiscal deficit that had to be covered out of the regular federal budget.

The steep rise in world oil prices (from an average of $25 per barrel, to $60 and more) in 2004-2005 created a new issue: how to spend the additional petrodollars that poured into the federal budget. The solution supported by Putin, on advice from the neo-liberal ministerial troika, was to set aside all revenue received from oil price margins above $27 per barrel, in a newly created Stabilization

Fund, which could be spent to repay Russia's external debt, but not used for domestic purposes. By January 2006, the Stabilization Fund had reached a total of 1.446 trillion rubles, equivalent to $51 billion, which should have been used for various investment and social projects in Russia. The government, however, refuses to do this, citing the danger of serious inflationary pressure.

In reality, there are various non-inflationary ways of spending the money, such as for the purchase of modern industrial equipment and technology abroad, for issuing long-term loans to finance infrastructure investment projects, and so forth. There are suspicions that Putin is saving this money as an emergency political reserve to be used in the Parliamentary and Presidential election campaigns of 2007-2008. In any case, the refusal to use the Stabilization Fund for productive purposes is effectively slowing down economic growth.

Another set of areas in which part of the surplus could be spent is defined by Putin's National Projects in education, health care, housing, and agriculture. As indicated above, they are greatly underfunded, despite the PR efforts to promote them. The money allocated for these projects in 2006 is 150 billion rubles, or less than 0.4 percent of total federal budget spending for the year. The funding for these projects could easily have been doubled by a less-than-20-percent reduction in the projected 776 billion ruble federal budget surplus. Instead, the surplus will be stashed away unproductively in the Stabilization Fund, raising it to new record heights.

The contradictory postures assumed within the upper echelons of the power structure have blocked any effective budget policy, including tax policy. This situation cannot fail to affect macroeconomic growth, down the road. Due to its structural imbalances, the Russian economy, in the absence of special budget incentives, is doomed to have mediocre growth rates, at best, and to lag ever farther behind the industrial nations of the West.

5.3 Credit and monetary policy

The aims of credit and monetary policy in the post-Soviet period have been to restrain inflation and attempt to regulate the money supply, the banking system, and the securities and currency markets.

After the decontrol of prices in 1992, inflation was virtually out

Table 5.5 The money supply in 1990-1998
(billions of rubles at end of the year)

	1990	1991	1992	1993	1994	1995	1996	1997	1998
Cash (M0)	0.08	0.19	1.7	13.3	35.7	80.7	103.8	130.4	187.8
M0 as % of GDP	12.5%	13.6%	8.9%	7.8%	5.8%	5.2%	4.8%	5.2%	6.9%
Money supply (M2)	0.42	0.96	6.4	32.6	97.8	220.8	288.3	374.1	448.3
Nominal GDP (for year)	0.64	1.4	19.0	171.5	610.7	1541	2163	2530	2741
M2 as % of GDP	65.6%	68.6%	33.7%	19.0%	16.0%	14.3%	13.3%	14.8%	16.4%
Real GDP, index		100	85.5	78.1	68.1	65.3	60.9	61.5	58.9
Real M2, index		100	42.0	21.6	15.9	13.6	11.8	13.3	14.1
M2 minus M0	0.34	0.77	4.7	19.3	62.1	140.1	184.5	243.7	260.5
Population's Sberbank deposits	0.22	0.37	0.66	3.97	17.6	51.1	96.4	115.2	126.8
Population's Sberbank deposits as % of non-cash money	59.5%	48.1%	14.0%	20.6%	28.3%	36.5%	52.2%	47.3%	48.7%
M2 minus M0 as % of GDP	53.1%	55.0%	24.8%	11.2%	10.2%	9.1%	8.5%	9.6%	9.5%
Foreign currency deposits	–	–	4.5	12.1	39.0	55.0	69.0	83.1	180.3
Quasi-money (M3)*	–	–	10.9	44.7	136.8	275.8	357.3	457.2	628.6
M3 as % of GDP	–	–	57.4%	26.1%	22.4%	17.9%	16.5%	18.1%	22.9%

* M2 plus foreign currency deposits.

Sources: *Obzor ekonomicheskoi polititki v Rossii za 1998 god* (*Review of Economic Policy in Russia for 1998*), Bureau of Economic Analysis (Moscow: ROSSPEN, 1999), p. 613; RET2, #10, 2002, Table 17.

of control for several years. As we have shown, this was due chiefly to the disruption of economic ties, attempts to maximize profit in monopolized markets, and artificially maintained shortages of goods. But inflation also had a monetary component: the Central Bank's printing of money consolidated the rise in prices that had taken place spontaneously, and to a certain extent fuelled it.

The years 1992-1994 saw a sharp contraction of real money in circulation, while its nominal volume was fantastically bloated (Table 5.5). Cash in circulation (M0) and the total ruble money supply (M2), which also includes current and fixed-term accounts in banks, nominally grew more slowly than GDP in current prices. Nominal GDP in 1994 was 436 times greater than the 1991 level, due to hyperinflation, while the total ruble money supply (M2) increased only by a factor of 102. Money is required for circulation of goods and services, yet the quantity of money grew at less than one-fourth the rate of growth of the total value of that turnover. In practice, this was equivalent to a sharp reduction of the money supply. By the end of 1994, the money supply, expressed in comparable prices, had fallen to one-sixth of its 1991 level, while real GDP had dropped only by one-third.

This process continued uninterrupted throughout these years, albeit at a slower rate. In 1991, the money supply in cash and bank accounts was equal to 68.6 percent of goods and services turnover. In 1992, this indicator dropped by more than one-half, to 33.7 percent. In 1993, it declined to 19 percent, and in 1994 it was 16 percent. There were two aspects to the macroeconomic effect of this shrinkage. It had a detrimental effect on production, making it more difficult to sell output. At the same time, it contributed to the gradual reduction of the rate of inflation. During 1992, consumer prices increased 24 times over. In 1993, they rose by a factor of 9.4, and in 1994 another 3.2 times.[12]

It would be a stretch to say that the relative contraction of the money supply resulted from a deliberate policy of the Gaidar and Chernomyrdin governments. Most likely the dominant processes were poorly guided, spontaneous ones, stemming from "shock therapy" and the lack of adequate market institutions. One thing that took place during those years, for example, was the mass devaluation of deposits belonging to the population and to businesses, which was equivalent to withdrawing from circulation practically all of the money accumulated before 1992, including cash balances. The devaluation of previous and current accumulation continued over the next two years, accompanied by a significantly faster decline of goods and services turnover. The portion of total non-cash money, accounted for by the population's bank deposits, fell from 60 percent in 1990 and 48 percent in 1991, to 14 percent in 1992. As a result of these processes, the relationship between the money supply and goods and services turnover underwent a fundamental shift.

It is often asserted that money played a secondary role in the planned economy, not performing the functions it typically has in a modern market economy. This claim is only partially true. Money actually functioned rather well as a medium of exchange and payment in the planned economy. The process of payments between enterprises through branches of Gosbank went on without serious interruptions.

The so-called market reforms disrupted normal monetary circulation and payments procedures. Even as non-cash transactions failed to develop to a level comparable with what exists in the West, the ratio of cash to GDP fell to Western levels, while the ratio of non-cash money to GDP dropped catastrophically, to only 25-30 percent of the level considered normal in Western economies.

The result was paradoxical: the transition to a market economy was accompanied by a reduction of the role of money in the economy. With inflation continuing at a strong pace, there was patently not enough money to service the turnover of goods and services, which naturally had a very negative impact on the process of production. The disruption of the payments system, particularly as a result of the lack of money, led to two specifically Russian phenomena, which began to develop especially after 1995: the overall growth of indebtedness, and a sharp increase in the direct exchange of goods: barter.

Enterprise arrears had equalled only 5.2 percent of GDP in 1993, but they rose to 13.3 percent in 1995, 29.1 percent in 1997 and 47.8 percent in 1998.[13] The greater part of this indebtedness was accounted for by non-payments to suppliers for products received, non-payment of taxes at various levels of the budget, and wage arrears.

Contrary to widespread belief, the planned economy was not primarily barter-based. Even in the first year of the market shock,

1992, barter represented only 6 percent of total sales by industrial enterprises. The sharp increase of the share of barter occurred during the market reform years, when the amount of money in the economy plunged. By 1994 it had risen to 18 percent, and then reached 40 percent in 1996 and 51 percent in 1998. Another 20 percent of the turnover was serviced using various monetary surrogates, especially enterprises' own IOUs.[14] In that period, as much as 80 percent of industrial enterprises' payments for electricity and gas took place without the involvement of banks or cash transactions.

The high level of barter demonstrates that a significant number of Russian enterprises were effectively insolvent. In particular, they lacked sufficient working capital to continue functioning, even at the depression levels that characterized the crisis. In addition, barter was a way for enterprises to survive under conditions where payments through the banking system had broken down. And it was a way for them to sell their output in the absence of sufficient solvent demand in the economy. Without the widespread use of barter, the collapse of production would have been even more severe during those years.

It is striking that the Central Bank leaders at that time were among those who strongly resisted any proposal to return to that institution its function as a payments center for the economy. This attitude was due partly to hostility to the idea on the part of the government, which did not want to undermine the competitiveness of the private banks. The Central Bank would have been able to perform this function, only if enterprises concentrated their short-term deposits in the Central Bank's branch offices, rather than in private banks. For most enterprises, such a system would have been better than dealing with the private banks, which charged their customers high interest rates on loans and exorbitant fees for other services.

At the end of 1992, the average bank lending rate for enterprises and organizations was 203 percent per annum. In 1994, it reached 297 percent. Price inflation outstripped those figures, however, so some such loans even had a negative real interest rate. Under certain conditions, such as for borrowing for purposes of speculation, it became profitable to take out bank loans. By 1995, however, inflation had dropped to 46 percent, while the bank lending rate was 119 percent. In 1996, the bank lending rate (52 percent) was nearly triple the rate of inflation (18 percent). In 1997, the lending rate was

29 percent and the rate of inflation was 12 percent.[15] In other words, credit became truly expensive for the first time. Starting in 1995, the rising cost of credit was fuelled by the issuance of GKOs to cover the budget deficit. The lending sector's scant resources were largely sucked up by these instruments, thus raising the real cost of credit for all borrowers.

The government's currency policy also affected the economy adversely. During those years it consisted of actions to restrain the rate of devaluation of the ruble against foreign currencies, compared with its devaluation on the domestic market. The exchange rate of the ruble, that is, was kept artificially high. From the end of 1991 through the end of 1997, the value of the ruble inside Russia fell by a factor of 2,253, while the dollar rose against the ruble only by a factor of 35. In 1995-1997, even though the rate of inflation had levelled off, the policy continued unchanged, under pressure from the IMF. The IMF demanded that the ruble be kept within a strict currency corridor. From the end of 1994 through the end of 1997, the dollar rose against the ruble only by 70 percent, while the domestic rate of inflation in that period was 310 percent.[16] Although the gap between the external and internal rates of devaluation narrowed, it nonetheless stubbornly persisted. The upshot was that, after the August 1998 crisis, it had to be corrected through an 80 percent devaluation of the ruble.

We showed in Chapter 1 that maintaining such a gap benefitted the incipient financial oligarchy, whose members took advantage of it to multiply their own money. Harm was done to the economy, meanwhile, by the cheapening of imported goods in comparison with Russian-produced goods, which helped push the latter out of the domestic market. The share of imported goods in total retail trade turnover was 50-54 percent in 1995-1997. After the sharp devaluation of the ruble, imports' share dropped to the 31-35 percent level in 1999-2000.[17]

Thus, the 1998 financial crisis was rooted not only in the government's wrongheaded fiscal policy, but also in its deliberately harmful monetary policy.

What changed in this area after 1998? First of all, it needs to be emphasized that all of the most substantial correctives to the previous policy were made by the Primakov government in 1998-1999. The fairly steady credit and monetary policy, developed during

Table 5.6 The money supply in 1998-2003
(billions of rubles at the end of the year)

	1998	1999	2000	2001	2002	2003
Cash (M0)	187.8	266.5	419.3	584.3	763.2	1147.0
M0 as % of GDP	6.9%	5.5%	5.7%	6.4%	7.0%	8.6%
Money supply (M2)	448.3	704.7	1,144.3	1,602.6	2,134.5	3212.7
Nominal GDP (for year)	2,741	4,805	7,335	9,063	10,834	13,285
M2 as % of GDP	16.4%	14.7%	15.6%	17.7%	19.7%	24.2%
M2 minus M0 (non-cash money)	260.5	438.2	725.0	1,018.3	1,371.3	2,065.3
Population's Sberbank deposits as % of non-cash money	44.3%	41.9%	40.3%	45.2%	51.2%	56.3%
M2 minus M0 as % of GDP	9.5%	9.2%	9.9%	11.2%	12.7%	15.5%
Foreign currency deposits	180.3	280.2	415.7	520.1	673.2	762.5
Quasi-money (M3)*	628.6	984.9	1,560.0	2,122.7	2,807.7	3,975.2
M3 as % of GDP	22.9%	20.5%	21.3%	23.4%	25.9%	29.9%

* M2 plus foreign currency deposits.
Source: Calculated on the basis of RET2, 2002, #10, Tables 1, 17, 19.

that period, was continued under Putin, thanks to the authority and perseverance of Victor Gerashchenko, who returned to the post of chairman of the Bank of Russia in the autumn of 1998 and remained there until March 2002.

From its very first moments in office, the Primakov government confronted a new wave of inflation. Year-end consumer prices in 1998 had risen by 84 percent, compared with the end of 1997, as against only an 11 percent rise in 1997.[18] They climbed by 36 percent in 1999. The government and Central Bank leadership both considered, and rightly so, that the jump in inflation had been caused primarily by the pressure of sharply higher prices on imports, which rose proportionally to the devaluation. Therefore no particular restraints were applied in the area of monetary policy, other than an austere budget policy. The money supply (M2) as a percentage of GDP declined by only 2 points in 1999 (Table 5.6). In the years that followed, the money supply began to grow more rapidly than nominal GDP growth, as it climbed to the level of 24.2 percent of

GDP in 2003. Including foreign currency deposits in Russian banks, the ratio of M3 to GDP rose to 29.9 percent, a new high for the reform period. Nonetheless, the money supply continued to lag behind the corresponding figures for industrially developed countries, where it regularly exceeds 50 percent or even 100 percent of GDP. As prime minister and then president, Putin was unable to make a breakthrough in this area.

The main factor in the lag continues to be non-cash money, meaning bank deposits belonging to the population and to businesses. Chapter 2 analyzed the underdevelopment of Russia's banking sector, compared with those of other countries. The financial crisis dealt it yet another blow, bankrupting several privately owned commercial banks, including some of the largest. The years that followed saw attempts to reform the banking system in order to stabilize it and, most important, engage it in the process of economic development. But no substantial results were achieved, in part due to resistance from the oligarchical groups. They viewed banking reform chiefly as an opportunity to consolidate larger banks, which would concentrate on servicing the large companies within the oligarchical groups. The oligarchs also sought to eliminate competition from state-owned banks, especially Sberbank.

What might the government and the Central Bank do to end the banking sector's relative stagnation and bring the lending function of Russian banks into correspondence with the role banks play in industrially developed market economies? The first step might be to speed up the passage of legislation to create a bank deposit insurance system. Secondly, the government needs to do more to promote the development of mortgage and consumer credit, which not a single industrially advanced economy does without. To date, government activity in the area of mortgage credit has been very weak. Next to nothing has been done with respect to consumer credit. The Russian subsidiaries of some foreign banks have moved into this field on an experimental basis. But domestic banks are hesitant to get into the consumer credit business, staying within the very limited bounds of credit card accounts with installment payments. As for deposit insurance, it currently applies only to some banks, and only to deposits up to 100,000 rubles (the equivalent of $3,500), which is too low to be effective. Interest on deposits remains lower than the rate of inflation, providing no incentive for the public to put their money in the bank.

In comparison, 1999 data showed that mortgage lending accounts for 44 percent of all commercial bank credit issued in the United States, consumer credit accounts for 16 percent, and retail lending as a whole makes up more than half of bank lending. U.S. bank lending to industries and other businesses is a comparatively modest 28 percent of total lending. That same year, U.S. corporations raised three times as much loan capital by issuing their own bonds, as they obtained in bank credit.[19] Since the banks are still the chief lending institutions in Russia, their role will remain extremely important for financing the real economy in the foreseeable future. Without the development of retail banking services, however, their possibilities for growth will be quite limited.

Lastly, measures need to be instituted to expand the use of non-cash transactions in the economy. The period of economic growth coincided with a sharp reduction of the share of barter in settling accounts between enterprises. It fell on average from 51 percent in 1998 to 11 percent in mid-2002.[20] Most interesting of all is the fact that this took place without any particularly interventionist actions by the government or the Central Bank. It resulted from the growing ability of enterprises to make payments, as their markets expanded. In other words, a growing economy facilitates the spontaneous solution of certain acute problems, which in a stagnating economy appear to be intractable.

For most enterprises the reduction of barter did not, however, bring about a fundamental expansion of the role of payments made through banks. Companies' bank deposits, for example, are growing extremely slowly, since businesses can find other, more profitable—and, most importantly, safer—places to put their money. A significant portion of potential lending resources departs abroad, where it does not even necessarily earn a higher rate of return.

The main shortcoming of this system is that enterprises avoid using banks for the very simplest transactions, though the banks' lending potential could be substantially increased, were they to do so. For instance, by far the greater part of not only off-the-books wage payments, but also completely legitimate wages, is paid in cash, rather than being transferred into employees' bank accounts. The government could certainly introduce legislation to require these and other such transactions to be made through banks.

Indeed, all payments made or received by businesses are supposed to be subject to strict tax accountability. If a significant number of these payments are made in cash, rather than through the banking system, the opportunities for concealing actual taxable revenue and sales become substantially greater. Thus the government even has a purely fiscal interest in having practically all business payments made through banks.

That is the prevailing economic practice in the West. Payments transacted outside of the banking system are almost automatically seen as attempts to conceal the funds and avoid taxation. The role of the banking system necessitates the widespread use of checks, as well as debit and credit cards, even for small retail purchases, not to mention larger payments, for which it is not the general practice to use cash.

Switching to such practices would automatically shrink the shadow economy, which accounts for such a large portion of Russia's economic turnover. Neither petty bribe-takers nor big business magnates are in the least interested in doing that. That may be why not a single one of the measures proposed for expanding credit resources within the Russian economy has been put into practice.

Instead, the government and the Central Bank leadership after 2002 focussed on relaxing regulations for currency operations. The minimum amount of dollar or euro earnings that goods and services exporters are required to convert to rubles was reduced. Capital export procedures were simplified. Though some currency controls remain in place, most of them were lifted.

Leading financiers, as well as the left opposition, strongly opposed this relaxation of the currency regulations. In their view, these measures promote capital flight, which has a detrimental effect on domestic capital investment and, consequently, on economic growth rates. The advocates of currency liberalization, among whom are the neo-liberals in the government and the oligarchical leadership of the RUIE, maintain that lifting the controls, on the contrary, encourages businessmen to invest more at home, since they are assured of their ability to take their earnings abroad. Foreign investors and the financial oligarchy in the West have supported the latter viewpoint.

What actually happened in 2002, when the currency liberalization took effect, was contradictory. Several officials claim that capital flight did decline. On the other hand, there was also a sharp drop in the growth rate of domestic capital investment. But if there really was a reduction in the outflow of capital and, as Minister of Economics Gref claimed, this had a positive impact on the economy,[21] then the question arises of why domestic investment shrank and GDP growth slowed.

The key to the puzzle is that only *legal* capital export decreased after 2002, whereas the total outflow of capital abroad remained enormous and may even have increased. Ministry of Finance analysts estimated total capital export in 2002 at $25.1 billion, as against $22 billion in 2001. The majority of experts at Russian investment banks believe that capital flight has not shown any tendency to decline. The fluctuation that was observed, remained in the relatively narrow range of $20-25 billion.[22]

How could it be otherwise, if currency controls were relaxed, yet there was no increased desire to invest capital inside the country? Until the situation changes radically as the result of an industrial policy that favors development of the domestic economy, these tendencies are not likely to change for the better.

5.4 Economic policy as a whole

We conclude this chapter with a short review of various aspects of economic policy during the period when Russia's latest phase of capitalism was being established and began to develop.

1. Economic policy prioritized reforms that did more to make it possible to proclaim the advent of a market economy and capitalist society, than to promote stable, crisis-free economic growth using fiscal and monetary regulatory methods. This pattern was particularly stark in the first half of the 1990s, when overall national economic stability was sacrificed, and the economy plunged into a prolonged period of crisis and stagnation, all for the sake of destroying the planned economy as quickly as possible, handing out state property to private capitalists, and creating conditions for the initial accumulation of oligarchical capital. Frightened by the 1998 financial crisis, the authorities initially retreated from the structural demolition process, but they renewed it when the economy started to grow spontaneously as it recovered from the prolonged crisis. In order to bolster confidence in the regime, however,

the policy of prioritizing capitalist reforms was now pursued much more cautiously, than under the "shock" methods of the early 1990s. Under Putin, the policy of further transforming Russia's economy and society in a capitalist direction has continued, but far more circumspectly.

2. Throughout this new capitalist period, the government has made virtually no use of fiscal policy, neither to overcome the initial crisis, nor subsequently to provide incentives for economic growth. The architects of Russia's economic policy were encumbered by the monetarist dogma of limiting and cutting budget spending in order to reduce the budget deficit to a minimum, and then to maintain a budget surplus. At first this was done under the pretext of fighting inflation. Later, the announced reason was to pay off the foreign debt promptly and in full. In both instances the impact on the economy was negative, first prolonging the crisis and stagnation, and then curbing the spontaneous growth rate.

3. For a long time Russian governments were guided both in structural policy and in fiscal and monetary policy by "recommendations," which in effect were orders, from financial circles in the West, who dictated their preferences through the IMF and the conditionalities it imposed in exchange for extending credits. The dogma of mandatory budget-balancing, and of budget austerity in order to achieve it, helped bring the financial crisis to a head in 1998. Thus, in real life, these principles gave rise to the construction of unpayable short-term government debt pyramids. In the view of many experts, the secret springs of this adventurist policy were to be found in a plot between Russian and foreign financial interests, who were out to make their fortunes by appropriating a portion of the IMF loans.

4. The government's currency policy also fuelled the financial crisis. It, too, was subject to IMF pressure, and it consisted in regular support for an artificially high exchange rate for the ruble. Besides its detrimental financial consequences, this policy artificially enhanced the competitiveness of imported goods on the Russian domestic market, from which they drove out domestic products.

5. Under the influence of oligarchical groups of financiers, Russian governments restrained the development of the banking system. In the mid-1990s, this encouraged the sharp reduction of the role of money in the economy, the effective collapse of the system of making payments through banks, and the predominance of barter as a means of settling accounts between enterprises. In later years the non-payments crisis resolved, to a certain extent, under the influence of spontaneous economic growth, but the banking system continues to lag behind the economy's requirements, because the oligarchical groups that control the major banks direct them toward servicing their own companies, rather than providing credit to the economy as a whole.

6. Despite official declarations of a desire to end the export bias of the Russian economy, the President and governments have systematically refused to adopt a targeted industrial policy, which would use the surplus money capital, accumulated in the export sectors, to develop the manufacturing and high-technology industries. Contrary to announcements made on the necessity of ending unrestrained capital flight, the regime since 2000 has liberalized currency regulations, which helps the oligarchical groups to export capital.

7. The neo-liberal dictum on reducing the regulatory function of government to a minimum harms the development of the national economy. In Russia's specific circumstances, unregulated development leads to imbalances and skewed economic relationships, which condemn the economy to systematic backwardness. Only active government intervention can straighten out the skew and ensure balanced, harmonious national economic development.

NOTES

1. RSY 2000, p. 561.
2. Ibid., p. 303, 341, 346.
3. Ibid., p. 249, 503-04.
4. RET2, 1995, vol. 4, #5, p. 12.
5. RSY 2000, p. 507.

6. RET2, #2, 2000, Table 15.

7. Ibid., Table 13.

8. Ibid., Table 11.

9. Ibid., calculated on the basis of Tables 9, 11 and 16.

10. RET1, 2002, #4, p. 100.

11. Ibid., p. 68.

12. *Obzor ekonomicheskoi politiki v Rossii za 1998 god* (*Survey of economic policy in Russia in 1998*) (Moscow: ROSSPEN, 1999), p. 610.

13. RET1, 1999, #1, p. 122; RET1, 2002, #4, p. 102.

14. RET1, 1999, #1, p. 123; RET1, 2002, #4, p.103.

15. *Survey of economic policy in Russia in 1998*, op. cit., p. 615.

16. Ibid., pp. 610, 628.

17. RET1, 2002, #4, p. 100.

18. Ibid., Table 6.

19. *Statistical Abstract of the United States*, p. 512, 538.

20. RET1, 2002, #4, p. 103.

21. Interview with German Gref, reported by Interfax on Jan. 9, 2003.

22. "Utechka kapitala vyrosla v 2002 godu, schitaiut mnogie ekonomisty" ("Capital flight increased in 2002, economists say"), *Moscow News,* Jan. 15, 2003.

6 Russia, the World, and the Future

6.1 Russia in the global capitalist system

Russia's place in the world economy changed fundamentally with the transition to capitalism. The Russian Federation had been part of the Soviet Union, which was a leading world producer both in its own right, and in combination with its Comecon allies in Eastern Europe. At the same time, it was a relatively isolated economy, attempting to be self-sufficient and functioning by the laws of a planned economy, which differ from those of the market and of capitalism. As it shifted to capitalism, Russia separated from the Soviet Union and became intertwined with the industrially developed capitalist world, but its role in the world economy contracted sharply in quantitative terms, and changed qualitatively as well. It turned from the leader of a large economic bloc and a center of gravity on a broader world scale, into part of a dependent area on the periphery of the world capitalist system.

Table 6.1 shows the quantitative parameters of this radical shift. The data shown for the Soviet period differ from the international comparisons, published in our official statistics at the time. The statistical handbook *National Economy of the USSR in 1988*, for example, said that the combined national income of Comecon member countries was equal to one-fourth of the world total.[1] Given the relative weight of the Soviet economy and those of the other Comecon members, the USSR's share (according to those data) would have been approximately 18 percent of world national income at that time. That comparison, however, counterposed national incomes in the strict Marxist definition of the term, denoting only net output in the sphere of material goods production, and

Table 6.1 Relative share of the USSR/CIS, Russia, Eastern Europe and selected other countries in world GDP
(% of total)

	1950	1960	1970	1980	1989	1998	2001
USSR/CIS	9.6	10.0	9.8	8.5	8.3	3.4	3.6
As % of USA	35.2	41.3	43.9	40.3	38.6	15.5	16.8
Russia	–	–	–	–	4.3	2.0	2.3
Eastern Europe	3.5	3.6	3.4	3.4	2.7	1.9	2.0
USSR/CIS and Eastern Europe	13.1	13.6	13.2	11.9	11.0	5.3	5.6
USA	27.3	24.2	22.3	21.1	21.5	21.9	21.4
Western Europe	26.3	26.8	26.3	24.3	22.5	20.6	20.3
Japan	3.0	3.4	7.3	7.9	8.3	7.7	7.1
China	4.5	5.3	4.6	5.2	7.7	12.0	12.3

Source: Calculated on the basis of data in Angus Maddison, *The World Economy: A Millennial Perspective* (Paris: OECD, 2001), pp. 274-75, 304, 329, 339, and Angus Maddison, *The World Economy: Historical Statistics* (Paris: OECD, 2003), p. 261.

excluding the larger part of services. The share of non-material services in Soviet GDP was much smaller than in countries with a market economy. Net output of non-material services made up 10 percent of Soviet national income in 1988,[2] for example, whereas in the USA that ratio was over 50 percent. This analytical approach artificially overstated the relative weight of the socialist countries, before even taking into account such factors as the exaggeration of material output growth rates in the USSR through the inclusion of repair and other types of work that are not strictly part of the final product. Also less than reliable are the purchasing power parities used in this comparison, which were based on an insufficiently representative selection of types of products, especially with respect to quality.

The series given in the table, which were calculated by the well-known Scottish economist Angus Maddison, correct for these shortcomings in Soviet methodology. At first glance, his data on the relative weight of the USSR and East European countries appear to be understated: in 1950-1970, the Soviet Union's share in world GDP held steady at 9.6-10 percent, while that of Eastern Europe was 3.5 percent, for a combined share of 13-13.5 percent. If we correct for the difference in the share of services, it turns out that the gap between Maddison's estimates and those of Goskomstat is not very great.

The ratio of Soviet to U.S. GDP, according to Maddison's data, rose steadily in the 1950-1970 period, reaching 44 percent in 1970. This would appear to be a fairly realistic estimate. The unofficial calculations made at the time by our researchers, including at the Institute of World Economy and International Relations (IMEMO), were close to these data. But in the 1970s, it was out of the question to publish calculations that differed so strikingly from the official figures.

After 1970, and especially from the mid-1970s on, economic growth in the USSR slowed. According to the Goskomstat data, average GDP growth declined from 7.6 percent for the 1966-1970 period, to 6.2 percent in 1971-1975, 4.8 percent in 1976-1980 and 3.7 percent in 1981-1988.[3] Maddison calculates a somewhat different pattern of decline in the growth rates: 4.8 percent in 1966-1970, 2.4 percent in 1971-1980 and 2 percent in 1981-1989. In other words, this Western author shows growth rates that were approximately 50 percent lower than what Goskomstat reported, but the tendency is the same.

According to Maddison's data, overall average annual world GDP growth was 5 percent in the 1960s, 3.8 percent in the 1970s and 3.1 percent in the 1980s. The world rate was declining, but it was still higher than GDP growth in the USSR. Consequently, the Soviet Union's share in world GDP dropped during this period from 9.8 percent in 1970 to 8.5 percent in 1980 and 8.3 percent in 1989. The relative weight of Eastern Europe also fell, with its share in world GDP dipping to 11 percent from its 1970 level of 13.2 percent.

In this same time frame, the ratio of Soviet to U.S. GDP began to fall for the first time in many years. Maddison's calculations show Soviet GDP at 44 percent of U.S. GDP in 1970, but only 38.6 percent in 1989. The Soviet economy grew more slowly than the American economy during those two decades.

The USSR's relative high point of development was achieved somewhere in the early 1970s, after which a period of relative backsliding began. Nonetheless, despite all the problems encountered by the planned economy in those years, the combined share of the European socialist countries in world GDP was 11 percent. Together with China, they accounted for 19 percent.

Table 6.2 Share of G8 member countries in world GDP, %

	1989	2001
USA	21.5	21.4
Japan	8.3	7.1
Germany	4.9	4.1
United Kingdom	3.5	3.2
France	3.8	3.4
Italy	3.4	3.0
Canada	2.0	1.8
Russia (for 1989, USSR)	8.3	2.3
Total, 8 countries	55.7	45.3

Source: Maddison, op. cit.; our calculations.

The transition to capitalism put an end to this relative stability. The Russian economy sank into a profound crisis in the 1990s. Moreover, it was separated from the rest of the former USSR. The result was that CIS member countries' share in world output had dropped to 3.6 percent in 2001, while the share of Russia proper was only 2.3 percent. There had been a sharp, nearly 80 percent contraction from the relative peak around 1970.

Since 2002, Russia has been a member of the Group of Eight (G8) leading industrial nations, whose annual summits define certain shared policy commitments, including in economic policy. Table 6.2 shows the GDP data for these countries, including Russia, and compares them with the USSR's performance by the same indicators, but in 1989.

The Soviet Union, before its collapse, could have laid claim to a leading role in the G8, alongside the USA and Japan. Today, Russia ranks next to last among these nations, trailed only by Canada. This goes to underscore, once again, the secondary role Russia plays in the world capitalist system.

Might the result have been different, had the Soviet Union been able to resist the centrifugal forces that dismantled it, and had market reforms not proceeded in such a catastrophic way? The Chinese experience demonstrates that it is possible for central planning to cohabit with a market economy in a certain kind of arrangement, and that this may create conditions for very rapid economic growth. During two decades of following such a course, China has been able to increase its share in world output substantially, even surpassing Japan, as the latter stagnated in the 1990s. Russia, however, by plunging down the capitalist road and discarding central planning altogether, has fallen not only far behind almost all of the leading industrial nations, but also behind China. Even discounting for the imperfection of Chinese statistics, the contrast is glaring.

Of course, it is important to avoid the other extreme, which would be to understate the size of the Russian economy. There are Western commentators who do this habitually, out of a desire to exclude Russia from the ranks of the great powers. The most primitive approach they use is to convert Russian GDP data from rubles to dollars at the currency market exchange rate, rather than according to purchasing power parity (PPP), as is the practice at the international financial organizations and in all competent statistical studies. In 1999, for example, Goskomstat gave the dollar's PPP with respect to the ruble as 4.7 rubles to the dollar, whereas the average exchange rate that year was 24.6 rubles to the dollar.[4] Using the exchange rate for such comparisons automatically understated Russia's GDP by a factor of 5.2.

Thus, when such writers wanted to express their indignation over Russia's being invited to join the G8, they claimed that Russia's GDP was roughly equivalent to Denmark's, and lower than that of the Netherlands. Cross-checking with United Nations figures, however, it turns out that Russia's $996 billion GDP in 1996 was 7.2 times larger than the Danish GDP, and triple the Dutch. If the difference in population size is taken into account, of course, Russia's lead is less impressive.

Nonetheless, the lag in output per capita is an entirely different question. By that measure, the USSR was behind even the smaller nations of Western Europe. Under Russia's new capitalism, that gap has only widened. When Putin became Acting President, he proclaimed the goal of catching up to the most backward members of the European Union (EU; European Economic Community until 1992), such as Portugal, in per capita output. In an article published at the end of 1999, he said that this would require Russia to achieve 8-10 percent annual growth. Maddison's data show that Russia was below Portugal in per capita GDP by a factor of 2.9 in 1998, twice as bad as the situation had been in 1989, when Soviet GDP per capita was below Portugal's by a factor of 1.4. The prolonged crisis and stagnation, caused by the hasty shift to a market economy, created serious difficulties for Russia in approaching objectives that had been relatively simple for the Soviet planned economy.

Raw materials dependence

It was not only in absolute and per capita GDP, that Russia turned into an economy peripheral to the industrialized West. Equally important was the continuation, and even amplification, of its role as a raw materials supplier for the world capitalist system.

The objection may be raised that Russian capitalism inherited this role from the Soviet centrally planned economy. That is only formally the case. The Soviet economy was oriented chiefly toward developing the defense sector and other heavy industry, and was unable to meet its own needs for civilian-sector machines and equipment, food or consumer goods. Addressing this situation required the importation of goods that were in short supply, which imports, in turn, were paid for with earnings from the export of raw materials and fuel, but only those types of which there was a relative surplus.

The products that are Russia's main exports today, namely oil and natural gas, began to be available for export by the Soviet Union on a large scale only at the end of the 1970s, with the development of West Siberia's natural resources. That was when oil and gas output surged. Soviet oil production rose by 170 percent during the 1970s, from 353 million tons per year to 603 million tons, levelling out in 1980. Gas output continued to rise throughout the 1970s and 1980s, increasing from 198 billion cubic meters in 1970 to 770 billion in 1988, a 390% rise. This increased production made it possible to boost oil exports from 67 million tons in 1970 to 144 million tons in 1988, and gas exports from 3.3 to 88 billion cubic meters in the same period. Counting refined petroleum products, the Soviet Union in its last years was exporting 33 percent of the oil it produced and 11 percent of the gas.[5]

On the eve of the breakup of the Soviet Union, fuels and metals accounted for 53-55 percent of Soviet exports (average for 1986-1988), while the above-mentioned three categories—civilian-sector machines and equipment, food, and consumer goods—made up 70 percent of its imports.[6] The composition of the Russian Federation's foreign trade was similar.

It changed little after the transition to a market economy, although the Soviet emphasis on the defense sector and other heavy industry virtually disappeared, while production of gas, and especially oil, dropped sharply. But Russian industry, plunged into a deep crisis and then stagnating, was unable to reorient toward producing to meet domestic demand. Right up until the devaluation of 1998-1999, it could not compete with the flood of relatively cheap imported goods. For the extractive industries, exporting their output meant they could convert natural rent into cash at world prices. This opportunity made exports their preferred type of activity. The incentives for exports and imports substantially changed, but the narrow specialization of Russia's international economic relations, far from disappearing, became more pronounced.

Not counting trade with other CIS member countries, 68.4 percent of Russia's exports in 1992 were extracted resources, metals, and gemstones; by 1999, they made up 71.3 percent of exports. In 1992, 76 percent of imports from non-CIS countries comprised machinery, equipment, food, and light industry products; in 1999, these categories accounted for 67 percent.[7]

These data only begin to give a picture of the extreme domination of exports by raw materials. In 1999, for example, half of the exports that were *not* counted as fuels and metals, but formally came under manufacturing exports, were actually raw materials or semi-processed goods: chemicals industry products, timber, pulp and paper, fur, leather, etc. The only large export heading for finished products was weapons (around 4 percent of exports in 2001 and 2005). As for civilian-sector manufactured products, light automobile exports fell sharply from the Soviet-era level of 341,000 in 1988, to 67,000 in 2003.[8]

While the composition of Russia's foreign trade turnover was preserved, its geographical distribution shifted. The share of the former Comecon countries, which had accounted for a little more than half of Russian exports and imports in the last years of the Soviet period, fell to 11 percent of exports and 5 percent of imports in 1999. The industrially developed EU member countries became Russia's main trading partners, accounting for 33 percent of its exports and 30 percent of its imports in 1999 (not including trade with Central and Eastern European nations that joined the EU later). Other major trading partners were the USA, with 6.7 percent of exports and 5.9 percent of imports; Switzerland, with 4.5 and 0.8 percent, respectively; and Japan, with 3.0 and 1.2 percent. These countries' combined share made up 47 percent of Russia's exports and 38 percent of its imports. CIS countries accounted for 16.4 percent of Russia's exports and 24.9 percent of its imports, as of 1999.[9]

The dominant role of the industrially developed countries in Russian foreign trade follows from its raw materials export-dependence, as well as, to some degree, its imports of equipment and other advanced technology. Although Russia has managed to end its need to import food grain, imports of processed foods and other manufactured consumer goods continue play an important role.

The President and the government have repeatedly declared it a priority to make foreign trade less skewed, through shifting to the export of more manufactured and science-intensive products. As the years pass, however, the composition of Russia's foreign trade has not changed. Objective circumstances are partly to blame. The persistent wide gap between domestic and world prices makes it practically impossible to halt the spontaneous export of fuels, metals, and other raw materials, since that would conflict with the interests of the big firms that dominate those sectors.

The problem of competitive power

Eagerness to export oil and gas is explainable on the basis of the pragmatic fiscal considerations of Russian budgetary policy and the drive by oil and gas companies to maximize profit, but it is more difficult to explain why, after more than a decade, the new Russian capitalism has been unable to launch the competitive export of manufactured products, which might not replace oil, gas, and metals, but could at least reduce their share in exports.

The simplest explanation is that Russian capital took an easier route: it exploited the positions in foreign markets that had already been established under the planned economy, but it was not willing to experiment or take risks in areas where the old socialist system had not created a base beforehand. The new Russian capitalists showed only slight interest in an area like weapons exports, for which a fairly solid base had been inherited from the previous regime. That sector was heavily politicized. It remained under government control, with only crumbs available for private capital. And the main markets for Russian armaments were China and India, while Russia's big capitalist interests looked to the West.

It is generally a mistake to attempt to study the competitiveness of a country's industry by looking at its foreign markets in isolation from the domestic economy. In most capitalist countries, major industries got established by producing for domestic consumption. They turned to export only after having won a place in the domestic market. In Russia, however, it became clear during the transition to capitalism that only some sectors of heavy industry could compete in the domestic market, and they happened to be the same ones that were able to sell their products abroad: metals producers, some of the chemicals and petrochemicals industry, the timber industry, and pulp and paper. In almost all cases, they could compete by selling semi-manufactures, rather than their final products. In areas like consumer goods, or machinery and equipment (except for weapons), Russian industry could not compete with imports. Exporting Russian products from these sectors, of course, was out of the question.

Yet, the development of these sectors depends on a combination of rising demand for their output, and resources to make capital investments in modernization. Whereas increased demand for domestic products depends on their quality and comparative price, it takes a certain level of profitability before funds will flow into investment. In an unregulated economy, it will take long years of waiting, before companies' turnover and the anticipated return on investment are high enough to attract capital, and before they can produce goods that are both less expensive and of higher quality than imports.

This objective would be more easily attainable, if the country did not possess export-oriented sectors that are highly profitable due to natural rent. In that case Russian money capital would have had no opportunities (niches) other than those that emerged in the domestic market. The anomalous situation, where capital is diverted from possible investment in non-export industries, will persist in Russia as long as there is a gap between the low cost of extracting and producing fuels and other raw materials, and the higher world market prices for those products.

For several years, closing that gap was one of the conditions set by the EU for Russia to be recognized as a country with a market economy. The relatively low domestic price of fuels and raw materials in Russia was viewed as a covert export subsidy, or dumping. This demand was dropped in 2002, under strong internal and outside pressure. The problem remains acute, however, from the standpoint of the prospects for Russian economic development.

The problem is not merely that the existence of different levels of profitability in different industries promotes the skewed composition of the Russian economy. Matters are compounded by the prospect that raising domestic fuel and raw materials prices to world levels would make all domestic products significantly more expensive, generally driving prices up. It would only be possible to launch this process, if domestic income were simultaneously raised by an adequate amount. Otherwise, the change would push the economy into a new phase of stagnation. And since the steady growth of real income is possible only on the basis of rising productivity, the process of equalizing domestic and world prices can go forward only slowly and gradually. Furthermore, a paradoxical situation could come about: levelling out the profitability of different sectors should promote an influx of capital investment in industries producing competitive finished products, but the cost of producing them would also rise, impeding their ability to compete.

In any event, correcting the raw materials tilt of the economy in the absence of regulation would be a prolonged and uncertain undertaking. Imagine, for example, that the exporting sectors' high profit were substantially invested in the purchase of equipment. As we saw in Chapter 4, a significant part of the growth of investment in 1999-2002 went for such purchases. Where is the guarantee, that domestic producers of machinery and equipment, as opposed to foreign manufacturers, would get most of the orders from oil, gas, metals, and other exporting companies? It is apparent that this would be unlikely to happen without special government support.

Government support could come either from producers that are state-owned or state-controlled MIC companies, or from consumers, among which are the quasi-state-owned natural monopolies. The only private-sector component of this scheme would be the oil companies, which could be a major source of demand for domestic manufactures. Even if such measures succeeded, they would even more firmly cement the economy's dependence on oil and gas exports, by orienting the machine-building industry primarily toward servicing the needs of the fuel and energy complex. It is doubtful that this would help Russian machine-building firms break into world markets.

In the majority of capitalist countries, government-imposed protectionism was the traditional means of defending industry while it was being established. In the second half of the 20th century, a number of developed capitalist countries adopted a national industrial policy, which became the most prevalent form of support for domestic industry. The core of this approach was selective government subsidies and other forms of assistance to certain sectors that the government had an interest in promoting, for one reason or another. France, and especially Japan, which developed its automobile, electronics and computer industries in this way, succeeded with the industrial policy approach.

Japan's experience in this respect is of particular interest, because until the 1960s it had these industries only in embryonic form, and it had to win a place for them in markets dominated by stronger competitors. In a single decade, Japan gained the ability to supply its domestic market entirely with Japanese products, almost eliminating imports, while also seizing strong positions in the U.S. and Western European markets. And Japan, unlike Russia, had no ready-made niche in the world market that it might have used as a source of financing for the industries in need of subsidies. Its main market-winning tool was a flowering of engineering and design ideas, which bore fruit in the form of the constant introduction of new, higher-quality and more competitive products.

Russia does have the advantages of a very big niche, in the form of natural rent from the export of oil, gas, and metals. Russia's other special qualification is its enormous engineering, scientific, and technological capabilities, which, however, are concentrated in the military-industrial complex and thus are used only slightly, or not at all, for modernizing non-military manufactures and creating new types of civilian-sector products. The key to solving the problem of competitiveness largely comes down to uniting aspects of these two niches: using a portion of the natural rent from the first, and the scientific and technologically capabilities from the second, to finance and develop a competitive manufacturing sector.

President Putin and leading members of the government have expressed this idea many times in their speeches, but it has not been implemented. The main obstacle is resistance on the part of the exporting monopolies, which do not wish to share the natural rent with the government. The government's own inertia is also a factor, since it fails to put forward realistic plans for developing the other sectors of industry.

One of the reasons Russia lags behind the advanced industrial nations is the underdevelopment of its automobile industry, its highway network and other roads, the computer industry, and telecommunications. Russia lacks a modern consumer goods industry and industries that produce equipment for consumer goods production. In short, Russia has not yet made it through the advanced phase of industrialization, which was typical for Western Europe and Japan in the last decades of the 20th century. Filling in that blank, by developing the relevant group of industries and related infrastructure, would create enormous additional domestic markets for Russian products, as well as jobs, and would make it possible to modernize the country's entire economic capacity, providing a material basis for accelerated growth of the economy as a whole. Rather than rushing into a post-industrial phase, as some of our economists advise, it would make sense to tackle the more modest objective of completing the industrial stage of development. We have the internal resources needed, but what's lacking is a government mechanism to turn the market economy in the right direction. It won't go there on its own by force of inertia.

A sector that not only has significant growth potential, but is also capable of serving as a locomotive to pull the economy as a whole out of its backward condition, is the automobile industry. In its day the auto industry lifted the economies of the United States, Western Europe and Japan into the era of "consumer abundance," some of them earlier, some later. The Soviet auto industry developed in small bursts, delimited by the campaigns to build a few automobile manufacturing plants, that took place in the 1930s and then again in the 1970s. At the end of the Soviet period, light car production was far behind the West, both in volume of output (1.1 million cars in 1990, as against 5 million in Germany, 6 million in the USA, and 8 million in Japan) and in quality, with Soviet cars getting low marks in practically every area except tolerance of rough terrain. There was no growth of output after 1975, when the AvtoVAZ plant in Togliatti was completed. The stagnation continued under the transition to capitalism.[10] Increasing demand was met primarily by imports, most of which were used cars.

The government exhibited interest in developing the auto sector only after Putin took office. In June of 2001, he laid out a number of demands, geared to curing the industry's backwardness, to a Kremlin conference of automobile industry businessmen and officials. It is not acceptable, Putin said, for Russia to "produce the cars of yesteryear." He said that it was important for society, and "an overriding task for our industry," to provide the population with "good-quality and affordable domestic products." The meeting outlined several incentives for the industry: raising tariffs on imported used cars, reducing them on imported equipment and parts ordered by auto plants, debt restructuring for auto producers, tax breaks for capital investment, etc. This package was designed as a stimulus for the industry to make a "great leap." Within five years, by 2006, light automobile production was to rise by 300,000 cars, a 30 percent increase.[11]

This conference took place on the momentum of aluminum magnate Deripaska's and steel baron Mordashov's entry into the auto industry. As the latter put it, "The time has come to coordinate the policies of various individual groups."[12] The need to attract major foreign investors to the industry was discussed.

One would think that the combined pressure from above (Putin) and below (the industrialists) would have gotten things moving. Ten months passed, however, before the government scheduled a cabinet discussion of the Ministry of Industry, Science and Technologies program for development of the auto industry. Now the objective under discussion was to double output by 2010, but without building a single new large automobile plant. It was clear that neither AvtoVAZ, GAZ, nor any of the other car makers, which were experiencing ever greater financial difficulties, would be able to handle plant modernization or to build new assembly lines and related capacities. The government evidently was hoping that foreign giants such as General Motors, Ford, VW, et al., would enter the Russian auto industry. But the relevant subsidiaries of those foreign companies planned to produce only some tens of thousands of automobiles in Russia, far fewer than the government was counting on. The program mentioned no measures to promote highway construction, and made no reference to developing consumer credit, without which a revolution in car production was next to impossible.[13]

The only factor that could have shifted the situation would have been large capital investment by the government in the industry and in sectors associated with auto. The failure of government plans for an upsurge in the auto industry stemmed more from the overall economic situation, than from bureaucratic chaos or intrigues by competing oligarchs. The industry provides a clear illustration of how ineffective Russia's industrial policy has been.

Some changes began, albeit slowly, after AvtoVAZ came under government control in late 2005. Plans were announced for a new large assembly plant, nearby the old Togliatti site, to be largely financed by government credit. The old plant would also be modernized. It remains to be seen, however, how rapidly those plans are brought to life, if at all.

Things were no better in the aircraft industry, which would seem to have had decent prospects. Here the main impediment was the small size of its market, caused by the catastrophic plunge of domestic air travel with the transition to capitalism. In 1990, 91 million passengers traveled by air, but by 1999 the number was only 22 million, more than a 75 percent decline. If we exclude international flights, the drop-off was even more striking. Ilya Klebanov, who was minister of industry, science, and technology in 2001, acknowledged that "the situation in the domestic market is critical: an absolute majority of airlines are losing money, and only 3 percent of the population flies."[14]

With the transition to a market economy, air transportation was privatized. In place of the monopolistic Soviet airline, Aeroflot, a number of independent companies appeared. Their financial situation was far from the best, due to the decline of domestic air travel, but they became the main customers for domestically produced aircraft. Although they had inherited a huge fleet of aircraft from Soviet times, the planes were systematically underutilized. Even so, they could not last forever. The need to purchase new planes became more and more acute.

There were two quite different markets. Domestic carriage was largely unprofitable, while international flights allowed the same companies to make a certain, sometimes substantial, amount of profit. In the international market, Russian companies had to compete with foreign airlines and were forced to purchase foreign-produced aircraft. Domestic airlines faced no such necessity, but their financial situation was such that purchasing even domestically produced planes was a difficult proposition. The Russian aircraft industry suffered in both cases. A significant part of the domestic market was gone, yet the Russian industry was unable to compete with foreign manufacturers. Russia passenger plane production contracted by a factor of 12, nearly 93 percent, during the 1990s.

Only in 2001, a decade after the reforms began, did the government act to help the aircraft industry. It was decided that the government would finance leasing, or aircraft rental. It was proposed to acquire 21-25 planes on this basis, including six Ilyushin IL-96-300 planes, ten Tu-204s, and four Tu-214s, for Aeroflot, Transaero, Dalavia, and Krasnoyarsk Airlines. The leasing formula involved bank financing in foreign currency, with government subsidies compensating the banks for the difference between the preferential lending rate of 11 percent and the 13-14 percent market cost of credit. Government-controlled Sberbank and Vneshtorgbank were to finance the leasing operations, with 85 percent of the credits being state-guaranteed. The 2002 federal budget allocated 2.4 billion rubles to develop the industry, almost double the previous year's level. It turned out not to be enough.

The problem here is not only to attract private capital, but to establish large civilian aircraft-building firms, independent of the MIC, that could launch the modernization of aircraft production, with appropriate government financing. The inevitable problems of how to maintain existing technological relationships between manufacturers can be solved, given a rational approach and targeted state intervention. But this cannot be expected to happen in an unregulated capitalist system.

The problems are similar in the machine-building industries that specialize in producing consumer durables. Unlike passenger car production, these manufacturers were generally under the control of the military-industrial complex.

With the transition to a market economy, they all sank into a deep crisis, from which many failed to emerge even when the overall economy began to grow again.

Every type of goods production in this group experienced a decline that was far worse than the average for industry as a whole. The sharp contraction of weapons production can be explained by the significant reduction of orders and purchases by the Ministry of

Defense. The drop in production of machines and equipment was associated with the overall reduction of capital investment. But the collapse of consumer durable goods sales was much steeper than the decline of the population's real income. Between 1990 and 1998, output of most consumer products fell by at least 90 percent, while the real income of the population was merely halved. Consumers were now spending most of their income on basic necessities, leaving less money available to purchase durable goods. In 1998, the share of televisions, radios, motorcycles, bicycles, and clocks in total retail turnover was 2.6 percent, as against 3.9 percent in 1990. During the same period, however, the share of passenger cars in retail turnover *rose* from 2 percent to 6.3 percent, and light automobile output fell only 25 percent from its pre-reform levels.[15] Thus, even with a substantial decline of real income, people found funds with which to purchase cars, but not electric lamps, radios, television set, and video cameras.

Competition from imported goods no doubt played a role, especially for electric household appliances and communications equipment. In 1998, for example, Russia produced 956,000 refrigerators and imported 526,000 (equivalent to 35 percent of domestic consumption), though only 33,000 came from outside the CIS. Domestic refrigerator consumption, however, was 60 percent lower than in 1990. Imported color television sets made up 80 percent of all color TVs purchased in 1997, but 55 percent fewer of them were purchased than before the reforms. Imported video cameras virtually completely replaced domestically produced ones, but 47 percent fewer of them were purchased in 1997 and 90 percent fewer in 1998, than at the end of the Soviet period. After an initial explosion of interest in such imports, demand for them receded, in parallel with real income.

When overall economic growth recommenced, the output of most consumer durables increased relatively strongly (with the exception of PCs, automatic coffee machines, tape recorders, and video cameras). The main factor in this process was not so much the increase of people's income (the pre-crisis level being reached only in 2002), but the temporary drop in dollar prices for these products. Even where there was a sharp uptick (four times as many color TV sets were produced in 2000 than in 1997, for example), output remained far below pre-reform levels. The crisis in this sector of the economy did not end.

It is unlikely that Russian capital will pour into consumer durables production, even if the government were to institute special incentives. But this sector is not a priority even on paper; it is not a formally announced target of government subsidies. Nonetheless, it makes no sense for a country the size of Russia to continue to satisfy its demand for consumer durables exclusively or primarily through imports. As in the case of the aircraft industry, it should be possible to establish large government-controlled concerns that would produce competitive products of sufficiently high quality to win consumers over.

One possible approach is to set up mixed public-private companies, and offer export-oriented companies generous tax incentives to invest in consumer durables production. It is entirely possible, for example, that oil, aluminum, and other exporting companies would prefer to invest their money in such manufactures, in return for partial control and for tax relief in their main operations, rather than to pay their taxes and watch those funds be invested in government-controlled consumer durables production.

The problem of foreign investment

From the very outset of the market reforms, people in the government, businessmen, and neo-liberal economists hoped for an influx of foreign capital into Russia. They thought such foreign investment would play a doubly constructive role: it could be an important supplemental source of financing for capital investment within the country, while also serving as the main channel through which advanced technology could be brought in from abroad. A decade and a half into the development of Russian capitalism, we have to say that these hopes were not justified. Total foreign investment in the Russian economy has been fairly small. Productive foreign investment is limited to a very few industries. The import of new technologies by way of foreign investment is negligible.

There are few official statistics on foreign investment. Goskomstat publications reflect it in three guises: (1) data on total investment by foreign investors, beginning in 1995; (2) balance of payments data on investment flows into and from Russia; (3) data on the participation by foreign capital in capital investment at enterprises

Table 6.3 Foreign investment by type

	1995 Millions of $	1995 % of total	1999 Millions of $	1999 % of total	2000 Millions of $	2000 % of total	2001 Millions of $	2001 % of total	2002 Millions of $	2002 % of total	2003 Millions of $	2003 % of total
Total investment	2,983	100%	9,560	100%	10,958	100%	14,258	100%	19,780	100%	29,699	100%
Direct investment	2,020	67.7%	4,260	44.6%	4,429	40.4%	3,980	27.9%	4,002	20.2%	6,781	22.8%
Capital contributions	1,455	48.8%	1,163	12.2%	1,060	9.7%	1,271	8.9%	1,713	8.6%	2,243	7.5%
Credits from foreign co-owners	341	11.4%	1,872	19.6%	2,738	25.0%	2,117	14.8%	1,300	6.6%	2,106	7.1%
Other direct investment	224	7.5%	1,225	12.8%	631	5.7%	592	4.2%	989	5.0%	2,432	8.2%
Portfolio investment	39	1.3%	31	0.3%	145	1.3%	451	3.2%	472	2.4%	401	1.4%
Stocks and equity	11	0.4%	27	0.3%	72	0.6%	329	2.3%	283	1.4%	369	1.2%
Long-term securities	28	0.9%	2	0.0%	72	0.6%	104	0.7%	129	0.7%	32	0.1%
Other investment	924	31.0%	5,269	55.1%	6,384	58.3%	9,827	68.9%	15,306	77.4%	22,517	75.8%
Trade credits	187	6.3%	1,452	15.2%	1,544	14.1%	1,835	12.9%	2,243	11.3%	2,973	10.0%
Other credits	493	16.5%	3,349	35.0%	4,735	43.2%	7,904	55.4%	12,928	65.4%	19,220	64.7%
Other	244	8.2%	468	4.9%	105	1.0%	88	0.6%	135	0.7%	324	1.1%

Note: These data omit financial regulatory agencies, and commercial and savings banks.

Sources: Our calculations; RSY 2000, p. 249, 265-66, 594.

(beginning in 1993). There are discrepancies among these sets of data, which it is not always possible to reconcile.

Three types of foreign investment are defined in the statistics: direct, portfolio, and other. Direct investment includes investment by foreign companies or individuals in enterprises which they either fully own, or in which they control at least 10 percent of the shares or equity capital. It includes so-called contributions to capital in the form of purchases of shares and credits from foreign co-owners (direct transfers of money from abroad in the form of credits). Portfolio investment includes purchases of shares, bonds or other securities of Russian enterprises, at levels below 10 percent of the equity capital. The "other" investment category includes various types of government and private credits, as well as foreigners' bank deposits.

Table 6.3 makes clear that until 1996, two-thirds of all foreign investment in Russia constituted direct investment. That is because foreign government credits and loans from international financial institutions were comparatively small in the first years of the market reforms. Beginning in 1996, however, this type of credit increased sharply to a level of several billion dollars annually, pushing the share of direct investment down to 23 percent of total foreign investment by 2003.

Speculative capital flows in the 1996-1999 period were a major destabilizing factor in world markets, and helped cause the financial crisis in Russia.

Even direct investment, which was far more stable than portfolio and short-term investment, was hit by the financial crisis. Foreign direct investment rose in 1995-1997, more than doubling in 1997 alone, but dropped off sharply in 1998, before resuming relatively slow growth, reaching $6.8 billion by 2003.

The amounts involved are relatively small on the scale of the Russian economy. Total foreign capital has not exceeded 4 percent of the value of fixed assets within Russia. The output of enterprises in which there is foreign participation is no more than 5 percent of total national output of goods and services. Direct investment is equal to 10 percent of gross capital investment.[16] These are also miniscule figures, on the scale of the world economy. In 2002, the foreign direct investment stock in China, for example, reached $448 billion, or 19 times more than in our country ($23 billion), while the

Table 6.4 Foreign investment by industry

	1995 Millions of $	1995 % of total	1999 Millions of $	1999 % of total	2000 Millions of $	2000 % of total	2001 Millions of $	2001 % of total	2002 Millions of $	2002 % of total	2003 Millions of $	2003 % of total
Total investment	2,983	100%	9,560	100%	10,958	100%	14,258	100%	19,780	100%	29,699	100%
Industry	1,291	43.3%	4,876	51.0%	4,721	43.1%	5,662	39.7%	7,332	37.1%	12,330	41.5%
Fuels	262	8.8%	1,700	17.8%	621	5.7%	1,023	7.2%	1,943	9.8%	5,305	17.9%
Chemicals and petrochemicals	174	5.8%	103	1.1%	243	2.2%	275	1.9%	334	1.7%	503	1.7%
Machine-building	197	6.6%	395	4.1%	470	4.3%	703	4.9%	490	2.5%	769	2.6%
Timber, pulp and paper	174	5.8%	193	2.0%	257	2.3%	241	1.7%	312	1.6%	599	2.0%
Food	296	9.9%	1,415	14.8%	1,786	16.3%	1,557	10.9%	1,210	6.1%	1,024	3.5%
Construction	217	7.3%	97	1.0%	86	0.8%	95	0.7%	126	0.6%	255	0.9%
Transport	11	0.4%	521	5.5%	1,020	9.3%	758	5.3%	174	0.9%	402	1.3%
Communications	88	2.9%	386	4.0%	927	8.5%	501	3.5%	436	2.2%	681	2.3%
Trade and public dining	507	17.0%	1,622	17.0%	1,954	17.8%	5,290	37.1%	8,800	44.5%	10,516	35.4%

Note: Noncommercial credits have been excluded.

Source: RSY 2003, Table 22.16.

annual inward flow of direct investment, $53 billion, was 22 times greater than in Russia ($2.4 billion). Foreign investment in Russia for the entire period of market reforms up to 2002 was less by a factor of 2.5 than a single year's foreign investment in China.[17]

Many explanations have been published for why so little foreign capital has come into the Russian economy. Among the reasons cited are foreign investors' complaints about insufficiently precise legislation covering various aspects of how foreign companies may conduct business, numerous bureaucratic obstacles, the unusually great extent of the illegal economy, corruption and organized crime, the lack of infrastructure, and so on. Few people complain about low profitability. Evidently, the return on investment would suit foreign investors, but they are deterred by the specific high risks in the Russian market.

Despite the obstacles, there has been some degree of foreign investment, especially in certain industries. Table 6.4 shows which branches and sectors of the Russian economy have particularly attracted the interest of foreign companies.

In the period under consideration, the three sectors of the economy that received the most foreign investment were the fuels industry (17.3 percent of total foreign investment), food and allied industries (16.3 percent), and trade (25.2 percent). These three sectors accounted for around 60 percent of all foreign investment.

We saw in Chapters 2 and 3 which subsectors and companies are involved. What foreign investors were looking for in the fuels industry was to gain control over at least some part of crude oil extraction, while acquiring minority ownership shares in the natural gas industry. These attempts only partially succeeded. The British multinational BP managed to acquire a 10 percent stake, with management rights, in Sidanco, which was ultimately taken over by the Russian company TNK, a component of the Alfa industrial financial group. After several years of disputes, the rivals reached a compromise, under which BP received 25 percent of the shares in Sidanco, but its right to manage the company expired in 2003. (On the merger of BP and TNK, see below.) The U.S. oil company Conoco, after a prolonged dispute, lost the oil industry holdings it had acquired in northern European Russia, but later acquired a minority share in Lukoil. Foreign companies received oil development concessions on Sakhalin Island.

Despite talk about the desirability of attracting foreign capital, some Russian oil companies take a dim view of attempts by powerful transnational corporations (TNC) to break into their holy of holies.

Another side of Russian companies' interaction with foreign capital is that Russian owners are eager to increase the capitalization of their firms, in order to be in a position to sell their control to transnational corporations at some point. This turned out to be a live option due to the rapid growth of the Russian oil industry.

Agreement was reached in February 2003 for BP to buy half of the shares in a new holding company, created out of TNK, Sidanco, Rusia Petroleum and several other Russian oil enterprises. The new company would produce 60 million tons of crude annually, becoming the third largest firm in the industry.

The establishment of this new holding company was christened the "deal of the century," for two reasons. First of all, it really was the new Russian capitalism's largest deal, as measured by the amount of foreign money invested, namely $6.75 billion. That was greater than annual foreign direct investment in Russia for any year since 1993. Secondly, many Western experts voiced the opinion that the BP deal could open the doors to broader foreign investment in our economy, since this was the first truly first-rank transnational corporation to decide on risking substantial capital in Russia, which had a bad reputation in the West as a zone of lawlessness, corruption and organized crime. A deal of this size with a respectable international company, it was supposed, would open a window to the world for Russia, helping to integrate the country into the global economy.

What was the outcome of the BP deal? Note that its main Russian participants were not Russian oil companies, but rather two financial groups: Mikhail Fridman's Alfa Group, and Access/Renova, headed by Victor Vekselberg. They still owned controlling equity stakes in TNK and the other Russian oil enterprises that made up the new holding company. The deal amounted to the sale of half of their stakes to a foreign company, which agreed to pay $3 billion in cash and another $3.75 billion over the next three years in the form of BP stock. Although formally this money was a contribution by BP to the holding company's equity capital, it by no means represented real investment in oil fields, refineries or other production facilities. It was merely a monetary payment for the right to manage these assets. BP received half ownership of the new holding company, as well as the right to name its chief executive officer. The actual management and control of the concern passed into foreign hands.

There was no immediate real benefit to the Russian oil industry. All that happened is that a group of oil companies changed ownership. How the new foreign partners will behave in the long run, and how much they will actually invest in the productive capacity of the industry, remains to be seen. Considering BP's many years of experience as one of the world's leading oil business operators, it is difficult to imagine that the new owners will do any worse than Fridman and Vekselberg, who were never oilmen.[18]

What made BP decide to take a serious step like the TNK merger, even though its previous relations with TNK and its owners had been less than stellar? It had to do with the fact that in 2000-2002, the years-long stagnation in the Russian oil industry gave way to rapid growth. The main reason for this was the sharp rise of world oil prices, resulting in a corresponding increase in the amount of rent available to be collected from the difference between the domestic costs of production and the foreign sale price of oil. Overall Russian crude production grew by 25 percent between 1999 and 2002, from 305 million tons to 380 million tons. Oil exports rose by nearly one-third in the same period. Superprofit from the extraction and export of oil increased several-fold. Oil industry sources, in forecasts that reflected their intentions, projected a doubling of exports by 2010. By that time, or slightly thereafter, Russia should have surpassed Saudi Arabia in oil production. BP, which had gotten a foothold in the Siberian oil fields in 1997, wanted to take part in this colossal new expansion. In 1998, BP paid $48 billion for Amoco, the American oil company, followed by $20 billion for another one, Atlantic Richfield. It would have been a strategic blunder to miss this "Russian chance," which was available much more cheaply.

BP itself announced that it planned to recoup its investment, with some profit, within four years, by earning $7.5 billion from its Russian subsidiary through crude production and superprofit from exports. One Western expert commented, "Pumping more barrels of oil is important, of course, but what's even more important is the profit on each barrel." In other words, BP's overriding interest was to boost Russia's role as a supplier of oil to the world market.

The BP-TNK deal was not, however, followed by other major foreign investment in Russian oil. In 2003-2004, Khodorkovsky's notion of selling most of the shares in Yukos to ExxonMobil was nipped in the bud by President Putin, who already had his sights on Yukos.

As for the natural gas industry, foreign investment has been constrained by the existence of a de facto government monopoly in the form of Gazprom, and the long-standing prohibition on the sale of its shares to foreigners beyond a certain limit. Nonetheless, alongside the government's controlling equity stake (38.4 percent, raised to 51 percent during 2005), foreign investors came to own 10.3 percent of Gazprom's shares, according to the company's own corporate reports. Around 4 percent belongs to the German company E.on Ruhrgas, with which Gazprom had long-standing close cooperation. A Ruhrgas executive sits on the Gazprom board of directors.[19] With the lifting in early 2006 of restrictions on foreigners' trading in Gazprom shares, foreign ownership of those shares is bound to increase substantially.

We saw in Chapter 2 that foreign investors' interest in the food and allied industries has focused on tobacco, beer breweries, and the confectionary industry. Foreign companies quickly took over the Russian tobacco market, with a significant number of the industry's enterprises coming under foreign control in the very first reform years. These incursions, combined with imports, gave foreign companies control of 80 percent of tobacco product sales in Russia.[20] This example illustrates two points. First of all, foreign cigarettes turned out to be a very profitable niche, and a large one, having a strong growth tendency (unlike in Western markets). Secondly, domestic capital showed little interest in this industry and did not put up much resistance to the foreign expansion. The situation in the beer industry was similar.

Finally, there is foreign investment in the retail trade, which has mainly taken the form of setting up supermarket chains and trade centers, including special outlets for selling imported products (for example, the Swedish furniture company IKEA). As of 1999, there were 3,700 Russian retail and public dining facilities with foreign co-ownership. Between 1993 and 1999, a total of 14.6 billion rubles was invested in their equity capital, or 29.3 percent of total investment in this sector of the economy. These companies' share of the sector's total business, however, was substantially less—only 4 percent.[21]

On the whole, foreign investors have taken a pragmatic approach to investing in Russia, despite their endless complaints about the difficulties of doing business there. They invested readily in areas like the food and allied industries, or trade, where it was known that the investments would be profitable, and Russian companies raised no serious obstacles. In areas where foreign companies faced hurdles such as resistance from Russian capital, or the presence of state-controlled monopolies, they have not, as a rule, succeeded in getting control of Russian firms, although they have eagerly made portfolio investments.

There will be certainly more portfolio investment in Russian companies, as a growing number of them start to quote their shares on the London and other foreign stock exchanges. This is the case not only for private companies in the food and allied businesses, but also some government-controlled concerns, like the large oil company Rosneft, that are eager to raise capital in foreign financial markets. They are liberalizing trade in their shares and attracting minority foreign institutional and individual investors, while retaining government ownership of controlling stakes. There is also a general view that Russian companies are undervalued in foreign markets, and that liberalizing trade in their shares will substantially increase their market capitalization. This is exactly what happened with Gazprom's shares in January 2006.

In most cases it was not lawlessness, rampant crime, and corruption that scared off foreign capital, as much as the limited size of the Russian market. The auto industry is a good example. Foreign companies have established themselves in this sector in virtually every country of Eastern Europe, generally by taking over the main light automobile factories. In Russia, however, there has not been a single attempt by foreign investors to purchase control over an existing auto plant, in the entire period of capitalist development. New factories built by foreign interests have been small and play no palpable role in the market. The plans announced in 2005-2006 by a number of international auto companies, to build relatively small assembly plants, whose total capacity would not exceed a few hundred thousand cars per year, represent only a slight shift. As shown in Chapter 2, demand in the Russian domestic market has been limited to relatively inexpensive cars, either domestically produced light automobiles or used imports. Demand for more expensive imported cars is no greater than 100,000 annually. This market was of no interest to major foreign investors. Nor was the utilization of existing plants to produce for export to third countries seen as a promising area.

Russian capital's transnational connections

We looked at the export of capital from Russia in Chapter 2. Conservative estimates put it in the range of $180 billion in the reform period (see Table 2.2). That is at least triple the total amount of foreign investment in Russia during the same period. Even according to the official balance of payments data, Russia's direct investment abroad was $12.1 billion in 1994-2001, or half the level of foreign direct investment in our country. The World Investment Report published by UNCTAD tallied Russia's outward stock of foreign direct investment at the end of 2002 at $18.0 billion and inward direct investment stock at $22.6 billion.

The inconsistent reports make it difficult to put together an accurate picture of the role Russian capital plays abroad. Part of the problem is that the flow of direct investment out of the country leads to the purchase of foreign companies or of control over them, turning the Russian firms that make such investments into TNC. Such companies typically own a network of foreign enterprises and play a part in the output and exports of other countries. Even if we take the larger of the estimates of Russian direct investment mentioned above, $18 billion, it is equal to only 0.26 percent of the world's total direct investment stock.[22] This negligibly small amount indicates how small the role of Russian capital is in relations among transnational corporations. Not a single one of the world's 25 largest transnational corporations is headquartered in Russia. The list of the 15 largest TNC in Central and Eastern Europe, published in the UNCTAD World Investment Report for 2003, included four Russian corporations, of which three were shipping lines (included because their vessels are registered in various countries), and only one was an industrial firm: Lukoil. They are listed in Table 6.5.

Setting aside the shipping companies, whose property abroad is almost entirely vessels sailing under foreign flag, the only really major transnational corporation headquartered in Russia is Lukoil. According to Lukoil, it has or participates in concessions in Azerbai-

Table 6.5 Russian transnational corporations
(UNCTAD classification, millions of $, 2001)

1 Foreign enterprises
2 Total for company

	Assets 1	Assets 2	Sales 1	Sales 2	Employees (1000s) 1	Employees (1000s) 2	TNI, %
Lukoil	5,830	15,859	8,771	14,892	13	40	35
Novoship	999	1,134	302	392	0.1	6.9	56
Primorskoye Shipping	267	438	115	146	1.3	2.6	63
Far East Shipping	123	377	101	318	0.2	5.6	23

Note: The TNI, or transnationality index, is calculated as the average of three ratios: foreign assets to total assets, foreign sales to total sales, and employees at enterprises abroad to total employees.

Source: *UNCTAD World Investment Report, 2003*, Table 4.

jan, Kazakhstan, Libya, Egypt, and Iraq, as well as controlling oil refineries in Ukraine, Romania, and Bulgaria, and filling station chains in the USA, Poland, Romania, Bulgaria, Turkey, and the CIS. Thirty percent of its refinery capacity is located abroad, as is 60 percent of its retail network and 4 percent of its crude oil reserves.[23]

No other Russian oil company comes close to Lukoil in this respect. Yukos, which before its break-up rivaled Lukoil in crude output, had only one oil refinery outside Russia (in Lithuania), an oil transport company in Slovakia, and sales outlets in other Eastern European countries.[24]

Yukos's international connections were stronger than it might have seemed. As owner, Khodorkovsky cultivated such ties. Earlier than most Russian companies, he shifted to internationally accepted financial accounting standards, and introduced a relatively high degree of transparency. Although the majority of Yukos shares remained in his hands, it is believed that up 10-12 percent of them were circulating on U.S. markets in the form of American Depository Rights (special certificates of indebtedness, which are officially registered in the United States to function in lieu of a company's stock shares).[25] Senior management at Yukos included fifty foreigners, while the company was represented in London by the former British Foreign Minister, Lord Owen.[26] These international connections did not, however, save Khodorkovsky and his company from criminal charges of tax fraud by the Russian government, ending in his imprisonment in a Siberian penitentiary.

UNCTAD's criteria for classifying Russian companies as TNC are open to criticism. For instance, there is hardly any good reason to exclude Gazprom from the list, particularly since in recent years it has expanded its pipeline network well into most of Europe, through buying into foreign gas transportation and distribution companies, while the market valuation of its assets has put it, in terms of capital, on an equal footing with other major international energy corporations.

So far, however, purchases of foreign enterprises by Russian companies have generally been limited largely to the CIS countries, the Baltic states, and former Comecon members, with which there are ties dating from the Soviet period and a business environment in which Russian entrepreneurs feel more comfortable. Countries like Poland, the Czech Republic, Slovakia, or Bulgaria also present less of a language barrier to Russian-speakers than other countries do. Russian ownership or co-ownership of foreign enterprises beyond this zone is still a relative rarity.

This picture is now changing, albeit very slowly at first. In 2002, for example, there was a report that Rusal might invest in a joint venture to build an aluminum plant in Australia. It did acquire, from the U.S. group Kaiser Aluminum, a 20 percent stake in Queensland Alumina. Rusal's other foreign holdings are enterprises in Armenia, Ukraine, and Romania.[27] In late 2001 the OMZ (United Machine-building Factories) group purchased 30 percent of an American company called Biolink Technologies, a computer peripherals and biometrics specialist. The acquisition was a firm of Russian origin, having come out of a company owned by émigrés from Russia, and dealing in computers in the U.S. market.[28]

In 2003 Severstal bought control of the bankrupt Detroit steel producer Rouge Industries; Norilsk Nickel acquired Stillwater Mining, the USA's only producer of platinum; and SUAL made a deal with Britain's Fleming Family & Partners to consolidate operations in the aluminum and bauxite field (which deal went sour in early 2006). Roman Abramovich has been expected to invest on a large scale in the West—beyond the Chelsea Soccer Club he bought in 2003—after selling off most of his businesses in Russia (though fresh investments by Abramovich in Russian companies, like his 2006 Yevrazholding and Rosneft share purchases, are also not excluded). These overseas acquisitions represent a new trend that should be watched; its tempo picked up, with the acquisitions by Gazprom, mentioned in our Introduction.

The reason for Russian companies' limp investment performance abroad has been not so much a lack of capital, as it is the absence of either the ability to organize a competitive operation, or readiness to overcome the obstacles presented by an unfamiliar, often hostile environment. Russian oligarchs are often incapable of making a go of businesses that produce for the domestic market, and they have trouble selling their finished products in foreign markets. Setting up such businesses abroad is an even taller order for them.

But the examples of Lukoil, Gazprom, Norilsk Nickel, Severstal, and others show that Russian capital is capable of carrying off an intrusion into Western markets, when it feels confident. Lukoil's purchase from Getty Oil of a chain of gas stations in the USA could happen because the Russian company had not only the money, but also the managerial experience needed for the project.

Another such example is Norilsk Nickel's 2002 purchase of a controlling equity stake in Stillwater Mining, the American platinum group metals producer. The acquisition cost Norilsk $41 million, and would enable Norilsk to break into the American palladium market, the largest in the world, where its market share had previously been rather modest.[29]

In other cases, Russian companies were prepared to purchase foreign ones, but they encountered political obstacles. In the mid-1990s Holland's famous Fokker aircraft company, which was partially owned by German capital, was on the brink of bankruptcy. One option was to sell the entire company to a different foreign investor, in order to save several thousand jobs, including highly skilled ones. The Russian government, representing the interests of our aircraft industry, was one of the potential buyers. But the Dutch government, which held a controlling stake in Fokker, refused to sell it to Russia or China, citing strategic concerns. The upshot was that no suitable buyer was found, the plant was closed and the workers were laid off.

Russian connections with international capital may well develop in the way indicated by BP's deal with the Alfa and Access/Renova financial groups. It resulted in these Russian groups taking co-ownership, on an equal footing with BP, of what became the third largest oil company in Russia. Although the joint corporation's capital is divided fifty-fifty, BP has the right to appoint its chief executive (president or CEO), who runs the company with an international staff. The chairman of the board of directors is a Russian, whose role in the company is as more that of an observer, than a decision-maker.

Thus TNK-BP, the new company created out of what had been TNK, Sidanco, Rusia Petroleum, and several smaller firms, effectively became a part—and not even the most important part—of the huge BP empire, which not long before had swallowed Amoco, Atlantic Richfield, and Germany's Veba Oil, the largest gas station chain in Western Europe, on top of its other transnational holdings. Lord Browne, the top boss of this empire, called its Russian component, "a new, sixth profit center."[30]

As we have seen, it was not size alone that qualified the BP operation as the deal of the century. More important was its role as a precedent for Russian oligarchs to follow in selling their holdings in oil, nickel, aluminum, etc. The pattern was noted in Chapter 2: in cases where financial groups took over raw materials concerns, they have viewed their companies not only as a foundation for increasing their own economic and political influence in Russia, but also as potential commodities for resale to foreign corporations and integration into the Western system of corporate connections. For that reason their top priority has been to increase the capitalization of their companies in whatever way possible, so as not to miss the moment when they think the market value of these holdings has peaked. The most important thing for these financiers was not ownership, as such, but control over the companies in order to be able to profit from reselling them.

For financial oligarchs, controlling one company or another is merely a stage in their enrichment program. They don't particularly care what company or what industry they invest in, as long as the investment risk is low and the prospective profit fairly high. The best companies for them are ones they can buy relatively cheaply, at several times below their prospective market value. They can always find managers who are ready to transform the purchase into "candy," which can deliver the result they want. The profit may be invested in the next target of their purchase and resale operation.

The New York Times observed about this practice, "Takeover followed by makeover has been Mr. Fridman's signature strategy in Alfa Group's various investments. He refurbished and sold a Russian candy maker to Danone Group, the maker of Dannon yogurt; a glass maker to Asahi Glass of Japan, and a cement producer to Holcim of Switzerland. ... 'Any business should be sold if you're offered the right price,' Mr. Fridman said. 'If you don't, the market will punish you. Or God. Or maybe they are the same thing.'"[31]

Russia's professional oilmen view their control of the companies they head in a different light from the financiers. For the oilmen, the company is a base for their own power and wealth. They don't want to give up control, because they feel unsure of themselves outside the oil industry. Historical examples from around the world show that such owners sell their companies only in the twilight of their careers in industry, and if they have no heirs to continue the business.

A similar situation developed in the aluminum industry. In early 2003, the second largest company in this industry, SUAL, signed the above-mentioned agreement with the British firm Fleming Family & Partners, establishing a joint venture that was to have brought brought together aluminum, alumina, and other enterprises owned by the two parties. SUAL, headed by Vekselberg, was believed to have acquired a 77 percent stake in the new concern, while Fleming got 23 percent. Here the main objective of the Russian owners, according to their own statements, was to "enter the Western markets," that is, to profit by selling the company to a foreign investor somewhere down the road. Accordingly, a British-selected foreign executive, South African Chris Norval from the transnational mining giant BHP Billiton, became the first CEO of the new entity, and was succeeded in 2004 by Brian Gilbertson, another South African veteran of BHP Billiton.[32] In early 2006, the Vekselberg deal fell apart. But it illustrates the potential desire of the Russian oligarchs to sell out to foreigners when the opportunity presents itself and they believe the price is right.

These cases illustrate a new model of the further development of Russian capitalism: foreign transnational corporations would take over from Russian magnates in the role of oligarchs. Such a turn of events would imply a changed correlation of forces in the upper echelons of Russian society. Will the political authorities go along? For the officials who hold political power, maintaining equidistance from an array of homegrown oligarchs is a more manageable proposition, than trying to keep balance against the more powerful Wall Street and City of London transnational groups.

It has to be recognized that all of the forms of integration into the world economy, reviewed in this chapter, represent varieties of dependence—whether with respect to trade, investment, or finances—that define Russia's place as being on the periphery of the world capitalist system, not at its center. In fairness, we should state that this dependence has not yet risen to the level of neo-colonialism. Russia's main industries, including the export-oriented sectors, are not yet controlled by foreign capital, and the levels of profit that transnational corporations make in Russia and export from Russia are still relatively small. Given current raw materials price patterns, our country will most likely be able to gain more than it loses from the unequal terms of trade, for some period of time to come.

Nonetheless, it is important to understand the prevailing tendencies, stemming from the way in which Russian capitalism is developing today. Dependence on the raw materials sector is the inevitable result of the bias in the economy, expressed in the industrial financial groups' lack of desire to invest in industries that don't offer the opportunity to receive superprofit. While accumulating large capital surpluses and taking them abroad, these same groups also avoid attempts to position themselves in the advanced industries of the developed countries. The parasitical behavior of making money by reselling easily acquired assets, which were created by the state, while avoiding the development of the industrial base in one's home country, leads to the surrender to transnational capital of control over key industries.

Shifting these tendencies will require a fundamental change in how the Russian economy functions and, accordingly, in government economic policy. Is this possible? We shall try to answer these questions in the final section of this chapter and the book.

6.2 The inertial system of Russian capitalism

The picture presented in the preceding chapters, and sections of the present chapter, reveals a Russian economy in which there took shape, with the transition to capitalism, a self-perpetuating system, which moves on its own characteristic trajectory and is extremely difficult to change.

The principal institutional characteristics of the system are these:

- monopolistic practices prevail over competitive ones;
- oligarchical financial groups dominate, while banking is relatively underdeveloped;
- the oligarchy is closely intertwined with the government, which does very little by way of economic regulation;
- the share of gross profit in national income is excessively high;
- the shadow economy is inordinately large, as is the portion of the national product, swallowed by corruption and organized crime.

These characteristic features of the system give rise to certain patterns in the behavior of economic agents, as well as in macroeconomic dynamics.

The prevalence of monopoly—or oligopoly, to put it more precisely—causes companies to orient, typically, toward obtaining profit more by maximizing the gap between the costs of production and sales price of output, than by increasing the volume of output and sales. This pattern of behavior set in during the first few capitalist years, when output was either declining or stagnating, while price inflation roared ahead. Since it made no sense to increase output under such conditions, the only available rational tactic was to maximize short-term profit by playing on the price spreads. In practically no case during those first years did a company attempt to best its competitors by lowering prices. On the contrary, every pretext and opportunity to raise prices was seized, even when there would seem to have been a possibility of increasing sales at the expense of a company's competitors. This may not always have held true for small business operators, who regularly practiced competitive pricing, but it was the case for the major concerns and even for medium-sized enterprises, which dominated local markets and preferred non-economic means, often involving physical violence, to eliminate their rivals.

The overall competitiveness of Russian producers in the domestic market rose after the financial crisis of 1998, thanks to the steep external devaluation of the ruble. This created an opportunity to get ahead of imported goods sellers. For the first time, profit could be accumulated on the basis of a company's volume of production and sales, rather than only through a high share of profit in the price of the output being sold. Even in this new, more favorable situation, however, production was geared up at a pace that was calculated not to reduce profitability. The result was a faster rate of increase of domestic prices than market conditions justified, leading to a fairly rapid loss of the competitive advantages provided by the devaluation.

In modern economies, the dominance of oligopoly and lack of competition in pricing often stimulate companies to improve product quality and develop new products and market niches, which bring them superprofit, even if only temporarily. This type of behavior did not materialize in Russia, which instead set about to prove Lenin's dictum that monopolies cause rot; they act as a brake on technological progress, including product differentiation.

Our companies do not harbor some principled hostility to the possibility and necessity of exploiting new niches. They readily do so, but generally only when some new type of product has already been developed abroad and needs only to be adapted for the Russian market. The rapid proliferation of mobile telephones and the Internet are typical examples. But there are practically no examples of starting up production of new items that have been developed in Russia. Even our automobile and aircraft companies, which are large and would appear to have potential strengths in this respect, and which are doing business in industries where constant product updates are essential to competitive success, have proven incapable of organizing the production of new models that incorporate significant advances.

One of the reasons for such lack of motion is the established inertial aversion to investing in the modernization of productive capacities or construction of new plants. Indeed, the experience of companies in the West demonstrates that constant product updates entail large, regularly incurred extra costs, with the expectation that they will be recouped only in the medium-term or more distant future. Most Russian companies, even large ones with ample resources, simply do not have any such long-term strategy. In well over a decade of its existence, Russian capitalism has not built a single new factory, contenting itself with using existing capacities and exploiting natural resource deposits that were explored and essentially developed earlier.

Even in a superprofit-laden sector like oil and gas, new construction has largely been restricted to building pipelines to the relevant export markets. This has been done by the government at public expense. Only in very recent years have the privately owned oil companies shown some signs of interest in participating in pipeline construction. Once again, their primary interest is in pipelines designed for export markets: to the port of Murmansk, with eventual deliveries to the USA, to Daqing in China, and to Nakhodka on the Pacific Ocean, for sales to Japan.

The oligarchical financial groups' dominant position in the economy has similar results. Most of these groups were founded by capitalists who made their careers in financial and other speculative operations. They had little interest in developing or improving the process of production; their overriding concern was to grab the most profitable pieces of formerly state-owned property and use them for purposes of personal enrichment. In most cases the targeted properties were export-oriented fuel and raw materials enterprises, which, upon falling into the hands of a few power groups, as we have seen, were organized on a strictly oligopolistic basis. In certain of the groups, banks served as the chief initial source of money-capital, which was subsequently directed into the main niches where reliable natural rent and superprofit were to be had. The niches then became the basis for the further growth of the financial groups, and so their corporate centers were relocated into those industries.

Gradually, especially after the financial crisis of 1998, the banks faded in importance as a source of profit from currency and other types of speculation. They became merely an ancillary component of the groups, servicing and coordinating the financial streams of the companies with which they were associated. It was a pattern that retarded any normal development of the banking sector into a branch of the economy that would service the economy as a whole, rather than only certain select groups of clients.

Here is one published description of the operations of MDM Bank, which is part of the financial group associated with Abramovich, Deripaska, and their companies (former companies, in the case of Abramovich): "For many years, the bank did no normal banking business. Loans were issued mainly to group insiders, while the bank itself often functioned as a treasury for the group's enterprises, organizing their financial flows so as to minimize their tax liability. Let the Russian bank that *hasn't* done that sort of thing cast the first stone at MDM."[33]

At a certain stage of the process, it suits the main shareholders in the financial groups to have the banks play this narrow role. But the banks' pressure may begin to conflict with their interests, if they want to emphasize a different objective, such as increasing market capitalization with an eye toward selling to foreign investors. A bank that is a closed institution with a limited number of customers and a small deposit base is of little interest to a foreign buyer. Therefore, the main owners have to consider how to extend the bank's branch network, expand its retail operations, improve transparency, and separate, to the extent possible, its normal commercial banking activity from its offshore and other money-laundering operations. Without taking these steps, Russian banks will not be able to be listed on foreign stock exchanges, which is a precondition for boosting their capitalization.

Couldn't Russian banking be normalized without being integrated into the world system of financial institutions? The bank executives themselves ought to be interested in developing commercial lending, beyond the limits of their "home" groups, including loans for medium-sized and small businesses, and expanded consumer and mortgage credit operations. But a shift in that direction is obviously a very slow process, not only because of the small domestic market for such lending and the limited number of relatively well-off customers for bank services. The axiom that profit must be maximized in the short term dictates that the banks prioritize servicing the industrial financial groups with which they are associated.

This pattern of banking activity is not limited to the major banks. Regional and local banks have tried to set up their operations according to the same model, whereby they emphasize the interests of their controlling shareholders and associated companies. These are also industrial financial groups, but on a regional or local scale. Having their own bank gives them advantages that would be hard to turn down, especially since they have effectively no access to financing from the large Moscow banks. Nor do they need it, if they can live tolerably well using their own financial institutions.

The close intertwining of the oligarchy with the state at all levels of government—central, sectoral, regional, and local—and the state's extremely weak regulatory ability also act to retard economic development. There are two fundamentally different models in a modern capitalist economy. In one of them, the government acts on behalf of the interests of the capitalist class as a whole. Being truly equidistant (and not just proclaiming this to be the case) from the main oligarchical financial groups, the government can act in the interests of the system as a whole, providing it stability and a situation of relative equilibrium. If the system gets out of balance and slips into crisis, the government moves to correct whatever biases may have emerged in the economy, even if doing so conflicts with the interests of certain groups within the monopolistic elite.

Under the second model, the government is directly dependent on, if not formally subordinate to, one or several of the oligarchical groups. Since the conditions that would ensure overall stability not infrequently clash with the interests of those groups, the government inevitably does less to correct imbalances and biases. The government has to trail after those private interests, a practice that often has an adverse effect on the overall economic situation, impeding the economy's development.

Neither of these models functions cleanly, as if in the abstract. The economies that actually exist in the world most often are a mixture or combination of these two models. But it is always possible to identify which model is dominant.

In Russia, the interweaving of the government and business is quite complex. Some sectors of the economy are so firmly subordinate to local oligarchical groups, that it is difficult, or impossible, for the central or regional government to have any control. Under Yeltsin, his so-called "Family" of businessmen and officials who were especially close to the President was essentially bought off by a few oligarchs. Beyond those relationships, a significant part of the bureaucratic apparatus answered to various oligarchical groups and did what the latter wanted. In one period, the state apparatus as a whole was nothing but a well-organized feeding trough for various clans of businessmen and corrupt officials, interwoven with criminal groups.

When Putin took office, he instituted the principle of government equidistance from all the oligarchs. It was announced that the state, or at least the President, should be an arbiter, superior to the capitalist elite. It appeared that the end had come for the system in which the upper echelons of officialdom were intertwined with the interests of specific oligarchs. Yet the practice of regular one-on-one meetings between the President and leading businessmen—none other than the oligarchs—continued, and even became more of a regular phenomenon, at least during Putin's first term. At the same time, certain indications emerged that the President was close to several new groups, which had been lower in the pecking order under Yeltsin and now wanted to take advantage of the new situation in order to get their hands on profitable, not previously distributed, pieces of the state-owned pie. Some of these grabs worked, while others did not. The Mezhprombank group, rumored to be close to the President, did not succeed in its efforts to seize control of Slavneft. But Alexei Miller, whom Putin installed at Gazprom to replace Rem Vyakhirev, and his fellow Petersburgers did manage to consolidate their control over the natural gas monopoly. The same group decisively beat back rivals at another feeding trough, namely, control over arms exports. In the electric power industry, however, the older groups were able to come out ahead of the new ones. What became clear is that the "government as arbiter" model also involves rivalries within the government over the allocation of property and niches where superprofit may be earned. It remains unclear, whether or not the first model will prevail. The rise of the powerful Kremlin group of companies and banks during Putin's second term, as well as the Kremlin-initiated breakup of Yukos, gave a clear indication that the proclaimed "equidistance" principle does not work.

The neo-liberal economic policy model also incorporates certain pretensions to the role of arbiter, insofar as the government is assigned merely to look after the creation of an overall favorable atmosphere for economic development, by implementing pro-business reforms, while minimizing its regulatory role, as such, and avoiding direct participation in the economy. It is on this model that the policy of the governments under Putin has been based. Broadly speaking, it requires that the government refrain from attempts to restore economic equilibrium.

In practice, the neo-liberal model is in conflict with the expansion of the Kremlin group, which promotes the direct involvement of the state in a number of key industries. The liberal model also effectively restricts the active use of fiscal policy to stimulate macroeconomic aggregate demand and rapid economic growth.

In principle, the liberal model has proven more or less successful only in evenly developing economies, free of major imbalances. In such economies the regulatory role of the government can indeed be reduced to a minimum, since the economy smoothes out imbalances and biases spontaneously. For the Russian economy in its current condition, this model is not only inappropriate, but harmful.

Let us return briefly to the question of the economy's tilt toward the fuels and raw materials sectors. As we have explained, what underlies this phenomenon is the uneven distribution of gross profit (surplus value), which is a self-feeding process that will not sort itself out automatically. In a well-functioning competitive market system, no sector's profitability (rate of profit) should deviate greatly from the average rate of profit in the economy as a whole. If some industry does have a higher-than-average rate of profit, capital will be attracted there from other sectors, until the profitability of the various sectors evens out. But this levelling will not occur in the presence of economic or natural barriers. The oil and non-ferrous metals industries in Russia entail barriers of both types. The oil fields have been seized by a small group of companies, which used their natural and geographical delimitation to shut out new competitors. Conversely, the profitability gap blocks capital formed in the fuels and raw materials industries from being invested in other sectors, where the rate of profit is much lower. Thus we have a trap, the vicious circle we discussed earlier.

The competitive economy model escapes from this dilemma by forcibly levelling the rate of profit. The ultimate owner of the raw materials (the landowner) is given the right to collect rent, which includes profit in excess of the average rate. In Russia, as in many other countries, private ownership of land has been legalized, but the state continues to own the land under which oil, gas, and ores are located. Development of these subsoil resources by private companies takes place under license from the government. Hence derives the right of the state to collect the relevant share of natural rent. In the period of primitive accumulation, subsoil resource development rights were handed out at ridiculously low prices, essentially for free. But that was by no means a final decision. If the government decides to collect a significantly greater share of the natural rent, it has every right to do so. How much should be collected is a question of economic expediency. The failure to move in this direction is less a matter of technical considerations about how to structure the needed tax legislation, than a question of overcoming resistance from the oligarchical groups, which have long considered themselves the owners of Russia's natural riches, and have no desire to share them with other sectors of the economy.

Broadly speaking, the failure to solve this problem is a brake on the country's economic growth. GDP growth depends on the rate of growth of its components in each industry. If half of Russia's capital investment, or more, continues to go into the fuel and raw materials sector, that sector will determine the overall GDP growth rate. Since those industries are oriented toward export, their growth rates will be tied to the growth of demand abroad; that is, they will depend on average world economic growth rates. In that case, Russia can forget about faster overall growth and catching up with industrially developed nations in terms of GDP and living standards.

Fast GDP growth can be achieved only if the manufacturing industries grow rapidly. Whether or not they do is determined by the potential capacity of the domestic market, which is by no means limited to average world economic growth rates. But the only way for manufacturing, and the economy as a whole, to achieve higher rates is by redistributing some of the capital, created in the rent-generating industries, to other sectors. Such a redistribution will only happen through active government intervention. The government is the only agency capable of carrying out that maneuver, but it will only be able to do it, if it is truly freed from its position of subordination to the oligarchical groups.

Not only with respect to this fundamental problem, but in general, the government's regulatory role is very weak in today's Russia. The government has next to nothing resembling an active budget policy. It makes no use whatsoever of the growth incentives that are employed, and have proven effective, in the West: government purchases of products for which demand has dropped off temporarily, or state investment in infrastructure. Even in tax policy, the only fiscal area in which government regulation is even slightly visible, the government is extremely indecisive, often prioritizing short-term fiscal objectives above the long-term goals of stimulating economic growth. Russia has virtually no monetary and credit policy. The Russian government has also been weak and inert in reforming institutions that play a key role in any normal market economy, such as the banking system and capital markets.

The oligarchical domination of the economy results in a persistently excessive share of gross profit (surplus value) in national income. The share of labor income is correspondingly low. Quite apart from the structural bias in favor of the fuel and raw materials sector, this discrepancy produces the persistent problem of a domestic market that is too small to accommodate fully the capital generated in the country. Even if the raw materials tilt were eliminated, the disproportionately high ratio of gross profit to labor income would make it impossible for Russia to realize its potential for faster overall economic growth.

The share of gross profit in GDP has been around 40 percent in recent years, while labor income's share (after deducting net indirect taxes) stands at only 44 percent. Accordingly, the share of personal consumption in GDP barely reaches 50 percent. Combined with gross capital investment's average share (17 percent of GDP), that means that only 66 percent of GDP is utilized in the economy as the result of aggregate private demand. In other words, Russia's produced output can be fully sold only if government purchases and net exports together absorb 34 percent of the total national product. Since half of that portion is consumed by government purchases (17 percent), fully 17 percent of what Russia produces has to go to net exports: that much has to be exported in excess of imports. This can happen only in the extreme situation where an unnaturally large portion of the national product is being sold abroad.

It would be unrealistic to count on that situation to endure for long. A more sensible approach would be gradually, but steadily, to increase the share of labor income, and hence of personal consumption, in GDP. Such an approach would expand the domestic market for Russian manufactured goods and thus ensure faster growth of the whole economy.

We can better visualize the problem by comparing the Russian indicators cited here, with the proportions of the U.S. economy over a long period of time (Table 6.6).

Table 6.6 Comparison of dynamic proportions of the Russian and U.S. economies
(% share in GDP, 1998-2005)

	Russia	USA
Gross profit	38.9	35.4
Labor income	44.3	57.7
Personal consumption	49.1	69.3
Gross capital investment	17.0	16.2
Personal consumption and capital investment	66.1	85.5
Government purchases	16.8	18.3
Net exports	17.0	–3.3

Sources: U.S. data are from National Economic Accounts, Bureau of Economic Analysis, http://www.bea.gov/bea/dn1.htm; our calculations. Russian data from NAS, Goskomstat, http://www.gks.ru/bd-1.asp; our calculations.

In the USA, where the relative shares of gross profit and labor income are more normal, the total share of personal consumption and gross capital investment in GDP reaches 85 percent. Since government purchases account for 18 percent, practically all of U.S. national output (in value terms) is sold inside the country, while the relatively small share of exported goods and services is more than compensated for by imports.

Increasing the share of labor income and reducing the share of gross profit would relieve the Russian economy of its excessive dependence on external markets and create a solid foundation for sustained economic growth, oriented mainly toward the domestic market. There is no need to decrease the share of capital investment in GDP. It should suffice to increase the share of gross profit spent on investment, for the purpose of modernizing and expanding productive fixed assets. Such spending will reduce the capital-output ratio and increase the economic efficiency of investment.

This turnaround is unlikely to occur within the framework of the neo-liberal model, at least not in the near- or mid-term perspective. It is therefore easy to project the direction of further economic development in Russia in the absence of the needed corrections.

1. At best, the economy would continue to grow at moderate speed, insufficient for any substantial reduction of the gap between Russia and the industrial nations of the West in per capita GDP and standards of living. In the worst case, a

drastic fall in oil and raw materials prices will put a brake on growth, and the income gap will widen.

2. Russia will be unable to escape from its current position on the periphery of the world economy and will retain its extreme dependence on the leading centers of world capitalism for at least one or two decades. It is quite possible that foreign transnational corporations will capture control over key Russian economic assets, making the dependence even greater.

3. At average growth rates and with a further decline in the share of government economic activity in GDP, the redistribution of income to public sector social programs will contract further, with conditions for financing education, health care, science, and the arts becoming even worse.

4. At the same time and for the same reasons, it will become impossible to maintain Russia's military power at levels that would guarantee the national security. The country's role as a great power with global interests would further diminish.

Such prospects are not to the liking of either the Russian elite or the majority of the population. The question arises, therefore, of what alternatives might be available.

6.3 Possible alternatives and policy solutions

To find alternatives to Russia's economic inertia means determining ways to change the mechanism described above.

The *maximalist* ways that have been suggested amount to destroying the very foundations of monopoly and oligarchical control, making the state a truly independent and active agent that helps to shape long-term economic processes, both in the various industrial sectors and in the economy at large. Among these suggestions is renationalizing some key industries and operating a large state-owned sector within the framework of a mixed economy, which would largely retain the principal contours of private entrepreneurship and a market economy.

It is the consensus of most Russian economists, that retaining and expanding the market is necessary in order to maintain equilibrium at the micro, meso, and macro levels. But it is also admitted that, while markets are necessary to maintain long-term proportions, they are not in a position to correct major structural imbalances when the latter become too large and rigid. To make the necessary adjustments, the state should play a more active role. But a substantial number of economists would argue that large-scale renationalization at this point would be destabilizing from the political, social, and economic perspectives.

A more realistic approach would be to tackle the same issue, but avoid a wholesale breakdown of the oligopolies and oligarchical groups, by placing certain limitations on their activities. This will be possible if the state is transformed into a truly independent power, able and willing to induce the oligarchs to adhere to certain clearly defined rules of economic behavior and refrain from attempts to unduly impose their will on the formulation of policy.

In practice, even this *minimalist* approach could lead to sharp confrontation with forces within the elite that are closely connected to the oligarchs and defend their interests. It is no secret that most of the leading newspapers in the country belong to oligarchical groups, and that at least some electronic mass media are under their strong financial influence. Some political parties fighting for seats in the parliament are known to be financed by big business. Its strong influence can be also seen at the level of important provincial governors and large city mayors. It is extremely difficult to fight for meaningful anti-oligarchical reform under these conditions.

Yet, it is quite possible, indeed indispensable, to educate the elite and the population to see realistic alternatives to current economic policies, and the dire need for them to be implemented in the national interest. It should be borne in mind that there is no unanimity on these issues at the top of the government. For instance, Putin made quite a sensation in his annual Message to the Federal Assembly in 2001, when he suggested redistributing mineral rent to other sectors of the economy. Following the President's initiative, some taxes on oil companies were indeed raised, but these changes were relatively minor and did not resolve the major macroeconomic imbalances.

One of the neo-liberal dogmas (to which the present Russian government still largely subscribes) is that the state should not be actively involved in the economy. This may be true in countries

Table 6.7 Profitability in sectors of industry, 1999-2001
(profit as % of output value)

	1999	2000	2001
All industry	25.5	24.7	18.5
Oil	57.9	66.7	46.5
Gas	22.6	30.0	17.4
Steel	28.2	25.6	12.5
Non-ferrous metals	57.4	51.6	34.4
Electric power	13.7	13.5	15.7
Machine-building and metal-working	17.4	14.1	13.6
Chemicals and petrochemicals	22.3	17.0	11.5
Timber, pulp and paper	23.9	16.5	11.5
Construction materials	8.6	9.0	9.8
Light industry	9.5	7.2	5.4
Food industry	13.0	10.1	11.5

Source: RSY 2003.

where private business is active in all areas that are crucial for maintaining a healthy and balanced economy. But in Russia this is not the case. For instance, the major structural imbalance between mineral resources and manufacturing would not have come about, had the government retained ownership of the largest oil companies instead of transferring them practically for free to private owners. Had that not happened, the issue of taxing mineral rent would not have emerged as a major structural problem, and private capital would not have been deflected from manufacturing and the high-tech sector.

What did develop in the Russian economy was an abnormally large gap between profitability levels in various sectors of industry. This discrepancy impeded any even-handed redistribution of capital and financing to the various sectors.

Goskomstat data (Table 6.7) show that profitability in industry as a whole averaged in the 18-25 percent range in 1999-2001. In most sectors it was substantially lower, in some it hovered around the average, and in just two—oil and non-ferrous metals—profitability was far above the average (46-67 percent and 34-57 percent, respectively).

The only way to free the economy from this bias is through active government intervention, in contravention of neo-liberal dogma. Two events occurred in the 2004-2006 period, which, it would seem, should have helped to extract the economy from its inertial dead end. Both resulted from government actions, though the first was deliberate and the second happened virtually of its own accord.

The first event was the crushing of Yukos Oil, described in Chapter 2, and the government's offensive in the oil industry: the seizure of most of Yukos's production assets by the state-owned Rosneft oil company and the purchase of Sibneft by the state-owned Gazprom. As a result, state-owned companies got control of over one-fourth of Russian oil production, as against the previous 7 percent. This means that an appreciable portion of the oil rent now comes under the control of organizations that, at least formally, are largely owned by the government, not by private capital. It also means that the government can influence domestic prices on oil and oil products, and use that capability as a means of restraining inflation.

There is reason to suspect, however, that the strengthened position of state-owned organizations in industry will be used not in the national interest, but in the private interests of the Kremlin industrial financial group, under whose control they are now operating. This would mean the use of the rent collected by Rosneft and Gazprom to expand those companies, rather than to support key manufacturing industries. There is also some danger that these companies, together with the private oil firms, will take part in an oligopolistic plot to crank up domestic prices on gasoline and other liquid fuels even farther than has happened already. In that case, the state-owned companies would dissolve into the overall system of oligarchical capitalism, losing any independent, stabilizing role they might have played in the economy.

The second event occurred in a more spontaneous way. A new tax on raw materials extraction was instituted in 2002-2003, with the rate directly linked to world prices. As long as the price of crude hovered in the area of $20-25 per barrel of crude oil, this tax remained relatively low and soaked up only a small portion of the oil rent. When world prices more than doubled during 2004-2005, however, the rate of taxation rose even more steeply (Table 6.8), in accordance with the formula chosen earlier.

In a period of four years, the tax rate increased by a factor of 6.2, or twice as rapidly as the domestic oil price. The result was that

Table 6.8 Average raw materials extraction tax rate
(in $ per barrel of oil)

	2001	2002	2003	2004	2005
Tax	1.7	3.0	3.5	5.6	10.6
Domestic price	7.4	9.5	10.2	14.5	21.9
Tax as % of price	23%	32%	34%	39%	48%

the share of the tax in the domestic price rose from one-fourth to one-half, which goes a long way toward explaining why gasoline and other petroleum products became significantly more expensive for the Russian consumer. The government increased its share of the oil rent, but did so more at the expense of the population, than of the oil companies. In addition, the government had established an uncalled-for automatic mechanism, which translated world price prices into domestic inflation.

Duties on exported oil also rose during this period (Table 6.9). The government's immediate objective in imposing those duties was to restrain fuel exports and reduce inflationary pressure in the domestic market. But exports continued to grow, while domestic inflationary pressures intensified. It should be noted that the rise in duties was also directly dependent on world prices and was adjusted quarterly according to a predetermined formula.

The export duty increased by a factor of 14.2 in 2001-2005, while the external (export) price of oil rose by only 250 percent. If we sum the extraction tax and the duty, their total share in the final sale price of oil on the world market rose from 16 percent to 66 percent in this four-year period. At the beginning of the first decade of the 21st century, the government was collecting only a small fraction

Table 6.9 Export duty, tax and external price of oil
($ per barrel)

	2001	2002	2003	2004	2005
Tax	1.7	3.0	3.5	5.6	10.6
Duty	1.8	3.0	4.1	10.6	25.6
Tax + duty	3.5	6.0	7.6	16.2	36.2
External price	22.3	23.3	26.0	35.8	54.8
Tax + duty as % of price	16%	26%	29%	45%	66%

of the oil rent, but by its mid-point, the greater portion went to the state. What the oil lobby had resisted so vigorously was achieved under the "neo-liberal" Putin, despite that opposition. With Khodorkovsky's empire crushed and Abramovich's company coming under Kremlin control, none of the oil oligarchs was prepared to oppose Putin openly.

It would appear that the crucial part of the goal set by the President in 2001 had been achieved. Finally, the petrodollars were streaming into government coffers. There remained just the little problem of finding the best use for them. And there a major obstacle arose. Legislation adopted in 2004 directed the majority of the petrodollars not into the current federal budget, but into the newly created Stabilization Fund, which was earmarked exclusively for payment of the state's external debt, including ahead of schedule. Spending it inside the country was prohibited. This law effectively brought to a halt any plans to redirect the oil rent into manufacturing, high-tech, and infrastructure. Though the government accumulated huge surpluses that could have been used for financing industries that needed it, this could not be done. The inertia of stagnation, discussed in Section 6.2, continued to exert its force without any perceptible weakening.

Overcoming that inertia will require radical changes in several areas of government economic policy. First of all, as noted in Chapter 5, the Stabilization Fund should be unfrozen, so that some of its resources may be used to develop the domestic economy, starting with major national investment projects in key manufacturing industries and economic infrastructure.

At the same time, there needs to be a steady reduction of the portion of petrodollars diverted into the Stabilization Fund. The government took a first step in that direction by raising, as of Jan. 1, 2006, the cut-off point (the level of oil export price, above which the relevant foreign currency revenue is put into the Stabilization Fund) from $20 per barrel to $27. The resultant increase of funds going into the regular federal budget will be $14 billion for the year as a whole, or almost 2 percent of GDP. This is a small, but not unimportant contribution to faster economic growth. The cut-off point ought to be raised still further in the future.

Minister of Finance Kudrin, one of the neo-liberal members of the cabinet, strongly opposed the decision to raise the cut-off point.

He and his allies believe that increased government spending will necessarily fan inflation. In their view, the influx of petrodollars into Russia is an inflationary factor, in and of itself, since it automatically increases the domestic money supply, creating excessive money demand that the economy is unable to absorb. According to them, the only way to deal with this inflationary influx is to isolate ("sterilize") the money in the Stabilization Fund and prohibit spending it inside the country.

There are several logical errors in this dogmatic neo-liberal line of argument.

Dollars that enter Russia only increase the domestic money supply when they are exchanged for rubles and deposited in Russian bank accounts. But far from all of the foreign currency earnings of Russian oil companies or other exporters returns to Russia. A significant portion remains abroad, where it is either spent or saved. Furthermore, the Bank of Russia does not automatically issue rubles to match its foreign currency reserves; currency emission occurs only to the extent that new rubles are needed to facilitate the circulation of goods and services and to effect money payments.

Finally, not all spending, and not all government spending, gives rise to inflationary pressures. If a country has excess production capacity, in a normal market economy any growth in money demand will be covered by a corresponding increase in supply, that is, by the additional production of goods and services. Under such conditions it is reasonable to expect even a *reduction* of prices due to economies of scale.

The point of principle is that if spending goes for capital investment in expanded production capacities, it will not, by definition, increase inflation. On the contrary, such investment may help reduce inflationary pressure over the long term. Investment in basic economic infrastructure works in the same way: building a modern highway network (which Russia so sorely lacks), installing modern communications systems, modernizing air transport, putting up new electric power transmission lines, building ports, etc. Such infrastructure development will obviously be accompanied by a growth of output in the industries that produce infrastructure components and equipment, and thus help to accelerate economic growth.

The government, which at present suffers from no lack of funds, but rather is regularly operating with budgets in surplus, is obliged to assume part of the responsibility for funding national investment programs. Such financing may take the form of long-term state credits, which would allow private companies to participate in such investment schemes. For this purpose the government and the private sector need to develop a comprehensive long-term economic development plan, for which adequate financing and material resources are allocated. Plans of this sort have been used with success in a number of countries with market economies, in order to boost economic growth. Indicative government plans of this kind are fully compatible with market principles.

Another pressing issue is how to ease the way for excess private capital to move from the oil and non-ferrous metals industries into manufacturing, particularly high-tech industries. Apart from creating additional government-run financial institutions such as specialized public development banks, to compensate for the underdeveloped private banking sector, the government should adopt special measures to promote the expansion of the capital market as a channel of capital flows into capital-deficit industries. More attention should be given to reforming the banking industry into a genuine public utility, and expanding the insurance business, mortgage and consumer credit, and various forms of mutual and other investment funds. When private capital is unwilling to invest adequately in these activities, the government should, at least on a temporary basis, set up its own institutions to close the gap.

The same is true of state-owned companies that could take the lead in developing competitive manufacturing industries, where private capital is slow and reluctant to do so. The automobile, aircraft, and computer industries come to mind. Mixed ownership could help to spur these largely dormant areas.

In this respect, there was a certain turn for the better in the very recent period. In the fall of 2005 Rosoboronexport, the state-owned armaments exporter, acquired a controlling stake in AvtoVAZ, Russia's largest car manufacturer, located in Togliatti, and then took over the truck producer KamAZ. Then, in January 2006, Boris Alyoshin, head of the Federal Industry Agency (Rosprom) proposed the merger of AvtoVAZ, KamAZ, and GAZ (in Nizhny Novgorod) into a single, state-controlled auto company. Alyoshin wants 5 billion rubles ($180 million) in state budget funds to be allocated for the modernization and development of these plants.

The plans of the new AvtoVAZ leadership go farther, according to reports. They intend to build a new auto plant in Togliatti with the capacity of producing 450,000 cars a year, which are to be new designs, developed in collaboration with foreign specialists. Since it is practically impossible to innovate using the existing manufacturing capacities, the new executives at AvtoVAZ believe that building a new plant is the only workable approach. They anticipate the first new cars coming off the line within two-and-a-half to three years. The existing lines at AvtoVAZ will also be modernized, effectively doubling total capacity. The needed investment will run into the billions of dollars, making government assistance indispensable. But without such spending, the company will be hard put to survive.

In February 2006, the Russian government decided to create a large aircraft-building corporation by merging half a dozen existing entities. Not all of the details of this project have been clarified. Past attempts to consolidate Russia's numerous aircraft factories and design bureaus have come to naught. Sukhoy and other leading firms in the industry fought for their independence. The multimillionaire Alexander Lebedev tried and failed to engineer such a merger. This time, however, President Putin's support could make the project happen.

The Russian government's indecisiveness in handling the stream of petrodollars entering the country is reminiscent of what happened with one of the Asian "tigers," South Korea. In 1961, it was a primarily agrarian country, with almost no modern industry. But the dictator Park Chung-hee, who came to power that year, decided to replicate in South Korea the successes of the Japanese zaibatsu, the large banking-industrial conglomerates, which launched the industrialization of Japan at the end of the 19th century. Park nationalized the banks, turning them into sources of financing for Korea's own conglomerates, the chaebols. He installed the country's most capable entrepreneurs to lead them, with the assignment of creating modern industries from scratch, in partnership with the state.

Lee Byung-chull, the founder of Samsung, began the production of color televisions, video equipment and other household electronics in South Korea, essentially from scratch. Another entrepreneur, Chung Ju-yung of Hyundai, carried out President Park's orders to found a modern ship-building industry, which could launch the biggest supertankers in the world. Another businessman, Kim Woo-choong, founded Daewoo, which was funded by the government to become one of the world's leading car manufacturers. For two decades, South Korea sustained annual growth rates of around 9 percent, largely because of what the chaebols were doing, and became one of the highest-ranking countries in the world in average per capita income, which reached $12,000 in 2003, or quadruple Russia's level.

Might South Korea's experience be of use for Russia? Indeed it might, if the government began to take an active part in the economy, if only in the form of Kremlin "chaebols." What is lacking for this to happen?

The first missing factor is a clear understanding on the President's part, that state financing and organizational leadership have to function as the main engine of economic growth, at least for a certain period of time. We need to give up the flawed monetarist dogma, according to which spending our petrodollars on productive investment will breed inflation. Money spent on the creation of new production capacities cannot cause inflation.

I have always advocated the creation of large manufacturing concerns in key Russian industries, since this would be the only type of entity, capable of generating competitive output by taking advantage of economies of scale in production for the domestic market, as well as for export. This is exactly what became the norm in the oil and raw materials industries. In manufacturing, however, the government is only now, belatedly and, so it would seem, grudgingly moving to create such concerns. But it is the right direction, and bolder action is in order.

Lastly, Russia clearly lacks innovative entrepreneurs who are capable of building new modern industries, instead of simply exploiting plant and equipment inherited from Soviet times. Or, rather, they exist, but they are stymied at every turn. So far, the Kremlin men are distinguished by their loyalty to the President, rather than by any great economic leadership capabilities. At least the defense people who have taken over AvtoVAZ are thinking on a grand scale. That is well and good, but it needs to be supplemented, as in South Korea, with government financial support. We have many capable airplane designers, but few genuine organizers, businessmen who would be able to make that unique capability commercially effective. Seeking and finding people with these rare talents is another priority for the President, his staff, and the government.

To date, the people promoted to the status of oligarchs by this regime have been either, in the worst cases, interested solely in lining their own pockets, or, at best, capable of staying afloat without allowing their businesses to fall apart. Now the need is to seek and find genuine creative entrepreneurial talent, as was the case in South Korea. Then things might pick up. At his January 2006 annual press conference, Putin confessed that he doesn't feel he has the talent to be a businessman and, therefore, would not want to head Gazprom when he leaves office in 2008. Of course, a head of state need not have such capabilities. The ability to distinguish talent from mediocrity in others, however, and the readiness to promote the former, are very desirable qualities in a President.

The billionaire Potanin said, in one of his TV interviews, that only a private property owner can succeed in business, because he has a personal interest in his company's success. I must beg to disagree. Over the past 100 years, capitalism in the USA and other industrially developed countries experienced the famous "managerial revolution," during which an array of successful managers emerged. In the majority of cases they, rather than the owners as such, are running the largest corporations in the world. A lot depends on the personal qualities of these businessmen. Of course, there are incompetent managers, who are capable of nothing more than "stripping" and looting their companies. At the same time, the ranks of property owners include not only clever financial operators, but talented innovators like Henry Ford, Sr. and Bill Gates.

Our Russian billionaires, as a rule, regrettably do not belong to this latter category. A few years ago, when Deripaska acquired control of GAZ and Mordashov took over the Ulyanovsk Auto Plant (UAZ), many people supposed that these major, successful businessmen would be able to revive the auto industry. But they did scarcely better than the former "red director" Kadannikov, who left AvtoVAZ semi-comatose, after a few years of running it in conjunction with the SOK group.

Active financial and organizational support from the government for the revival of stagnating manufacturing industries represents only one aspect of the constructive economic policy that needs to be adopted. Another essential area of an alternative economic policy would be the consistent improvement of macroeconomic

Table 6.10 Macroeconomic proportions in the USA, 1929-2005
(billions of $ in selected years, representing the high points of economic cycles)

	1929	1937	1948	1957	1966	1973	1981	1989	1999	2005
GDP	104	92	270	461	788	1,383	3,116	5,439	9,248	12,479
Labor income	51	48	142	258	443	813	1,828	3,152	5,332	7,119
As % of GDP	49%	52%	53%	56%	56%	59%	59%	58%	58%	57%
Personal consumption	78	67	175	287	482	852	1,941	3,595	6,255	8,746
As % of GDP	75%	73%	65%	62%	61%	62%	62%	66%	68%	70%
Ratio of personal consumption to labor income	1.53	1.39	1.23	1.11	1.09	1.05	1.06	1.14	1.17	1.23
Gross fixed capital investment	15	10	42	70	117	225	528	798	1,577	2,084
As % of GDP	14%	11%	16%	15%	15%	16%	17%	15%	17%	17%
Government purchases	9	13	41	100	174	288	633	1,085	1,629	2,360
As % of GDP	9%	14%	15%	22%	22%	21%	20%	20%	18%	19%
Net exports	0.4	0	5	4	2	1	−15	−80	−257	−726
As % of GDP	0%	0%	2%	1%	0%	0%	0%	−1%	−3%	−6%
Gross profit	46	35	108	165	283	455	1,056	1,897	3,226	4,513
As % of GDP	44%	38%	40%	36%	36%	33%	34%	35%	35%	36%
Ratio of fixed investment to gross profit	34	29	39	42	41	49	50	42	49	46

Sources: *National Income and Product Accounts of the United States, 1929-1994* (Washington: 1998), Vol. 1, pp. 1-54; *Economic Report of the President, 2000*, pp. 306-336; National Income Accounts, http://www.bea.gov/bea/dn1.htm, our calculations.

proportions, in order to achieve normal expansion of the domestic market and adequate overall economic growth. The comparison with the USA, illustrated in Table 6.6 above, shows the inordinately low share of labor income in the Russian economy. But the share of labor income in the USA was not always as high as it is today. For instance, Table 6.10 shows that it was only 49 percent of GDP in 1929, practically the same low level as in today's Russia. In the decades that followed, it increased to 58-59 percent, and has been oscillating around that level for the last 30 years. If such an improvement was possible in the typical market economy of the USA, it should be also possible in Russia, and does not represent any violation of market rules.

In the USA, this shift transpired as a result of major structural and institutional changes. Most of these occurred in the first two decades after World War II, largely under the administrations of the Democratic Party (Truman, Kennedy, and Johnson), which pursued reforms in the spirit of John Maynard Keynes and the welfare state. There was a substantial increase in the share of government purchases in GDP and a larger role of trade unions in determining wages. Consequently, the structure of domestic macroeconomic demand changed drastically.

In 1929, personal consumption accounted for 75 percent of final domestic demand, gross investment for 14 percent, and government purchases for only 9 percent. This structure is consistent with relatively low taxes, which represent no substantial deduction from either personal consumption demand or companies' resources for capital investment. In 1929, tax deductions accounted for only 2.7 percent of total personal income and 13.5 percent of corporate gross profit.

Big business in Russia today considers that to be an ideal macroeconomic structure. But that 1929 structure led to the Great Depression, in which consumption demand turned out to be grossly inadequate and the economy was helpless in the absence of government anti-cyclical policies and built-in automatic stabilizers. That lesson has been largely forgotten today, but it is worth recalling. Russia is not immune from depressions of the type the USA experienced 70 years ago.

Following World War II, American leaders were so apprehensive about a possible repetition of the Great Depression, that they drew the right conclusions. By 1957, the share of personal consumption in GDP had fallen to 62 percent, while government purchases rose to 22 percent, fully making up for the potential loss in aggregate demand, while gross investment remained practically unchanged at 15 percent. The new composition of final demand reflected the increased role of government as a factor of economic stability and was consistent with higher taxes. Tax deductions from personal income rose to 11.5 percent (on average), and taxes on corporate profit climbed to 48.7 percent. The personal tax increase of 8 percentage points "ate up" part of the consumer demand, but because labor income's share rose by 7 percentage points, from 49 to 56 percent of GDP, one compensated for the other. It is also noteworthy that a 3.5-fold increase in the corporate profit tax did not negatively affect the share of gross investment. In fact, business now spends nearly half its gross profit for capital investment, instead of only one-third, as was the case in 1929.

The rise in labor income peaked in 1981, by the end of the welfare state reforms. Thereafter the share of labor income began to decline, particularly as a result of Reaganomics and the neo-liberal dogma of minimizing the role of government. This turnaround marked the end of government cooperation with the trade unions, and the start of a more aggressive policy toward labor.

In 1929-1957, aggregate labor income rose at an average annual rate of 6 percent, faster than the 5.5 percent growth of nominal GDP. During that period, the unions succeeded in imposing the practice, according to which rising labor productivity, as well as consumer price inflation, should be matched by growth in money wages. This principle was recognized in collective bargaining agreements and, while it helped create a somewhat inflationary environment, it also promoted growth in aggregate demand and contributed to making recessions weaker and shorter.

Russian trade unions have very little impact on wages, so it is up to the government to correct this deficiency. An alternative income policy would need to include legislation to guarantee a more active role for labor, and faster growth of aggregate labor income compared to GDP for a substantial period of time. Russia could make use of the experience of indicative planning in France, where the government determined macroeconomic proportions, including the absolute and relative growth of labor income, in collaboration with the trade unions and industrialist associations.

Such a policy is likely to encounter strong opposition from big business, which tends to consider any rise in the share of labor income as a reduction in profit. But this is not necessarily true. Given proportions that guarantee rapid overall economic growth, profit tends to rise in absolute terms, even though its share in GDP may be reduced.

Another important point is to convince the business community that it has to separate the issue of reducing taxes from that of reducing government spending. Lower government spending will further reduce aggregate demand and slow economic growth. It will not necessarily free up more resources for capital investment.

Policy recommendations

To summarize, a minimum program of proposed measures can be formulated in the following few points:

- The state, as ultimate proprietor of the nation's mineral resources, should maintain effective control over an adequately large share of the natural rent and rechannel it via the government budget and private capital markets into chronically capital-deficient sectors of the economy.
- One of the basic principles of business tax policy should be to equalize profitability in the various sectors of the economy. Sectors with higher profitability should pay higher taxes.
- The government should retain its presence as owner and manager of businesses in those economic sectors where private capital is slow and unwilling to invest in modernizing and expanding competitive production. This should apply to key manufacturing industries, as well as to lagging areas of finance and other business infrastructure.
- State-owned and mixed companies should especially be promoted in sectors with a high potential to compete in foreign markets.
- Government income policy should center on jointly determining, with the trade unions and business associations, essential macroeconomic proportions that guarantee fast and stable economic growth. Particular atten-

tion should be paid to a carefully coordinated program of raising the share of labor income in GDP to about 60 percent of GDP and drastically reducing the relative size of impoverished and near-poverty income groups in the population.
- Implementing reforms of this type will naturally raise the question, sooner or later, of the destiny of capitalism in our economy. If the economic system to emerge from such reforms turns out to be clearly superior to oligarchical capitalism, the question will solve itself. In any event, the optimal relationship between capitalism and other forms of economic organization should be decided in the course of specific, practical competition between them, rather than on the basis of ideological debates. Practice, not ideology, should determine what is valid.

NOTES

1. NKh1988, p. 658.
2. Ibid., p. 5, and our calculations.
3. Ibid., p. 8.
4. RSY, 2001, Table 25.20; RET 2002, #10, Table 22.
5. NKh1988, p. 381, 637.
6. Ibid., pp. 647-48.
7. RSY 2000, pp. 582-83.
8. Ibid., Table 25.16; NKh1988, p. 637.
9. Calculated on the basis of RSY 2000, p. 578, 580.
10. RSY 2000, p. 332, 612-13.
11. "Svetloe budushchee rossiiskikh avtoliubitelei" ("A bright future for Russian car lovers"), Rbc.ru, June 6, 2001; "Chto khorosho dlia AvtoVAZa, khorosho dlia kogo?" ("What's good for AvtoVAZ is good for whom?"), Smi.ru, June 6, 2001; "Vladimir Putin: nel'zia mirit'sia s vypuskom avtomobilei vcherashnego dnia" ("Vladimir Putin: we can't accept production of yesteryear's cars"), Strana.ru, June 6, 2001.
12. "Aleksei Mordashov: pod egidoi gosudarstvennoi vlasti dogovarivat'sia proshche" ("Alexei Mordashov: it is simpler to reach agreement under government sponsorship"), Strana.ru, June 7, 2001.
13. *Moscow Tribune,* March 29, 2002.

14. Strana.ru, Aug. 23, 2001.

15. RSY 2000, p. 332, 454; our calculations.

16. Our calculations; RSY 2000, p. 249, 265-66, 594; our Table 6.5.

17. Our calculations, based on the *World Investment Report* (Geneva: UNCTAD, 1992 and 2002).

18. "Dolia riska" ("A Share of the Risk"), *Izvestia,* Feb. 12, 2003; "TNK prodana britantsam" ("TNK Sold to the British"), *Slovo,* Feb. 21, 2003; "Rynok ustal zhdat' informatsii ot BP" ("The Market Is Tired of Waiting for Information from BP"), Strana.ru, Feb. 11, 2003; "Krupnaia investitsiia BP pomozhet reformam Putina" ("Major Investment by BP Will Help Putin's Reforms"), Reuters, Feb. 10, 2003.

19. Gazprom.ru and MMNK.ru (site of the Moscow International Oil and Gas Club).

20. "Rost s dymkom" ("Smoking Growth"), *Izvestia,* Jan. 1, 2003.

21. RSY 2000, p. 547, 551, 594; Russian IOT, 1998-1999, p. 161; our calculations.

22. See UNCTAD *World Investment Report,* 2003, Annex Table B.4; our calculations.

23. Lukoil.com.ru.

24. Yukos.com.ru.

25. *Finansovye Izvestiia,* Feb. 28, 2002.

26. *Der Spiegel,* April 24, 2003.

27. *Izvestia,* Sept. 26, 2002.

28. *Vedomosti,* Dec. 6, 2001.

29. *Izvestia,* Nov. 22, 2002.

30. "Pioneer deal or Russian roulette? BP's Lord Browne is heading an oil rush into the East—but it's not without risk," *The Independent,* Feb. 12, 2003.

31. Sabrina Tavernese, "A Rocky Road Led to Big Russian Oil Deal," *The New York Times,* Feb. 19, 2003.

32. *Izvestia,* Jan. 16 and 23, 2003.

33. "MDM-bank prodaetsia inostrantsam" ("MDM Bank to be sold to foreign interests"), Gazeta.ru, March 15, 2003.

Glossary

Acronyms

ABM Treaty. Anti-Ballistic Missile Treaty.
AFK. Automobile Finance Corporation.
AIOC. Aluminum International Organization Company.
AME. Armaments and military equipment.
APK. Agro-promyshlennaya kompaniya, agro-industrial company.
AvtoVAZ. Volga Auto Plant.
AVVA. All-Russian Automobile Alliance.
BEA. Bureau of Economic Analysis.
BrAZ. Bratsk Aluminum Plant.
CIS. Commonwealth of Independent States.
DC. Defense complex; the military-industrial complex.
FGUP. Federalnoye gosudarstvennoye unitarnoye predpriyatiye, Federal State-owned Unitary Enterprise.
FPG. Finansovo-promyshlennaya gruppa, industrial financial group.
FSB. Federal Security Service.
GAZ. Gorky Auto Plant.
GKO. Gosudarstvennaya kratkosrochnaya obligatsiya, short-term government bond.
GLONASS. Global Orbital Satellite Navigation System.
GMK. Gornometallurgichesky kombinat or kompleks, mining and metallurgical works.
GOK. Gorno-obogatitelny kombinat, ore-processing combine.
IAPO. Irkutsk Aircraft Production Association.
INDEM. Information Science for Democracy Foundation.
IOT. Input-output tables.
KamAZ. Kama Auto Plant.

KMK. Kuznetsk Metallurgical Combine.
KrAZ. Krasnoyarsk Aluminum Plant.
KV. *Kommersant-vlast,* weekly magazine.
LOMO. Leningrad Optical Instrument Association.
MAPO. Moscow Aircraft Production Complex.
MFK. International Finance Company.
MIC. Military-industrial complex.
MIB. Interregional Investment Bank.
MK. Metallurgichesky kombinat, integrated iron-and-steel works.
MMK. Magnitogorsk Metallurgical Combine, "Magnitka."
MP. *Malye predpriiatiia, Small Businesses,* Goskomstat publication.
MPS. Ministerstvo putei soobshcheniya, Ministry of Railways.
MVD. Ministerstvo vnutrennykh del, Ministry of Internal Affairs.
MVZ. Mil Helicopter Factory.
NAS. National Accounts System, figures published in the series *Natsionalnyye scheta Rossii (National Accounts of Russia).*
NEP. New Economic Policy, Lenin's initiative of the early 1920s, which permitted limited free-market activity in Soviet Russia.
NGZ. Nikolayevsk Alumina Plant.
NII. Nauchno-issledovatelsky institut, scientific research institute.
NkAZ. Novokuznetsk Aluminum Plant.
NKh. Serial publication *Narodnoe Khoziastvo SSSR (The National Economy of the USSR).*
NLMK. Novolipetsk Metallurgical Combine.
NTMK. Nizhnetagil Metallurgical Combine.
NPK. New Programs and Conceptions.
NPO. Nauchno-proizvodstvennoye obyedineniye, science and production association.
OKB. Opytno-konstruktorskoye byuro, experimental design bureau.
OMON. Otryad militsii osobogo naznacheniya, national police special forces.
OMZ. United Machine-Building Factories, formed by Kakha Bendukidze on the basis of the Soviet-era machinery giant Uralmash.
OVK. Mutual Credit Societies, a retail banking network consolidated with Rosbank.
PMU. Puskovaya mobilnaya ustanovka, mobile launch unit.
RAO. Rossiyskaya aktsionernaya kompaniya, Russian Joint Stock

Company. The term designates a company accorded special national significance.
RET. *Russian Economic Trends*. In our notes, RET1 refers to the quarterly and RET2 to the monthly publication.
RTS. Russian Trading System, the country's main stock exchange.
RSY. *Russian Statistical Yearbook*.
RUIE. Russian Union of Industrialists and Entrepreneurs.
SaAZ. Sayansk Aluminum Plant.
SeAZ. Serpukhov Auto Plant.
SMC. Strategic Missile Corps.
SPS. Soyuz pravykh sil, Union of Right Forces political party.
SUAL. Siberian-Ural Aluminum Company.
TNC. Transnational corporations.
TNK. Tyumen Oil Company.
TWG. Trans-World Group.
UAZ. Ulyanovsk Auto Plant.
UES. Unified Energy Systems, the Russian national electric power company.
UGMK. Ural Mining and Metals Company.
UST. Unified social tax.
VSNK. East Siberian Oil and Gas Company.
ZIL. The Likhachov Factory, a famous Moscow auto plant.
ZSMK. West Siberia Metallurgical Combine, "Zapsib."

Other abbreviations, terms, and Russian words

Comecon. Short form of Council on Mutual Economic Assistance (CMEA), the economic bloc of the Soviet Union and its close allies in Eastern Europe and elsewhere. The term has Cold War overtones, but is better recognized than the acronym.
Goskomstat. Russian acronym for the State Statistics Committee. The agency was renamed the Federal Service for State Statistics in 2004. This book uses the traditional name and abbreviation.
Near Abroad. Countries that were formerly republics within the Soviet Union, and now are the Russian Federation's nearest neighbors.
Nomenklatura. The Soviet hierarchy of official positions, with attendant power and privileges.

Rosoboronexport. Russian Defense Exports, the state-owned exporter of weapons and military equipment, formerly called Rosvooruzheniye.

Rosvooruzheniye. Russian Armaments, reconstituted as Rosoboronexport in 2004.

Sberbank. Russia's state-owned savings bank.

Vneshtorgbank. Russia's Foreign Trade Bank, a state-owned institution.

Index

Some companies and other entities are indexed by acronym only, with expansions provided in the Glossary. Government institutions of the Russian Federation, as well as constituent territories of the RF and other major cities and regions, are listed under Russian Federation. Companies ending in "-energo" are electric power utilities.

ABM Treaty, 180
ABN AMRO Bank (The Netherlands), 60, 173
Abramov, Alexander, 102-3, 135, 150, 191, 195
Abramovich, Roman, xiv, 36n, 81-2, 96, 126, 133-5, 147, 150, 157, 166, 173, 187, 190-1, 193, 195, 199, 201, 344-5, 351-2, 364
Access Industries 80, 144-5, 150
Access/Renova, 80, 144-6, 149, 338, 345
Achinsk oil refinery, 77
Admiralty Shipyards, 123, 191
Aeroflot (airline), 61, 127, 133-4, 149, 187, 330-1
Aerospace Equipment (defense industry), 123
AFK (auto), 110, 195
Africa, 90
Agroprombank, 129
Agros project, 138-9, 141
AIOC (aluminum), 91-3

Aksyonenko, Nikolai, 174-5
Albright, Madeleine, 80
Alekperov, Vagit, 35n, 73, 75, 147, 149-50, 191, 199, 201
Alexandrov, Vladimir, 191
Alfa Bank, 59-60, 62, 126, 130-2, 136, 138, 144-6
Alfa-Eco, 112-3, 125-6, 146, 191
Alfa Group, 78-80, 93, 97, 101, 103, 105, 113, 125-6, 130, 136, 139, 144-50, 337-8, 345, 347
Alfa Telecom, 145-6
Al-Invest, 94
Alliance Group (oil), 154n
Almaz-Antey (defense industry), 187
Almaz NPO (defense industry), 123, 182, 230n
Almaz USA, 154n
Alrosa (diamonds), 191
Alyoshin, Boris, 366
Amoco (USA), 80, 339, 346
Angara Petrochemicals Company, 77-8

Anisimov, Vasili, 97
Antey (defense industry), 122-3, 191
Apatit (phosphates), 128, 141
Applied Mechanics NII (defense industry), 182, 230n
Arcelor (steel, Luxembourg), xxiii
Armenia, 344
Arzamas Machine-building Factory (defense industry), 121
Asahi Glass (Japan), 347
Ashurbeli, Igor, 230n
Asia, xxii, 100, 189, 367
Association of Expeditors, 175
Atlantic Richfield (USA), 339, 346
Australia, 344
Austria, 100
Aven, Pyotr, 78, 93, 125-6, 131, 136, 145
Avionika design bureau, 120
Avtobank, 60
Avtopilot magazine, 129
AvtoVAZ (auto), xiv, 61, 108-11, 127, 149-50, 155n, 188, 195, 328-30, 366-9
AVVA (auto), 109-10, 127, 195
Azerbaijan, 128, 342-3

Babayev (confectionary), 114-5, 126
Baikal-Amur Mainline (BAM), 173
Balaeskul, Vladimir, 150
Balkar Trading, 36n, 72-3
Baltic Bank, 174
Baltic Beverages Holding, 114
Baltic Construction Company, 174
Baltic Factory (shipbuilding), 120, 123, 183, 191
Baltic republics (later, states), 243, 344
Baltika (beer), 114, 194
Bank of Moscow, 60, 138
Bank of New York (BONY), 142
Bank of Russia (Central Bank), 12, 46-7, 65, 168, 187, 226, 291, 305, 307, 309-12, 365
Baranovsky, Yuri, 193
Baring (UK), 114
Basic Element (holding company), 96, 135, 137, 150
Bazhayev, Ziya, 79, 154n
Belarus, Republic of, 75, 193
Belgium, 37n, 75, 114
Bendukidze, Kakha, 35n, 44, 118, 150, 191
Benkov, Valeri, 191
Berezovsky, Boris, xiv, 35-6n, 81-2, 87, 96, 109-10, 125-7, 130, 132-4, 136, 147-8, 157, 164, 187, 189, 192
BHP Billiton (Australia), 347
Biolink Technologies (USA), 344
Blavatnik, Len, 144-5, 150
Bogdanchikov, Sergei, 191
Bogdanov, Vladimir, 74-5, 138, 150, 191, 195, 199, 201, 231n
Bolloyev, Taymuraz, 114, 194
Bolshakov, Alexei, 174
Bolshevichka (garment industry), 116
Bolshevik factory (confectionary), 114
Borodin, Pavel, 193
Borovik, Artyom, 79
Boyko, Maxim, 194
Boyko, Vasili, 91
BrAZ (aluminum), 90-3, 95-6, 154n
Brevnov, Boris, 163
British American Tobacco (BAT), 112
British Petroleum (BP, BP-Amoco), xxii, 45, 63, 78-80, 83, 139, 142, 145, 148, 217, 337-9, 345-6
Browne, John (Lord Browne), 346
Brudno, Mikhail, 143
Brunswick UBS Warburg, 119
Bulgaria, 343-4

Bulygin, Alexander, 196
Burnham, James, 15-6
Bush, George H. W., ix
Bush, George W., xxiii, 179
Bykov, Anatoli, 92-5, 152n, 194

Campina (The Netherlands), 115
Canada, 285, 320
Cargill (USA), 115
Carnegie Foundation, 252
Castro, Fidel, 137
Cayman Islands, 170
Central Asia, 91, 243
Chase Manhattan Bank, 57, 79, 152n
Chelsea Soccer Club, 134, 344
Cheney, Richard, 80
Cherepovets Metallurgical Combine (see Severstal)
Cherkizovsky (meat-packing), 115
Chernogorneft (oil), 78, 80
Chernomyrdin, Victor, 74, 87, 118, 161-3, 167-71, 183, 199, 231n, 279-80, 305
Chernoy brothers (Lev, Mikhail), 35n, 44, 91-7, 104-5, 154n
China, Peoples Republic of, xx-xxi, 116, 120, 122-3, 127, 179, 181, 183, 208, 221, 318-21, 325, 335, 337, 345, 351
Chineysk ore deposit, 173
Chubais, Anatoli, 87, 95-6, 98, 100, 122, 129, 136, 139, 163-6, 170, 188, 191-2, 194, 196-7, 228, 279-80, 284
Chung Ju-yung, 367
CIS, 318, 320, 323-4, 332, 343-4
Citibank, Citigroup, 60, 63
Clinton, William J., x-xi, 36n
Coase theorem, 153n
Coca-Cola (USA), 115
Comecon, ix-xi, 243, 265, 317, 319, 323, 344

Communist Party of the Russian Federation, 122, 132
Communist Party of the Soviet Union, 8, 49, 243
Conoco (USA), 45, 337
Corporation of Ferrous Metal Producers (Roschermet, steel), 98
Cuba, 77, 86-7, 127, 137
Cyprus, 79, 113, 122
Czech Republic, 344

Daewoo (Rep. of Korea), 368
Dalavia (airline), 331
Danone (France), 114-5, 347
Dart, Kenneth, 142
Delovaya Rossiya (Business Russia) association, 208
Dengi magazine, 129, 133, 189-90, 193-5
Denmark, 321
Deripaska, Oleg, 36n, 44, 94-7, 108-10, 121, 134-8, 147-50, 152n, 166, 190-1, 199, 201, 228, 329, 351, 369
Djilas, Milovan, 16
Domovoy magazine, 129
Donskoye Pivo (beer), 114
Dubinin, Mikhail, 150
Dubov, Vladimir, 143
Dukat (tobacco), 112
Dyakov, Anatoli, 162-3
Dybenko, Alexander, 75

Eastern Petroleum Company, 74, 77
East Siberian Oil and Gas Company (VSNK), 77
East-West United Bank, 168
EFKO Group (food), 115
Egypt, 343
Ekho Moskvy (radio), 128
Elgin coal deposit, 173

Energiya Corporation (aerospace), 146, 191
E.on Ruhrgas (Germany), 45, 340
Ernst, Konstantin, 191
Europe, xxii, 15, 19, 45, 95, 100, 179, 189, 344
   Eastern Europe, ix, 66, 243, 317-9, 323, 341-3
   Western Europe, ix, xi, 116, 167, 243, 285, 318, 321, 327-8, 346
European Bank for Reconstruction and Development, 100
European Union, 321, 323, 325
Expert magazine, 129, 138
ExxonMobil (USA), 63, 340

Fadeyev, Gennadi, 174, 176
Fain, Alexander, 191
Far East Shipping, 343
Federal Grid Company, 166
Fedulov, Pavel, 103
Fetisov, Gleb, 145
Finans magazine, 100, 106, 143, 200
Finland, 86
Fitom (holding company), 110
Fleming Family & Partners (UK), 344, 347
Fokker (The Netherlands), 345
Forbes magazine, 73-4, 143, 169, 199
Ford, Henry, 369
Ford Motor Company (USA), 108, 329
Forus (Switzerland), 109
Fradkov, Mikhail, 165, 279-81
France, 110, 112, 320, 327, 372
Fridman, Mikhail, 78-80, 93, 125-6, 131, 136, 145, 150, 190-1, 195, 199, 201, 228, 338-9, 347
Fukuyama, Francis, 1
Fyodorov, Alexei, 119

Gaidar, Yegor, 118, 126, 161, 167-8, 264, 279-80, 282, 284, 305

Galbraith, John Kenneth, xi, 228
Gallaher Group (UK, tobacco), 112
Gates, Bill, 369
GAZ (auto), 108-10, 121, 155n, 329, 366, 369
GAZ-Invest (holding company), 109
Gazprom (natural gas), xiv-xvi, xxii, 35-6n, 45, 61, 70, 83, 102, 132, 134, 138, 146-8, 152n, 161, 167-73, 186-8, 191-3, 196, 199, 230-1n, 340-1, 344-5, 354, 362, 369
Gazprombank, 60, 64, 138, 146-7, 188
Gazprominvestholding, 147, 191
Gazprom-media, 197
General Motors (USA), 329
Georgia, Republic of, 44, 118, 287
Gerashchenko, Victor, 309
Germany, xi, 45, 63-4, 115, 142, 152n, 320, 328, 345-6
Getty Oil (USA), 345
Giffen, James, 36n
Gilbertson, Brian, 347
Gini coefficient, 243-5
Gipronikel Institute, 86
GKO bonds, x, 51, 132, 292-3, 295, 308
Glencore (Switzerland), 93
Globex (bank), 60
Gloria Jeans Company, 116
Golden Telecom, 145
Goldman Sachs, xxiii
Goldovsky, Yakov, 172, 192-3
Golitsyn Bus Factory, 109
Goncharuk, Alexander, 150
Gorbachov, Mikhail S., 9, 15, 126, 291
Gosbank (Soviet), 64, 126, 306
Gosinkor Corporation, 119
Gosplan, 264
Great Depression (1930s), xxiv, 131, 371
Greece, 94

INDEX

Gref, German, xvi, xxiii, 281, 284, 301, 313
Group of Eight (G8), 320
Gusinsky, Vladimir, xiv, 35n, 87, 128, 130-3, 147, 170, 192
Guta Bank, 60, 187-8
Gutseriyev, Mikhail, 191, 193

Halliburton (USA), 80
Harvard Business School, 10, 36n, 144
Hay, Jonathan, 36n
High-Speed Railways (VSM), 174-5
Holcim (Switzerland), 347
Hungary, 94
Hyundai (Rep. of Korea), 367

IAPO, 119-20
IKEA (Sweden), 340
IlimPulp (pulp and paper), 149-50
Illarionov, Andrei, 165, 284, 301
Illingworth Morris (UK), 116
Ilyashenko, Valentin, 73
Imperial Bank, 168
INDEM Foundation, 222-5, 227
India, 120-1, 123, 179, 181, 325, 343
Ingosstrakh (insurance), 135
Inkombank, 114-5, 119-20, 126-7, 130-1, 147
Institute of World Economy and International Relations (IMEMO), 319
Interbrew (Belgium), 114
International Bank for Reconstruction and Development (World Bank), 149-51, 167, 245, 279
International Finance Company (MFK), 78, 128
International Monetary Fund, 167, 279, 291-2, 308, 314
International Moscow Bank, 60
International Space Station, 182

Interregional Investment Bank (MIB), 118-20, 156n
Interros (holding company), 78, 80, 87-8, 105-6, 119-21, 129, 131, 138-9, 141, 150
Investment Bank and Trust, 60
Iraq, 155n, 343
Ishayev, Victor, 183
IST Group, 120-1
Italy, 115, 320
Itera (natural gas), 147, 169, 171, 191
Itogi, 128
Ivanov, Sergei, 124, 180-1
Ivanov, Victor, 187
Izhmash-Avto (auto), 108
Izhora Works (*see Uralmash-Izhora*)
Izvestia, 129, 136, 138, 188

Janjgava, Givi, 156n
Japan, xi, 63-4, 112, 142, 152n, 189, 318, 320-1, 324, 327-8, 347, 351, 367
Japan Tobacco International, 112
Johnson, Lyndon B., 371
Jordan, Boris, 78, 105, 196

Kachkanar Mining and Ore-processing Combine, 101, 103
Kadannikov, Vladimir, 110, 150, 195, 369
Kagalovskaya, Natalya, 142
Kagalovsky, Konstantin, 143
Kaiser Aluminum (USA), 344
KamAZ (auto), xiv, 61, 366
Kanashi Auto Parts Plant, 109
Kantor, Oleg, 92
Kantupan (holding company), 79
Kapital (holding company, auto), 109
Kaskol (defense industry), 121
Kasyanov, Mikhail, 164, 183, 193, 195, 213, 226, 279-81, 300-1

Kazakstan, 36n, 93, 95, 343
Kazitsin, Andrei, 150
Kennedy, John F., xi, 371
Keynes, John Maynard, 371
Khaidarov, Jalol, 103
Khakamada, Irina, 208
Khan, German, 145, 150
Khloponin, Alexander, 88
Khodorkovsky, Mikhail, xiii-xiv, 36n, 76-7, 82, 116, 121, 127-8, 130-1, 136, 140-4, 147, 150, 154n, 166, 190-2, 195, 199, 229, 281, 339, 343-4, 364
Khristenko, Victor, 104, 123, 183
Khrunichev State Research and Production Space Center, 191
Kim Woo-choong, 367-8
Kiriyenko, Sergei, 279
Kislyak, Mikhail, 102
Klebanov, Ilya, 118-9, 183, 330
Klishas, Andrei, 106, 139-40
KMK (steel), 101-3, 155n
Kokh, Alfred, 87
Kola Mining and Smelting Company (non-ferrous metals), 88
Kolibri (meat-packing), 115
Kolpakov, Serafim, 98
Kolpakov, Yuri, 91-2
Kommersant, 129, 133-4
Komsomol (Soviet Communist Youth League), 126-7
Komsomolskaya Pravda, 129, 136, 138
Komsomolsk-on-Amur Aircraft Factory, 120, 183
Komsomolsk-on-Amur Shipbuilding Factory, 123
Konversbank, 147
Korea, Republic of, 189, 208, 367-9
Koshits, Yevgeni, 172
Kotz, David, 21-2
Krasnoyarsk Airlines, 331

Krasnoyarsk Combine Factory, 73
Krasnoyarsk Non-Ferrous Metals Processing Plant, 86, 88
Krasnoye Sormovo (shipbuilding), 118, 123
KrAZ (aluminum), 90-7, 154n, 194
Krazpa Metals (aluminum), 93
Kredobank, 101
Kremlin oligarchical group, xv-xvi, xviii, 83, 110, 144, 173, 184, 188, 229, 281, 354-5, 362, 364, 368
Kress, Victor, 165
Kristall Factory (beverages), 113
Kudrin, Alexei, xvi, 164-5, 281, 284, 364-5
Kukes, Simon, 80, 194-5
Kukura, Sergei, 150
Kurgan Bus Factory, 109
Kurganmashzavod (defense industry), 121, 123
Kuybyshevnefteorgsintez (Samara refinery, oil), 75-6, 154n
Kuzbassenergo, 96
Kuzbassugol (coal), 104
Kuzmichev, Alexei, 145
Kuzmin, Anatoli, 154n
Kuzyk, Boris, 194
Kyantrishvili, Otari, 76
Kyrgyzstan, 287

LaRouche, Lyndon H., Jr., xix, xxiv
Lazarenko, Pavlo, 226
Lebed, Alexander, 94
Lebedev, Alexander, 367
Lebedev, Platon, 77, 128, 143, 150
Lebedinsk GOK (mining), 147
Lee Byung-chull, 367
Lenin, Vladimir I., xx, 3, 5, 19, 350
Leningrad Institute of Economics and Engineering, 100
Libya, 155n, 343
Likin Bus Factory, 109

Lisichanskneftegorgsintez (oil and gas), 80
Lisin, Vladimir, 94, 105-6, 149-50, 191, 193, 201
Literaturnaya gazeta, 128
Lithuania, 343
Loans-for-shares (*see Privatization*)
LogoVAZ, 96, 109, 127
LOMO (defense industry), 119, 129, 138
Lomonosov Porcelain Factory, 116
London Metals Exchange, 90, 154n
Lopukhin, Vladimir, 161-2
Lopukhin, Yuri, 99
Louis Dreyfus Group, 139
Lukoil (oil), 35n, 45, 61-2, 73-5, 79, 82-3, 145-50, 196, 337, 342-3, 345
Luxembourg, xxiii, 168
Luzhkov, Yuri, 110, 132

Maddison, Angus, 318-9, 321
Maganov, Ravil, 150, 196
Makarov, Igor, 169
Makhmudov, Iskander, 102-4, 135, 150, 155n, 191
Mamut, Alexander, 58-9, 136, 152n
Mandel, Ernest, 37n
MAPO (defense industry), 122
Mars (USA), 114
Marx, Karl, 5, 14, 21
Masharin, Victor, 75-6
Maslyukov, Yuri, 122, 183
MDM Bank, MDM Group, 58-60, 135-8, 141, 147-50, 166, 351-2
Mechel (mining and metals), 149-50
Media-Most (*see Most Group*)
Medium- and Small-Tonnage Shipbuilding Concern, 123
Medvedev, Alexander (of Khrunichev), 191
Medvedev, Dmitri, 171-2, 187

Megionneftegaz (oil and gas), 62, 146
Melamed, Leonid, 196
Melnichenko, Alexander, 135-6, 150
Melnikov, Vladimir, 116
Menatep, Bank, 76, 127, 130-1, 136, 140-2, 154n
Menatep, Group, 77, 140, 142-3
Menatep-Impex, 77
Metalloinvest, 149-50
Mezentsev, Alexander, 182, 230n
Mezhprombank, 60, 193-4, 354
MiG (defense industry), 122-3
Mikom, 95, 102
Mikrodin (trading), 44
Mil Helicopter Factor (MVZ), 118, 123
Miller, Alexei, 171-2, 187, 191-3, 228, 231n, 354
Millhouse Capital, 134, 150
MMK, Magnitka (steel), 98-9, 103-4, 126, 150, 195
Mobil Oil (USA), 73
Monaco, 154n
Mordashov, Alexei, xxiii, 99-101, 108-9, 149-50, 155n, 190-1, 201, 329, 369
Moscow City Telephone Network, 61
Moscow Financial Institute, 140
Moscow State University, 1, 95
The Moscow Times, 128
Mosenergo, 61
Moskva-3 cooperative, 129
Moskvich (auto), 108, 110, 155n
Most Bank, 130-2
Most Group (holding company), Media-Most, 128, 132-3, 170, 192
Mutual Credit Societies (OVK), 138-9, 141

National Projects, 287-8, 303
National Reserve Bank, 60, 146-7, 163, 166
Nazdratenko, Yevgeni, 165
Neftesam (oil), 75-6, 154n
Nemtsov, Boris, 139, 163, 170
Nestlé (Switzerland), 114
The Netherlands, 285, 321, 345
Nevzlin, Leonid, 143
New Economic Policy, 6, 20-1
New Holding (holding company), 79
New Programs and Conceptions (NPK) (holding company), 121, 138, 194
New York Stock Exchange, 89, 145
Nezavisimaya Gazeta, 127, 133
NGZ (aluminum), 95-6
Nizhnevartovskneftegaz (oil and gas), 79
NkAZ (aluminum), 90, 92, 94-6
NLMK (steel), 98-9, 104-6, 129, 138, 149-50, 193
Norilsk Mining and Ore-enriching Combine, 86
Norilsk Mining Company (non-ferrous metals), 61, 88-9, 154n
Norilsk Nickel (non-ferrous metals), 36n, 61, 71, 86-9, 105, 129, 137-8, 140-1, 154n, 344-5
Norimet (non-ferrous metals), 88-9, 154n
Norval, Chris, 347
Nosta Pipe Mill, 126
Novaya Gazeta, 128
Novitsky, Yevgeni, 150
Novoship (shipping), 343
Novosibirsk Aircraft Factory, 120
Novyye Izvestia, 133-4
Noyabrskneftegaz (oil and gas), 81
NTMK (steel), 101-3, 105
NTV (television), xiv, 128, 132, 170, 188, 197

Oboronitelnyye sistemy (Defense Systems), 122-3
Obshchaya gazeta, 128
Ochakovo (beer), 114
Ogaryov, Alexei, 191
Ogonyok, 127
Oktyabrskaya Railroad, 174
Olenogorsk Machine Works, 86
Olivest (oil), 82
Olympic Bank, 146
OMON, 113
Omsk Petroleum Refinery, 81
OMZ (*see Uralmash-Izhora Group*)
Onaco (oil), 74, 80-1
Oneximbank, 87-8, 118-21, 128-31, 136, 138, 140
Oppenheimer (USA), 119
Orenburgneft (oil), 81
Organization of Petroleum Exporting Countries (OPEC), 33
ORT / Channel 1 (television), xiv, 126-8, 133, 187, 191-2
Orwell, George, 16
Oskol Metallurgical Combine, 147
OST (beverages), 112
Otchertsev, Valeri, 191
Owen, David (Lord Owen), 343

Paris Commune factory (textiles), 116
Park Chung-hee, 367
Parmalat (Italy), 115
Paulson, Henry, xxiii
Pavlovsk Bus Factory, 109
Pechenganikel (nickel), 86
Pension Fund, 298, 302
PepsiCo (USA), 115
Perm Motors, 129, 138
Pernod Ricard (France), 112
Petrokommerts (bank), 60, 145-6
Petrosoyuz (food), 115
Petroleum Finance Company (NFK), 81, 127

Philip Morris (USA), 112
Philips Electronics (The
   Netherlands), 100
Philips Petroleum (USA), 80
Plastinin, Sergei, 150
Pogosian, Mikhail, 119-20, 191
Poland, 343-4
Popov, Sergei, 136, 150
Port of Odessa, 76
Portugal, 321
Potanin, Vladimir, 36n, 44, 78-80,
   85, 87-9, 105-6, 119-20, 128-31,
   136-41, 144, 147-50, 166, 188,
   190-1, 199, 201, 369
Pozner, Vladimir, 222
Prikhodko, Sergei, 187
Prima (tobacco), 112
Primakov, Yevgeni, xiv, 117, 122,
   132-3, 163-4, 176, 183, 279, 287,
   308-9
Prime-TASS (media), 138
Primorskoye Shipping, 343
Privatization, xiii, xix, xxi, 5-6, 9-11,
   36n, 39-45, 49, 64, 65-71, 77, 80,
   85-7, 90-1, 94, 97-9, 101, 109,
   116-8, 132, 137, 157, 161, 163,
   167-9, 173, 175, 184, 189, 282-4,
   330
   Loans-for-shares, 9, 78, 87-8, 98-9,
      101, 119, 129
   Voucher auctions, xiii, 9, 67, 86,
      90-1, 99, 105, 109, 118, 162, 168
Prof-Media, 138, 141
Prokhorov, Mikhail, 140, 150, 201
Promstroybank, 120
Promsvyazbank, 64
Pugachov, Sergei, 193
Pumpyansky, Dmitri, 150
Purgaz (natural gas), 171
Putin, Vladimir V., ix, xiii-xvi, 1, 7,
   82-3, 87, 104, 113, 117, 121,
   124, 132-4, 136-8, 144, 163, 165,
   171-2, 176, 178, 183, 187-8, 191-
3, 202, 208-9, 222, 249, 279-81,
284, 287, 295, 299-303, 309-10,
314-5, 321, 324, 327, 329, 340,
353-4, 360, 364, 367-9

Queensland Alumina (Australia),
   344

Raiffeisenbank, 60
Ramen Instrument-making Design
   Bureau (defense industry), 156n
Rashnikov, Victor, 104, 150, 195
Razgulyay-Ukros (food), 115
Reagan, Ronald, 279, 372
Red October (confectionary), 114-5
Refine Oil, 81
Regent Gaz Investment Company,
   170
Renaissance Capital, 129
Renault (France), 110
Renova, 80, 96-7, 144-5, 150
Ren TV, 164
Rich, Marc, 36n, 91, 93
Rimashevskaya, Natalya, 251
RJR International, 112
Romania, 343-4
Rona-Tas, Akos, 252
Roosevelt, Franklin D., xi-xii
Rosbank, 60, 136, 138-9, 141
Rosenergoatom, 231n
RosLada (auto), 108
Rosneft (oil), xiv, xxii, 74, 78, 83,
   135, 143, 172-3, 187-8, 191, 341,
   345, 362
Rosoboronexport (arms exports),
   xiv, 110, 121-2, 183, 187-8, 366
Rospan (natural gas), 171
Rosprom (I, holding company),
   116, 121, 128, 140-1
Rosprom (II, *see Russian
   Federation, Government,
   Ministry of Industry and
   Energy*)

Rossel, Eduard, 102
Rosspirtprom (beverages), 112-3
Rostelecom, 61
Rostextil (holding company), 116
Rosvagonmash (rail), 173
Rostvertol (defense industry), 121, 123
Rosvooruzheniye (arms exports), 121-2, 183, 191-2
Rot Front (confectionary), 114-5
Rouge Industries (USA), 344
Royal Dutch Shell, 64, 217
RTR (television), 187
Rubin Design Bureau (defense industry), 123
Ruhrgas (*see E.on Ruhrgas*)
Rusargo (food), 115
RusElCo (food), 139
Rusia Petroleum, 138, 145, 338, 346
Ruspromavto (auto), 108-9, 135, 137
Russian Academy of Sciences, 36n, 165, 251
Russian Aluminum (Rusal), 36n, 71, 96-7, 109, 121, 134, 137, 155n, 196, 344
Russian Civil War, 6, 19
Russian Commodities and Raw Materials Exchange, 102
Russian Credit Bank, 93, 119
Russian Federation
  Constituent territories (including cities in them of the same name)
    Altay Territory, 112
    Chechnya, 127, 132, 154n
    Chelyabinsk Region, 104
    Chukotka, 134
    Ivanovo Region, 250
    Kaliningrad, 108
    Kalmykia, 82
    Kemerovo Region, 95-6, 102, 155n
    Khabarovsk Territory, 183
    Khakazia, 77
    Krasnodar Territory, 112, 114
    Krasnoyarsk Territory, 86, 88, 94
      Taymyr Autonomous District, 86, 88
    Leningrad Region, 74, 250
    Moscow, 44, 76, 79, 87-8, 104-6, 110, 112-3, 116, 118, 127-9, 133, 149, 155n, 174, 194, 250-1, 352
    Moscow Region, 250
    Murmansk Region, 250, 351
    Nizhny Novgorod Region, 118, 121, 155n, 250, 366
    Novosibirsk Region, 77
    Omsk Region, 114, 123
    Penza Region, 114
    Primorsky Territory, 165
    Ryazan Region, 79-80, 250-1
    Sakhalin Region, 337
    Samara Region, 75-6
    St. Petersburg, xv, 78, 86, 112, 114, 116, 120, 128, 140, 171, 174, 176, 183, 193, 250, 354
    Saratov Region, 78, 112
    Sverdlovsk Region, 102
    Tatarstan, 149
    Tomsk Region, 77, 165
    Tyumen Region, 79-80, 92, 250
      Yamal-Nenets Autonomous District, 168, 171
    Ulyanovsk Region, 108, 155n, 250-1
    Voronezh Region, 250-1
    Yaroslavl, 109, 128
  Federal Assembly, xiii, 202, 360
    Federation Council, 226
    State Duma, 88, 133-4, 165, 291-2

INDEX 391

Russian Federation, *continued*
  Government, xiii, xxi, 14, 37n, 80, 83, 87, 104, 117-9, 124, 126-7, 129, 132, 134, 136, 157, 159, 161, 164, 166, 170-4, 178-9, 181, 183, 187, 191, 193, 202, 208-9, 218, 221-3, 226, 229, 279-83, 286, 291-2, 294-5, 301-3, 307-11, 314-5, 324, 327-8, 345, 349, 353-7, 360, 362-7, 369, 373
  Accounting Chamber, 217
  Central Bank (*see Bank of Russia*)
  Committee on Metallurgy, 92
  Federal Currency and Export Control Service, 91-2
  Federal Energy Commission, 159
  Federal Market and Securities Commission, 88
  Federal Security Service (FSB), 193
  Ministry of Agriculture, 113
  Ministry of Defense, 117-8, 124, 127, 164, 176-82, 222, 226, 230n, 260, 331-2
  Ministry of Economic Development and Trade (since 2000), 38n
  Ministry of Economics (to 2000), 22-3, 38n, 122, 229n
  Ministry of Finance, 128-9, 226, 313
  Ministry of Fuel and Energy (to 2000), 75-6, 154n, 161
  Ministry of Industry and Energy (since 2004), 122-4, 183
    Federal Industry Agency (Rosprom), 124, 183, 366
  Ministry of Industry, Science and Technologies (2000-2004), 122-3, 329
  Ministry of Internal Affairs (MVD), 92-3, 127, 260
  Ministry of Nature, 91
  Ministry of Railways (MPS), 159, 173-5
  Presidential (Kremlin) Administration, 37n, 73, 82, 133-4, 136, 144, 151, 166, 171-3, 179, 187, 192, 222, 369
  Prosecutor General's Office, xiv, 37n, 87, 219
  State Council, 165, 209
  State Customs Committee, 127
  State Property Committee, 78, 87, 98, 168
  State Statistics Committee (Goskomstat), 8, 24, 26-7, 38, 205, 211-3, 215, 219-20, 225, 232n, 235-6, 240, 245, 260, 271, 278n, 300, 319, 321, 333, 361
Other cities and areas
  Cherepovets, 100
  Far East, 165, 250
  Izhevsk, 108
  Klin, 114
  Kuzbass area, 95-6, 102
  Magnitogorsk, 104
  Monchegorsk, 86
  Nakhodka, 351
  Nefteyugansk, 75
  Nizhnevartovsk, 73
  Nizhny Tagil, 102-3, 123
  Norilsk, 88
  Pechenga, 86
  Rostov-on-Don, 114, 116
  Sayanogorsk, 95
  Serpukhov, 108, 155n
  Siberia, 36n, 44, 73, 76, 79, 121, 135, 149, 250, 322, 339, 344
  Surgut, 73, 75
  Syzran, 108

Russian Federation, *continued*
    Togliatti, 155n, 328, 330, 366-7
    Ural area, 96, 102-3, 135
    Yamal, 171
    Yekaterinburg, 44, 128
Russian Metallurgical Company (steel), 105
Russian Metallurgy (steel), 98
Russian Railways, 175
Russian Revolution of 1905, 19
Russian Revolution of October 1917, 4, 19, 113
Russian Socialist Federation of Soviet Republics (RSFSR), 69
Russian State Service Academy, 221
Russian Steel, 105
Russian Trading System (RTS) index, xxiii, 51, 84, 199
Russian Union of Industrialists and Entrepreneurs (RUIE), 1, 58, 136, 175, 301-2, 312
Russky Telegraf, 129
Rust (beverages), 112-3
Rutskoy, Alexander, 76

SaAZ (aluminum), 90, 93-5
Samara Metallurgical Company (Sameco), 95, 126
Samara Neft (oil), 75
Samaraneftegaz (oil), 142
Samotlor oil field, 79-80
Samsung (Rep. of Korea), 367
San Capital, 114
San-Interbrew (beer), 114
Saratov oil refinery, 78
Satarov, Georgi, 222-3
Saturn (defense industry), 123
Saudi Arabia, 339
Savelyev, Vitali, 196
Sberbank, 58-60, 62, 64, 65, 80, 152n, 304, 309-10, 331
SBS-Agro Bank, 129-31

SeAZ (auto), 108, 155n
Sechin, Igor, 173, 187
Segodyna, 128
Sementsov, Vladimir, 92
Semibankirshchina (Reign of the Seven Bankers), 106, 125, 146, 148
Semyonov, Yuri, 191
Serov Ferroalloy Plant (steel), 101
Seven Days (publishing), 128
Severnaya Verf (Northern Shipyards), 120, 122-3, 138, 183, 191
Severonikel (nickel), 86
Severstal (steel), xxiii, 61, 98-101, 103-4, 108-9, 149-50, 344-5
Sevmash (defense industry), 123
Shakhnovsky, Vladimir, 143
Shepherd, Robert, 79
Sheremet, Vyacheslav, 169, 172
Shibitov, Andrei, 119
Shleifer, Andrei, 36n
Sholk (textiles), 116
Shtyrov, Vyacheslav, 191
Shulyakovsky, Oleg, 191
Shvidler, Yevgeni, 194-5
Siberian Aluminum (Sibal), 93, 95-6
Sibneft (oil), xiv, 36n, 61, 74, 77, 81-3, 89, 96-7, 126-7, 130, 133-4, 147, 150, 154, 173, 187-88, 193-4, 362
Sibneft Oil Trade, 217
Sibur (petrochemicals), 121, 171-2, 192-3
Sidanco (oil), 74, 78-81, 85, 88, 129, 139, 145, 154n, 337-8, 346
Silovyye Mashiny (Power Machines), 138, 141
Simonov, Mikhail, 119-20
Simonov, Valeri, 191
Sins (holding company), 81
Sistema (IT), 149-50, 191
Skuratov, Yuri, 87

Slavneft (oil), 74, 80, 154n, 191, 193-4, 217-8, 232n, 354
Slavneft-Belgium, 217
Slovakia, 343-4
Smirnoff vodka, 113-4
Smirnov, Boris, 113
P.A. Smirnov and Descendants (beverages), 113, 145
Smolensky, Alexander, 129-31, 147
Smushkin, Zakhar, 150
Sobinbank, 60, 145-6
Sobitex (textiles), 116
Soglasiye Insurance Company, 138-9, 141
SOK Group, 369
Sokol Aircraft Plant (defense industry), 121, 123, 126
Soros, George, 79, 139, 144
Soskovets, Oleg, 91-2, 98-9, 162
South Africa, Republic of, 142, 347
South America, 90
Soviet Union (*see Union of Soviet Socialist Republics*)
Soyuz Bank, 135, 137
Soyuzkontrakt, 120
Soyuzmetalresurs (mining and machine-building), 135
Splav Science and Production Enterprise (defense industry), 123
Sputnik (investment fund), 105
Stabilization Fund, 302-3, 364-5
Stalin, Joseph, 20
Stillwater Mining (USA), 344-5
Stolichny Savings Bank (see SBS-Agro)
Stolitsa magazine, 129
Stolypin, Pyotr, 19
SUAL (aluminum), 96-7, 144, 146, 155n, 344, 347
Sukhanov, Yuri, 193
Sukhoy (defense industry: aircraft), 119-20, 122-3, 138, 183, 191, 367

Surgutneftegaz (oil and gas), 61, 74-5, 79, 83, 138, 141, 149-50, 195
Surgutneftegazbank, 74, 141
Surgutneftestroy, 74
Surkov, Vladislav, 187
Svet (holding company), 76
Svyazinvest (telecommunications), 129, 139
Sweden, 243, 285, 340
Switzerland, 36n, 76, 91, 93, 109, 324, 347

Tabakprom (tobacco), 112
Taganrog Scientific-Technical Aviation Complex, 119
Taiwan, 208
Takhaudinov, Shafagat, 150
Taopin brewery (beer), 114
Tarasov, Artyom, 72
Tariko, Rustam, 113
Tatarenkov, Vladimir, 94
Tatneft (oil), 84, 149-50
Tekhnokomplex (defense industry), 123, 156n
Tekhnosnabexport, 147
Tetraplast, 75
Thatcher, Margaret, 279
Timan bauxite deposit, 96
TNK (oil), xxii, 45, 74, 78-81, 97, 125-6, 144-5, 148, 193-4, 337-9, 346
TNK-BP (oil), 80, 83, 146, 338-9, 346
Tokaryov, Victor, 94
Tomskneft (oil), 77, 142
Transaero (airline), 331
Trans-CIS Commodities (non-ferrous metals), 94, 154n
Transkreditbank, 173
Transmash (defense industry), 123
Transnational Aluminum Company (Tanaco), 92

Transneft, 187, 191
Trans-World Group (TWG), 91-6, 104-5, 154n
Trotsky, Leon, 15-6, 37n
Truman, Harry S, 371
Trust and Investment Bank (Trast), 140
Tryokhgornaya Manufaktura (textiles), 116
TsEPKO (holding company), 114
Tula Arms Factory (defense industry), 122
Tuleyev, Aman, 95-6, 102
Turkey, 116, 221, 343
Turkmenistan, 169
Turushev, Mikhail, 91
TV-6 (television), 126-7, 134, 164, 192
Tyumen Aviation Group, 79
Tyumenneftegaz (oil and gas), 79

UAZ (auto), 101, 108-9, 155n, 369
UES (electric power), 61, 70, 95-6, 136, 152n, 162-8, 172, 188, 191-2, 196-8, 230n
UGMK (steel), 101, 103, 149-50, 155n
Ukraine, 76, 80, 95, 114, 134, 169, 171, 226, 287, 343-4
Unilever (The Netherlands, UK), 115
Union of Right Forces (SPS), 163-4
Union of Soviet Socialist Republics (USSR), ix-xi, xiii, xx, 6-9, 15-6, 32-3, 36n, 39, 42-3, 49, 64-7, 69, 75, 85, 89, 94, 98, 113, 115-8, 124, 126, 138, 152n, 155n, 157, 167, 173, 176-8, 180, 189, 208-9, 217, 235, 237, 240-4, 247, 249, 253, 255, 258, 260, 265, 274-5, 279-80, 285, 290-1, 306, 317-24, 328, 330, 332, 344, 368
United Bank, 109, 127, 130
United Kingdom of Great Britain, xxii, 63-4, 82, 105, 112, 116, 134, 144, 152n, 154n, 279, 320, 343-4, 347-8
United States of America, ix-xi, xvii-xviii, xxiv, 15, 19, 25, 31, 36-7n, 55, 63-4, 79-80, 89, 93, 97, 100, 112, 115-6, 118-9, 125, 131, 135, 142-4, 152n, 154n, 166, 169, 178-80, 182, 189, 196, 206-8, 216, 226-8, 240-1, 253, 260, 267-8, 279, 285, 311, 315, 318-20, 323, 327-8, 337, 343-5, 348, 351, 357-8, 369-71
  Central Intelligence Agency, 169
  Democratic Party, 371
  Department of State, 80
  Ex-Im Bank, 79
  Federal Bureau of Investigation, 226
Uralmash-Izhora, Uralmashzavod, OMZ (machine-building), 35n, 44, 61, 100, 118, 150, 191, 344
Uralvagonzavod (defense industry), 123
Urengoy gas field, 171
Urinson, Yakov, 122, 164
Uritsky Factory (tobacco), 112
Usmanov, Alisher, 191
Uzbekistan, 72, 155n

Vainshtok, Semyon, 191
Vaknin, Sam, 252
Vasilyev, Vladimir, 76
Vavilov, Andrei, 226
Veba Oil (Germany), 346
Veblen, Thorstein, 227
Vekselberg, Victor, 91, 96-7, 144-5, 150, 166, 190-1, 201, 228, 338-9, 347
Venezuela, 93
Vester (oil), 82
Video International, 194

Vinogradov, Vladimir, 126, 130-1
Vinoram (beverages), 113
Vishnevsky, Igor, 93
Vladimir Tractor Factory, 36n, 144
Vneshtorgbank, 59-60, 64, 80, 110, 187-88, 331
Volga Motors (auto), 109
Volga Pipe Factory, 141
Volkswagen (Germany), 329
Voloshin, Alexander, 166
Vyakhirev, Rem, 35n, 168-72, 191-3, 199, 231n, 354
Vyakhirev, Yuri, 171
Vympelcom (telecommunications), 145
Wimm-Bill-Dann (food), 114-5, 150, 191
World Jewish Congress, 132
World War I, 4, 6
World War II, xii, 371

Yafyasov, Vadim, 92-3
Yakoboshvili, David, 150, 191
Yakovlev, Yuri, 231n
Yakunin, Vladimir, 176
Yanovsky, Kirill, 150
Yava (tobacco), 112
Yedinaya Rossiya (United Russia) Party, xiv
Yedinstvo (Unity) Party, xiv, 133
Yeltsin, Boris, xiii, 16, 40, 76, 91, 98, 132-3, 157, 168, 170, 176, 183, 208, 222, 279-80, 300, 353-4
Yeltsin "Family," 133, 280, 353
Yerevan Cognac Factory, 112

Yevrazholding (steel), 101, 103-5, 134-5, 150, 155n, 195, 345
Yevrofinans (bank), 60
Yevrosib (transport), 174
Yevrosibenergo, 135, 137
Yevtushenkov, Vladimir, 149-50, 191, 201
Yuganskneftegaz (oil), xiv, 75, 77, 142-3, 172, 187-88
Yugorsky Bank, 92-3
Yug Rossii (food), 115
Yukos (oil), xiii-xiv, 36n, 49, 51, 61, 74-9, 81-4, 128, 131, 134, 140-3, 145, 150-1, 154n, 172, 187, 190, 192, 229, 340, 343, 354, 362
Yunco (oil), 154n
Yuzhno-Russkoye gas field, 171
Yuzhuralnikel (non-ferrous metals), 86

Zaitsev, Anatoli, 174
Zalog Bank, 93, 95
Zapsib, ZSMK (steel), 99, 101-3
Zavolzhsky Engine Plant, 101, 109
ZhASO (insurance), 173
Zhivilo, Mikhail, 92-3, 95-6, 102, 194
ZIL (auto), 44, 129
Zingarevich, Boris, 150
Zmeinogorsk Liqueur and Spirits Factory, 112
Zubov, Valeri, 88
Zurabov, Mikhail, 281
Zyuganov, Gennadi, 132
Zyuzin, Igor, 150

About the Author

The economist Professor Stanislav Menshikov is one of Russia's leading experts on the United States, as well as on Russia's own economy. He draws on over half a century of research and experience in both countries. After teaching at the Moscow Institute of International Relations in the 1950s, Dr. Menshikov worked at the Institute of World Economy and International Relations (IMEMO) of the Soviet Academy of Sciences, and the Institute of Economics and Industrial Organization, which is affiliated with the Siberian branch of the Academy. In the1970s and 1980s, he headed Economic Projections at the United Nations in New York and was a consultant to the Communist Party Central Committee in Moscow. He has taught at Moscow State University, Novosibirsk State University, Tinbergen Institute and Erasmus University in Rotterdam, and the University of Aalborg, Denmark. Since 1997, he has co-chaired ECAAR-Russia, the Russian branch of Economists Allied for Arms Reduction.

Professor Menshikov's books about the American economy, and U.S. political tendencies and factions, provided a differentiated picture that was unusual during the Cold War. Among them were *U.S. Corporations in World Markets* (1958), *Millionaires and Managers* (1966), and *The Economic Cycle* (1975). Toward the end of the Soviet period, the book *Capitalism, Communism, Coexistence* (1988) appeared, comprising a series of conversations between Menshikov and his longtime friend and professional associate, the late John Kenneth Galbraith.

During the past fifteen years, Dr. Menshikov turned his keen eye to developments within Russia, and its relationship with the globalized economy, in *Catastrophe or Catharsis? The Soviet Econ-*

omy Today (1990, 1991), and *The Russian Economy: Practical and Theoretical Aspects of Transition to a Market Economy* (1996). His columns in the *Moscow Tribune* and *Slovo* weekly are read eagerly by people who want to understand what is happening in Russia.

Professor Angus Maddison of the University of Groningen (The Netherlands) and the University of Brisbane (Australia) writes, "*The Anatomy of Russian Capitalism* is the latest of many books by Stanislav Menshikov, and the fifth to be translated into English. He is the most cosmopolitan of Russian economists, with an insider view of the old style command economy and the problems of transition. He has a comparative perspective gained by nearly fifty years scrutinizing the performance of Western capitalist economies. In the 1960s, when I first met him, he was the leader of a brilliant team of Americanologists at the Institute of World Economy in Moscow. In the 1970s, he was Director of Planning and Projections in the UN Secretariat in New York, where he interacted closely with leading American economists, including Nobel laureate Lawrence Klein and John Kenneth Galbraith. In the 1980s, he was a high official in the International Affairs Department of the Party secretariat in the Kremlin. Since then he has worked as an independent journalist and academic in Prague and Amsterdam, continuing his scrutiny of the world economy and publishing a couple of James Bond-style mysteries."

Translator's Acknowledgements

The translation was made from the Russian edition of *The Anatomy of Russian Capitalism* (Moscow: Mezhdunarodnyye otnosheniya, 2004), as revised by the author. Professor Menshikov's assistance with terminology and his efforts to achieve precision in the updating process have been invaluable. I would like to thank the colleagues who helped me prepare the English text, including Nancy Spannaus, Kenneth Kronberg, and Allen Douglas, as well as members of the Ruslantra online translators' group, whose brainstorming abilities sorted out more than a few tangles: Andrei Azov, Marina Burkova, Vladimir Dorofeyev, Alexei Glushchenko, Irina Hood, Eugenia Kanishcheva, Konstantin Lakshin, Natalia Mikhailova, Victor Nikolaev, Alexander Okunev, Natalie Shahova, Yan Shapiro, Alla Toff, Saule Tuganbayeva, Elliott Urdang, and Ekaterina Usilova.—*RBD*